DAYS OF DEATH, DAYS OF LIFE

DAYS OF DEATH, DAYS OF LIFE

Ritual in the Popular Culture of Oaxaca

KRISTIN NORGET

COLUMBIA UNIVERSITY PRESS   NEW YORK

COLUMBIA UNIVERSITY PRESS
Publishers Since 1893
NEW YORK, CHICHESTER, WEST SUSSEX

Library of Congress Cataloging-in-Publication Data

Norget, Kristin.
Days of death, days of life : ritual in the popular culture of Oaxaca /
Kristin Norget.
p. cm.
Includes bibliographical references and index.
ISBN 0-231-13688-9 (cloth : alk. paper)
ISBN 0-231-13689-7 (pbk. : alk. paper)
1. All Souls' Day—Mexico—Oaxaca de Juárez.
2. Funeral rites and ceremonies—Mexico—Oaxaca de Juárez.
3. Oaxaca de Juárez (Mexico)—Social life and customs.
I. Title
GT4995.A4N67   2006
394.266'0972'74—dc22   2005051850

Columbia University Press books are printed on permanent and
durable acid-free paper
Printed in the United States of America

c 10 9 8 7 6 5 4 3 2 1
p 10 9 8 7 6 5 4 3 2 1

For my father,
John Gunther Norget

CONTENTS

ACKNOWLEDGMENTS

THIS BOOK REPRESENTS a long journey; the path has not always been straight or always smooth. I want to acknowledge the many people who have accompanied me along the way.

How did I end up in such a welcoming neighborhood? The gods were surely smiling on me. My greatest debt of gratitude goes to those who gave so much of themselves to welcome so warmly a stranger into their midst: *muchísimas gracias*, especially, to María de Jesus (Chucha) Cruz Ortiz and family, Lidia Blas Cruz and family, Lupe Mendoza, Reynaldo Cabrera, Mauro Cruz, Avelia Mandonado, doña Otilia Sandoval, Fezali Zavaleta, Marino Betanzos, Elias Betanzos, Candelaria Maldonado, José Zarate, Rosa Trujillo, Francisco and Gustavo, Alfonso Santiago, and Padre Hermenegildo Pérez.

Heartfelt *gracias* to my *comadre*, Valeriana Pizarro, and family: Paulino, Camilo, Claudio, Tiburcio (!), Felix, Telésforo, and dear Patricia, whose deep intelligence and love have taught me much about resilience, spirit, and extraordinary solidarity and the possibilities of what a family can be. Life in Oaxaca would not have been the same without Dorothy Cline, a source of great wisdom and emotional support as both friend and "mother." Since those early days, Jayne Howell has shared with me the delight, humor, and sorrows of life in Oaxaca. I admire her spirit and courage. Michael Higgins, Art Murphy, Ramona Pérez, Martha Rees, Lois Wasserspring, Ronald Waterbury, Jack Corbett, and Jorge Hernández have for many years represented for me a terrific and supportive community of fellow "Oaxacanistas."

My graduate research in Oaxaca benefited tremendously from the resources at the Instituto Welte de Estudios Oaxaqueños, including the sound points of guidance and efficient help offered by Cecil Welte and Ursula Greenberg. From its beginnings in the cramped quarters above the pizza place on the Andador, to its current site in the north of the city, "the Welte" has evolved into a vital research center for serious scholars of Oaxaca. I have relied regularly on the aid and friendship of its librarian, Gudrun Dohrmann. I also wish to thank the Department of History at the Universidad Autónoma Benito Juárez de Oaxaca for inviting me to become an affiliate during the initial phase of my research. Of particular help were the department's administrative assistants, who patiently transcribed some of my interview material. Enrique Marroquín was a gracious and encouraging guide when I was struggling to understand the enigmatic complexities of religion, and the Catholic Church, in Oaxaca.

Muchas gracias also to Padre Juan Ruiz, Padre Wilfrido Mayrén, and Madre Guadelupe Cortés. I am proud to consider them among my friends. I also want to thank Sergio Sánchez, Rosa and Luis Arroro, Eustolia Sánchez, Raul Herrera, David Poisal, Lowell Greenberg, and Sergio Bátiz—all of whom understand why Oaxaca is the place where I am always renewed.

I owe a special debt to Amparo Rodriguez, who on a cold, rainy day in London introduced me to the Day of the Dead and to the other side of the fiesta that was not represented by the colorful objects of "folk art" in the glass cases of a somewhat sterile museum atmosphere. There are many people I appreciate from my early graduate student days; they left an indelible mark on me in ways they may not realize. Part of my contentedness at the Department of Social Anthropology at Cambridge University was due to the positive and supportive atmosphere of a vibrant and dynamic community of scholars. Thanks particularly to my supervisor, Stephen Hugh-Jones, who was a great teacher, inspiration, and example. Peter Wade was important to me as friend and adviser, as was David Lehmann. Keith Hart and his iconoclastic spirit arrived back in Cambridge, just as I was finishing writing up my dissertation, to inspire a critical (re)engagement with anthropology that I still nurture. I am also grateful to Anita Herle at the Cambridge Museum of Anthropology, Elizabeth Carmichael at the Museum of Mankind, Susana Rostas, Valentina Napolitano, the late Ernest Gellner, and Robin and Catherine Porteous. Other members of my graduate cohort provided provocative discussion as well as friendship. Special thanks to André Czegledy, Nicole Toulis, and Louise de la Gorgondière. Nicholas Röhl and Rebecca Porteous were steadfast and generous friends who added much to my life in England.

I want to express my appreciation to Eric Worby, Janalyn Prest, Sean Brotherton, Bob White, John Hall, and the staff and colleagues in the Department of Anthropology at McGill University, especially John Galaty, Bruce Trigger, Mike Bisson, and Sandra Hyde, and the wise counsel of Ellen Corin, Laurence Kirmayer, and the wonderful Rose Marie Stano. It has made a huge difference to have near me fellow Latin Americanists who are both excellent scholars and generous people: thanks to Phil Oxhorn and Daviken Studnicki-Gizbert, and especially Catherine LeGrand, for their enduring support, encouragement, and friendship. Pierre Beaucage at the University of Montreal has been an exceptional mentor, colleague, and friend in both Montreal and Mexico. The formidable combination of his razor-sharp mind, rich experience, and generous social consciousness makes him a great anthropologist and rare human being; I have learned much from him. Igor Ayora and Gabriela Vargas have been sources of inspiration and companionship at critical moments over the past decade.

Research for this book benefited greatly from the assistance of students at McGill, including Monique Skidmore, Anna Fournier, Stephanie Pommez, Miranda Ortiz, Antoine Libert, and, especially, Mauricio Delfin, who is an integral part of many of my best memories of Oaxaca. Santiago Olguín collected final bits of information in Oaxaca, which allowed me to fill in important details.

Columbia University Press enthusiastically picked up this book project and ran with it, with sparkling professionalism, integrity, efficiency—and good humor. My sincere gratitude goes to Suzanne Ryan, Wendy Lochner, and the masterly copy-editing skills of Rita Bernhard and, especially, Irene Pavitt, who patiently fiddled with the countless photos of graves that flooded her e-mail inbox. An additional thank you is owed to the anonymous reviewers whose comments, I believe, made this a better book.

Those of us who, over the years, have made our lives in more than one place depend greatly on friends who will tolerate our somewhat schizoid imaginaries. Deborah Allan, Tom Baxter, Nicholas Boston, Pauline Conley, Anne Drost, Mark LaPrairie, and Amanda Vincent have been faithful friends despite the distances that have often divided us. Thanks also to Gabriel Gbadamosi, Robert Lee Adams Jr., and Lázaro Patterson, for pushing me to grow. True organic scholars and bonnes vivantes Marika Finlay de Monchy and Karin Cope saved me when I needed to be saved. Through their deep intelligence, humanity, and passion for life, they showed me that being a misfit is not necessarily fatal. I am indebted to the extraordinary editorial talents of Karin, in particular, for midwifing this book through the most difficult of its births.

In England, my research was supported by the Canadian Federation of University Women, the Radcliffe-Brown Fund, the Cambridge University Ling Roth Fund, and an Allen Scholarship. I am also grateful to the Fonds Québécois de la Recherche sur la Société et la Culture (FQRSC) and the Social Sciences and Humanities Research Council (SSHRC) for generous funding of research that allowed this book to develop in new directions. A stay at the idyllic Rockefeller Bellagio Centre in 2000 gave me time and peace for writing an initial draft of this book. Much of the section "The Church and 'Popular' Religion Today," in chapter 2, was published in "Progressive Theology and Popular Religiosity in Oaxaca, Mexico," *Ethnology* 36 (1997): 67–83.

I want to acknowledge the support and love of my family, especially my mother, Judith Norget, and my father, John Norget, to whom I dedicate this book. My sister, Susan; brother, David; Charles Kahn; Uncle Walter and Aunt Olga; and John, Tammy, and family have also always been there for me. Finally, completion of this book was made possible by my darling daughter, Adaeze, who helped me to close one cycle and open a new one.

Que Dios les bendiga.

DAYS OF DEATH, DAYS OF LIFE

Introduction:
Death and Life in Oaxaca

Mexican death is the mirror of Mexican life. . . . Our contempt of death is not at odds with the cult we have made of it. Death is present in our fiestas, our games, our loves and our thought . . . death revenges us against life; strips it of all its vanities and pretensions and converts it into what it really is: a few neat bones and a dreadful grimace . . . but all of this boastful familiarity does not rid us of the question we all ask: What is death?

— OCTAVIO PAZ, *The Labyrinth of Solitude*

IN THE SOUTHERN MEXICAN CITY OF OAXACA, a funeral cortège moves slowly through the city core, a pace that gives the heterogeneous muddle of onlookers plenty of opportunity to assess the parade of figures passing through the street. It is not hard to recognize many among the group of mourners as wealthy Oaxacans: women dressed in black clasping bunches of white roses and gladioli surround the shiny lozenge-shaped coffin borne in the back of a dark blue limousine; men in dark suits and ties follow solemnly; they carry enormous wreaths bearing the names of their donors, embossed in large letters on wide dark satin ribbons. A group of musicians accompany the mourners; their instruments wail a melancholic and hauntingly beautiful dirge.

In Oaxaca, the streets are still used for public events and processions of all kinds, religious and secular. But this particular occasion is unmistakably a funeral, and, although in some ways it is clearly a carefully crafted and ostentatious display for all to see, the meanings, emotions, and practices that lie behind such moments of public ceremony are less evident. Although death is an obvious and unavoidable universal phenomenon, the cultural meanings that attach to it, and to the rituals that attend it are not. Indeed, even within a given geographic or cultural space—a city such as Oaxaca—the way that death is treated, and its manifold meanings, may vary considerably, from one social group to another, and from neighborhood to neighborhood. How rituals of death are practiced often says a great deal about how a given community regards not only life but the relations between life and death, the living and the dead, self and other, and now and any other time, whether past or future.

Days of Death, Days of Life had its beginnings in a doctoral research project undertaken at Cambridge University from 1989 to 1993 on the annual celebration of the Day of the Dead in the southern Mexican city of Oaxaca de Juárez. From a focus on Day of the Dead celebrations, my interest quickly expanded to include everyday death rituals, funerals, other rituals, and commemorations that take place around the calendar year, for it became apparent to me that I could not begin to fathom the significance of various popular practices around the Day of the Dead if I did not also have a sense of how death, in its immediate and everyday forms, was greeted and experienced in the community where I lived. When I began my first period of fieldwork in Oaxaca in the early 1990s, the people I spoke with kept directing me to the celebrated ancient ceremonial ruins of Monte Albán and Mitla; they appeared to believe that my expressed interest in contemporary funerary practices was a mistake: what, *por Dios*, could I want to learn about death today? Thus in the *colonia* (neighborhood) where I lived during the course of my fieldwork, my interest in death was the source of much amusement; I was continually the brunt of local jokes that made light of my apparent fixation with talking about or hanging around *los muertos* (the dead). At the same time, it was evident that my neighbors themselves recognized the importance of death in their everyday lives, and, apart from the festive time of the Day of the Dead, when such invitations were more commonplace, they also made a concerted effort to invite me to and include me in funerals, wakes, prayer sessions, and other rituals related to death. This might seem surprising, above all, to people in the United States and Canada, where death, on the whole, is a private and highly sanitized affair. When I told people outside Mexico about my research, they often asked if it bothered me to invade others' "private" moments of mourning by going to funerals and wakes when I was not a close friend of the family. But such preoccupations with the privacy of emotion, common in the United States and Canada or in western Europe, do not necessarily apply to other cultural settings, where the event of death is configured in a significantly different way.[1] While there is certainly a danger in overemphasizing the differences in emotional repertoire from one culture to another, at the same time real differences should be recognized and are important. In Oaxaca, for example, I found that a curtain of private mourning is rarely drawn around funeral events; my neighbors' readiness to speak about death frankly and honestly took some getting used to, but it was also my saving grace.

Aside from the several deaths I encountered in Oaxaca during my research, at a more personal level, too, death was with me at every step of the way. About a month after my initial fieldwork began in 1989, my father died in Canada, following a year-long battle with cancer. I returned to British Columbia to spend a week with my family after his death, and then came back to Oaxaca at the end of October, just in time to participate in preparations for the Day of the Dead. When I think back, much of that time is still a blur, as I deflected grief over my father's death by throwing myself into my research. But I do recall that upon my arrival back in the city, death was everywhere: he was a skeleton made of papier-mâché in a shop window; he was the candies, fruits, and treats that children screamed for as they ran through the streets; he was embodied in the bread for sale in the buzzing city markets. And I am thankful that death was such a tangible presence then, for if it had been otherwise, I am sure that I would have felt more despair and anger than I already did.

"Death is never an easy topic," writes Nancy Scheper-Hughes in the introduction to *Death Without Weeping*, her eloquent and moving ethnography on the culture of mothering and infant death in a shantytown in northeastern Brazil. Scheper-Hughes's research experience forced her to deal with personal anger and indignation in confronting the pervasive hunger, sickness, and suffering of women dwelling on the political-economic fringes of Brazilian society. Although the degree of poverty and illness that I witnessed in the marginal neighborhoods of Oaxaca where I was working was not as severe as the suffering Scheper-Hughes found in her fieldwork setting, I did see people around me regularly denied access to the medical treatment they needed. I also observed or otherwise learned of adults and children—especially those who lived in the poorer *colonias populares*, such as the neighborhood where I lived—who died sometimes as a result of shocking medical negligence or for other "unnecessary" reasons. The fact of my father's death added an unusual layer of significance to the suffering I witnessed: it was impossible for me to have a detached, primarily intellectual engagement with death during my research; above all, it made me realize that the often frighteningly immediate, emotional, and visceral comprehension of death was inseparable from the larger quest for understanding I had embarked on.

Thus it was that the long days of my first experience of fieldwork in Oaxaca were lived in the shadow of my father's death; the reality of his death confounded me and at a deeper level terrified me, although I could not admit that at the time. In those confusing early days, I first met several members of a family that later more or less adopted me, when one of the family sons suffered a violent and unexpected death. The support and understanding that this family so generously offered me, their words of comfort, their warmth and example, not only cemented my relationship with them but also gave me space to mourn my father's death, to face and accept my own disorientation and profound sense of loss.

I can now see that other aspects of my fieldwork also came to play a part in my process of mourning and my attempts to heal. Initially most of my exposure to death and its rituals in Oaxaca fell within the parameters of fairly conventional modes of anthropological research: I attended wakes, funeral ceremonies, and the adjunct series of funereal rites or prayer evenings known as *novenarios*. In my first year of research, I attended roughly twenty funeral-related rituals in Oaxaca and the surrounding countryside; these ranged from wakes and funerals to death anniversary ceremonies (known as *cabo de año* [end-of-the-year] celebrations). In the dozen years since then, I have gone to many more. The deceased who were celebrated came from all points on the social spectrum—the very young to the very old, women and men, rich and poor—yet most were related to residents of the five popular *colonias* belonging to the parish of Cuauhtémoc. Increasingly, when someone in the neighborhood died, I attended these events as an "expected" member of the local community. I also participated in other rites and rituals held in the parish and beyond, as part of my "duty" as a member of the Legión de María (Legion of Mary), an international group dedicated to the cult of the Virgin Mary, or of Pláticas Bíblicas, the *colonia*'s Bible discussion group. On occasion, if I happened to be with friends who were on their way to a funeral or *novenario* celebration, I joined them, even if I was not expected or did not know the person who had died. My initial discomfort with the context of death disappeared once I experienced the open and welcoming ambience that pervaded most death rituals in the area. My presence at local funerary events came to be expected, and when a death occurred that was even remotely in the vicinity, I was one of the first in the neighborhood to be informed.

"Research" for me was thus a multifaceted learning process. Apart from the informal knowledge and understandings that I absorbed by virtue of simply living in Oaxaca and having the chance to exchange personal thoughts and reflections on death with my neighbors, I conducted approximately seventy-five formal but open-ended interviews on death-related themes with a diversity of Oaxacans. These interviews served to enrich immeasurably my understandings and perceptions of death, its meanings, and its rituals in Oaxaca; statements taken from these interviews appear throughout this book. Sometimes the interviews were quite straightforward; at other times, the dialogue followed a chaotic, winding path, the conversation alternately touching on existentialist philosophers, sentimental reflections on family members gone but not forgotten, stories of ghosts, or recipes for tamales. Although I based my interviews loosely on a general list of questions or topics, I allowed each conversation to take its own direction, for I quickly discovered that this was the best way to allow space for the sudden insights or leaps of thought that sometimes happen when one speaks of such a profound but everyday topic. I used a small tape recorder to document most of the interviews; I learned that the presence or absence of the recorder did not seem to make much difference to what was said during these conversations. Exchanges lasted anywhere from forty-five minutes to several hours. I also made extensive videotapes of the Day of the Dead and even, on occasion, when the family permitted it, of various funeral rites; surprisingly, perhaps, these efforts of documentation seemed to be welcome in many venues; sometimes neighbors inviting me to a wake would even remind me to bring my camera.

Despite the variety in the details of individual descriptions of death-related customs, and the reach of my own observations from the many ritual events I attended, patterns did emerge. I have tried, then, in my representation of death rituals in Oaxaca, to offer a few specific accounts, which, although they cannot stand for all such rituals, share significant characteristics and meanings with other events I witnessed and recorded but could not include here because of space limitations. Likewise, in my use of statements made by neighborhood residents about death, life, belief, ritual, and survival, I have tried to allow room for the range of voices and opinions I encountered. Sometimes these voices or opinions contradicted or criticized one another radically. This is to be expected: not only do many ideas, identities, and lifeways commingle in an urban setting such as Oaxaca, but discussions of life and death also open onto vast terrains of debate, based on differences in beliefs that rest on, but are not simply ascrib-able to, subjective differences in experience, origins, age, economic status, level of education, and religion. Many of the beliefs people discussed with me were not absolute but were subject to change, criticism, or contradiction; as I hope my discussion of them makes clear, these beliefs, like the rituals that often serve to frame them, are mutable, if patterned, forms. I cannot say, then, how *old* the rituals I observed were, nor can I predict how long they may continue to be practiced in the ways I witnessed. What I documented was how certain rituals were framed, thought about, and carried out in several poor, largely "indig-enous" neighborhoods in Oaxaca in the 1990s. My interest here, in this book, is not simply to supply some of this documentary material but also to reflect on what it means in and for the lives of marginal people and communities in contemporary Mexico. As I promised them, I have changed the names of all the people who shared their experiences, explanations, insights, and wisdom with me, as well as the names that identify the community and parish where I lived during much of my fieldwork. On their consent, the real names of representa-tives of governmental or other public organizations whom I interviewed appear in full.

This book is intended to be a contribution to the ethnography of contem-porary, particularly urban, Mexico, to popular religion and popular culture, and to current anthropological literature on cultural practices surrounding death. By locating popular religious practice at the center of processes of social and cultural change in contemporary Oaxaca, I hope to offer an original perspective on the significance of religion in Oaxacan and Mexican culture, especially the role of religion in informing certain particularly salient aspects of identity.

THOUGHTS ON DEATH AND MEXICO

Long before I ever visited Oaxaca, I had formed an impression of the meaning of death in Mexican culture. Readings of the claims and rhetoric of various staple writings on "the Mexican character," including Octavio Paz's eloquent argument regarding the supposed devil-may-care attitude of Mexicans toward death, or novels that poetically rendered a long-past magical existential landscape, shaped much of this impression. To be powerless, resigned by poverty or misfortune to the awful dictates of fate, not to care, to laugh in the face of death: these romantic tropes that I found in my readings of fiction set in Mexico were further embellished by Oscar Lewis's evocative ethnographies of the pathos-filled lives—and deaths—of the Sánchez family in mid-twentieth-century Mexico City. But as I learned during the course of my fieldwork in Oaxaca, attitudes toward death are far more complex than such instances of "national" rhetoric might suggest. Nevertheless, in order to fully understand what is particular about my findings, perhaps a brief review of various Mexican rhetorical formulations of "the Mexican character" and "the meaning of death" in Mexico might be helpful. Consider the following four "sound bites":

> You have killed only as I have killed, thoughtlessly. That's why no one knows what it is like and no one can tell us about it. If I could come back, if I could come back and tell what it is to hear the rifles and feel it in the chest and face; if I could tell the truth about that, maybe we would no longer dare to kill, never again; or maybe it would be that no one would mind dying. It may be terrible . . . or it may be as natural as birth. What do we know, you or I?
> Carlos Fuentes, *The Death of Artemio Cruz* (1964)

> Here [in Mexico] one thinks about death without apprehension, its attractiveness becoming stronger in proportion to the amount of Indian blood in our veins. The more *criollo* [Spanish] one is, the more afraid one is of death, for that is how we are taught.   Xavier Villaurutia, *Obras* (1966)

There are very few countries in the world that demonstrate an indifference to death the way Mexico does; our difference consists in not fearing death while awaiting it; we wait, not simply peacefully, but with a smile of indifference, with stoicism, or perhaps even with interest dignified of greater cause.

From the newspaper *El Oaxaqueño* (31 October 1934)

La vida no vale nada . . .	Life is not worth anything
Se nace siempre muriendo.	One is born always dying
Se vive siempre llorando,	One lives always crying
Y asi termina la vida	And so life ends . . .

From José Alfredo Jiménez's song "La vida no vale nada"
("Camino de Guanajuato," 1954)

There are many ways that a nation gathers its people into a common fold or, in the words of Benedict Anderson, into an "imagined community." Such gatherings are particularly challenging for plural, multicultural nations like Mexico, whose beginnings are rooted in the experience of colonialism. In 1821, after some three hundred years of colonial rule, the territory we know today as Mexico (which then included large portions of the American Southwest, most of the territory of present-day California, New Mexico, Nevada, Arizona, Texas, and Utah) gained its independence from Spain, and, in 1824, the Republic of Mexico (Los Estados Unidos de México) was established. But the country's difficult birth as an independent nation did not culminate until the time of the Mexican Revolution at the beginning of the twentieth century. And ever since the adoption of the federal constitution in 1917, political leaders in the Mexican nation-state have been preoccupied with an unending need to create a singular national subjective identity, one that can cohere, contain—and represent—a diverse population profoundly divided by local and regional histories, and by multiple axes of religion, ethnicity, privilege, and poverty. Drawn in the image of colorful vibrant folk heroes such as Pancho Villa and Emiliano Zapata, and embellished by nineteenth-century liberal ideas, this ideal national Mexican subject consisted of a fusion of indigenous and Spanish ancestry; as such, the national type was figured as a hybrid and tragic figure, anchored in his or her cultural heritage, yet secular, modern, and rebelliously independent and forward-looking. The self-identification of Mexican revolutionaries as mestizo, or of mixed ancestry, set the stage for an important rhetorical reformulation of modern Mexican national culture as mestizo culture; although in effect, such a rhetorical turn identified the political elite with "the people," it also provided an ideological platform for a protectionist economy and a strong state that continued to deprive many of "the people," even as it guaranteed them full citizenship and equality under the constitution.[2]

Still another way that this national character, as a fusion of "folk" practices and intellectual ideas, was invented and popularized in the twentieth century has to do with a purported special relation with or attitude toward death.[3] There is no doubt that, in Mexico, the enshrining of a certain fatalism or devil-may-care insouciance before death—loudly celebrated in mid-century intellectual writings—is marked by a history that has been bloody and particularly mortal for the poorest and most indigenous of Mexico's inhabitants. But any true remembrance or recounting of this history is not particularly evident in the statements and stereotypes that characterize this national folk culture of death, as the four "sound bites" offered earlier testify. Rather, as the contemporary Mexican intellectual Roger Bartra has argued in his book *The Cage of Melancholy*, a particularly *Mexican* insouciance toward death has become one of the "socially accepted *forms of subjectivity*":[4]

> The first steps [along a road to self-discovery] have been marked with the sign of death, a death lived and suffered at every moment in a supposedly unique form by dint of being exclusively Mexican. The Mexican treatment of death is so perfectly inscribed in the archetype of melancholy that it can inspire the deep philosophical speculations of Mexico's existentialists, the anxieties of her poets, the processes described by her novelists, the analyses of her sociologists, and the patriotic exhortations of her politicians.[5]

In a similar vein, the anthropologist Carlos Navarrete has suggested:

> The idea of the Mexican who laughs and dances with death, who drinks *pulque* with the skeleton [*calavera*], who is not afraid of death but instead venerates it held sway until the thirties and forties. Octavio Paz, in *The Labyrinth of Solitude*, repeats almost the precise words of Diego Rivera: the idea of the Mexican who does not fear death, who says "si me han de matar mañana que me maten de una vez" [if they must kill me, let them do it once and for all], etc. So this concept is not false, but it stems from a postrevolutionary interpretation, rooted in the moment when the Mexican is searching for himself, searching for his roots.[6]

Formulated from a wish to offer a portrait of the popular, lower classes that will take into account, in emblematic form, the peasants' historical aspirations and exalted struggle for land and social justice—thereby lending "a shared sense of the past and a unified gaze towards the future"[7]—the idea of the Mexican who cares nothing for death became a way for postrevolutionary intellectuals to dramatize and romanticize, as *typical*, a character who perhaps existed nowhere.

The figure can thus be everyone, because, in fact, it is no one. More insidiously, as Bartra comments, the myth neatly rests on two common bourgeois views of the "folk": first, the perception of a religious fatalism among the popular "masses" (an attitude regarded by some social commentators today as encouraging the poverty of indigenous peasants and the urban proletariat), and, second, a disdain for the lives of these popular social groups as a whole.[8] Their lives do not matter; they must know this, and act accordingly—voilà, in a nutshell, the famous "character."

As is often the case with generalized representations of other elements from indigenous or popular Mexican culture, cultural projections of this peasant tradition are rife with pathos and fundamentally dichotomous. The heroic romanticized image of a great indigenous preindustrial past is ambivalently articulated alongside a rhetoric that speaks of peasant backwardness as the sorry ball and chain that slows down the development and maturation of the nation as a whole. Likewise, the common peasant archetype of "aggressive emotionalism"—immortalized in the classic films of the *bandito*-Lothario Pedro Infante, in the popular personage of Cantinflas, and in the novels of Carlos Fuentes—is also figured as an ambivalent dual identity in which the well-known revolutionary, stoic, patriotic macho is melodramatically fused with a passive, melancholic alter ego. The metamorphosis of the modern Mexican arises, apparently, rhetorically, from such doubled combinations: thus the "modern" nation emerges, embodied by an integral "reborn" secular, rational mestizo self, a metaphysical zephyr who ascends, victorious, from the ashes of a violent but heroic past, the very self of a nation "both timelessly ancient and moving forward."[9] Perhaps it should not be surprising, then, that even in a relatively recent contemplation on the Mexican character—tellingly entitled *The Day of the Dead and Other Mortal Reflections*—Frank González Crussi continues to rework the features of the national archetype:

> Merriment alone does not characterize the Mexican attitude. There is also an element of fatalism. The Aztecs lived with the pervasive feeling of the futility of human aspirations; their pessimistic philosophy must have endowed them with plenty of resigned acceptance of man's vulnerability. Moreover, it is hardly necessary to invoke the intervention of highly debatable pre-Columbian atavisms. Stoicism and resignation are bulwarks against misfortune, and Mexico has known repeated large-scale catastrophe. . . . As in other latitudes, dark humor and a shrug of the shoulders have expressed this powerless resignation. In Mexico, the expression "*Ya le tocaba,*" the equivalent of "his number was up" or "his turn finally arrived," often condenses the only possible reaction in the face of ineluctable doom.[10]

González Crussi's narration of "the" Mexican character takes place in a voice that is at once solemn and earnest; as with other elite or intellectual voices that have preceded him, he has assumed the task of interpreting for the "outside" world the psychological intricacies of his countrymen, or *paisanos* (at least one of the stories in the collection appeared in the *New Yorker*). His descriptions of the "hallucinatory land" of Mexico and its people's timeless, "ancient tradition of a joking familiarity with death" resonate readily with Octavio Paz's famous remark, "The Mexican's indifference to death is fed by his indifference to life."[11] As always, behind such a psychological profile of stoic indifference in the face of death brews a violent and darkly sardonic sense of humor: in short, laughter is given as the only means for confronting an existence in which one has no choice but to leave one's lot in the hands of external, even metaphysical, forces; what will be is what is destined to be.

Certainly, if one looks for them, what appear to be reflections of such dark humor and indifference may readily be found everywhere in Mexico, particularly in everyday parlance. Death is constantly embodied, given shape, anthropomorphized: thus it is called, variously and affectionately, *la flaca* (skinny), *la calaca* (skeleton), *la pelona* (baldy), and *la dientona* (long-toothed one). Synonyms for dying are similarly multiple and colorful. Those I heard most frequently in Oaxaca included *estirar la pata* (to stretch the foot, or the paw), *colgar los tennis* (to hang up one's tennis shoes), *comer tierra* (to eat dirt), *entregar el equipo* (to surrender the equipment), *irse al hoyo* (to go into the hole), and *petatearse* (to stretch out on the *petate* [reed mat used for sleeping, especially in rural indigenous communities]). But how far the existence of such expressions may be taken to characterize the existential quality of a national character remains a matter of extreme, psychological speculation. (Consider, for example, whether the common idiomatic English phrases "to kick the bucket" and "to buy the farm" suggest that English-speaking North Americans typically avoid speaking of death directly, that death is intimately linked to agrarian life, or that they have a particularly funny sense of humor about death.)

As Bartra observes, such generalized Mexican nationalist imagery frequently identifies peasants—the ostensible protagonists of the revolution—as deeply melancholic, dramatic characters; they are victims of a violent history, the residue of which is said to be a pronounced inferiority complex. Another, complementary image, that of the urban lower-class *pelado*, the hero of the modern age, offers a further elaboration of the stereotype. A distinct set of atavistic behaviors typically accompanies the profile of the *pelado*: as a result of a life of profound existential insecurity, this peasant or mestizo urban working-class Mexican character is figured as stubborn, undisciplined, and duplicitous; tales about him are pervaded by double and triple entendres and deceit, for he is a born nihilistic skeptic who uses kindness to mask his distrust. Particularly in such tales, contradictions found deep within the fissures of the collective psyche of Mexicans are said to be revealed discursively—in puns, understatement, indirection, and nuances of expression—what Jorge Portilla, in a classic essay on Mexican character, called the complex of *relajo* (slacker).[12] Naturally this stereotypic "Mexican" who is no one and everyone, who embodies the hopes and emotional tenor of the nation, as well as carrying its defeats as scars on his body, is a male hero. He plays brazenly with death and laughs defiantly in its face. He is a common man, but he almost becomes—for a moment at least—in the daring of his laughter and the breadth of his indifference, a god.[13]

Drawing on well-known representations of rapacious and bloodthirsty Aztec culture, in which men approached gods and the states of gods, the psychological roots of this generalized Mexican's intimate and nonchalant relationship with death were further elaborated by a twentieth-century literary and artistic production that makes colorful use of Mexico's tumultuous "modern" history, from the violence of the Conquest to various states of unrest, lawlessness, and banditry, punctuated by the bloody wars of independence and revolution. Thus literary classics such as Juan Rulfo's *Pedro Páramo* and Carlos Fuentes's *The Death of Artemio Cruz*, as well as a number of works of visual art—for example, the much-celebrated turn-of-the-century engravings of José Guadelupe Posada or the dramatic postrevolutionary paintings of Diego Rivera and José Clemente Orozco—added depth and monolithic dimensions to the portrait of a melancholic macho who cavorts with death in a landscape of surreal and supreme fatalism. But the elaboration of this portrait of the national character was not simply to be left to novelists or painters or to the discourses and pronouncements of various philosophers and essayists like Paz;[14] before long, anthropologists also got into the act, and, alas, too few of us have truly left this particular traveling road show behind—especially when it comes to talking about the Day of the Dead, one of the best known of Mexican popular or "folk"-Catholic festivals.[15]

Certainly, much of the sensationalism that attends accounts of El Día de los Muertos, both inside and outside Mexico, draws on the fiesta's purported strong links with pre-Columbian indigenous traditions, where death and sacrifice within a polytheistic religious system were undeniably central cultural preoccupations. Fantastical accounts of a brutal, sadistic, and obsessive Aztec love of death are very much a part of any contemporary imaginary of "Death in Mexico," a matter that is reflected in the explanations by many Mexicans of the meaning and significance of the Day of the Dead. I, too, have been complicit in such forms of romantic fantasy; after all, as a student of anthropology, before I really knew anything about the subject, on the basis of its mystic and macabre draw and probable exciting color, I elected to focus my research on the theme of death rituals in the Day of the Dead in Oaxaca. Soon after committing myself to the topic, in my first research "foray," as it were, I went to an exhibition of artwork surrounding the Day of the Dead festival. It was 1987, and the exhibition was held at the Serpentine Gallery in London's Hyde Park. My first exposure to what I then regarded as the eerily seductive images of dancing skeletons—including a series of "larger-than-death" skeletons, or *calaveras*, created by the celebrated Linares family of Mexico City, whose works draw hefty sums on the international "folk art" market—this exhibition cemented many of my preconceptions: here, indeed, were colorful figures of death who laughed at death! In the years since, I have attended many other Day of the Dead exhibitions in museums and other institutions, in both Europe and Mexico; I have also read countless catalogues of exhibitions that have taken place elsewhere in the world. My fascination, you see, continues, unabated, although I know that, with few exceptions—like perhaps the Museum of Mankind's excellent exhibit "The Skeleton at the Feast" in 1993—many such depictions of Mexican "death" offer little but sanitized, static, folkloric views of the festival, and contribute mightily to the illusion of a unified Mexican national sentiment and sensibility concerning death.

Such emphasis on a unifying attribute, the Mexican "attitude toward death," is, in part, a result of the increasing importance that scholars, artists, politicians, and others have placed on the discovery of continuities between the cultural traditions of pre-Hispanic New Spain and contemporary Mexico. As the anthropologist Stanley Brandes recently argued: "Mexican and foreign scholars alike reportedly cite [the Day of the Dead] as something peculiar to Mexico, a remnant of ancient Aztec funerary rites and an expression of a uniquely Mexican relationship to death." Contrary to many reports that the Day of the Dead is the result of a neat fusion of pre-Hispanic and Catholic elements, Brandes suggests that "the evidence indicates that the Mexican Day of the Dead is neither Spanish nor Indian but, rather, a colonial invention, a unique product of colonial demographic and economic processes."[16] Intent as he is on eroding some of the exotic veneer of the Day of the Dead, and challenging simple views of its "indigenous" origins, Brandes remains preoccupied with the "true" origins of the festival as they may be read in the mirror of its material culture. Such preoccupations also appear in Hugo Nutini's *Todos Santos in Rural Tlaxcala*, his dense ethnography on the "expressive culture" of the Day of the Dead in a central Mexican town.[17] These concerns about identifying the origins of contemporary practices may help us distinguish more clearly the importance of various acts of idealization of the past by contemporary festival goers; what such studies rarely tell us, however, is how specific contemporary actors *use* ritual and festivals and other sites of commemoration to affirm a relation to a past, a future, and a present community and to mark themselves off as members of a distinct community. This book, then, endeavors to address this absence by attending closely to the beliefs and statements that people append to such crucial performances of cultural identity.

In the context within which we consider the use that individual actors and intimate communities make of various festivals, stereotypes, and historical invocations, it seems to me especially significant that many Mexicans today, whether they speak of themselves as "indigenous" people or not, do seem to point proudly to a pre-Hispanic, indigenous legacy as the root of what is unique, and indeed valuable, about them as a nation.[18] At the same time, as an anthropologist, or observer-interpreter of culture, part of my task is not simply to take everything at face value, for such claims about the glories of a national or an individual past are made, in various settings, in every nation, for a variety of rhetorical purposes. My problem is to sort out, in the settings where I hear such claims, what each claim means, for they do not all seem to amount to the *same* claim. Indeed, individual speakers may and do lay claim to this past for opposing reasons, or the claim may depend very much on the context within which it is made: sometimes, the goal is to claim an indigenous past proudly; other times, the goal might be to subsume such a past in a mestizo present or future. Some claimants might also speak of this past as an imperial past, thereby arguing for present continuities with one—or more—of the world's great ancient civilizations and so forth.

Thus in the chapters that follow, I am concerned not only to describe what I have seen and to transcribe and select certain statements about life, death, and the ritual form that attend them, but also to interpret the material that I have collected according to the way that it is meaningfully deployed or used in various settings. This book, in part, is an exploration of the role of religion, particularly popular religion, in the shaping of people's senses of themselves. As we will see, despite the fact that Oaxacans use religious and other ritual arenas to compete with one another for status and prestige, and certain popular celebrations, such as the Day of the Dead, have been subject to some commercialization, the popular death rites I discuss are also means by which members of the popular classes project and affirm aspects of a unitary identity, in certain contexts. My interest, then, is not in accepting the statements and opinions of my informants as reflecting some kind of essential "truth"—indeed, my informants often contradicted themselves! Rather, I am interested in *why* they say what they say and what these rhetorical statements may indicate about Oaxacans' views of themselves and of the world around them, in a setting of rapid change.

Adding yet another layer of complication to this work of interpretation is the importance of distinguishing between the way that I have used, both privately and professionally, the rituals I have attended—how, for instance, research into death rituals is attached to my professional advancement or to my private mourning—and how others in the community where I work have used and continue to use the same death rituals to build and maintain particular alliances and community sensibilities and identities, alliances and sensibilities that, over the years, have incorporated my presence in various ways but do not really depend on it.

Some readers may note the conspicuous absence in the main text of this book of attempts to enter into direct, explicit conversation with other theorists or theoretical debates within anthropology. Rather than foregrounding my theoretical frameworks, I have left them largely implicit in the belief that often they distract from, rather than augment, a reader's unfolding understanding of an ethnographic work. Where relevant, such corollary arguments and citations may be found in the notes.

Life and Death in Oaxaca

In *Days of Death, Days of Life*, I offer a series of explorations of the experience of death in the city of Oaxaca, where death is part of a *live* culture woven tightly into the fabric of everyday life. In the end, I have come to feel that my account of death in Oaxaca works to refute the text of Mexican nationalist discourse so briefly and stereotypically rendered earlier—in part by giving voice to people and communities that do not feel themselves to be subsumed into such a national culture. Perhaps, too, like just about any anthropologist writing today, I have also wanted to refute many of the gestures of anthropology. I am less sure that I have succeeded at this latter undertaking; what matters most, perhaps, is that I have tried, to the best of my ability, to hear and to take account of the meanings that rituals of death have for the ongoing lives of their practitioners, as both individuals and members of a community with a certain moral, normative cohesion. For it seems that in a political and economic landscape that is, as it is for many marginal Mexicans, uncertain and unstable, and where death, suffering, and violence are tangible presences in everyday life, many of the people that I write about have seized on the special power of death and the social practices occasioned by it to signify to themselves—and to one another—what is most important to them. My aim is thus not to idealize the practices I discuss; I could hardly here claim to have "discovered" (thereby enacting yet another form of conquest) some sort of "authentic" pocket of traditional culture and identity. Rather, what I hope I have rendered is an account of some of the ways that death is experienced in the marginal community where I did my work—not simply as an event to be suffered but as a site in which profound and life-sustaining dramas of connection and relation play out.

A NOTE ON THE WORD "POPULAR"

One of the concepts to which I have a great deal of recourse in this book is the notion of the "popular" (Spanish, *popular*). This word does not mean, as it so often does in everyday English parlance, "prevalent," "accepted," "standard," "in vogue," or "current"; "popular," in the context of Latin American studies, has a more specific, technical, and pervasively political meaning, and can refer to any group of people that falls outside dominant culture or the inner circle of powerful or wealthy elites. Nevertheless, it is important not to regard popular culture as a bounded realm of consciousness, behavior, and practice that is particular to a specific social group, but instead to be cognizant of its internal complexities. My approach toward popular culture harmonizes with both classic and recent literature that works against reductionist and idealizing perspectives, treating popular culture as always in flux, produced from struggles underwritten by relations of power.[19] Popular culture in Mexico, as elsewhere, is a highly contested domain. For example, throughout the nation's history, popular cultural expressions, as well as invocations of the term "popular" itself, have been harnessed to social and cultural agendas of both the state and the church, in efforts to define the nature of popular culture and to win the allegiances of those who represent it. A romantic idealization of popular culture is part and parcel of nationalist rhetoric, in which "folk" or popular cultural forms, heavily inflected with indigenous elements, are upheld as symbols of national identity. At the same time—made in the realm of the everyday, slippery, protean, and always shifting—pieces of the territory of popular culture always remain outside the foothold of dominant social sectors.

Thus when I speak of popular culture, I am not talking about mass media or the latest rock videos; I am speaking of the cultural forms that belong to a marginal population that may be made up of a mixture of urban workers, urban poor, indigenous peoples, peasants, unemployed, and other social actors who cannot be readily placed on the ascending ladder of class categories familiar to most Europeans or North Americans. Indeed, over the course of a lifetime, one individual may belong to all these categories or to several at one time; each is therefore not a distinct class position, but all are marginal and often not party to many of the promised benefits of the modern nation-state, including equality before the law and free exercise of democratic rights. In the heterogeneous community that is any "popular" neighborhood, popular culture is best seen as a *process*; it is produced from day-to-day negotiations of interests, discourses, and perspectives that can partly be explained by differences in age, gender, wealth, and so on. Sometimes a marginal, "popular" status leads to unified political action or the articulation of revolutionary points of view—for example, within the current Zapatista movement, which first exploded with the rebellion of the Ejército Zapatista de Liberación Nacional (EZLN, Zapatista Army of National Liberation) in 1994, and later gained momentum with the rallying cry "Todos somos Chiapas!" (We are all Chiapas!). But, more often, certain expressions of popular culture play an important communal role in critiquing or exposing the decadent or unjust values of dominant culture and reaffirming different values and a different view of the world.

It is in popular religion especially that this social critique may be seen, heard, and felt. Despite areas of overlap with more publicly defined religious traditions, in certain ways popular religion is importantly distinct. I use the qualifier "popular" to refer to the role of religion as a set of beliefs and practices associated with "the people," as opposed to elite social sectors or to its form as disseminated by the institutional church. As Roger Lancaster says of popular religion, it is a means by which the "poor assume interpretations and meanings of religion from their own point of view, as distinct from elites with whom they share a general system of meaning."[20] The "traditional" ethical foundation of Oaxacan popular religiosity reflects a moral economy with roots deep in traditional Oaxacan rural, indigenous culture. This specification need not be limited to only Catholicism; while the "official/elite" religion tends to be more concerned with a tight adherence to doctrine and with individual (as opposed to collective) salvation, "popular" religiosity—whether of Catholic or Protestant kinds on the surface—is born of different material needs and concerns, and the same tendency toward "magical practicality," as Max Weber termed it, will be evident.[21]

Ritual provides a particularly appropriate focus for getting at this special religious sense. As we will see, Oaxacan death rituals display the distinct material, sacred logic of popular religion, characteristics that permit popular religion to sustain a sense of local identity in an especially profound way. In the *colonias populares* where I did my research, I found that death was not a sudden or punctual event, but a protracted social process that followed and accomplished the transformation of the deceased from a member of the community of the living to that of the dead. In and through this process, a particular social poetics of death was formulated, and a popular social consciousness was articulated.

The rituals documented in this book do not simply express a strong and persuasive ethical vision in which the profane world is turned upside down—the poor better the rich, and the living go on relating to the dead. Rather, the sensuous, protracted, demanding, and extravagant character of popular ritualizations of death that I witnessed served to build and cement reciprocal communal relations within a framework that strongly articulated the nature of the "good." It has seemed to me, then, that rituals of death are one of the primary zones in which what might be called the "social idiom" of these marginal, poor urban communities reproduces and maintains itself. In addition, the notion of personhood articulated in these rituals extends well beyond the boundaries of the autonomous, biophysical individual so celebrated by Western modernity; in the *colonia popular*, it is the responsibility of the living to ensure the well-being of the dead; not to do so puts the whole community in danger. At the micro- or individual level, then, ritual is negotiated through relationships; through dreams, fantasies, dramas, prayers, enactments, and the serving or consumption of food or alcohol or both; through exchanges of goods and money; through the care and dressing of the image of a saint or the making and filling of altars for various purposes. Each of these acts, ritually undertaken, points well beyond the body of any individual actor or community member, and toward a continuous community consisting of both the living and the dead, whose well-being depends on these ritual actions. Instead of referring to an actual, geographically fixed, unified, and bounded group of people, the image of the "traditional popular community" that emerges within such popular religious arenas is contingent, formed from the rhetorical claims and ritual practices of many poor Oaxacans, in spite of the very real and salient differences among them.

Because Oaxaca is not a city especially known for its Day of the Dead celebrations, and thus, until quite recently, Day of the Dead celebrations were largely internal community affairs, it seemed a good place to examine the relationship between the Day of the Dead and other popular ritualizations of death as they are practiced by people for whom they have more than just national cultural or commemorative value. What are the meanings, for those who most intensively undertake them, of these popular rituals of death? How does the Day of the Dead function in relation to ordinary funerary practices carried out by a specific community rather than—or in addition to—the church or the state? What sorts of changes, if any, has a move from country to city brought about in these celebrations? What sorts of pressures do urbanization, globalization, and the expansion of the tourist industry place on these manifestations of "popular" culture in poor and relatively marginal communities? Do these changes matter to the residents of the *colonias populares*; do they tend to accept or reject them?

Based on fieldwork first conducted in a parish that consisted of seven *colonias populares* on the outskirts of Oaxaca City from 1989 to 1991, and revisited almost yearly for the last decade, *Days of Death, Days of Life* attempts to pose and answer such questions. A contribution to an urban anthropology of "popular" classes, this book documents a set of practices that carve out a strong communally oriented identity for marginalized, poorer residents of the city. Although both this population and its practices are in flux—as any study of popular culture must recognize—one of the constants documented here is the use of death rituals by *colonia* dwellers in order to enunciate and to create, practically, locally, and temporarily, a view in which some form of communal egalitarianism and justice is meted out to the poor and marginal: good for those who have not inherited the goods of the national state. These ritual spaces contrast in important ways with most of the texture of everyday life. Not only is death itself a great leveler—as many *colonia* residents will testify, "we all have to die"—but the popular ritual practices surrounding death also serve to cement a sense that it is the poor and marginal who are best positioned to die "well"; it is in such communities that the living still know the importance of attending to their dead, perhaps in part because death is never very far away. The popular ritualization of death thus serves to articulate and materialize an ethics that is significantly at odds with the values of a consumer-oriented urban culture; the forms of nourishment, exchange, kinship relation, resource pooling, and time called for or required by popular death rituals provide opportunities for certain *colonia* residents to demonstrate their lived and concrete adherence to an ethics that celebrates sacrifice and sharing over acquisition and self-advancement.

Whether such an ethics will survive the inevitable incorporation of the *colonias populares* into the municipal core of Oaxaca, as well as more general pressures of out-migration and globalization, remains to be seen. Although it is possible to imagine, too, that such an ethical ideal might be at the basis of indigenous rights movements or other pressures of popular and democratic reform in Mexico, the chief role of the worldview articulated in and through the ritualizations of death studied here seemed to be the formation and maintenance of both individual and communal senses of well-being, despite death, poverty, violence, and other forms of adversity. In such a view, then, a good life is bound up with treating death and the dead properly, in giving them their due—as several of the more colorful Day of the Dead stories documented in chapter 5 testify. This is not exactly an argument for the revolutionary potential of carnivalesque inversions; rather, what I have tried to provide here is a documentary that suggests the ongoing importance of a sacred dimension in forms of popular culture that stand at some odds with the economic rationalities of consumer capitalism. What the ritualizations of death in the *colonia popular* nurture are forms of resilience more so than resistance; as outsiders looking in, particularly at *death* rituals, we should be cautious about privileging opposition over elasticity, figuring the latter as giving in rather than going on. For who opposes death for too long and gets away with it? What an outsider might learn from such rituals is something about a dimension where an ethics of sustainability takes place.

OUTLINE OF THE BOOK

Days of Death, Days of Life is divided into three general thematic parts, each of which contains two chapters. Part 1, "Rites of Popular Life in Oaxaca," outlines some of the basic contours of daily life in the *colonia popular*; part 2, "Rites of Popular Death in Oaxaca," discusses various rituals and funerary practices that ordinarily attend death in the *colonia*; and part 3, "Living the Day of the Dead," focuses specifically on practices that surround the Day of the Dead in Oaxaca. Although the chapters may be read independently, each one builds on the vocabulary and elaborations of previous chapters, and overall, the book moves from general description to interpretation.

Chapter 1, "Anthropology in a Mexican City," sets out in some detail the geographic, social, and historical setting of my fieldwork: a parish consisting of seven *colonias*. My work focuses on one of these neighborhoods, a place that I call Colonia San Juan. This chapter introduces several of the residents of Colonia San Juan and discusses some of the ways in which kinship and mutual aid associations are organized in the parish community.

Chapter 2, "Practicing Popular Religion in Oaxaca," sketches the alliances, divergences, and confrontations between official church-sponsored religious practices and the more popular or folk practices that are the central concern of this book. After looking at some examples of a contemporary cult of the saints, this chapter surveys some of the complex interactions of church, state, and area indigenous communities from the beginning of the colonial period to the reforms of the Second Vatican Council (Vatican II) in the mid-1960s. While far from providing a complete investigation into the origins and development of various popular indigenous religious practices, this brief survey aims to offer several historically informed theories about the roots and development of popular religious forms that lie outside official church- or state-sanctioned practices or both.

The traditional ethical foundation of Oaxacan popular religiosity reflects a moral economy with roots deep in traditional Oaxacan rural, indigenous culture. Also, the special kinetic, performative, and sensuous qualities of contemporary popular religion have a long history. It is outside my aims to substantiate my arguments concerning the functions of popular religiosity by trying to anchor present popular practices in past, more "authentic" cultures. I want only to offer a more dimensioned sense of where certain contemporary practices, and the sensibility they embody, may derive from. Popular religion is a reservoir of symbols, significances, and associations that people may draw on; it is certainly not specific to a bounded community except in imaginary, ideal terms.

Over time, the content of the amalgam of "popular" religious practices and beliefs in Oaxaca has changed considerably. Its manifestations in today's urban Oaxaca are wide-ranging, reflecting a diverse population living in an ever globalizing world. Yet, despite transformations to the religious landscape, I argue that the ethical essence of this popular sacred bricolage remains and can be seen in the logical structure that underlies many popular religious practices.

The last section of chapter 2 examines the ongoing and uneasy relationship between the official church and popular practices; often the same actors participated in both venues, but, despite the efforts of the contemporary church, in its participatory renewal program, La Nueva Evangelización (New Evangelization), to mobilize, appropriate, or incorporate many popular forms, *colonia* residents have insisted on maintaining some sites of distinct separation for their practice of "popular" religion. The relationship between the official church and popular religion thus remains uneasy; likewise, as examples from subsequent chapters demonstrate, the obligations entailed by popular practices typically carry far greater moral weight than those required by the church. (Although I discuss the rising rates of conversion to various groups, as the majority of my informants—indeed, of Oaxacans—are Roman Catholic, and popular religious practices have grown up alongside of and in reaction to Catholic practices, "official church" here always means the Catholic Church in its various local parishes.)

Chapter 3, "Living with Death," documents, with photographs, transcriptions, and lengthy descriptions, the form that popular wakes, funerals, and burial practices typically take. The first time these intensive, elaborate, and multiday popular Oaxacan practices have been documented in this sort of detail, the chapter is concerned to track, as carefully and as fully as possible, the stylized and routine activities and forms of behavior enjoined by popular funeral rituals and rites. Here I begin to show some of the very specific ways in which Oaxacans of the popular classes use the particular elements of these highly charged ritual environments to enact performances of heightened altruism and sentiment and to make moral distinctions between themselves and wealthier, more elite residents of the city. I discuss what a good death in popular moral terms means, and why it matters to the community.

Chapter 4, "The Drama of Death," continues the discussion of the "good death"; it details several specific wakes and funerals, and discusses and analyzes many of the comments made by various participants about what they are doing and why. This chapter is specifically concerned to track what I refer to as "the social idiom of the community"—that is, how these rituals aid in the formation and reinforcement of certain popularly valorized forms of community and communal exchange.

Chapter 5, "Days of the Dead in Oaxaca," begins with several stories I was told about the importance of honoring the dead at Day of the Dead ceremonies. These stories demonstrate the extension of the popular morality discussed in chapters 3 and 4, and serve to show how Day of the Dead celebrations fit into and reinforce other, more occasional popular death rituals, practiced throughout the year. This chapter surveys Day of the Dead celebrations particular to Oaxaca and discusses the month-long practice of rotating "cemetery days" in the city, as well as the meanings, forms, and contents (offerings, or *ofrendas*) of typical and specific altars to the dead. The celebration of the Day of the Dead thus not only serves to reinforce certain ethical ideals of generosity and care for members of the popular community, but also extends those ideals beyond the community of the living. In the preparation of altars and offerings, in visits to gravesites, in the extensive preparations for the return of the dead as for an honored guest, Day of the Dead celebrations prepare the living to die and serve to invite the dead into a social, sensuous, and reciprocally affective relation with the living, a reciprocity that significantly challenges the limits of the rational, bounded, autonomous individual so glorified by Western modernity.

Chapter 6, "Spectacular Death and Cultural Change," explores the pressure that the increasing commodification of "popular" culture for tourism and the introduction of North American holidays, such as Halloween, have put on popular ritual and practices in and around Oaxaca. In this chapter, I document a series of changes to Day of the Dead celebrations in Oaxaca as they have increasingly become the province of official metropolitan organization; I also track the rather indifferent popular response to these changes. Certainly, these officially instituted changes have provoked some reflection on and discussion of culture, tradition, cultural possession, and change by *colonia* residents, but as I found, perhaps not surprisingly, my concern about the disappearance of important traditions, or their incorporation into official state-sponsored holidays, was not shared by most of my informants. In the end, of course, I have had to confront my own idealisms and romanticisms; I had wanted the popular traditions that I encountered and studied to be and to remain some radical other to the forms of culture I already knew, but this desire for cultural purity was mine and not a "popular" wish. Death, my informants told me, would not go away. Why should I be afraid that rituals around death would disappear? Through the foregrounding of my own romanticization of popular "tradition," and my own difficulties with the idea that the rituals I had documented were changing, this chapter attempts to pose some significant questions about the risks and frameworks within which popular cultural forms might be studied, as well as to inject some irony into the desire for the authenticity of the other that so often undergirds ethnographic work.

PART 1

Rites of Popular Life in Oaxaca

The culture of poverty in Mexico is a provincial and locally oriented culture. Its members are only partially integrated into national institutions and are marginal people even when they live in the heart of a great city. . . .

Some of the social and psychological characteristics include . . . a strong present time orientation with relatively little ability to defer gratification and plan for the future, a sense of resignation and fatalism based upon the realities of their difficult life situation, a belief in male superiority which reaches its crystallization in *machismo* or the cult of masculinity, a corresponding martyr complex among women, and, finally, a high tolerance for psychological pathology of all sorts.

— OSCAR LEWIS, *The Children of Sánchez*

CHAPTER 1

Anthropology in a Mexican City

Death is our destiny: from the moment we are born we carry with us how many years we will live, the moment we will die. This is the destiny of life and death. But being poor is not our destiny, since there are many people who ended up rich after being born in poverty. It's your goal to work, make money, and take care of it; if you don't know how to take care of it you will never be anything but poor.

—DOÑA LUISA, AGE FORTY-FIVE

STUDIES OF DISTINCT RURAL COMMUNITIES made up the bulk of early-twentieth-century ethnographies of Mexico, especially those produced by North American anthropologists.[1] Then, in the 1960s, as urban growth exploded and various forms of popular culture began to be of interest to anthropologists and other theorists of culture, a number of researchers began to study distinct urban communities or subgroups. One developing branch of this new urban anthropology was concerned with seeking general models that could account for lifestyles of the urban poor. This focus on the urban poor was generated, in part, because anthropological interest in urban Mexico (and urban locales elsewhere in Latin America) first followed the paths of rural migration to urban centers. Initially, researchers regarded the vast peripheral "squatter settlements," visible in urban regions across Latin America, as zones of transition between traditional rural village existence and "modern" urban life; in such spaces, it was argued, the poor lived out their marginal station in life. Notions of "adaptation" and "acculturation" were developed to describe a process of rapid life change and accommodation to urban norms. Most discussion of "adaptation" or "accultura-tion" assumed that, in a fairly short time, new migrants to urban spaces were swallowed up by urban life and the capitalist economy, that they found a steady place in the city, even if that place was near the bottom of the economic heap.[2]

In 1961, in his well-known study *The Children of Sánchez,* the anthropologist Oscar Lewis proposed one of the most influential and remarkably persistent early models for making sense of life in an urban squatter community, the concept of the "culture of poverty."[3] As he wrote about it, the notion of "the culture of poverty" moved from an examination of the poor objective material conditions shared by many inhabitants of a marginal urban neighborhood to a whole set of inferences about shared values, normative structures, and behavior considered to be "characteristic" of such a place. Thus, having vividly described the texture of everyday life for a handful of residents, Lewis arrived at a series of conclusions about the "culture" or "consciousness" of poor squatters' lives and communities. On the basis of such a paradigm of assumed shared consciousness or "culture" of poverty, parallels were sometimes drawn between widely geographically separated communities; further, center–periphery or dependency models, used in the analysis of international political and economic relations, were applied, by analogy, to interclass relations within the same society. Thus, for many years, those neighborhoods that stood physically, politically, and economically at the margins of a city were believed, quite simply, to also embody a set of attitudes and lifeways that stood at the cultural margins of the urban mainstream.

One of several anthropological attempts to conceptualize an "ideal type" of squatter settlement, which could then be analyzed within a larger framework in order to more fully interpret patterns of social interaction in urban spaces, the "culture of poverty" model aligned rather neatly with other, equally appealing, idealizing theories about "folk society," including the celebration of such "rural" or "peasant" values as egalitarianism, social cohesion, and the centrality of family relations.[4] Such idealized communities were often imagined according to theories that diametrically opposed them, as remnants of some happy past, to the disorganizing, secularizing, divisive forces and influences of modernized and "fallen" urban society. Despite the great evidence of social, political, economic, and cultural change entailed by large-scale movements of people to the cities, most idealizing community-based theories of the mid-twentieth century had little room for change; the communities they discussed were therefore all too frequently taken to be internally homogenous and economically, culturally, and geographically circumscribed.[5] Even when the subject of study was *how* members of particular marginal communities were assimilated into the social, economic, and cultural "core" of a given city, rural life and urban life were frequently understood as static, dualistic, oppositional categories: a person was *in* one or the other, and historical connections between the two zones—complex modes of exchange, dependence, exclusion, privilege, and movement—were often downplayed or overlooked.

Criticism of static center–periphery models began in earnest in the 1970s, and, more recently, better accounts of the complex interactions between "culture" and "capital," including a good deal of concern with patterns of movement—of people, goods, money, and various cultural forms associated with the globalization of trade—have considerably complicated the sorts of claims that may be made by an anthropologist who studies "marginal" urban communities.[6] Distinct forms or patterns of cultural expression and behavior may indeed be found in such communities (as they are found in every community), but where these forms and patterns have come from, and what they mean in the lives of participants and the history of the community, neither is singular nor can be simply stated, as I hope this chapter will show.

Recent ethnography on Mexico has pointed to the need to recognize modes of cultural creation that cannot readily be pinned to specific, readily identifiable social communities or collective groups, but are products of the interaction between profound structural changes—such as urbanization, globalization, and the transition to "modernity"—and processes of social diversification.[7] In these terms, then, "popular culture" subsumes a process of identity creation that is shaped by relations of power. In this book, I use the term *colonia popular* to designate a particular kind of neighborhood, but it is not equivalent to the popular community in its full significance. I am concerned with the "popular community" as formulated from a habitus or an ethos—a cluster of images, values, and deeply felt associations—that is produced in the course of daily social interaction. The "popular community," then, is a *dimension* of social life in certain Oaxacan neighborhoods but does not represent it in any complete, unified way. In popular religious settings, a "popular self" is constructed at the interface of social interaction, certain moral schemes that prioritize "traditional" collective social relations, and ritual performance.

AN INTRODUCTION TO OAXACA

I first visited Oaxaca on a holiday in 1987. Struck by the beautiful colonial façades, the tranquility of the place, and the sweep of low mountains hanging protectively over the city's northern edge, I found Oaxaca a welcome relief after the constant cacophony of traffic and human noise—not to mention the bothersome and persistent pollution—of Mexico City. Oaxaca was my introduction to the southern region of Mexico; it gave me my first sense of several of the very different economic and social landscapes enclosed within the country's borders. In Oaxaca, I saw people whom I thought looked authentically "Mexican"—that is, Indian. Their appearance corresponded to some inner dream of an other, authentically *Latin American* place. Through a lens distorted by my fantasy, I saw in them extreme formality, deference to authority, and fervent religious devotion. Like other tourists, I was excited by sights such as the mystic ruins at

Monte Albán and Mitla; by the indigenous peasant villages that surrounded the city, each devoted to a separate kind of artisanal production; by the rich cuisine; and by the warmth of the people I met—truly here was the "otherness" of experience I had been seeking.

In the decade and a half since my first visit, Oaxaca has changed enormously. Ten years ago, I was oddly shocked by a video game parlor that had opened up by the *zócalo* (town square). Today, Internet cafés are more ubiquitous in the city than in many urban centers in Canada or the United States; whenever you like, you can sip a foamy cappuccino or a café latte while checking your e-mail. These establishments compete for space in the now high-rent city center, or *centro*, with everything from companies doing Web sites, to pizza places, pricey art galleries, sushi restaurants, and vegetarian juice bars. On the street, cellular phones are more common than bicycles; a film by Federico Fellini or Woody Allen, shown at an alternative cinema, might be interrupted by the annoying whine of someone's pager. A special sightseeing tram now takes visitors (mostly Mexicans, since foreigners still demand some colorful dream of authenticity) past noteworthy sites in the city center. Since I began my fieldwork in the city, traffic lights have been installed at many intersections where traffic was previously almost nonexistent; an increasing number of beggars and mounting problems of air pollution, water supply, and sewage all reflect the aches and pains of zealous growth and urbanization.

The old blind man I first saw more than thirteen years ago still sings his plaintive and beautiful songs on the cobblestoned Andador Turístico (Tourist Walkway), which runs from the colonial *zócalo* to the busy roadway leading to Mexico City that skirts the northern edge of the *centro*; occasionally, you can still see burros tied up outside the beautiful church and former convent of Santo Domingo, and people from indigenous rural towns may be heard speaking their local languages as they traverse the streets, some selling flowers, tamales, alfalfa, *chapulines* (grasshoppers), or furniture. An unmistakable greenish glow still emanates from the earthquake-proof, thick-walled limestone buildings that line the *zócalo* and streets nearby, lending a unique and undeniably mystic ambience to the city. Sweethearts still fill the benches in city parks on late afternoons and weekends. But such picturesque snapshots, as though of a disappearing past, although prized by visitors, cannot really stand as representative images of the place Oaxaca has become.

Oaxaca de Juárez (known simply as Oaxaca), the capital of the state of Oaxaca, is a city of some 250,000 people located approximately 180 miles south of Mexico City (figure 1.1). Both city and state are frequently characterized as spaces of pronounced cultural traditionalism, poverty, and a significant number of residents of indigenous background. The majority of the state's 3.4 million

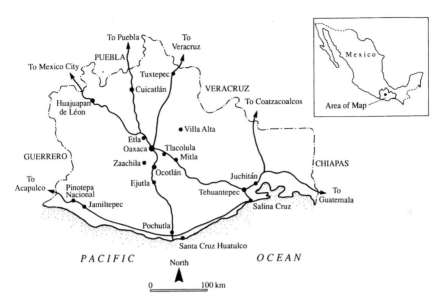

FIGURE 1.1   Mexico and the state of Oaxaca. (From Arthur Murphy and Alex Stepick,
Social Inequality in Oaxaca: A History of Resistance and Change [Philadelphia:
Temple University Press, 1991])

inhabitants live in rural, indigenous settlements; there are 570 municipalities
in the state of Oaxaca, in which sixteen distinct languages (excluding dialects)
are spoken, which suggests a rather wide dispersal of political and administrative power in the state. Roughly 70 percent of the inhabitants of the state are
of indigenous origin, giving Oaxaca the highest proportion of Indians in the
country: about 18 percent of the nation's total indigenous population.[8] While
the largest indigenous groups in the state are Zapotecs and Mixtecs, there are
also Triquis, Chinantecs, Chontales, Mixes, Chatinos, Mazotecs, Chochos, Cui-
catecs, Huaves, Zoques or Tacuates, Ixcatecs, Amuzgos, and Nahuas; there is
also a small but significant Afro-Mexican population. This strong indigenous
presence, and the paradoxical way it is used as the presentation of state identity,
especially in tourism, is critical to understanding the texture of life in Oaxaca
City; it has contributed to Oaxaca's distinct cultural profile and to its political
and economic marginalization relative to other Mexican states.

Being indigenous in Mexico is usually synonymous with being poor. Oaxaca
is located in the southeastern belt of predominantly indigenous states, which
include Chiapas, Guerrero, and Veracruz. Per capita incomes in Oaxaca are
less than half the national average (Oaxaca has the second-lowest national per
capita income, after Chiapas); state statistics are likewise comparably high for

illiteracy, unemployment, death by curable disease, and lack of access to potable water, electricity, and well-maintained roads. Using these indexes, residents of 75 percent of Oaxaca's 570 municipalities have been classified as existing in a condition of "high" or "very high" marginalization.[9] In Oaxaca City, socioeconomic prospects for many residents are quite dim, despite the sanguine, energetic promises of slogans seen on political signs or billboards around the city: "Oaxaca: adelante!" (Oaxaca: forward!).

To complicate matters, rapid urbanization in the state has sharpened tensions and contradictions between urban (mestizo) and rural, peasant (indigenous) ways of life. In addition to widening the rift between rich and poor, government-propelled, neoliberal economic reforms and efforts to democratize the national political culture (partly responsible for the milestone victory of the Partido de Acción Nacional [PAN, National Action Party] over the dinosaur Partido Revolucionario Institucional [PRI, Party of the Institutional Revolution] in the presidential election of 2000) have been met by a blossoming of organizing from popular sectors, including a multifaceted indigenous movement that is fighting for indigenous autonomy. The effects of a regular out-migration of Oaxacans, especially to the United States, and the transformation of Oaxaca's urban landscape to fulfill the increasing demands of international tourism, have accentuated the heterogeneity of the city's population and urban culture. Indeed, Oaxaca may be seen to concentrate many of the contradictions and paradoxes of Mexico's contemporary development in a globalizing world.

The boundaries of the city of Oaxaca have, over the course of the last several decades, expanded to include formerly rural towns. Although residents of many of these outlying *colonias populares* retain a number of ideas and practices common to rural indigenous communities, there is no doubt that the culture of Oaxacan urban neighborhoods, like *colonias populares*, consists of a mixture of the "new" and the "traditional." While migrants from rural areas make an effort to adapt to city lifeways, they may also continue to sleep on reed mats, or *petates*; they may speak an indigenous language at home or consult a local healer, or *curandero*; they may use herbs when ill or when a doctor is beyond their means; they may keep and practice a number of popular or folkloric religious observances such as the death-related rituals I discuss in detail in this book. At the same time, as city dwellers, residents of the *colonias populares* are active participants in a service-oriented, capitalist economy characterized by access to the abundance of consumer goods, images, values, and worldviews found in comparatively wealthy areas of Mexico or in any developed country.

"Doing anthropology" in the city of Oaxaca—above all, in the marginal, "popular" communities that house the bulk of the city's population—thus requires developing a "hybrid ear," a sensitivity to the particular cultural mixtures and forms developed, maintained, and cultivated by *colonia* residents. Despite their rural roots and origins, *colonia* dwellers are urbanites; they are not rural folk in a state of transition. "Popular" practices in the marginal communities of Oaxaca cannot be understood in terms of rural survivals, on the one hand, or urban acculturation, on the other. Here the two terms are not at odds with each other; rather, the notion of the popular, as it has developed in Latin America over the past two decades, defines not a specific group or geography but a relation of marginality. Thus those who belong to the popular classes may include recent migrants to the city, members of indigenous populations, the urban poor, and other politically and economically marginal groups that do not belong to a powerful cosmopolitan or governing elite. The definition of popular culture in this context means, most simply, "the symbols and meanings embedded in the day-to-day practices of subordinated groups."[10]

Brief Historical Sketch

Given a comparatively mild climate, fertile soil, plenty of water, and a large and settled indigenous population, the Valley of Oaxaca presented propitious conditions for Spanish settlement. Long before the arrival of the Spanish in 1521, however, the region already had a long history as a center of power in southern Mexico. The site where Oaxaca City lies today began as an indigenous settlement populated by Mixtec and Zapotec peoples; the ruins of Monte Albán, now located just outside the city, attest to a wealthy and powerful civilization, and Mitla, famous site of the ruins of a Zapotec ceremonial center, was a focal point of a cult dedicated to ancestral worship and the underworld.[11] Later, the garrison of Huaxyacac (Nahuatl, "in the nose of the *guajes*," a tree, ubiquitous in Oaxaca, bearing a podlike legume) was established sometime around 1450 by Mexicas (Aztecs) from the north, who eventually succeeded in subjugating the local Mixtec and Zapotec peoples. The Aztecs were then conquered and assimilated under Spanish rule, a process that began in 1521, when the infamous conquistador Hernán Cortés sent his envoy, Francisco de Orozco, to open a southern route to the sea. Cortés later declared himself marqués del Valle, and a settlement, known as Antequera, grew up, located advantageously at the confluence of three fertile valleys and a natural stop for traders traveling between Mexico City and parts farther south. Cortés and the Spanish Crown wrangled for years for control of this settlement: the Spanish wanted to concentrate power and wealth in the city, and Cortés, in order to frustrate Antequera's growth, initiated the establishment of indigenous settlements on the outskirts of the town. Thus settlements such as Santo Tomás Xochimilco, Santa Anita, Jalatlaco, Santa María del Marquesado, San Juan Chapultepec, and San Martín Mexicapan came into being—the last two now distinct municipalities, separate from Oaxaca proper. In 1532 the Crown finally solved its problems with the marqués del Valle by dividing the city of Antequera between Oaxaca del Marqués, a settlement for indigenous peoples, and Antequera del Rey, which was for the Spanish.

Antequera thus followed the standard plan of Spanish colonial cities, with its central core occupied by Spanish residences and all administrative and commercial activity, and its periphery made up of various indigenous communities that, over time, were gradually incorporated into the urban center. The colonial city effectively inverted the forms of pre-Hispanic cities, where the center was an empty core, surrounded by regions dedicated to various activities.[12] Antequera was where tribute was collected and the labor of indigenous populations orchestrated and controlled under the colonial *encomienda* (land-tenure and commission) system.

Once Pope Alexander VI made his 1493 declaration that any land discovered west of the Azores would fall under the rule of the Spanish Crown, as long as Spanish explorers and settlers made "God's name known" wherever they went, colonization went hand in hand with evangelization. In 1528 the first missionary order, a group of Dominican friars, arrived in the fertile Valley of Oaxaca; within seven years, they had established an ecclesiastical center in Antequera, the Bishopric of Oaxaca, and begun to set up parishes in the surrounding area. Although there were more than twenty separate indigenous groups in the region of Oaxaca at the time, the Dominicans concentrated primarily on converting Zapotecs and Mixtecs, perhaps as a way of combating the influence of the highly important, visible ceremonial centers of Monte Albán and Mitla.

Antequera de Oaxaca grew very slowly over the course of the sixteenth and seventeenth centuries. By 1579 there were just five hundred households, or a total population of six thousand, in the city.[13] According to one historian, whatever increase in the number of residents did take place was the result of the in-migration of Indians from elsewhere in the valley and the surrounding area, not to a real growth in the population.[14] Spanish political functionaries as well as those who served the marqués; owners of *encomiendas* and haciendas, mines, mills, and cattle; representatives of the church of various kinds; and artisans resided in the city, whereas Indian populations—primarily Zapotecs, Mixtecs, and Aztecs—settled on the outskirts in communities such as Jalatlaco and Santo Tomás Xochimilco (figure 1.2). Consequently, the populations of these outlying communities fluctuated quite a bit during the sixteenth and seventeenth centuries. Many of the residents of these indigenous communities found work in Antequera's textile workshops; they also serviced the Spaniards as carpenters, bakers, shoemakers, tanners, tailors, potters, metalworkers, masons, and silversmiths—and, in turn, developed a strong dependence on the urban economy, becoming assimilated into the local occupational structure. Artisanal production was structured around *gremios* (guilds), which did not permit access to the rank of master or guild official to those who were not "pure of blood" and longtime Christians. (These *gremios* later became the basis of important indigenous religious brotherhoods, or *cofradías*, although such organizations were not nearly as important in urban Oaxaca as they were in rural indigenous communities.) At the same time, however, particularly during the seventeenth century, the Spanish in Antequera depended on the outlying Indian settlements for their food supply: agricultural production from the Valley of Oaxaca nourished the entire region.

On the whole, divisions between the Spanish and the indigenous peoples were quite strictly reinforced by a system of ethnic distinction that rendered the European "core" as the functional and symbolic (moral) center of life and

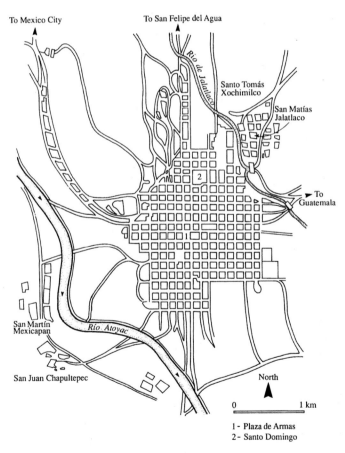

FIGURE 1.2 The colonial city of Antequera. (From Arthur Murphy and Alex Stepick, *Social Inequality in Oaxaca: A History of Resistance and Change* [Philadelphia: Temple University Press, 1991])

opposed the urbanized *gente de razón* (rational people) to outlying rural, "uncivilized," "savage" *indios*. Spanish-born *peninsulares* were at the top of the colonial
heap, while their lesser cousins, the New World–born *criollos*, stood above the
indios. (Traces of such practices and discourses remain in force in Mexico, in
the opposition between a national, valorized mestizo identity and more marginalized, if increasingly self-conscious and oppositionally organized, *indios*.)
Nevertheless, it is important to note that early examples of what we might today
call "hybrid cultural spaces" were numerous in colonial Antequera. Important
liminal figures that, in their movements between Indian and Spanish worlds,
blurred geographic, racial, and moral separations included indigenous nobles,
or *caciques*; hereditary rulers or chiefs, who adopted the Spanish language and
customs; and indigenous artisans, healers, temporary laborers, Indian nannies,
and *curanderas* (female healers, sometimes hired by nuns).[15] The world traversed
by such liminal figures could be quite broad, for not only was Antequera the
religious and administrative center of the Bishopric of Oaxaca, but it also served
as a stopping place for travelers and merchants going from New Spain to Central
America; it was also the way station for commodities, including *añil* (indigo)
and other dyes, wine, and cacao, on their way north to Mexico City or Veracruz
from Guatemala, and on to the Oaxacan port of Santa Cruz Huatulco.

Important, too, was that, unlike in many other settlements in New Spain, the
large landed estates, or haciendas, that appeared in the Valley of Oaxaca were
relatively small. Owing in large part to the relative strength of Oaxacan *caciques*
under the Spanish, the few haciendas that did exist did not result in great losses
of land for the indigenous populations, who were able to retain large tracts of
their lands and hence some independence from the Spanish for their own subsistence needs. Agriculture in the Oaxaca region thus remained mainly geared
to subsistence and an indigenous market economy, and throughout the colonial
period the focal point of the local economy was a rotating market system, established by the Spanish, that joined city, small marketing centers, and the rural
hinterland. Although it played a critical role in the colonial economy of the
Valley of Oaxaca, by allowing the Spanish to procure a wide range of goods, this
market system was also crucial to the local indigenous subsistence economy—it
remains, even today, very strong in some respects.

Still the requirements placed on the haciendas in the region and the obligations
that tied Indians to them in order to satisfy the demands of the Spanish population
in Antequera were extreme. Harsh working conditions and the onslaught of a series
of devastating illnesses brought by Europeans to the New World, including smallpox, typhoid, measles, whooping cough, and malaria, resulted in a steep decline
in the number of native peoples; after dropping sharply toward the end of the sixteenth century, the indigenous population reached its lowest point around 1630.

By the late sixteenth century, Franciscans, Jesuits, Augustinians, Carmelites, and Mercedarians had established footholds in Antequera, and by the end of the colonial period, despite considerable intraclerical strife, the church was the leading Spanish landowner in the Valley of Oaxaca, controlling nearly one-quarter of the productive rural property in the region and funding a number of entrepreneurial enterprises from its coffers. Indeed, by the eighteenth century, most orders owned significant amounts of both grazing land and urban real estate.[16]

This amassing of wealth—and, with it, political power—in the hands of the church was by no means unique to the Valley of Oaxaca. Similar concentrations of wealth and power elsewhere in Mexico led to the 1804 decree by King Charles III of Spain, requiring all church funds to be turned over to royal control. Complying with the decree meant that church officials were forced to call in loans and other investments in business enterprises, and colonial Mexico plunged into economic chaos. When Napoleon invaded Spain in 1808 and restricted political authority in Mexico to Spanish loyalists in Mexico City, disaffected members of the clergy began to plot their revolt. The Grito de Dolores (Cry of Dolores), the Mexican declaration of independence, was issued by Padre Miguel Hidalgo y Costilla on 16 September 1810, and the fighting began. Eleven years later, in 1821, a treaty was signed with Spain, which guaranteed the religious hegemony of the Catholic Church, a constitutional monarchy, and equal rights for Mexican-born residents of mixed Indian and Spanish ancestry (mestizos) and Mexican-born Spaniards (*criollos*). Notably, *indios*, considered by the engineers of independence to be an obstacle to development, were excluded from the agreement. Within two years, the new monarch had been overthrown, and, in 1824, the constitutional republic of Los Estados Unidos de México was established.

While Oaxaca remained peripheral to the struggle for independence—most significant battles took place in Mexico City and farther north—independence slowly brought changes to the region as political power began to shift into the hands of nonclerical mestizos. The urban center, no longer known formally as Antequera, but as Oaxaca City, remained quite small, however, partly because of laws that prevented Indians from settling in the city. In addition, in the mid-nineteenth century, the decline, as a result of the beginning of the War of Independence, of the important cochineal industry, which manufactured a bright red dye for export from the crushed, dried, red bodies of a cactus-feeding insect, helped to further marginalize the city. National liberal reforms designed to wrest power and wealth from the church and to provide for greater educational opportunity, instigated under the governorship, beginning in 1848, of the Oaxacan native son and Zapotec lawyer Benito Juárez (later the president of Mexico [1868–1872]), had some effect on the growth and well-being of Oaxaca City. (Although Juárez was, himself, of indigenous background, the situation of indigenous peoples was made far worse by the reforms: the two primary liberal policies, the Juárez Law [1855] and the Lerdo Law [1856], subjected Indian groups to an expropriation of their lands, resulting in the disintegration of many indigenous communities.)

Although the modernization of educational systems, the encouragement of foreign investment, and the expansion of networks of transport were continued under Porfirio Díaz, for the next twenty-eight years (1876–1911), at his authoritarian behest, both free elections and a free press were suspended, and the gap between rich and poor, in Oaxaca and elsewhere, widened. The population of Oaxaca diminished in the wake of the Mexican Revolution and the *reparto agrario* (land redistribution), under Lázaro Cárdenas, in the 1930s, as absentee landlords (many of them Europeans) lost their rural holdings and migrated elsewhere. In addition, a number of strong earthquakes in the 1930s caused a significant number of people to leave the area. By 1940 the population of Oaxaca City stood at thirty-five thousand.

If its marginal status during the colonial period had meant for a peaceful existence, marginality was also the theme of Oaxaca's fate in the postrevolutionary period—and, indeed, for much of the twentieth century. Owing to the comparatively small number of dispossessed peasants in the state, and its physical isolation, the revolution made a relatively insignificant mark in Oaxaca, and the state produced no revolutionary leaders or instances of radical mobilization. That, combined with Oaxaca's relative lack of infrastructure, caused national political leaders to view the state as relatively unimportant; not surprisingly, when the PRI consolidated its control over the national government in the 1920s, Oaxaca was consistently ignored by Mexico City and received few financial incentives to boost its development.

An international highway and rail links, completed in the 1950s, brought the Valley of Oaxaca into more regular contact with the remainder of the country and allowed a greater integration into the national economy. Over time, financial crises, and power struggles and tensions between political and economic elites and non-elites, emerged in Oaxaca City, especially those related to problems of a rising urban population including, housing and access to social and labor benefits. Yet, until recently, aside from sharp student-led political protests in the 1970s (which showed the willingness of the authoritarian state to respond with repressive measures),[17] popular resistance in Oaxaca was isolated and low-key, and the city remained fairly small, isolated, insular, and provincial.

Thus ideas of the popular and marginality as lived experience in Oaxaca cannot be understood outside the particularities of the history of Oaxaca's development on the geographic and political peripheries of Mexican national culture and society.

Oaxaca City Today

It remains the case that the majority of the residents of the state of Oaxaca are Indian peasants, or *campesinos*, living in medium-size towns and villages. Oaxaca City is by far the largest urban hub in the state, with approximately 7.5 percent of the state's inhabitants; Huajuapan de León is in second place, with roughly 1.5 percent. Located at the confluence of three valleys, Oaxaca City lies at the heart of the "Central Valleys," the most prosperous and densely populated area of the seven geographically and ethnically diverse regions comprising the state itself (figure 1.3).

Anthropologists have frequently argued that the state's indigenous rural character, mountainous topography, and poor communications system have contrib-

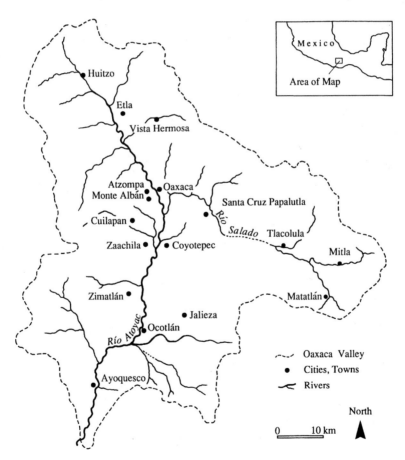

FIGURE 1.3 The Valley of Oaxaca. (From Arthur Murphy and Alex Stepick, *Social Inequality in Oaxaca: A History of Resistance and Change* [Philadelphia: Temple University Press, 1991])

uted significantly to the area's political and economic marginalization.[18] While its traditional economic profile will undoubtedly continue to change dramatically, the economic mainstays of Oaxaca remain agriculture, livestock, commerce, and tourism.[19] Terms such as "center" and "periphery" are not simply descriptive of geographic relations. There are no large industries in either the city or the state of Oaxaca; in addition to revenues generated by tourism, the wealth of Oaxaca is derived from its place as the commercial, political, and administrative center of southwestern Mexico—that is, its position as the center of a peripheral region.[20] Tourism is the only economic sector that has grown constantly since the mid-twentieth century; it is now the most significant source of income in Oaxaca City.[21] Despite minimal development to its economic infrastructure, the population of Oaxaca's urban center has escalated dramatically, especially over the course of the past several decades. From 1940 until the 1980s, the city averaged a rough annual growth rate of just over 4 percent; by 1990 the city boasted nearly 250,000 residents.[22] Between 1970 and 1990 alone, Oaxaca City more than doubled in size. Today, its official population is estimated at 256,130 inhabitants, although this figure is commonly regarded as a conservative estimate, since it excludes the seventeen officially recognized municipalities, other communities, and "irregular" settlements located just outside the metropolitan zone of Oaxaca itself.

A major source of Oaxaca City's dramatic rise in population is the continuous stream of peasant migrants from the rural regions of the state. Oaxaca has a long history of attracting indigenous labor from the *campo* (countryside). In the colonial era, Indians in the Valley of Oaxaca often came to the city of Antequera, in order to free themselves of the obligation to pay tribute on the hacienda estates of the Spanish; today they come in search of new opportunities—for employment, education, and new experiences. Unfortunately, most rural migrants who wish to escape rural poverty only succeed in becoming assimilated into the urban underclass. Estimates from 1990 suggest that 60 percent of the urban population work in the informal sector of the economy and earn less than the minimum wage. In 2000 official figures indicated that 41.46 percent of the economically active city residents earned less than two minimum wages daily (the equivalent of roughly U.S.$8).[23] The current inadequacy of employment opportunities, combined with the increasing difficulty of surviving in the countryside (especially in the past couple of decades, with the introduction of economic policies that have forced formerly self-sufficient rural peasants into a closer dependence on the market), mean that many members of rural indigenous Oaxacan communities now migrate in the hundreds, either seasonally or permanently, to the north of Mexico or to the United States.[24]

Rural to urban movement has thus been critical to Oaxaca's social and cultural development. It has been estimated that more than 80 percent of all Oaxacan urban household heads came to the city from rural areas of Oaxaca or from other parts of Mexico; some argue that the numbers have increased in recent years.[25] Historically, given the structure of the colonial city, poor indigenous immigrants were forced to settle in the less desirable neighborhoods on the city's periphery. In periods of rapid urbanization, beginning in the 1960s, this colonial settlement policy resulted in the blossoming of illegal squatter settlements on unclaimed land at the outer edges of the city. Within just a few years, by the mid-1970s, more than 60 percent of the metropolitan area of Oaxaca was covered with housing that had its origin in some type of "irregular" land occupancy.[26]

As its population expanded, Oaxaca proper grew beyond its early boundaries and swallowed up these peripheral squatter settlements and other formerly distinct neighborhoods located near its periphery. By 1980 densely populated *colonias populares* covered about half the city's geographic area and embraced most of Oaxaca's inhabitants.[27] Today, many formerly illegal land occupancies and squatter settlements have been formally registered and recognized as *colonias populares*, a term that both refers to the inhabitants—members of the popular classes—and officially designates the smallest municipal unit with political representation.[28]

If originally the term *colonia popular* was associated with the squatter settlements of the poor urban classes, now the word *colonia* is virtually synonymous with "neighborhood." It is important to recognize the unique position of such *colonias* in Oaxaca's social landscape. Today, internal social differentiation is ordered centrifugally, in much the same way that it was in the colonial era: the center of the city is distinguished socially from peripheral neighborhoods, or *colonias populares*; likewise, the urban mestizo character of Oaxaca City as a whole is distinguished from the "Indian" communities encircling it, which are, in turn, distinguished from those located farther away. Such distinctions mark especially strongly *colonias* located in or near what were formerly indigenous towns such as Jalatlaco, Xochimilco, Trinidad de las Huertas, and San Martín Mexicapan, or what are referred to as *pueblos conurbados*, formerly separate towns that are now virtually part of the city, such as Santa Cruz Xoxocotlán.

As one walks through the *colonias* at the very edge of the city, one easily encounters liminal landscapes that reveal themselves as an interface between, or merging of, rural and urban worlds: here are dirt roads and tin and adobe homes in yards with minimal fencing or none at all; water is fetched from a well up the hill or from a collective tap two blocks away; maize grows tall in small yards, while chickens graze freely and pigs, goats, and sometimes even burros are tied up outside a house. Such scenes, which multiply in number as one moves farther and farther away from the city center, contrast sharply with the urban core (figure 1.4).

The *centro*, where the greatest percentage of renters lives, is today home to a mixture of the very rich and the very poor. Less than half this population, how-

FIGURE 1.4   A scene from a *colonia popular*.

ever, consists of recent migrants, compared with figures as high as 80 percent in most *colonias*.[29] The middle to upper classes in Oaxaca are predominantly composed of two groups: old, established families with a long history in Oaxaca, whose wealth has been derived largely from commerce, and more recent arrivals who have come to work for the federal government or national—and, increasingly, transnational—companies and businesses.[30] The small community of foreigners (dominated by American "ex-pats," but with some Europeans) could be added to this group, as well as academics and researchers (both native and foreign) and other intellectuals and artists.

Noises and people flow throughout the public, collective spaces of the *centro*: itinerant vendors of bread, alfalfa, *chapulines*, furniture, neon-colored nylon balloons, weavings, carpets, or jewelry mingle with tourists, students, government workers, and professionals (figure 1.5). A broad cross section of Oaxacan society converges in the *zócalo*: rich kids from San Felipe hang out on the square's edge, and small children move among the tourists and Oaxacans seated at the restaurants and bars that ring the edge of the square, begging, hawking chewing gum and small items of *artesanía*, or offering to shine shoes (or sandals!); a *plantón* of demonstrators or hunger strikers chants in front of the municipal palace; a blind man sings; the mariachis and marimbas play; and Triqui artisans and

FIGURE 1.5   The *zócalo* of Oaxaca City.

tapete weavers from Teotitlán del Valle sell their wares alongside dreadlocked bohemian jewelry sellers, drummers, and *capoeiristas* from Mexico City.

While the *colonias* farther from the center were considered, for quite a time, poorer and less prestigious, as pollution and noise in the city core have worsened, many wealthy Oaxacans have chosen to settle in expensive new *fraccionamientos* (subdivisions) at some distance from the center. In these more recently established *colonias* and suburbs—where pizza parlors and McDonald's, a Sam's Club, and a six-cinema CineMax line the well-lighted wide streets—paler-skinned Oaxacans live among servants, manicured lawns and gardens, and new blocky "modern" architecture. Two cars are parked in many of the driveways by evening, but these communities boast a relative lack of both human traffic and communal meeting spaces. As the *centro* has become increasingly commercialized, dense, and noisy, upper-class peripheral settlements have become more common; as elsewhere, such movements are nostalgic reappropriations of the bucolic charm of the *campo* by the bourgeois classes. Thus, for example, in the town of San Felipe del Agua, in the north of the city, Diódoro Carrasco, the former governor of Oaxaca (and the former minister of the interior of Mexico [1994–2000]), as well as various better-off politicians, academics, and foreigners have constructed airy, spacious ranch-style homes. But most of the communities on the edge of the city are also "on the edge" in various other senses as well.

LIVING ON THE EDGE

I began my work in a place I call Colonia San Juan. Located on the northern fringe of the city, where the worlds of old and new, rural and urban lifestyles, come together in a coexistence that is energetic, if not always easy, Colonia San Juan is set on a flank of the Cerro del Fortín, the foothills stretching toward Mexico City (figure 1.6). San Juan is one of the older of the seven *colonias* that make up the parish of Santa María Cuauhtémoc. A busy roadway, paved in the mid-1980s, runs along the lower, north–south edge of the *colonia* and divides it from the barrio of Cuauhtémoc, formally an indigenous town that was incorporated into the city in the early twentieth century. The parish church is here, as well as public primary and secondary schools attended by most of the children in the parish. Residents of San Juan readily hear the church bells that chime each hour throughout the day and, more clangorously, during fiestas; likewise, every morning a crackly, amplified recording of the national anthem flies up the hill to San Juan from the school grounds. The streets radiating up from the roadway into the *colonia* are at a steep incline; the walk up makes even the fittest person break into a sweat. Colonia San Juan's setting discourages the regular through-traffic that plagues many other city *colonias*; it is thus a neighborhood where it is safe for children to play on the street. The *colonia* is noisy and busy; neighbors walk up and down the streets, kids play, dogs bark, and music and chatter from radios and stereos escape into the air. If you stand in the middle of the *colonia*, a magnificent view of the city spreads out before you. You can easily spot the distinctive blue and white–checkered cupolas of the Iglesia de Santo Domingo and the hazy outline of the low, dark green mountains that flank Oaxaca to the north and east, especially those of the northern sierra, or Sierra Juárez.[31]

Current demographic patterns suggest that Oaxaca is gradually becoming a city with a young, native, urban-centered majority and an older generation of migrants.[32] Nevertheless, many of the adult residents of the *colonias populares*, certainly most of those in Colonia San Juan, are first- or second-generation migrants from small towns and villages in the rural regions of the state. Many *colonia* residents, especially those born in the city and older migrants who arrived there as adults, are bilingual; that is, they speak both Spanish (*castellano*) and an indigenous language. Often, however, partly because of years of public disdain and hostility to native languages, such indigenous languages are spoken only in the home or other "private" spaces.

FIGURE 1.6   A view over Oaxaca City, with the mountains in the distance.

Unlike many other *colonias* located on the periphery of Oaxaca, San Juan did not begin as a squatter settlement, nor did it grow up from the illegal sale of lots.[33] San Juan was first established around 1955, thanks to the sale of cheap tracts of land by four people who apparently possessed legal entitlement to the property.[34] In its beginnings, San Juan was regarded—by *colonos* (residents of the *colonia*) and by other city residents—as cut off from the rest of the city. When asked to describe the early appearance of the place, my neighbors often used metaphors of isolation and an inhospitable "naturalness" to talk about the neighborhood. Older residents spoke of the *colonia* at the time of its founding as "abandoned" (*abandonado*), consisting of "bare mountain" (*puro monte*). It had no roads, no running water, no electricity, no drains or sewers; the only way to the center of town was by foot. Their descriptions were always framed by reference to the progress or improvements that have come with greater urbanization and the betterment of the material conditions of many *colonia* residents. For example, regarding the replacement of older dwellings of adobe or corrugated iron by more finished cement houses on her street, doña Isabel, a longtime San Juan resident, commented, "There are no longer any ugly houses here, because everything has been modernized." Nevertheless, especially in the older, lower sections of San Juan, the *colonia* encompasses a wide range of building materials and different kinds of homes.

Indeed, many urban Oaxacan *colonias populares* about the same age as Colonia San Juan showcase distinct zones or layers of temporal development: thus one may see architectural characteristics considered to be "traditional" or rural side by side with those viewed as "modern" or urban.[35] Both the five-star hotel built toward the end of the 1980s and the Lions Club—used since the early 1970s as a social club by Oaxaca's aspiring middle to upper classes—are set on the *colonia's* southern flank and are bordered by paved roads. But when I first arrived in 1989, most *colonia* residents still lived in fairly rudimentary dwellings and made do with quite skeletal city services, great "improvements" to the neighborhood notwithstanding. Rooms lit by single bare lightbulbs and an utter lack of indoor plumbing were the norm.

With its unpaved roads, minimal services, and shabby appearance of some of its residences, San Juan appeared uniformly poor in 1989. But, economically speaking, it was healthy and stable, and continues to be, when compared with many other Oaxacan neighborhoods, including others within the same parish. The majority of families in San Juan, especially in the *colonia's* older, lower half, own the properties they live on; home ownership, here as elsewhere in the region, is strongly valued.[36] The cost of constructing a rudimentary dwelling is relatively low (at the beginning of the 1990s a few hundred U.S. dollars was enough to build a simple house of tin siding; even today, construction labor is still very inexpensive), and many families at least own a basic home on land that might be borrowed or rented. Members of one extended family frequently live together on the same *solar* (yard), and sometimes a number of separate dwellings, one for each small family unit, is constructed in the same yard.

Even more than its architecture, the texture of life in the *colonia popular* is a complex mixture of the old and the new. Contrary to many anthropological predictions, residents do not simply abandon customs and practices from rural spaces as they "assimilate" into city life. Often, in fact, one sees the re-creation of customary rural patterns, alongside new, urban forms: ovens used for cooking stand beside grinding stones (*metates*) for pulverizing corn or coffee beans; beds are placed alongside reed mats (*petates*); store-bought flour tortillas are eaten along with those made by hand with corn flour (*masa*); and so on.

Likewise, in San Juan, residents tend to speak of themselves by invoking the associations attached to the rural spaces they have come from. Movement from a rural to an urban space is often configured as a positively valued, progressive movement and represents the hope of a new and better life. Living in the city often means access to higher education or chances of employment as a construction worker, restaurant employee, or maid—regular, if poorly remunerated, work. At the same time, however, many people in San Juan and the parish of Cuautémoc speak quite approvingly of San Juan as a particularly "traditional" barrio, where customs are preserved better and more richly than in other newer colonias.

Aiding in the preservation of such valued rural lifeways are the strong links that many Oaxacans, especially those of the popular sectors, retain with the town or village that they or their parents come from; for example, several of my neighbors regularly return to their native pueblos, especially on special occasions such as El Día de los Muertos (Day of the Dead), the town's annual *mayordomía* (patron saint's festival), or other important fiestas. Often a given house in the *colonia* is used by visiting kin, *compadres* (ritual co-parents, usually associated with sacramental rites such as baptism, first communion, or a wedding), or even nonrelatives from the country as a "home away from home," operating much like a satellite extension of the village community. One friend in a neighboring *colonia*, Lucía, who has been settled in Oaxaca City for more than two decades, regularly receives both short- and long-term visitors from the Sierra Juárez. She herself returns there at least once a year, normally on the feast day of the patron saint of her hometown.

New migrants to the city typically use exchange networks among kin, *compadres*, and friends to help them find employment and housing. Some migrants will have lived elsewhere in the city before being able to move to a space like San Juan and establish a more "permanent" residence. As a result of such patterns of movement, it is common for given *colonias* to become dominated by migrants from the same rural area, who are linked through family or *compadrazgo* (ritual co-parenting) relations and networks of exchange. One section of San Juan, for example, contains many families from the highland Oaxacan town of Huautla de Jiménez (home of the famous *curandera* María Sabina), while families from the state's Sierra Juárez region heavily populate a neighboring *colonia*. Some neighbors' homes are constantly filled with new arrivals, both individuals and families; the tendency for people to establish new households near their relatives seems very strong, especially among rural in-migrants, who are likely to settle, if not near kin, then at least close to other families from the same town. Even residents of small single-family dwellings in San Juan typically have relatives living nearby, either in the *colonia* or in a neighboring community. While some of the first settlers in the *colonia* were born in Oaxaca City, the majority came from small rural Oaxacan communities and, in time, shared their properties with their children and other members of their families. Early residents might have bought several parcels of land when the *colonia* first began; later, they were able to sell them or allow relatives to settle there.

As is true for the majority of Oaxacans, most individuals and households in San Juan depend for their survival on wage labor, whether skilled or unskilled.

It is rare to find an adult who has more than a few years of primary school education, although many make great sacrifices to provide their children or grandchildren with a university education.[37] A few of the latter have professional careers and permanent, salaried jobs with benefits and security; these few work as teachers, nurses, doctors, or lawyers. Other *colonos* with steady employment are low-paid workers in the service sector. Many of these workers are women who head single-parent households, their partners or husbands having left or died. Still others are self-employed laborers who work out of their homes; they might hire relatives or friends as employees and run a sustainable family business as a tailor, welder, *cuchillería* (knife-crafter), mechanic, or weaver.

Most such employment yields a very modest income. Life in San Juan and other *colonias populares* in the city calls for a great deal of creativity as residents struggle to make ends meet, let alone "get ahead." Locally owned corner stores are found throughout the neighborhood, where residents may buy small goods and beer, which is often sold illegally. These are complemented by numerous other small stores and entrepreneurial projects that are run out of people's homes. Some people will sell various items—such as vegetables and fruit, soft drinks, or (illicitly) mescal—on a casual basis from their homes, and solitary door-to-door vendors frequently move through the *colonia*'s streets, offering everything from handmade tortillas, fertilizer, or *atole* (hot drink made from maize and milk) to woven tablecloths, articles of clothing, vegetables, pots and pans, alfalfa, and even ladders or furniture. For some, such enterprises represent a primary source of income; most people, however, rely on such sales to bring in supplementary funds. Some households also minimize their expenses by raising chickens (for meat and eggs), turkeys, or even pigs on their properties.

RESPETO AND CONFIANZA

As in many other postcolonial social landscapes, an odd balance of insecurity, authority, restraint, and openness characterizes life in Oaxaca. In particular, deeply rooted hierarchical notions of domination and subservience form the core of the normative structure of Mexican and Oaxacan social interaction. An authoritarian principle is clearly articulated in the basic unit of socialization, the family, where a distinct pecking order of statuses and role expectations—especially gender roles—plays out. Yet nuances of such hierarchical relationships, structured by ideas of superiority and deference, resonate throughout the social field. In state-run primary and secondary schools, for example, children are taught to venerate the national *pátria* (fatherland) in disciplined ritual fashion on a regular basis: each Monday, for example, in the rite of honoring the flag

(Homenaje a la Bandera), through hymns, marching, and salutes, young Mexicans learn quickly that respect for their country, parents (especially their father), and other figures of authority is one and the same, and requires unquestioned reverence, self-sacrifice, and rigorous order. Likewise, especially in ritual settings, social interaction is directed by the concept of "respect" (*respeto*). Outside the family, "respect" influences interactions between individuals in relationships of a hierarchical nature—between *compadres*, old and young, between mestizo and *indígena*, rich and poor.

To understand how such relationships work, it is important to see that *colonias populares* have their own centers and peripheries. Despite the general accuracy of the description of a *colonia* such as San Juan as a poor, "marginal" neighborhood, it is worth noting that there are significant socioeconomic differences among *colonia* residents. (In part, such differences may be seen as an index of just how vast the disparities are in Mexico regarding wealth, education, opportunity, experience, worldviews, and so on.) Thus while the social structure of urban Oaxaca could be usefully read off in terms of an analysis of class, such an approach, by itself, can severely limit the researcher's appreciation of both the complexity of interpersonal relations and the nature of the relationships both among and within socioeconomic classes. In Oaxaca, for example, class differences among people have been mixed with processes of generational change, as well as specific linguistic and cultural variations; taken together, such factors produce a far more complex and interesting picture than a simple study of class stratification alone would allow. Important, too, is that Oaxacans themselves conceive of distinctions not through the lens of socioeconomic class so much as in terms of idioms related to sociality. In such a view, members of another "class" are, quite simply, those who do not belong to one's own psychosocial community.

Within such a psychosocial community, the relative intensity of reciprocal exchanges depends on several measures of relationship that may include formal relations (family, god-parenthood), physical proximity (one's immediate neighbor), or economic and psychosocial interdependence. This last zone is where a vital component of social interaction in the *colonias* comes into play in the practice of *confianza*, a relationship of mutual trust or mutual aid. Since the root of *confianza* is the family, it refers to a singular kind of trust, with overtones of affect and intimacy. Starting from the immediate family, the bounds of one's personal sphere of *confianza* move outward in a widening circle, typically embracing more distant relatives and members of one's ritual kin group, other friends and acquaintances, and so on. Those outside one's circle of *confianza* are strangers, people to be least trusted in one's social environment.

Confianza is the object of social practice; it is especially important in ritual contexts when *compadrazgo* links are made. Familial ties and obligations are linked with religious and life-cycle rituals and are extended by the relationships of ritual kinship. The *compadrazgo* system is therefore an important social institution modeled on the idiom of blood kinship. Webs of blood kinship among residents in Colonia San Juan exist alongside—and sometimes overlap—networks of *compadrazgo* relations. In the years of my study, nearly every adult in San Juan had at least one *compadre* or *comadre* who was also a *colonia* resident; some residents had close to a dozen such ritual co-parents.

Compadrazgo relations may be grouped into categories based on their relative importance. The most significant godparents—what we might call "first-order" *compadres*—are those who sponsor another person in the course of sacramental rites such as baptism, first communion, and confirmation. "Second-order" godparents are sought for other, slightly less important rites such as funeral *levantadas*, taking a child to be "raised" in front of a saint, and sponsoring religious figurines such as the Niño Dios. (All these ritual activities are discussed in subsequent chapters.) Finally, "third-order" *compadres* might play minor roles of sponsorship within larger sacramental celebrations or, alternatively, be tapped to sponsor some sort of secular life-cycle rite such as a school graduation. Customarily, verbal forms of reference or address mark out and enshrine relationships of first- and second-order *compadres*. Whether third-order *compadres* are addressed in the language of ritual kinship very much depends on the individuals involved.

Compadrazgo relations vary in intensity and perceived importance according to the sorts of responsibilities entailed by the link; even within each level or "order" of ritual kinship, the significance attributed to the tie will vary according to participants. Thus, for example, contact with a baptismal godparent who has moved away from the city may be lost altogether, while the importance of a third-order *compadre* link may be inflated and treated as especially significant, as in the case of my *ahijada* (goddaughter) from a kindergarten graduation, who still greets me with a traditional formal address: "Mano, madrina." The density and complexity of *compadrazgo* networks within many *colonias* are partly a result of rural migrants being helped by relatives or *compadres* to settle in the city; such density also reflects the use of *compadre* bonds to reinforce existing friendships between people who have lived together in the neighborhood over a long period.

While many observers (both scholars and casual commentators) seem to doubt that economic exchanges among *compadres* in urban settings like Oaxaca continue to be as strong as those found in rural locales, in San Juan I observed many occasions in which relations of *compadrazgo* functioned as a means of extending an individual's or a family's bulwark of financial security—above all, in cases of significant or unexpected expenditure. Ritual kin were tapped for money loans to help with the sudden costs of a medical emergency or a funeral, or—as I experienced on a couple of occasions—to pay an official or a lawyer a *mordida* (bribe) to spring someone accused of a crime from the city *procuraduría* (courthouse). Other examples of heavy financial burdens, which *compadrazgo* relations might be expected to help carry, involve important ritual occasions, such as sponsoring a *mayordomía* or hosting a life-cycle fiesta such as a baptism or *quinceaños* ("coming-out" party celebrating a girl's fifteenth birthday). The *compadrazgo* system thus provides an institutionalized, positively sanctioned means of amassing sizable funds fairly quickly. (In non-crisis situations, the favor implies stronger obligations of commensurate reciprocity but also, usually, concerns a much smaller amount of money.)

Today, first-order *compadrazgo* ties are typically made between individuals of fairly equivalent socioeconomic status, and, although economic exchanges between them may occur, most such relationships are primarily social. For the most part, then, the sorts of economic exchanges that take place between such *compadres* are limited to small items and favors. Indeed, a male neighbor of mine claimed there was no point in having a rich person as a *compadre*, since the two would not be able to *convivir* (socialize on an intimate level); in other words, *confianza* would not be possible in such an unequal relation. The practice of establishing secular *compadrazgo* links for comparatively unimportant occasions such as a kindergarten or primary school graduation would seem further to underline the increasingly social tone of the institution of ritual co-parenthood today.

Compadrazgo is thus most often seen as an institutionalized means of extending one's network of *confianza*, and most households in San Juan seemed to be tied up with one another in a network of *compadrazgo* relations. Among certain homes in my immediate neighborhood, visiting between households and patterns of interaction appeared to be regular and frequent, despite some claims from informants suggesting that this was not the case. Although some households did seem to isolate themselves from *colonia* "neighborliness," a strong and convivial internal network of *colonos*, well known to one another, appeared to anchor everyday social life in the area. The frequency of such meetings has, however, appeared to diminish over the years; increasingly, the only regular events involving concentrated gatherings of *colonia* residents have been those related to life-cycle rituals such as baptisms, birthdays, *quinceaños*, funerals, or other religious fiestas.

Thus while there is no doubt that *compadrazgo* relationships continue to be important, both economically and socially, in marginal communities like San Juan, it is also clear that these forms of ritual kinship and mutual obligation, so important to life and survival in outlying rural communities, have undergone and continue to undergo significant transformations in the move from country to city. Nevertheless, some aspects of relationships of *compadrazgo* sketch out the contours of a world in which certain important beliefs and values at some odds with individualistic or capitalist beliefs still obtain. In the next several sections, I outline the terms of several of the most important of these beliefs or values. These terms are not "scientific" or systematic; they belong less to the vocabulary of scholarly analysis than to the realm of self-description from within the *colonia*. Sometimes one term or one testimony appears to conflict with another, but, taken together, they describe the general, inhabitable practical and psychosocial universe of the *colonia popular*. Similar to Pierre Bourdieu's concept of "habitus," which is a way of explaining class as a lifestyle, my terms are a way of getting at predispositions deeply inscribed in residents' consciousness.[38] Again I stress that these predispositions should not be seen to characterize, in a deterministic way, the "popular classes." Rather, "the popular" in this sense refers to an *abstract* community; while this community may have a concrete *source*, it has no concrete, actual referent.

IMMUTABLE ESSENCES

In Oaxaca, as in many other parts of Mexico, who one "is," in terms of one's social prominence or character, has everything to do with one's origins, usually biologically understood. Such understandings may be vestiges of the colonial period, when social status was determined by legal caste designations premised on "racial" origins and informed by physical appearance and occupational status—to which were ascribed typical manners and morals.[39] Today, visible differences of "race" and class are frequently conflated or treated as distinctions inextricably linked and situated within an evaluative scheme that is highly morally inflected.

Thus, for example, notions of poverty as a morally charged immutable essence are deeply embedded in Oaxacan and Mexican cultural attitudes and expectations; popular Mexican soap operas, or *telenovelas*, watched by millions of people throughout the country, are good indicators of the prevalence and hegemonic character of such cultural norms and ideals. One especially popular telenovela, *El premio mayor*, was broadcast in 1995 (unlike long-running American soap operas and other Hollywood-model series, *telenovelas* typically have just a two-month run): the story of the members of a family of *corriente* (common) background who become multimillionaires. As the soap unfolded, one saw that, once again, birth was taken to be everything. Unable to handle wealth, the *corriente* family cannot escape its roots: family members engage in naïve and distasteful behavior; they cannot transcend who they "really are." There are, of course, many variations on this theme, some of them romantic and, for a time at least, quite hopeful. An internationally syndicated *telenovela*, *María la del barrio* (starring Mexian pop icon Thalía), tells, for example, a fairy tale about a girl of poor (*humilde*) background. Her beauty (her light skin) offers her a way out of her poverty, and, eventually, María marries a rich, handsome, and important man and embarks on a singing career. Inevitably, however, her "real" social essence comes back to haunt her as her mother-in-law, who disapproves of her daughter-in-law's low-class background, tries to thwart María's success; María cannot hope to escape her condition of birth—indeed, she will always be "*del barrio*."

The rich, then, are not simply those with money; rather, they are profoundly different from those who do not have money. "With money, even dogs can be made to dance" (Con el dinero, hasta los perros bailan), one *colonia* resident, doña Isabel, told me, in a humorous quip that nevertheless testifies to the surreal and qualitative distinctions that attend the world of those who are moneyed. Although most *colonos* I knew believed that hard work was the best path out of a situation of poverty and suffering—if not for oneself, then for one's children—people could never become truly separated from their roots. Such a belief carries with it some rather interesting corollaries: if through work one finds a means of "raising oneself," then others may aid by "remembering" one's origins. Of neighbors who had built a big house on her street in San Juan, doña Isabel commented:

> They made that house because they have money, no? The husband works, he's an architect, and Julia is a teacher and Rosa is an accountant with her own office. They have bucks [*lana*]. And now the other one is a doctor. . . . I have been in houses like that. . . . They can't ignore me because I knew them as children, when their father wasn't doing too well; he drank a lot. I knew them as children and they remember me too, and now that they're back in the *colonia* again, they're all married. So they've gone up a notch [*subieron de categoría*], but they don't close the doors to me.

Poverty, the experience of being poor or *humilde*, is, in such a view, an ontological condition; it confers an identity that cannot be erased, no matter how thoroughly it is covered up by dressings of wealth and of status. Conversely, one might live in the *colonia* and yet not be *of* it in some way, as doña Alicia, an older, educated middle-class woman, who lived in a finished stucco house, confided to me: "Those in the upper half [of the *colonia*], with little education, are not accustomed to seeing people with more money. I have suffered a lot with the people here, señorita, you have no idea!"

Plagued by vandalism and the envy of her neighbors, Alicia drew strong distinctions between herself and her neighbors. An anomaly within the *colonia*, she had minimal ties with others and did not participate in relationships of *compadrazgo*. There was, in short, little *confianza* in her life in the *colonia*.

RAISING ONESELF

An oft-repeated myth in political circles regarding informal economic groups of marginalized populations in Mexico argues that they are politically apathetic and therefore do not participate in public, civic sectors or work hard enough to better their situation.[40] In San Juan, I found that generally many residents were strongly conservative; while perhaps not entirely agreeing with such mythologies, they repeatedly rejected the idea that they represented an exploited class and frequently blamed their poverty on bad luck or the lack of "opportunities" in the city. Consider, for example, the testimony of one *colonia* resident in the epigraph that begins this chapter. Or this opinion, related by another of my neighbors:

> There are rich people who feed off the poor to be rich, and yes, that's a sin [but] many times it's a sin to be poor when one looks for poverty oneself; very often someone is poor because there aren't possibilities for getting ahead [*salir adelante*], but when one has them, it's a sin not to get ahead, to get out of that poverty.   Saúl, age fifty-four

Progress is thus commonly configured in terms of a personal ethic: if one has the chance to improve one's economic status, one *must* seize it. An individual's worth is measured in terms of not what or how much he or she owns, but how he or she makes use of the opportunities that present themselves. Framed in a biblical idiom, and suffused by metaphors of suffering and upward and forward movement, the rhetoric of economic improvement involves moving forward (*salir adelante*) or "raising oneself" (*levantarse*). These are fundamentally moral terms: "raising oneself" or "moving forward" describe attitudes involving self-respect and an ability to work. Such attitudes are buttressed by the views enshrined in sentimental national political rhetoric, which speaks of equality, democracy, and individual opportunity, although few *colonos* can truly lay hold of such things. In a manner that appears to epitomize Marx's notion of false consciousness, I found that while *colonos* might speak of limited economic opportunities, they rarely speculated on the systemic aspects or sources of the inequalities they experienced; instead, they maintained the hope that, through individual hard work and family solidarity, things would get better. And, indeed, sometimes it came about that by working long hours, holding several jobs, and pooling their resources the members of an impoverished household would manage to get by, and then, over time, in incremental bits, to improve their material situation. Such examples inspired others and served to underline the moral aspect of "raising oneself" or "moving forward."

It is also important to note that "raising" is not entirely a description of class mobility, for, as we have seen, the accumulation of wealth does not serve easily, in the eyes of *colonos*, to transcend the conditions of one's birth. In Colonia San Juan, for example, there were some well-to-do families that had only minimal interaction with others in the neighborhood; their spheres of everyday interaction were to be found elsewhere in the city (or even beyond), with others of a similar lifestyle. Some San Juan residents considered such families to be of the "upper class": they were described as "people with cars" (*gente de coche*), "people with good resources" (*gente de buenos recursos*), or "those who are well positioned" (*bien sentada*). By contrast, several other families that had previously been poor improved themselves and continued to play an active, integral role in everyday *colonia* life. Having grown up and *convivido* (lived) among others of a minimally educated, poor background before they bettered their own economic circumstances, members of these families remained socially rooted in the community.

In the *colonia*, consumer goods are strong markers of social distinction but so, too, are certain cultural practices; observing these cultural practices of distinction is crucial to both projecting and protecting one's "class" identity. Thus while prestige may be seen to reside in certain aspects of material wealth, it is also resolutely linked to one's honor or "presentation." This is why a wealthy family from which I rented a small apartment for a month at the beginning of my fieldwork informed me that they could not allow me to have Mexican visitors in my apartment (although fair-skinned foreigners seemed to be fine); they were, as they explained, a "decent" or honorable family (*una familia decente*). They felt that as their tenant and thus, in some respect, a representative of their judgment, I also had an obligation to maintain the social distinctions that their prestige was based on. A well-educated white Canadian of European background, my presence was an outward sign of their honor, but I had to comport myself as though I were a member of the family, a well-behaved daughter. Although when I later moved to Colonia San Juan, my behavior was still subject to the vigilance of my landlords and neighbors, they were not nearly as strict or openly judgmental.

Public perceptions of "decency" or moral uprightness are even more strongly related to the inviolability of the familial body this example would suggest. Thus in the *colonia*, a "respectable" young man is often spoken of redundantly as a "son of the family" (*hijo de familia*)—an odd usage that implies that a less respectable young man might be a son but not of the family. The family is overwhelmingly the unit from within which aspirations and distinctions are expressed; because of this, generational differences are important to take into account. Indeed, it may be useful to examine "class differences" as stages in a moral-developmental cycle envisaged and orchestrated from within the family.

In San Juan, for example, my neighbors Miguel and Carmen, a butcher and his wife, were both of poorly educated, humble background (neither had finished primary school). They had four children under the age of twelve, all of whom they sent to private schools in the city, an effort that caused them considerable financial difficulty. Providing the children with a better education than was available at many of the public state schools near San Juan—during my stay, many of the public schools were constantly plagued by strikes—was one goal; another objective was clearly to encourage the children to move in social circles quite different from those available to their peers in the *colonia*. Thus although Miguel and Carmen's children often played and socialized with others of their age in the neighborhood, they also frequently participated in other activities such as "scouts" and English-language classes, activities usually associated with middle- and upper-class lives. Similarly, through parent organizations at the school, the couple had established friendships and even *compadrazgo* relations with people of higher economic status. Such an effort at "raising themselves" was not, of course, strictly economic; it had everything to do with the bounds of propriety and distinction set out by the family as well. One had to be careful not to associate with others "beneath" oneself. Carmen, her sister, and her mother thus strongly disapproved of my friendship with a young man from a neighboring *colonia*; they viewed him simply as the son of a poor, *indio* family and wondered how he could be worthy of my attention. "Es de otra categoría," they told me, "he's from another class"—as though that information alone should serve to put an immutable boundary between him and me.

Several years later, however, Carmen's mother, Isabel, spoke approvingly of the mother of the young man; she had raised seven children on her own, and the four youngest had received a university education and had become professionals. Isabel compared the mother's "rise" with her own triumph over poverty: "Thanks to God that we recovered [*nos levantamos*]—little by little—but we did it. What satisfaction it is for her, and it should be for others like her . . . to see her children with good jobs, bettering themselves . . . you just have to pull through [*seguir adelante*]." Because the sons turned out well, their family was not, in the end, perhaps, *de otra categoría*.

I found that commentaries like Isabel's were frequently inserted into a wider discourse, a personal narrative with strong moral overtones that configured life in terms of absolutes and yet was all-encompassing in its reference. As Isabel explained, in one conversation: "Those who have money are never satisfied with just that—they always want something more—material things [*lo material*] are everything. . . . They never know true love, they never know pure spirituality . . . sure, money is important to a point—to have a house, food—but them, they have everything: their house is huge, but that doesn't permit them to be happy."

In such moralizing representations told from within the *colonia*, the rich are frequently figured as those who are morally bereft and spiritually impoverished: mean, unholy, uncaring. For example, another woman repeated a tale about a rich woman who would rather burn her old clothing than give it away. Generosity, happiness, a love of community, spirituality—these are among the positive attributes that a *colono* might have, regardless of material wealth.

Still, although "raising oneself" is measured in terms of the retention of or increase in such attributes, it also clearly, and sometimes quite contradictorily, has to do with changes in material wealth and aspirations toward upward (class) mobility. Themes of wealth and poverty are continually worked into the *colonos'* assessments of their social environment and thoughts about its changes. These are not immutable essences but are clearly the forces that work over and shape the terms of reference for everyone in the city.

DISCOURSES OF ETHNICITY AND "COMMUNITY"

If the *colonia popular* enshrines an ethics of individual hard work as the key to self-realization within a contemporary urban setting divided by glaring disparities in wealth, opportunity, and entitlement—disparities framed and hidden behind discourses of egalitarianism and democracy—it also embraces a set of principles and social practices that are more organic to life in rural, indigenous communities: solidarity, collectivism, altruism, and balanced reciprocity. The side-by-side functioning of this "double ethic" accounts, perhaps, for the degree of diversity, vacillation, and inconsistency in individuals' representations of themselves or of one another in the *colonia popular*.[41] In such a context, no theme is more complex or opaque, no topic of conversation more uncomfortable, than a discussion of ethnicity or race.

Officially Oaxaca is considered to be a mestizo city, which means that despite its numerous indigenous residents, the city is taken to belong "first" to a national ethnic culture (and those who embrace it wholeheartedly); indigenous cultural concerns are local matters, even if sites such as Monte Albán are considered national—and international—treasures. Although denotatively the term "mestizo" refers to people of mixed European and indigenous heritage, it is best understood as a cultural rather than a genetic category. Today the word "mestizo" is proudly embraced as the very "type" of national Mexican ethnic identity; in part, this pride reflects some of the gains of Mexican independence, when Mexican-born residents of mixed Spanish and Indian ancestry ceased to be second-class citizens in the eyes of the law. In the words of B. L. Margolies: "On all levels of society, Mexicans casually use egalitarian designations: we are all Mexicans, we are all *Mestizos*, we are all the same. . . . [Y]et a significant segment of the population behaves as though they are more *Mestizo* than others."[42] Nevertheless, behind the national celebratory account of "race mixing," or *mestizaje,* lies a historical ideology that equated national "progress" with whitening or Europeanizing. At the root of the positive, nationalizing account of *mestizaje* was a vision of an evolutionary process of "race" improvement: the goal was the very disappearance of indigenous peoples and their culture.[43] Although it has lost its overtly genocidal cast, the perpetuation of the concept of *mestizaje* today has produced various myths, among them the idea that "Mexico will progress with social justice for each and every Mexican because the nation is egalitarian."[44]

A primitivizing temporalization of indigenous peoples is one corollary of the national glorification of mestizo identity: whatever is *indio* belongs to the past, whether ways of life, practices, cultural artifacts, or people. Seen through such lenses, the lives of indigenous people become extensions of some exotic primordial pre-Columbian past that nevertheless belongs to everyone in the nation as a whole. This past is frequently called on to lend a mystical timeless quality to the nation itself: here are the mythological origins that confer on the nation its naturally bounded, internally integrated, homogeneous (in its mestizo generality) whole.

The label "Indian" is no less an illusory ethnic category; it, too, is falsely generalizing. This is not simply because of the significant ethnic variation among indigenous peoples in the state of Oaxaca but also because, for many individuals of indigenous background, the place one comes from overrides any considerations of what could be called "ethnic" identity. Indeed, Oaxacans of any "ethnic" background exhibit a strong affinity with their places of birth and will identify others in the same way. When asked for her "ethnic" affiliation, a person of indigenous origin is not likely to say "Zapotec" or "Mixe," but, instead, to name the region or the town she is from. A person is a *serrana* (from one of the sierra regions of the state) before she is a *oaxaqueña*. Even if he has been a longtime resident of Oaxaca, someone will be described as a *chilango* (a slightly disparaging term for someone from Mexico City) rather than as a Oaxacan or a Mexican. This form of identification carries over into the national sphere, where politicians are always identified by the states they come from; such points of geographic origin are considered to be deeply significant aspects of their identities. As an English-speaking North American, I was (and am) forever a *gringa*, although, in typical Canadian fashion, I often expressed dislike at being lumped in with those from the United States.

Nevertheless, it would be a mistake to see these examples as fixing a geographically or physically rooted way of conceptualizing "ethnicity." The culture of social relations emerges out of the terms of interrelation among groups of people who recognize one another as mutually distinct, what some might call a principle of alterity.[45] In a study published in the 1990s, the urban anthropologists Arthur Murphy and Alex Stepick argued that, among urban Oaxacans, "ethnic identity" faded once independent Indian neighborhoods were absorbed into the city and the population became more mestizo.[46] But in my experience in the *colonia popular*, ethnicity—in the sense of race or skin color and particular cultural practices—*does* matter. In the same way that "ethnic" is commonly used in North America to designate non-white others, in Oaxaca those who are considered to have "ethnicity" are indigenous—the designation *las etnias* refers to the various indigenous peoples in Mexico, who contrast with the "default" national mestizo norm. They are objectified as Indian people (*indios*), their identity determined officially by language use and unofficially by skin color, dress, and other social practices.

Expressions of the pervasive social philosophy that some call *malinchismo* also percolate through local social interactions. A word sometimes used to describe a penchant for customs, behavior, and goods from the United States, *malinchismo* also refers to the denigration of a dark-skinned indigenous identity in favor of light-colored hair and skin. The word is derived from Malinche, the name best known for Marina, an opportunistic young woman given, as the legend goes, by an Aztec chief to Hernán Cortés to act as his concubine, interpreter, and adviser. It turns out, of course, that this legend is not strictly true; in fact, she never lived with Cortés but with one of his "first officers." Nevertheless, her treachery is legendary; her part in divulging Aztec secrets has been credited with the downfall of the civilization, and, indeed, Cortés rewarded her handsomely. *Malinchismo* refers, then, to a willingness to sell out your own, an attitude of disdain toward your own country, people, or goods. In this view, all Indians are "backward" and live in misery. Their poverty is taken to be an affront to mestizo Mexicans, who associate it with pathetic ignorance (Indians are people who cannot help themselves) and a viscerally repugnant dirtiness (Indians are a blot on the mestizo national body). In the *colonia popular*, aspects of such thinking would show up in everyday conversation in the form of pejorative diminutives such as *indito*; the saying "No seas tán indio" (Don't be so Indian) is, for example, a way to express disdain for someone's behavior that is thought to be crass, ignorant, or uncivilized. Also, like many of those who exist, conceptually or actually, on the margins of the dominant society, Indians are also seen to be dangerous: hence my neighbors often warned that I had to be careful when I was in "popular" (indigenous) areas of the city or in *el campo*.

As one researcher has commented, "the process of *mestizaje*, sometimes seen as basically racial, is in fact social; *'mestizo'* is an achieved as well as an ascribed status—even though achievement may be difficult and, in the case of communities, may span decades."[47] The negative associations with "Indianness" so prevalent in Mexican culture mean that many individuals who might otherwise be regarded as indigenous describe themselves as mestizo, thereby affiliating themselves with national Mexican culture. As I observed throughout Oaxaca and in Colonia San Juan, individuals become "whitened" by means of the acquisition of wealth or the elevated status of an occupation; a "glass ceiling" rule, however, is often mentioned as a limit on the upward social mobility of individuals of indigenous appearance.

Ethnic identity as a referent for social differentiation, while informed by apparently "objective" characteristics such as skin color, proves, in practice, to be slippery and mutable terrain.

The "Popular Community"

As generally poor people with rural origins and an urban life, Oaxacans of the popular sectors operate within a double ethic, which involves both reciprocity and dependency.[48] Notions of self-worth and responsibility to others are thus bound together in unpredictable, contradictory, and fluctuating ways. Informed by highly charged ideas attached to race or color differentiation, the boundaries of "ethnic" groups are locally defined and therefore change continually. Further, San Juan residents necessarily subscribe, at least to some extent, to the values and norms of Mexican national culture and society. Nevertheless, while they assert their national mestizo identity in social practice, and manifest a desire to participate as integral citizens in the Mexican "familial body," many of the *colonia* residents hold out for still other, and more locally meaningful, identities. Popular Catholic practices are important sites of this firm stance; they encompass eclectic and highly locally inflected mixtures of "modern" and "traditional," "official" and "folk," "public" and "private" ritual.

In the *colonia*, "community" membership is defined by a certain set of subjectively determined markers used by individuals in order to affiliate themselves with—or dissociate themselves from—one another. Belief in "immutable essences"—what we might call a sharp essentialist tendency in the understanding of human natures in the *colonia*—leads easily into a disturbing xenophobia of "others," although, of course, the boundaries around the "other" are changeable, layered as they are with associations of affect and trust, or *confianza*. "Community," defined in these terms, circumscribes a largely imagined unit of imputed solidarity, "spirit," and collective opinion. Based on a familial idiom, such a concept of "community" is infused with the notion of *confianza* and is articulated in terms of kinship. I often heard women, within the bounds of the *colonia*, call one another *hermanita* (little sister). Among men, a parallel form of address is *carnal* (blood brother) or *compadre*. These terms are used even if the individuals concerned are not strictly related as kin or even ritual kin. Such words of proximity and affection suggest not only a common culture or common membership in a group but also a level of intimate relationship; community belonging thus carries with it all the love and hate and ambivalence that intimacy brings.

Thus although San Juan residents could be said to demonstrate an intense "class" consciousness—in the sense that they identified themselves as "the poor" with a high degree of internal solidarity—disputes between neighbors occurred often. Gossip, envy, resentment, and harsh criticism of others in the community were frequent; I heard neighbors accuse one another of poisoning their dogs, of damaging one another's property, or of stealing. Each instance would seem a fairly clear indication of an absence of or disintegration of *confianza*. Nevertheless, in other contexts, the very same individuals would lay claims to strong intra-*colonia* cohesion and egalitarianism, based on relations of trust and respect. An example of what Anthony Cohen, in his study of the symbolic construction of community, called "pragmatic egalitarianism," such shifts in alliance serve to mask internal conflict by means of the assertion of a veneer of social sameness and implicit harmony.[49] It is also the case, however, that, in social life, efforts to construct a bounded identity group involve continual changes and renegotiations.

Colonos would speak, for example, of the *colonia* as a socially cohesive, democratic unit in moments when they felt that the idea of community solidarity was important to meet collective needs. Fostered in part by the need for many *colonias* to rely on their own members in order to make infrastructural improvements—paving roads, delivering electricity, and so on—in San Juan strong sentiments of faith in the collectivity also served to express a strong distrust of the government, and even distrust of the local *mesa directiva* (*colonia* council). Thus the use of expressions of solidarity is always strategic, whether personal or political. It is not possible to claim that all such collective expressions are "resistant" to individualizing impulses of dominant culture; some are, and some are not.

TRADITIONAL PRACTICES

Many ethnographic accounts of the peasant economies of the state of Oaxaca highlight reciprocity as the core principal of traditional economic behavior; in such accounts, formal and informal gift giving and reciprocal exchanges of various kinds serve to establish and reinforce social relationships, even outside the *compadrazgo* network.[50] How deep the "traditional" roots of such principles of egalitarianism and communalism run is hard to say; most studies have extrapolated backward from social arrangements observed by anthropologists in rural communities in the twentieth century. Nevertheless, in Colonia San Juan, certain of these communal cultural practices, regarded as "traditional" by residents and ethnographers alike, persist. The examples that follow highlight several occasions where such "traditional" practices remain in force or are newly reinvented by urban residents.

San Juan's *mesa directiva*, which lobbies the municipal government on behalf of *colonia* residents, has been successful compared with other *colonia* councils in obtaining municipal help with the installation of public services. At the time of my first fieldwork, the leader of the council was an outgoing, articulate woman named doña Elisa; she was married but, to all appearances, ruled the roost in her large household, which consisted of both immediate- and extended-family members. Nevertheless, despite the successes of doña Elisa and the council, San Juan had to depend a great deal on self-help and local initiative in order to accomplish major work projects of benefit to the community. As in other *colonias* in the city, such projects were typically carried out through a system of cooperative labor referred to as *tequio,* an ancient form of collective labor that also served to describe the collective labor owed to Spanish landowners under the hacienda system.[51] In rural communities, *tequio* continues to refer to various collective work projects—some ad hoc, others annual—that will serve the community, such as repairing the church or a central public road, cleaning the school, or planting and harvesting (figure 1.7). Both men and women are expected to participate, depending on the activity.

FIGURE 1.7   *Tequio* in Colonia San Juan.

The system works in a similar fashion in the city. Local schools, for example, are maintained through the *tequio* system directed by both the *mesa directiva* and the *colonia* parents' association, Padres de Familia. The general rule is that, for each student, a parent or another family member is expected to devote a day now and then to help with tasks related to the upkeep of the classrooms and grounds. If unable to participate, the parent or family member must send a substitute or pay a preset quota. Unsurprisingly, perhaps, the *tequio* system always seems to work better in theory than in practice; one always hears complaints by one resident about another's unwillingness to participate. Such problems were no doubt inevitable, given that the same degree of commitment to the *colonia*'s "progress"—as represented, for example, by the paving of roads—was not shared by all neighbors; some residents, for instance, were renting their homes, and improvements were likely to benefit owners rather than renters.

Sometimes the term *tequio* was also used to refer to a more loosely organized, occasional work party. Such *tequios* were typically limited to a certain section of the *colonia*, as in the case of the paving of dirt roads, where only residents of a particular street were concerned. Yet in these cases, too, not everyone who was expected turned up; the preliminary clearing of the streets of large rocks and the leveling of hillocks was a labor usually carried out by just a portion of those who had been notified of the work party. In one particular road-clearing project, the failure of some residents to "cooperate" later caused conflicts related to the paving itself, since residents were also responsible for financing the section of the road corresponding to the length of their respective lots. While residents in these instances usually received some help from the municipality, which defrayed a portion of the cost of cement, such projects usually required a substantial investment by each household in order to cover the remaining material expenses and labor. Those living on borrowed or rented property were, understandably, reluctant to make such a financial sacrifice—or were simply unable to do so. As a result, when I left San Juan after my fieldwork in 1991, despite plans to pave continually, some streets remained a patchwork of paved and dirt patches and could not be traversed by car; all, however, have been completely paved since then, changing San Juan's appearance considerably.

Cooperative work groups, referred to as *tequios*, are also used for the maintenance and renovation of the parish church and grounds; for such work, people donate labor, materials, or money or all three on more or less strictly voluntary terms. Referred to as *cooperaciones*, funds for renovations and fiestas are also collected by volunteers on a door-to-door basis; these collections are orchestrated by the parish advisory board, which has representatives from each of the seven *colonias* in the parish of Cuauhtémoc. Although negative social sanctions applied to those who were unwilling to contribute (they were accused of "not cooperating" or being "cheap" [*no quiere cooperar; es muy codo*]), such mild disapproval seemed not to have much moral force.

I first observed the important Oaxacan tradition of communal gift giving, referred to as the *guelaguetza*, during a funeral. For a funeral or any significant collective gathering, individuals contribute food, small amounts of money, or other necessary items to the family who hosts the event. This is one side of the *guelaguetza*, for the whole process is a circular exchange that entails reciprocation between households or individuals of payments in equivalent kind and measure. Although in rural Oaxaca the *guelaguetza* system is often very formalized—items given are noted carefully in a special book to ensure "proper" or equal return—in the city, the form of *guelaguetza* is much looser, and the term is used to refer to any instance where a number of people contribute materially (or with their labor power) to a common enterprise for the benefit of one individual or family.[52]

Versions of the mechanisms of both *tequio* and *guelaguetza* exist in both rural and urban settings partly because of parallel needs: first, a lack of ready, liquid capital for financing certain projects or events; and, second, a way of spreading out costs over time. Other means of dealing with unstable flows of income in Oaxaca City include systems of credit that are similar to those in use in rural areas. Unlike most stores in the center of town, for example, several small *colonia* businesses, such as corner stores, offer credit as a normal aspect of conducting business. Many door-to-door salespeople allow customers to buy items in installments, or *bonos*; in fact, several of my neighbors told me that this was the only way they were able to afford to purchase their building lots.

Borrowing money was also not unusual, especially for poor families. While relatives and *compadres* were usually able to help with small non-interest loans, when larger amounts were needed (once sources from within the family were exhausted) residents were forced to look elsewhere to obtain funds. These usually took the form of "temporary" loans (although they often took years to pay back completely, if at all). Those approached for the loan were often *compadres*, but sometimes mere acquaintances—such as the neighborhood anthropologist—were also approached. A possible indication of the inability of *compadrazgo* networks to fulfill people's needs—especially in times of crisis—is the heavy reliance on "nontraditional" channels for managing large expenditures (such as repaying loans), including pawning personal possessions or getting a high-interest loan from a local money lender (San Juan, like other neighborhoods, had its local loan shark, or *prestadora*). Notably, government-run pawnshops in Oaxaca are especially busy after important fiestas like the Day of the Dead that involve heavy expenditures.

The invocation and reuse of traditional systems such as *tequio* and *guelaguetza* in the city serve to foster an ethic of neighborhood collectivism and a sense of community cohesion. I observed that appealing to the ideal of the community was often particularly compelling as a tool of mobilization in the *colonias*, although, quickly enough, tensions would erupt when a group with disparate interests in a project or strong differences of opinion attempted to follow customs encouraging unified collective action.

What can explain, then, despite such difficulties, the special resonance of the invocation of community in Oaxacan popular neighborhoods? In his exploration of the idea of "community" in the Oaxacan Mixtec town of Nyoo, the anthropologist John Monaghan argues that communal action is a "mode of sociability" that consistently refers to a particular moral ideal. Explaining that recent changes in the economic and political setting of Nyoo have exacerbated the tensions between households, Monaghan suggests that population increases, land privatization, and greater degrees of social stratification have meant that the household has emerged as the basic unit of survival in Nyoo. Households, he maintains, compete with one another for goods, and the community lies, both structurally and experientially, in the transactions that occur between households.[53]

According to such a view, a "community" does not just come into existence whenever a group of people shares the same space or a similar set of interests or needs; rather, "community" is precisely an entity that people create and experience through their interactions with one another. And, indeed, at popular Catholic rituals in Oaxaca, through the performance of traditions including the *guelaguetza* and other practices of reciprocity, such a moral ideal of community is voluntarily and forcefully enacted and reenacted. Indeed, in the *colonia popular*, it is above all in such cyclical and highly invested sacred settings that the *ideal of the community*—as well as the ties that create and bind it—comes into being, in a real and concrete way. Popular religious rites not only supply the forms for such communal bonds, but actively demand the participation of many individuals and households, both privately and collectively. Religion, in effect, constitutes a symbolic language and set of gestures that speak to and of ultimate truths and transcendent metaphysical power; consequently, it is able to create openings for self-determination, offer potential respite from oppressive social orders, and defend alternative visions of the world. The unique qualities of popular Catholicism in Oaxaca allow it to perform this function and also to contribute to the constitution of local identities in special and intriguing ways.

"TRADITION" AND RELIGION

Visitors to Oaxaca City will invariably be struck by the sheer quantities of religious centers and motifs. One sees not only numerous beautiful, centuries-old churches but stores crammed with religious icons, portraits, and other paraphernalia; colorful religious altars large and small in private homes, markets, and other businesses, including on buses; and—on practically any given day throughout the year—colorful and energetic religious processions, or *calendas*, belonging to some barrio's annual fiesta. At first glance, Oaxaca appears to be a bastion of staunch, traditional Catholicism; such an impression is valid to some extent when this city is compared, for example, with Mexico City. But this orthodox appearance is also deceptive, for it masks the rich and fluid complexity of religious currents the city encompasses.

Many anthropologists who have focused their attention on the city of Oaxaca have used a strong materialist perspective to analyze phenomena of socioeconomic stratification and to account for residents' rational adaptation to economic forces.[54] The materialist slant of Oaxacan urban anthropology has meant that these researchers tend to speak of religion as a largely epiphenomenal aspect of social life, a quaint system of belief that cushions the harsh realities of everyday life or, alternatively, mystifies the variety of social injustices that pervade the social and political environment. In his ethnography of a *colonia popular* in Oaxaca, for example, Michael Higgins claims that people "use their religion not for collective goals, but as part of an individualized interpretation, supported by religious symbols, which serves as a means of dealing with and maintaining their level of material worth."[55] Such a view, however, assumes that urban Oaxacans identify themselves first and most importantly as material or class actors, and that various forms of culture, including religion, play little part in informing their actions. Worth asking, then, in a space where religion seems so overwhelmingly evident, is the question: How does religion inform communal and individual identities? What role does it play in the structure and experience of people's lives?

It is important to note that one cannot make sense of popular religiosity—religion as it is practiced in an everyday way by members of the popular classes—simply in terms of expressed religious affiliation or religious denomination. As elsewhere in the city, the overwhelming majority of the residents of Colonia San Juan are self-avowed Roman Catholics, although a small number of Jehovah's Witnesses (Testigos de Jehovah), Mormons (Mormones, or members of the Church of Jesus Christ of Latter-Day Saints), and Pentecostals may also be found in the *colonia* and other popular neighborhoods.[56] Important as they are, these affiliations with various churches or temples do not predict or sum up the range of expressions of religiosity practiced by *colonia* residents. For example, it is not unusual for someone who regularly attends church to consult, in time of trouble, a "parapsychologist," a "spiritualist" (*espirituista*), or some other religious practitioner who heals through the manipulation of spiritual energies; a *curandera* or *curandero* (neighborhood healer, skilled in the use of herbs and alcohol *soplados* [blows] to cure); as well as the local minister or priest. Within the popular sphere, these are not competing practices, but complementary religious additions, and although some of the more conservative elements of the Catholic Church (and most other orthodox sects) take a dim view of the invocation of such additional religious resources, they have not been able to stamp them out.

This, perhaps in part, is because "Catholicism" in Mexico is far from being a body of official doctrine consciously learned, adopted, or practiced in most of the lives of the faithful; rather, it is a bundle of practices, beliefs, and customs that are assimilated through general pathways of socialization. Religion, particularly a practice as dominant as Roman Catholicism is in Mexico, becomes, in such a setting, part of quotidian experience; it is not an isolable realm of culture that may be reflected on and rationalized, chosen or discarded. Many Oaxacans I know, especially among the poor, see Catholicism as a kind of generic or default religious faith and identity. To be Catholic is simply to be a Christian, one who embodies moral personhood. Thus Jesús, a middle-aged neighbor, adamantly insisted, "Soy Católico, pero a mi manera" (I'm Catholic, but in my own way). It is assumed that those who are not Catholic belong to a Protestant sect or are adherents of at least some recognized spiritual affiliation; everyone, in other words, is expected to be a *creyente* (believer). In San Juan, I was most often asked two questions: What was my country of origin, and what was my religion? Although I replied that I was not a practitioner of any recognizable faith, the fact that I was baptized in the Anglican Church served to qualify me for moral personhood. As an older woman in San Juan said to me, "Son creencias de la fe católica, creo que todos las tenemos iguales" (They're beliefs of the Catholic faith; I think we pretty much all have them).

A steady proliferation of churches—even the emergence of divisions within the Catholic Church—has marked the past several decades in Oaxaca.[57] In recent years, there has been a notable and mounting presence of Protestant and Evangelical religions, especially in poor neighborhoods such as Colonia San Juan and others in the parish of Cuauhtémoc.[58] Although Protestants have been in Oaxaca since the late nineteenth century, the two decades from 1950 to 1970 saw a rising tide of neo-Evangelical churches in Oaxacan indigenous communities, including Pentecostal churches, Adventists, Baptists, Jehovah's Witnesses, and Mormons, many of them of U.S. origin. Compared with the state of Chiapas—Oaxaca's neighbor to the south—Oaxaca has the highest number of non-Catholics in the country, or approximately 10 percent of the total population.[59] Undoubtedly, seasonal or permanent migration to the United States has been an additional important factor in the increase of Protestants.

People living in neighborhoods at the edge of the city—a veritable marketplace for religious proselytizers—appear to be the most likely candidates for conversion to other sects. In response to this steady Protestant and Evangelical encroachment, the Catholic Church in Oaxaca has launched a series of interrelated movements designed to renew Catholicism and Catholics' faith. The program of Nueva Evangelización (New Evangelization) has taken various forms over the years since its beginnings in the 1980s; changes are largely dependent upon the ideological and theological orientations of both parish priests and diocesan directives. These movements have certainly affected Catholics' relationship to their faith, and marked the subtle ways that their religious identities overlap with other dimensions of social differentiation.[60]

Partly under the influence of the New Evangelization, the few non-Catholics in Cuauhtémoc, San Juan's local parish, are often referred to as *nuestros hermanos separados* (our separated brothers), a designation which implies that the "brothers" were once Catholic (often true) but have been led astray. Another equally common phrase speaks of such "brothers" in terms of the "error" of their ways:

nuestros hermanos equivocados (our mistaken brothers). Despite such language, I found a surprising amount of religious tolerance among my neighbors. Many Catholics have told me, for example, that when a member of a Protestant sect arrives at the door, they welcome the person in and are willing to listen to what he or she has to say. They may do so, in part, because, despite Protestants' different perception of the individual's responsibility toward God and community, they share similar views with Catholics on basic issues of respect and family duty. Unlike in rural towns, where conflicts between non-Catholics and Catholics are often bitter and even violent,[61] in my experience Protestants are not socially ostracized or subjected to overt expressions of antagonism by Catholics. Rather, because most Protestant and Pentecostal groups demand a great deal of time and energy in terms of structured worship, and they provide their members with a social community, people who belong to Protestant sects, in effect, appear to hold themselves apart from their Catholic neighbors. This was especially true for the families in San Juan who were Jehovah's Witnesses, since almost all were members of one extended family.

The horizontal authority structure of Protestant sects seems to foster strong affective bonds; there is greater lay participation in services and a ready-made community, regardless of social background. These attributes seem to be especially attractive to recent migrants to the city, particularly women in need of material and moral aid and support. In my experience, Evangelical Protestantism (a label that would include Testigos de Jehovah and Mormones), with its emphasis on rationality and self-discipline, is perceived—by both adherents and nonpractitioners—as a religiosity associated with modernity, a vehicle for "getting ahead." Yet in its relative sensual asceticism and its celebration of individual morality, it contrasts strongly with the sensuousness and aesthetics of popular Catholic practice.

The ideological forms of Protestantism, as Max Weber so persuasively argued, project values of self-restraint and disciplined work, motivated by values of "progress" that contrast with the communalistic traditionalism of popular religiosity. Protestant discourses, such as that of the Testigos de Jehovah, frequently criticize "traditional" Catholicism for its "vices": bureaucratic corruption, the accumulation of wealth, showy display, and the encouragement of drinking in ritual contexts. An interesting religious corollary to nationalist, secular narratives of modernization, "old" Catholicism is clearly identified, in such discourses, with hierarchical and decadent social elements that actively prevent the "progress" of society.[62]

Thus in Oaxaca, socioeconomic class distinctions intersect in complex ways with significant variations in religious practice. These distinctions are underlain by differences in affect and morality, as related to ideas of the "traditional" and the "modern." For most people of the popular classes in Oaxaca, of poor and of indigenous cultural background, religiosity encompasses a wide array of beliefs and ritual traditions, including a range of what are considered superstitious or "magical" customs. Brought to the city by rural immigrants, such practices and beliefs continue to thrive in the context of the maintenance of a broader cultural way of life. Such "folk" traditions are often unknown—or pointedly ignored—by upper-class, more mestizo Catholics, who tend toward religious expressions that are more orthodox in tone and tradition. They often make a strong effort to distinguish themselves from what they regard as the "inferior" indigenous ways of life that surround them. Thus for both Protestants and some Catholics, many folk indigenous—or quintessentially "popular"—practices are negatively valued, associated with backwardness, ignorance, and naïveté, and often blamed for holding their practitioners "down" economically. These negative associations explain, perhaps, the ambivalence that greets any inquiry into popular Catholic practices and festivals, including the Day of the Dead.

At the same time, I observed that popular Catholic practice used by Oaxacans in Colonia San Juan and elsewhere enriched and revitalized certain ideals and traditions crucial to their sense of communal identity. Such practices served to bring the community together—sometimes in actuality, at times only ideally—as well as to mark off its members from those who did not share in its rituals and parameters. In this context, Catholicism offered an idiom in which a sense of self and of community could be elaborated, and norms and values held in common could be articulated and explored. As Carmela, a middle-aged woman, explained, for example: "For God there is no distinction of anything; for God we can all be his children: all the poorest Indians [*inditos*] who have nothing, and those who are well off, who have a lot of money, who have everything; for God there is no distinction. Blacks, whites, brown-skinned, God loves all of us."

Doña Carmela's words explain that religion, in principle, is inclusive. But the argument that lies behind her statement suggests that not all people truly practice their faith as they should. The popular classes are those who keep their faith and who live out a narrative, dignified by the Bible, of poverty and struggle every day. "The poor are those who are most glued to the church. The rich may attend mass," one woman explained to me, "they give their *limosna* [offering], but they don't treat their workers well." Such self-perceptions and felt allegiances are revealed and affirmed through everyday popular religious practices and inform the vocabulary of everyday speech. In such statements, an oppositional dynamic is set out rhetorically: we—the poor, the moral, the traditional—hold fast to values lost or corrupted by them—the rich, the selfish, the materially greedy, the superficial. Poverty is thus equated with virtue and ontological rootedness. As one *colonia* resident testified eloquently, in a long speech on the relative virtues of poverty and wealth, and country and city life, as they relate to donations for festivals and religious celebrations:

> We the poor, we have more faith, because we have more needs. And here, if you go to ask from a rich person, he gives you nothing. He gives only as he wants; he'll throw you a little bit of money and he says: well, work, lazy! Or even if you ask them for work, they have fewer employees so that the employees must work harder. Sometimes you even ask them for something, and they give you nothing. And nevertheless, the poor person, how he sacrifices himself in order to wash, to iron. Or at least the *campesino*, cultivating his little piece of land, he has his chicken, his hen or a turkey, a goat, but he has to do something. This is the custom in the pueblos.

In this way, Oaxacans of the popular classes draw on the practices and systems of meaning represented by popular Catholicism to shore up situationally defined boundaries of community in the face of perceived threats to the social values and ideals of communalism, reciprocity, and social balance, values seen by many as distinctive to the idea of the "popular." As we will see in the next several chapters, in the zone of popular culture, discourses that call on "tradition" or invoke "traditional values" in fact represent active and changing social relations and are not simply references to survivals from the past.[63] They are, however, attempts to relate a valued set of practices to specific places, memories, and times, to hold on to a ritually maintained and bounded sense of a communal popular "self."

CHAPTER 2

Practicing Popular Religion in Oaxaca

Juquila, Oaxaca, December 1995

The tiny virgin some 30 centimeters high is perched on a stand covered in gold leaf and clothed in a white tunic spread out like a cape, giving her the appearance of a small white and gold triangle. Her hands are clasped, and a blue neon halo hovers over her crowned head. A heavy-set woman with thick, steel-gray braids whispers her fervent prayers hoarsely, but under her breath, as she kneels before the altar. She rises, places a folded note and some coins in the box before her, and then turns and walks slowly, pensively out of the church, passing the group of young cyclists who shout a loud cheer to their beloved Virgencita before turning their bicycles away from the plaza and the throngs of devoted.

POPULAR RELIGION IN OAXACA is a complex syncretic system that to any outsider may seem unpredictable and even esoteric in the apparently illogical nature of its beliefs and expressions. It reflects ideas and practices related to concerns of persons—primarily indigenous and poor—who are situated in a particular position in the broader social order. Bound up with determinations of power, morals, and ideas that swarm around social obligations, the integrity of popular religion stems not from a shared set of doctrines, but from a certain configuration of the social world.

GEOGRAPHIES OF SACRED AND PROFANE, POPULAR AND "OFFICIAL"

Every religious practice develops—or perhaps emerges from—particular conceptions of body, spirit, and being, as well as elaborating an account of the nature of human and divine, or supernatural, relationships and the world. Popular religious practice in Oaxaca is no exception. At its most basic, a popular account of the "person" in the parish of Cuauhtémoc argues that one is composed of a material, physical self—this physical self is often referred to as one's natural "shell"—and a spiritual self, which is synonymous with a "life" essence: the seat of sensitivity and certain kinds of emotionality. This spiritual essence, associated with interiority, is usually thought to reside in one's soul. In turn, the soul, it is argued, is located in the heart, which is both a physical place—the core of one's body, or life—and a metaphorical or metaphysical space, the seat of love, compassion, and moral feelings.

A child enters the "interior," moral, social world and is recognized as fully "human" with the rite of baptism. This is because it is widely believed, roughly following Catholic doctrine, that a person's spiritual persona is not born until baptism, when he or she becomes a member of the moral community. Accordingly, many newborn infants I knew in San Juan were not named until their baptism ceremonies. The introduction into the social domain at baptism is underscored by the importance of godparents during such a ritual. Not typically blood relations, *padrinos* (godparents) stand for the community outside the immediate family and formally connect the child with the realm of moral and spiritual sociality. Thus the child acquires its soul, or "inside," by being spoken for from the "outside," or the community. Socialization in the *colonia* envisages movement in two directions at once: inward and outward. Incorporation into the social sphere happens, in effect, as one is "en-souled."

Likewise, although sacred sites are sprinkled throughout the geographic territory (graves, shrines, and festival locations), the sacred domain for individuals is typically physically circumscribed, its two poles represented by home and church. Like the "heart" of the body, the home is steeped in complex significance and embodies sacred qualities of domesticated, if corruptible, interiority. Symbolic correspondences are drawn between home and church as a way of sanctifying the home, which is sometimes spoken of as "the domestic church" (*la iglesia doméstica*). Thus altars are established and kept in the home. Regularly decorated with flowers, candles, and objects of special significance, domestic altars, like church altars, feature figures or icons of special saints, the Christ Child, or, most often, the Virgen María, albeit in miniature.

In addition, many of the rites that take place in the church are replicated in *colonia* households—from simple praying before the altar to elaborate festivals such as the Posadas at Christmas, when Mary and Joseph's search for shelter is replicated and celebrated, and the Candlemas, which commemorates the presentation of the baby Jesus at the Temple in Jerusalem and Mary's subsequent purification. The two sacred realms of church and home are also connected during certain religious festivals when church images "go visiting" various houses in San Juan, and when parish homes are included as stations or links in a ritual processional round beginning and ending at the church, as happens during Via Crucis (Way of the Cross), Corpus Christi, and any fiesta procession or saint's day festival.

In keeping with an analogy that would view the home as "the domestic church," the official church promotes the Holy Family of Joseph, Mary, and Jesus as a paradigmatic ideal for the family. Popular religious observations operate their own twist on this paradigm, however, for while "male authority" is nominally underlined, at the same time the space is dominated and organized by a woman or women. Thus whereas in the culture at large, in accord with well-known gestures of misogyny and projection, women are frequently considered "polluted" and associated with treachery and "irrational" passions, in a "proper" popularly religious home a married woman with children may wield considerable power. For although, in their maternal roles, women are considered to be emotionally and physically delicate, this "fragility" also appears to help figure women as innately more spiritually sensitive, compassionate, and caring than men. Encouraged, above all, by certain popular ritual expressions to follow the Virgin Mary's model of humility, sacrifice, and maternal devotion, the pervasive popular ideal for women of *la madre abnegada*—a martyr-inspired identity supposedly ratified by both biological and "divine" law—may also lead to considerable, if mixed, glorification of women.[1] As we shall see in chapter 3, while women are barred from authority in the institutional church, popular religious practices, which are frequently based in the home, often permit them to re-create sacred centers where their power as sacred actors and as moral exemplars is significant.

If a woman may be identified with the role of the Virgin Mary, in the context of popular religious ritual a child may also be identified with the Child Jesus—El Niño Jesús or Niño Dios. Such emulative assimilation is implied, for example, by the popular rite of Presentación (Presentation), when, at age three, a child is taken to church for a special mass, the stated precedent being Christ's Presentation in the Temple in Jerusalem forty days after his birth. The identification of *colonia* children with the figure of the Niño Dios is also suggested during a traditional wake for a small child or baby, when the corpse is placed on a raised platform on top of a table and surrounded by a sea of flowers, the whole scene bearing a strong resemblance to the appearance of the Child Jesus on the household altar at Candlemas. As with the paradoxical force of female emulations of the Virgin Mary, the characteristically "popular" cult of the Child, celebrating the power of the small and the weak, represents a reversal of customary associations of diminutive size and potency.

Individuals may also be linked with the saints or Jesus by the common tradition of naming a child after the saint who is celebrated on the child's day of birth or after a favorite "saint of devotion." The bond is thus reiterated every birthday, a day that is often referred to as one's *santo* (saint [day]). Spiritual parenthood is likewise figured as a complement of biological parenthood by means of *compadrazgo* (ritual kinship networks). Not only do individuals acquire "spiritual parents" or godparents who help to shepherd them through moral (and economic) life in the social sphere, but the spiritual kinship link between human and supernatural is also made ritually concrete through the idiom of parenthood. At certain sacred times, such as the Posadas–Candlemas cycle (December 16–February 2), religious images are treated like children. A "godmother" (or sometimes a "godfather") is sought to sponsor one celebration or another and to dress a household image of the Child Jesus for blessing at the church. In reciprocal fashion, an earthly mother or father will often ask a Virgin to act as spiritual parent for a sick child when she or he places the child before a saint for a *levantada* (raising). So it is that intimacy, affective bonds, and reciprocal relations of varying sorts characterize the relationship between humans and saints. Through the establishment of a common bond of kinship between humans and supernatural beings, and underlined by links between their respective associated "dwelling places," a framework is erected for exchanges between them.[2]

Reciprocal as such relationships between saints and humans might be, the relations between mortal men and women, as they are figured in popular geographic and religious expression, are anything but reversible. A rigid double standard regarding male and female sexuality reflects the common Mexican cultural association of men with the public, external realm outside the home and women with the internal, morally pure, sacred domain of home and family. The traditional gendered division of labor and activity mirrors this conceptual segregation. Many adult men I knew spent comparatively little time at home, passing most of the day working or socializing with friends, some returning to their houses primarily to eat or sleep. In contrast, for many women in San Juan a trip to the market or to school to fetch their children was often their only moment away from the house alone. A woman, whether married or unmarried, who was seen frequently outside her home, without attending to a specific errand, was liable to become the object of gossip—as, indeed, I was. If, in relation to the household, men may be identified, more or less, with the responsible, "civilized," and docile Joseph, once outside domestic bounds they belong to the domain of the exterior, an amoral sphere often subsumed under the term "the street" (*la calle*). In stereotypical terms, in *la calle* men become part of the profane, dangerous world and are regarded as predisposed to engage in correspondingly profane behavior—drinking, violence, and illicit sexual relations—thought to fuel and further evoke their "animal" natures. (Such a popular version of the street, while figuring a spiritual "underworld" or "fallen" state, also represents a temporary inversion of Mexican nationalist associations between civil, political, and economic order, and the public domain. "Popular" men thus appear to be risky characters to both themselves and others. Frequently, these are the bodies in need of "salvation," both supernatural and political.)

In keeping with such polarized ideas, a marked segregation of the sexes is observable at almost every public occasion, especially fiestas. Whereas in the "official" church a male hierarchy guides all events, in popular religious zones women typically organize and occupy the interior, domestic arena and are at the forefront of processions, the singing of hymns, and other religious activity, while their sons and brothers and husbands carry on with "profane" behavior outside the bounds of the "sacred zone" and the home. In the course of popular religious celebrations, it is not unusual to see men lingering behind or on the periphery, often drinking or involved in dangerous activity such as lighting fireworks or wearing or running around with *toritos* ("bulls" constructed of firecrackers and wood). In this way, gender divisions appear, within social ritual contexts, to aid in the separation and objectification of various moral spheres. If "the people" in general are ordered by the (male) church hierarchy in the course of "official" church engagements, and if women are "disciplined" by men in most of their activities and public appearances in the profane world, ordinary men's profane activities and undisciplined "wildness" are called to account by women in the popular spiritual sphere.

For according to the popular cosmogony, the "profane" world outside the home is the realm of the unknown and the uncertain. This exterior sphere includes the natural domain, which for many has negative and even fearful connotations of potential danger, wildness, chaos, the uncivilized, the unknown, the unfamiliar. Thus many of my neighbors in San Juan told me that garbage tossed into the street or into a vacant lot was not a despoiling of the environment, but a practical disposal in wasteland. Victims of evildoing (like many of those that end up in the Red Cross amphitheater, where autopsies of anonymous cadavers are performed) are spoken of as being discovered—as often was the case—in the most "natural" of sites, usually on or beyond the margins of the city in ditches or rivers, the peripheries of moral geography. On the edges of this civilized moral geography, too, are the raunchy strip bars and live sex shows found in nightclubs like La Costa and La Trampa and sequestered in the newer outlying colonias.

The distinction between the realms of the "sacred" and the "profane" also has a temporal dimension. For example, at night *la calle* is considered particularly dangerous. The nighttime air is believed by many to carry "bad or evil air," or *mal aire*, and sickness, to which women and children are considered especially vulnerable; many (especially older) women in San Juan may be seen at night with *rebozos* (shawls) covering their heads and mouths, parts of the body vulnerable to the entry of *mal aire* or other agents of illness.

Such a symbolically charged local topography bears some resemblance to the categorization schemes of other Mediterranean and Latin American social landscapes. Robert DaMatta, for example, describes the distribution of Brazilian social life, and the generation of social discourse, with reference to three spatial domains: the home (*casa*), the street (*rua*), and the other world, or the supernatural domain. The site of the origin of one's identity, and the space of shared substance with one's family, the home is exclusivist, unique, and hierarchically ordered according to age and gender. This ideological orientation of the home exists in tension with the street, which reflects universal values and an individualistic ideology based on public equality. The supernatural sphere of the other world functions, then, as a mediating field and enables the reconciliation or containment of other contradictions between life in the home and on the street, and their respective ethical systems. As DaMatta explains, "in a system so structured, the social universe is perceived as divided, segmented, cross-cut by spaces and ethics that are distinct but complementary." The result is a perception of a social environment based on alternation and complementarity, which, during "extraordinary [ritual] moments," may be transformed into a "coherent totality by means of a single ethic and an exclusive pattern of behavior."[3]

It is in the social landscape that popular religious practice focuses its work. Indeed, popular religious rituals in Oaxaca frequently involve symbolic manipulation and extension of the bounds of the interior, spiritual realm as a way of taming or counterbalancing parts of the exterior, mundane dimension, transforming the latter temporarily into a positive, sacred setting. This occurs on both temporal and physical planes. It is significant, for example, that many religious ceremonies or events take place over a long period, from several hours to several days, representing a protraction of positive "sacred" activity.

Popular rituals thus work to erase certain divisions, at least for a time, even while the careful observation of certain popular rituals reiterates other divisions: between the faithful and the unfaithful, between women and men, between the popular and the official church. So it is that while many of the collective religious practices in Oaxaca are subject to some official control by the church or state—for example, the mass or certain public aspects of religious fiestas—much daily religious activity goes on outside of the physical confines of the church and its hierarchy's sphere of influence and direction. Most of the devotional expressions that attend the cult of the saints, for example, fall outside the bounds of the official church. Some of these expressions involve group undertakings, whereas others are largely familiar or private. A vibrant and deeply affective zone of "informal" worship, many of these extra-Catholic rituals form the core of popular urban (and rural indigenous) religious practice.[4]

THE SAINTS

A small number of sacred figures or saints are particularly well known and venerated throughout Mexico. The Virgin Mary, for example, in her manifestation as the beloved Nuestra Señora de Guadelupe (Our Lady of Guadalupe), the patron of Mexico, is the inspiration for a wide array of feast days and devotional cults. Her special feast day is December 12—one of Mexico's most important fiestas of the year. Aside from the millions who join pilgrimages from all over the country to Tepeyac, in Mexico City, where the Virgin is said to have first appeared in 1531, in Oaxaca, on December 11 and 12, thousands wait outside the Basílica de Guadalupe for a blessing at the Virgin's altar. For this day, as for the celebration of Corpus Christi in June, babies and children are dressed up as *inditos* (little Indians, the diminutive, sometimes used pejoratively, is here affectionate): little girls are brought to the altar in traditional embroidered blouses (*huipiles*), braided hair, and sandals, and little boys are dressed up in white *campesino* trousers, sombreros, and false mustaches.[5]

In Oaxaca, in addition to the many fiestas that honor various manifestations of the Virgin—the most important include the Virgen del Carmen, the Virgen de la Concepción or Virgen de Juquila, and the Virgen de la Soledad (Virgin of Solitude), the patron saint of Oaxaca—the Virgin is honored on Good Friday (Viernes Santo), when some women may be seen attired in mourning black; on September 8, a day known as La Natividad (Nativity of the Blessed Virgin Mary); and on August 15, the Virgin's Asunción (Assumption Day, which typically receives significantly more attention than Christ's Ascension Day, on May 9).[6] The official church has a role in some, but not all, of these festivals. In the parish of Cuauhtémoc, for example, where Colonia San Juan is located, the church dedicates the whole of the month of May to the Virgin. For the entire month, local schoolchildren are encouraged to visit the church every afternoon to offer her flowers and to recite prayers. In Cuauhtémoc, Mary is also honored as the Virgen del Rosario (Virgin of the Rosary) for two weeks in October, during the annual community *mayordomía* (patron saint's festival). This festival is judged by many practitioners to be the most important fiesta for the parish; it involves months of planning and the expenditure of millions of pesos.[7] And the Legión de María (Legion of Mary), a group of women dedicated to the Virgin's veneration, participates in and leads many popular rites, while maintaining a relationship with the "official" church.

In keeping with the independent orientation of many popular religious practices, however, individuals or families may pray to their own "saint of devotion," a guardian saint from whom they request personal favors. There is a saint for every need or desire: fidelity, fertility, safety in travel, luck in love, recovery of belongings, protection of children; the list goes on and on. Popular custom distinguishes these saints according to their associated specialties; just as you would not take your car to a bakery for repairs, just any saint cannot answer prayers directed at a specific topic.

The saints also function as icons that divide or differentiate geographic regions: every state, every pueblo, and many workplaces have their own *santos patronales* (patron saints); each such saint has a yearly *mayordomía*, which is celebrated by everyone in the locality or workplace. The cult of the saints also serves to unite separate neighborhoods or communities at particular times of the year, as neighborhoods encompassed by a given parish, for example, come together for major festivals celebrated by the church. Indeed, in many respects the official Catholic fiesta cycle is conflated with a reproductive cycle: there is the birth, teaching, Passion, death, and Resurrection of Christ. The stories that link and celebrate these events also inform the sacraments and life-cycle rites marking the days and years of individual, family, and community life. Thus baptism, communion, confirmation, and last rites knit together individual concerns and divine histories; they also mark the cyclical points of birth, death, and renewal so important to the agricultural calendar.[8]

The Holy Family and the saints are venerated as examples to be emulated, and when human frailty intervenes, they may be counted on as intercessors for the faithful, with a distant and authoritarian God. The cult of the saints thus involves an implicit and considerable hierarchy, a system of patronage and authority to be cultivated and placated. Commenting on the implications of such a vertical structure of authority, the distinguished historian of colonial Mexico William Taylor argues that in the colonial period the church advocated filial piety, the respect owed to parents by their children, as an apt model for the social order:

God is the father of piety, Mary the mother of mercy; kings, under the divine protection of God, are to be loved and revered as fathers of the state and its members; the Church is their mother. Rulers and the rich are enjoined to exercise prudence, piety and charity; subjects and the poor are instructed to be patient, tolerant and humble. Like God, the king was distant, aloof and shadowy father who could be approached mainly through benevolent intercessors.[9]

While it is tempting to hear echoes of such quiescent order in many contemporary popular practices surrounding the saints, what such a model leaves out is the way in which individuals, by developing special devotions to and relations with particular saints, also cultivate an intimacy with those saints and their powers. The saints—and individuals' relationships to them—are thus deeply personalized. Saints are sacred personas who inhabit the landscape of the everyday as honored and, usually, much beloved guests. Consequently, in popular practice, the idiom of reciprocal exchange is more important to the relations with the saints than the language of hierarchy and authority. What matters is an establishment of mutual obligation between mortal and saintly visitor. Such obligations thus serve to reframe the hierarchical "official" invocations of the saints and to replace the saints within the logic of an indigenous moral and material economy.

Unsurprisingly, then, an extremely important aspect of popular religious activity in Oaxaca consists of the fulfillment of vows or pledges (*mandas* or *promesas*) made to particular saints by individuals, families, or community groups. Taking part in a pilgrimage to a faraway shrine, bringing flowers regularly for a certain period to an image in church or at home, and engaging in some other concrete form of respect or devotion are common ways of satisfying such vows. Residents of San Juan repeatedly told me that misfortune is likely to befall one who fails to honor a *promesa* or to fulfill it with "true faith" in the heart. Pilgrims flock to pilgrimage shrines like Etla, near Oaxaca—where, on Good Friday, the local patron saint, El Señor de las Peñas, is honored—or to the shrine of the Virgin of Juquila, in the south-central highlands of the state, in order to place money or miniature figures representing a desired item or outcome—a little cow fashioned of mud, a house of straw or stones, a toy car—on the altar of the saint. According to popular wisdom, the greater the amount of money left, the better the chance that one's request for favor will be granted. Letters asking for protection against one's enemies or against envy, good academic results, romantic favors, or weight loss are also attached to the shrine or placed in a special mailbox alongside it (figure 2.1).[10]

And, from time to time, new saints are abruptly "discovered" through "miraculous" circumstances. In August 1995, for example, a rumor ran like an electric current through Oaxaca City, telling of a new Virgin who had appeared to a young man by a streambed just outside the nearby town of San Felipe Jalapa. Apparently, drought had left the streambed completely dry, and right near the site where the Virgin had appeared (in the form of a small carved wooden image), a spring had suddenly emerged, bringing water to the streambed.[11] Not long afterward, droves of visitors arrived in San Felipe, eager to see, with their own eyes, evidence of the miracle. They demonstrated their passionate devotion with tears and abundant offerings, as at any other pilgrimage site. Later in the year, the Virgin's appearance was exposed by the local media as a hoax, a creation by a few San Felipe residents interested in the lucrative prospect of establishing a pilgrimage destination in their town. (Pilgrims to Juquila, for example, serve

FIGURE 2.1 A pilgrim at a shrine dedicated to the Virgin of Juquila in
San Juan de Chapultepec (San Juanito), Oaxaco..

as that community's economic mainstay.) Despite the contentious origins of
the supposed "miracle" in San Felipe, the event does serve to illustrate one role
of the saints in helping popular communities to confront the vicissitudes of
social and economic flux. Like other, similar miracles that have characterized
moments in Oaxaca's past, this "vision" of a local apparition of the Virgin made
use of religious consciousness in order to try to negotiate some form of social,
cultural, and economic change in the midst of a period of great instability and
uncertainty.[12] The "use" that a handful of San Felipe residents tried to make of
an apparition of the Virgin Mary was thus not much different from the "use"
that individuals make of particular saints as they seek benediction, healing, or
economic or social benefit—although, as commentators were quick to point out,
the quality of one's intention, the "truth" of one's faith, matters absolutely.

For the affective texture of individuals' interactions with the saints is of paramount importance. In this folk-Catholic cosmology, unlike God, who acts at a
great distance from human lives, the saints are visible, tangible, plastic beings,
figures to whom are attributed human needs and emotional qualities, including
capriciousness, benevolence, anger, and sadness, as well as the power to grant
favors large and small. Sacred images on household altars (or, during fiesta
periods, in the church) are devotedly and fastidiously clothed, visited, offered
food and flowers, kept company, talked to, sung to, laid down, caressed, and

kissed—much as any beloved human being might be. In Cuauhtémoc, during the saint's day festival in October, a small image of the Virgin Mary is taken from the church to various homes in the parish; the Virgin is said to be "visiting" on such occasions. In turn, parishioners may drop in to visit the Virgin as they would a special guest in the neighborhood, showing her affection and *respeto*. Also, while a saint may be the object of love, saints, like people, are also the objects of "avoidance." If a believer concludes that invoking a particular saint always backfires, or seems to be unlucky, then that saint must be carefully avoided, excluded from devotions or prayers.[13]

The Niño Dios (Christ Child) is another very popular saint in Oaxaca and the object of celebration during the Christmas Posadas—which end with the Acostadita, or "laying down" of the image of the Niño Dios on Christmas Eve in a manger in the Nativity scene made in each home—through to La Candelaria (Candlemas)—also known as the Paradita, or "standing up," on February 2—a festival that commemorates Christ's Presentation at the Temple. For La Candelaria, women dress little images of the Niño and take them to church to be blessed. Then, from Candlemas to Ash Wednesday (Miércoles de Ceniza), small fiestas are held in individual homes, sponsored by *madrinas* (godmothers) of the Niño and attended mostly by women and children. As during the Posadas, candies, food, drink, whistles, candles, and *luces de bengala* (sparklers) are distributed among fiesta guests, and firecrackers are set off in the street. The Niño sits (often on a little wooden throne) in the house altar and is prayed and sung to (figure 2.2).

The cult of the Niño Dios reflects the common view that the small, the young, and the weak are closer to God. (Similarly, I have often heard believers claim that the Virgin of Juquila, whose image is less than a foot tall, is nonetheless very powerful.) Children, who are usually considered innocent of sin, are likened to the saints—whose souls have been washed clean by their holy actions. Frequently described as *angelitos* (little angels), children undergoing first communion or confirmation ceremonies are dressed in white clothing, often complete with haloes and paper wings. Children are also typically chosen to represent saints during religious fiestas in processions such as the Posadas or during *calendas*, parades that are a typical part of *mayordomías* (figure 2.3); they are frequently given important roles in religious rituals, with the hope that their purity of heart and spotless souls will guide other, more sinful parishioners to God.

The intimacy of emotional exchange with the saints is pervasive. One Good Friday, at a neighborhood chapel in Cuauhtémoc, I attended what was called a *velorio* (wake) for Christ. Participants said rosaries—the customary "popular" mode of prayer—before an image of the Virgin of Solitude and remained with

FIGURE 2.2 Baby Jesuses for sale at the Mercado Benito Juárez in Oaxaca City.

FIGURE 2.3 A neighborhood *calenda* for the Santísimo (Holy Spirit).

her the entire night in sympathy, just as they would have accompanied any neighbor who had lost her son. Another index of residents' fervent faith in the capacity of saints to endure emotional suffering may be found in the details of a scandal that rocked Oaxaca City in January 1991. One night, thieves broke into the Iglesia de la Soledad in the city center and made off with the valuable crown and rosary from the church's large image of the Virgen de la Soledad. In keeping with traditional mourning customs, soon afterward black bows appeared on cars, on buses, on the windows of houses, and above doors throughout the city. In the weeks that followed, people throughout Oaxaca—young and old, women and men—visited the offended Virgin en masse; they offered her flowers and hymns. Some of the faithful were even moved to donate their own jewels to make a new crown. At a Bible discussion meeting in San Juan following the incident, one of my neighbors, who had gone to visit the Virgin, solemnly declared that the face on her image had clearly shrunk and that tears could be seen in her eyes.

Intimacy and accident clearly do not diminish the power of the saints. Worshiped for day-to-day spiritual aid and for the critical conduit they offer to divine power, the saints function not only as intercessors, intermediaries between the spheres of the mundane and the sacred, but also as sources of joy and friendship. The ties between worshipers and saints often resemble the ties between *compadres* (ritual kin). These are relationships that carry obligations but that also may be depended on in times of sickness and of health. As Lucía, a middle-aged woman in the parish, told me, speaking of the saint whose image sat on her altar: "It's like a joy in my heart, I truly feel that. I speak with him, I pray to him; he is a joy for me, my little saint." The goal of this relationship between mortal and saint is a sense of well-being that is material and social as much as it is spiritual: here personal health and welfare are inseparable from notions of social balance and harmony—and the popular practices that work toward their achievement.

For example, the Niño Dios is especially popular in his form as the Niño Doctor (Child Doctor), and many people in need of a miraculous cure for themselves or for someone dear to them may adopt the Niño Doctor as a special saint of devotion. Reflecting this popularity of the Niño Doctor, for the Paradita, the house image of the Niño is often dressed in a little white doctor's smock; a black case is placed in one hand, a stethoscope hung around his neck, and a hypodermic needle placed in his other hand (figure 2.4). A *milagrito* (tiny two-dimensional metal replica of the ailing organ or appendage, a foot, say, or an arm) may be pinned to the Niño Doctor's smock, to help guide him to the correct remedy. One day, during my initial period of fieldwork, my neighbor, Julia, told me about a Posada party she had just attended in the house of a very poor

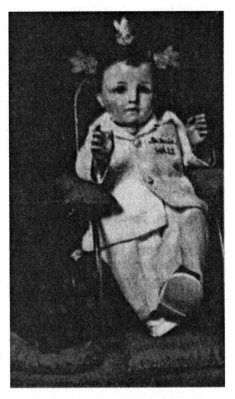

FIGURE 2.4 An image of the Niño Doctor.

(*muy humilde*) woman named Rosa. Rosa had just recovered from an illness; she had promised the figure of the Niño Antocha in Puebla that she would hold a party in his honor if she got better. She borrowed 300,000 old pesos (around U.S.\$50) from her employers (she earned just 200,000 old pesos [around U.S.\$40] a fortnight), purchased an image of the Niño, and then outfitted it in a tiny doctor's uniform. Because the saint answered her plea, Rosa felt called on to make a significant sacrifice in honor of him. This was the medium of her thanks, her reciprocal obligation to the saint whose care had saved her.

Similarly, a very ill child may be "raised" before a certain saint, in a rite known as a *levantada*. The mother of the ill infant takes her child to church or asks another woman to act as the child's "godmother" and take him or her. At the church, the mother or the *madrina* prays to a particular saint, usually some aspect of the Virgin, and then lights a candle and offers up the soul of the child, asking for a cure. The mother of one small girl I knew had her daughter "raised" before the Virgen del Carmen; soon afterward, the child recovered. As part of a pledge made to the Virgin by her mother, every day for a year, the little girl wore a brown dress, like that worn by the image of the saint.

Not every such pledge or vow involves positive outcomes, nor are they all made to such spotless or holy saints. La Santísima Muerte (Most Holy Saint of Death), is, for example, a popular "saint" to whom an *oración* may be said, ostensibly to bring illness or death to one's enemies. Some of the people I asked, however, refuted such an account of the nefarious powers of deadly saints, and maintained that La Santísima Muerte could not be asked to harm others, that her power could be invoked only to protect oneself or others against harm deliberately brought by others. In any case, candles bearing the saint's image and a prayer, or small packets of special dust (*polvo legítimo*) and a prayer for La Santísima Muerte, may be purchased from the herb or folk medicine stalls in most markets in the city. To win the saint's protection, the dust is sprinkled on one's body or on altar candles before lighting them. Sold in the cluster of stands typically found outside churches during many religious festivals, alongside a plethora of other sacred items—more orthodox printed prayers, portraits, scapulas, rosary beads, plaster images, and candles—the dust of La Santísima Muerte joins a range of quasi-religious folk substances like the "Dust of the Seven He-men" (apparently a cure for gossips) and special powders for increasing or decreasing sexual appetite. So it is that the saints, whether for bad or good, enter the thickness and fray of human life. They become, alongside the signs of human desires and foibles, the agents by which material and social goods circulate throughout the community.

This singular way of perceiving and interacting with the saints is part of the particularities of the "experiential script" of popular religiosity.[14] In popular communities in Oaxaca, the saints are revered not simply for the moral lessons they offer but also, crucially, because they serve as *human examples* that one should aspire to emulate or imitate. The more important the festival, the more dramatic this message. Thus, for example, festivals such as Semana Santa (Holy Week), which involves the dramatization of events preceding, during, and following Christ's Passion and death, and the Christmas Posadas, which play out Mary and Joseph's search for lodging on Christmas Eve, make these sacred histories tangible and vitally real for and within the community of believers. As neighbors play the parts of Mary and Joseph, knocking at your door to request aid and lodging, or act out the Passion, suffering, and crucifixion of Christ, in graphic detail, you are called to bear witness to the familiar human faces of these tales. You, too, play some part in this ritual story; you cannot escape the immediacy of the drama at hand. The saints are not abstractions or imaginary constructions; they are real and present and powerful. What is sacred is thus right here, immanent in the spaces and figures of daily life.

This is also why images of the Virgin, other saints, Christ, or simply the cross itself are often kissed, touched, or brushed with a piece of clothing, a flower, or an herb branch: the power of the divine is effectively present within the images or structures that represent whatever is holy. Consequently, whatever comes into contact with such an image is imbued with a kind of palpable, material divine essence. People return from pilgrimages with mementos or relics—scapulas, a religious pendant, a relic, rosary beads, or a small framed portrait of the honored saint or Virgin—that have been blessed by a priest at a saint's shrine or have been blessed by coming into contact with an already holy icon or image. Regarded as potent talismans of a spiritual blessing and strength that has been transferred from the realm of the divine into that of the mundane, such blessed mementos, it is widely believed, contain a sort of potency that one may draw on to satisfy individual needs, including simple material gains as well as physical or spiritual healing. Sacredness thus consists of an embodied and tangible reality; it belongs to the here and now of the every day, not some otherworldly or abstract dimension.

Building Communal Ties

An intimacy of relationship between profane and sacred, humans and sacred beings—both saints and the dead—is characteristic of popular religious values and expressions. Within a popular religious frame, one's actions are not simply a matter of personal responsibility but have an impact on the community as a whole. Whatever one does, then, is at once individual, social, and collective. When Rosa prayed to the Niño Antocha for healing, and her prayer was answered, she held a party, so that others in the community might share both her good fortune and her devotion. Having been granted favor, she returned the kindness, in a gesture that turned her sacrifice into abundance for others.

Such flows between the individual and the community, the sacred and the profane, also hold for popular conceptions of sin. While the official church regards persons as individually responsible for sins—in its view, sins are distortions in one's relationship with God, interruptions or imperfections in one's inner spiritual values—sin, according to a popular outlook, is not simply a matter of individual conscience. Crimes or negative behavior almost always affect the immediate social environment in the popular community; in particular, actions that stem from egotistical greed or ambition frequently threaten family (kin, or *compadrazgo*) or community relations or both.

In keeping with such "folk" beliefs, sins are conceived as deeds that induce uneasy disturbances or imbalances in the larger universe, with the possibility of detrimental results for self, family, and the community as a whole. Because popular religion is not especially preoccupied with concerns having to do with salvation—unlike the "official" church—in everyday practice the sacraments receive little emphasis compared with domestic liturgies, particularly those involving supplication of the saints. I learned quickly from people in San Juan, for example, that confession at the church does not carry the same valued moral weight as ensuring one's proper performance of funeral or Day of the Dead ritual obligations, building home altars, or setting out offerings to the saints or the dead. Popular religious obligations are typically about ensuring "good" outcomes, insofar as this is possible, for members of the community, both living and dead; such obligations are not about individual transcendence.[15]

Any given human body and the social body are thus profoundly linked in such a belief system; indeed, this linkage is a guiding principle in the "folk" pathology of illness. Illness articulates the sorts of symbioses that folk beliefs elaborate among the individual, the domestic group, and the rest of the community. *Susto*, for example, is a condition caused by severe shock or fright; it is often spoken of as the "loss of one's soul." Remedies must be undertaken immediately in order to recover or recapture the lost soul and restore it to the frightened person.[16] Likewise, anger, strong tension (*muina* or *coraje*), and envy (*envídia*) between family members or neighbors is seen to have real affective force, sufficient to cause harm, misfortune, or illness. Similarly, *mal de ojo* (evil eye), an ailment that overwhelmingly afflicts children—particularly beautiful children—is understood to be caused by the envious glance of an adult whose stronger person energies may inflict damage on a weaker child. In the same manner, trouble with the saints or with the dead that is caused by improper behavior—failure to keep a vow, or *promesa*, or to carry out expected ritual obligations—can have negative repercussions within and for the community.

Consequently, a combination of religious symbols, practices, and beliefs saturate folk medicine in popular practice in Oaxaca.[17] Both divination of the causes of illness and prescribed cures derive from a profound sense of the interrelationship between physical and moral life, individual and community. Analyzing medical practices in Oaxaca in the 1970s, in an urban *colonia popular* like San Juan, Cheleen Mahar found that illness and cures were frequently discussed in terms of balance; according to such folk beliefs, sickness and the condition of one's social relations are related. Sorting out how to remedy one area may also remedy the other. The task, with regard to healing, Mahar found, was to discover whether the force or cause from which an illness derived was supernatural or natural.[18]

More recent work by Linda Hunt on various conceptions of the etiology and treatment of cancer in Oaxaca City suggests that Oaxacans have come to distinguish between illnesses such as cancer, in which root causes are associated with "modernization," and illnesses such as *susto* and *mal de ojo*, in which certain traditional "imbalances" are suspected. Treatment methods, Hunt argues, are selected in part in accordance with the ostensible "origins" of an illness: a traditional illness requires a traditional cure (figure 2.5), whereas a "modern" or an "imported" illness—AIDS, for example, has often been associated with foreigners—requires a "modern" or an "imported" cure. However, Hunt claims that many people employ local health practices such using home herbal remedies, consulting a *curandera* or *curandero*, or making vows to saints in conjunction with biomedical treatments. Traditional curing methods, she argues, draw on culturally meaningful idioms in a way that the "official" health

FIGURE 2.5 *Limpia* (cleansing) to cure *susto*.

care system cannot. And while we must acknowledge that traditional healing methods are also much less expensive than modern ones (only some Oaxacans have health insurance), Hunt's work underscores the crucial relationship among "well-being," spiritual blessing, and the sacred sphere for urban members of the popular classes.

Hunt shows, for instance, that the efficacy of any cancer treatment for poor Oaxacans depends partly on its ability to purge and rectify a sense of disorder. Mediated conceptually through the body, healing involves the movement of polluting disorder from inside to outside. The healing process itself is envisaged in a religious idiom: moral purification (*purgar*) follows from the expulsion of evil, disease-causing agents from the afflicted person. Cures are often accomplished by what amounts to the use of homeopathic principles: a healing substance might be selected for a given treatment because it possesses qualities widely perceived to oppose the characteristics of the element causing an ailment. The premise of such cures is that the interaction of contrasting qualities neutralizes the malevolent effects of any negative force acting on a body. In her study, Hunt cites the popularity of snake meat as a cure for cancer: by eating the snake, one ingests a power equal and opposite to the maleficent impurities of cancer.[19] Like a pilgrimage, the process of healing requires movement, an externalization of inner unrest, and the acquisition of some sort of spiritual peace. The goal of any of these ritual processes involves the retrieval of a condition of harmony, balance, continuity, and pureness—and therefore a sense of order. Acts of healing are thus at once social and individual or physical; contradiction or discordance is addressed through transformations that repair the afflicted body and, through it, the social order itself.[20] The preoccupation with the magical and the practical evident in Oaxacan popular religiosity, especially in relation to healing, can be seen to reflect what Roger Lancaster calls an "ethical sub-religion," a materialist mode of faith concerned with the maintenance of values and practices that prioritize the interests of the collective group.[21]

The maintenance of a critical social balance and collective well-being happens in other ways as well. Numerous symbolic and material mechanisms of social leveling—primarily in the form of ritual exchange—and ideals of cooperation and communalism animate popular religious (and many secular) activities in communities such as Colonia San Juan in Oaxaca. The annual round of Catholic festivals and life-cycle rites—particularly baptism, first communion, and confirmation—offer opportunities for the trumpeting of personal wealth or social status, as well as for the symbolic reaffirmation of traditional ideals and values of communal solidarity in the context of reciprocal exchange and *convivencia*. To begin with, sacramental rites such as baptisms, weddings, and first communion and confirmation ceremonies allow for the establishment or reaffirmation of *compadrazgo* bonds—those non-kin social links that are so often activated by individuals in times of economic need. Outside the *compadrazgo* network, these ritual occasions also serve to affirm more general social ties in the form of the *guelaguetza*, or small-gift exchange. In rural and urban Oaxaca, the *guelaguetza* is a traditional exchange system that provides for individuals to contribute food, small amounts of money, or other items to a family hosting a religious celebration, thus permitting them to sponsor an event that they otherwise could not afford. Such contributions are reciprocated over time, when the givers themselves sponsor various ritual events. Often quite formalized in its expression in rural areas, the *guelaguetza* has taken on a looser form in Oaxaca City, but it remains the general rule for such expensive and expansive collective ritual occasions.[22]

Thus while certain popular religious rituals in Oaxaca may function as a forum for the competition for prestige, or in order to underscore certain factors of internal "distinction" on the basis of gender, ethnicity, or class,[23] they also serve to enact and to celebrate positive values related to collectivism, communality, and social equilibrium. I argue that by typically affirming the virtues of poverty and the world of the autochthonous and "traditional," such popular rites try to ensure the survival of a community in a rapidly changing urban setting; they tie individuals to a past and to others with concrete and material ritual actions, with hopes, desires, expectations, and mutual obligations. Discordant, in many ways, with the individualizing tendencies of consumer capitalism, and the transcendental spirituality of much orthodox Christianity, such ritually maintained and reaffirmed popular communal values may not offer an effective world-inverting resistance to the dominant order so much as an elastic resilience in the face of it.

Conquest, Evangelization, and the Rise of "Popular" Religion

At various points in the history of Oaxaca, the Catholic Church or "official" religious agents have been opposed to the interests of popular religion as an independent domain of social practice and identity creation. In diverse ways, the church has worked to expunge or appropriate the particular potency of popular religious forms and to frustrate their independence and autonomy. At the same time, however, popular religion has ultimately deeply affected the practice of "official" Catholicism in Mexico. But, as William Taylor has argued, "any given combination of Christian and 'pagan' elements . . . was not, in itself, a synthesis of religious or selective assimilation of one religion by another, but part of an incomplete process that might be reversed or redirected and could not be measured by traits added or subtracted."[24]

Taylor has carefully analyzed a number of factors informing the relationships between priests and parishioners, the official church and what he calls "local" or "folk" religious practices in eighteenth-century Mexico.[25] Situating his study more or less midway between colonial contact and conquest, and Mexican independence and modernization, Taylor examines the complex of relationships that emerged between conquering and subjugated peoples, cultures, and practices. Arguing that the Conquest was not a single violent event but a long process involving alliances between the Spaniards and a number of indigenous groups against the dominant Aztecs, that eventually, after the depredations of disease and war, resulted in a "coup d'état," Taylor takes care to mark such shifting and multifarious alliances in his account of the emergence of new forms of local religious practice and sacred space:

> Local religion in central and western Mexico during the eighteenth century was not unified, fixed, and uncontested from top to bottom, or simply set against the religion of Catholic priests. Any explanation of religious change there [thus] needs to account for the local conflicts over religious practices and the multiple meanings of religious symbols; for the understandings that were shared between rulers and ruled and the misunderstandings that could divide them; for the development of parallel and complementary practices, as well as mixed or fused ones; for ways in which religion could still be altered by groups and individuals in conflict.[26]

Such cautionary notes are important, for in examining the relationships between dominating international institutions such as the Catholic Church and locally resistant or distinctive practices in communities that are largely indigenous, it is easy to paint with too broad a brush, to overplay one element or another, whether conquest, resistance, or the supposedly easy syncretic mixing of cultural elements. Nevertheless, in order to better understand the sometimes uneasy coexistence between the Catholic Church in Oaxaca today and various popular or local religious practices, it is perhaps useful to sketch certain rather broad historical dimensions, which continue to inform contemporary relationships and interests in various ways.

While my aim is to furnish some background account of the emergence of popular religion in Oaxaca, in this brief history I also want to highlight the particularities of contemporary popular religion as an everyday, practical philosophy and way of engaging with the sacred. The anthropologist Marshall Sahlins has shown quite convincingly that historical change permits the persistence of culturally shared structures of meaning despite quite profound transformations elsewhere in society. In other words, history is not a series of events that unfolds haphazardly through time, but is organized by already existing, culturally formed frameworks for perceiving and understanding the world. In these terms, we can see historical processes such as religious syncretism as shaped by interpretive frameworks—or "paradigmatic structures," as Sahlins calls them—that give sense to people's actions. These interpretive frameworks are different lenses not simply for perceiving reality but also for experiencing it. For example, maligning the static "mix and match" models of syncretism often used in the history of Mexican religion, Inga Clendinnen argues that the notion of belief as a statement that someone may consciously assert does not capture the quality of a *lived faith*, where belief has as much to do with affect—emotional, moral, and aesthetic—as with ideas. Thus these culturally embedded interpretive frames are also frameworks for *being* in the world.

In applying these arguments to Oaxacan popular religion today, I do not presume a clear, direct continuation of an original "paradigmatic structure" of Oaxacan indigenous sacred experience. I argue, however, that, at the very least, we can still see elements of the general ethical orientation of past habits of sacred experience in contemporary popular religious practice. Let us look now at some of the historical underpinnings of this ethical foundation.

The numbers alone tell a grisly story. It is estimated that, in all of what is now Mexico, of an indigenous population of 25 million at the beginning of the colonial period in 1521, by 1600 only slightly more than 1 million people were still alive, the remainder having perished in war, under slavery, or by disease. Indeed, in the Valley of Oaxaca, from the beginning of the Conquest until 1630, the indigenous population fell from 350,000 to between 40,000 and 45,000, a decline of almost 90 percent in just over one hundred years.[27] More profoundly, the cultural rupture that began with the Conquest also represented a symbolic violence enacted on surviving indigenous bodies and communities; it involved a shattering and displacement of dominated orders of meaning, traditional referents of identity, and sources of expression—in effect, the entire world, imaginary and geographic, human and supernatural, was remade. The Conquest was thus not simply an economic and military exercise but a collective act of consummate symbolic aggression. And, despite important exceptions,[28] friars, priests, and other agents of the Catholic Church were among the principal architects of colonization; they designed and maintained various power structures and systems of control that aimed at the domination of the bodies, minds, and souls of conquered peoples.

The Spanish learned the Indians' languages, converted the Indians to Christianity, and, in an attempt to change their subsistence patterns, instructed them in European methods of cultivation and crafts and introduced new livestock.[29] The conquerors proselytized the Indians and performed rapid baptisms. They also destroyed existing buildings to impose their own architectural forms and remake the world in their own image. Sumptuous churches, cathedrals, monasteries, and convents were built on the razed ruins of indigenous temples or sites of worship—only after smashing the idols of "pagan" gods they had been housed in the temples, burning manuscripts, and deposing or exterminating native priests. The parish church of Mitla, in Oaxaca, for example, was constructed over the ruins of a Mixtec temple, and, in Mexico City, the ruins of the Templo Mayor, the main temple of the Aztec city of Tenochtitlán, are found right alongside the cathedral in the capital's *zócalo*. And in the city of Cholula, hundreds of chapels and churches were erected over pilgrimage temples, including the famous Iglesia de Nuestra Señora de los Remedios, which stands over a large pyramid.

The division and reordering of indigenous geographic and social space was a further dimension of the imposition of order in the course of the Spanish colonizing project. Under the *encomienda* system, particular Indian communities were assigned to serve individual colonists. The first *encomienda* grants were made by Hernán Cortés in 1522 to reward his soldiers for their work in the conquest of New Spain. These *encomiendas* provided the labor for agricultural, mining, and cattle-raising activities, which were to become the mainstay of the colonial economy. In addition to the *encomienda* system, beginning in the mid-sixteenth and early seventeenth centuries a scheme of forced labor called the *repartimiento* reorganized the indigenous population outside the *encomiendas*. Indigenous laborers were recruited and then assigned to various managers of the properties of royal functionaries to work in the mines, on particular ranches or haciendas, or in the construction of roads, bridges, churches, and other public works.[30] Indians were also obliged to pay heavy tributes to the Crown; those who failed were often imprisoned and tortured. The abuses of both these systems incited the wrath of friars and various representatives of the church, for they found that their efforts at evangelization were impeded by the alienation and suffering of the Indians.

The church thus played a dual role. On the one hand, the *repartimiento* and *encomienda* systems served to bring Indians into rural landholdings or haciendas where, in addition to providing labor for and tribute to Spanish landowners—and to convents and members of the church—they were "protected" and educated in Christian doctrine. This meant that priests did not have to travel to the countryside to find subjects to evangelize, but, quite literally, they had captive audiences. The Indians also provided a significant labor force for the monasteries; their exploitation contributed to the rapidly rising wealth of the clergy. Native communal village lands were expropriated and added to church lands—villages were burned when people refused to leave them—and indigenous children (especially the children of the nobility) were gathered into monastery schools where they received Catholic baptism, were indoctrinated into the Christian faith, and were instructed in Spanish and Latin. Saving souls and enriching the church appeared, sometimes, to be mutually supportive activities. But as the increasingly evangelized indigenous population began to decline rapidly, both workers and souls disappeared, significantly complicating the relationship between Indians and conquerors, "Christians" and "pagans."

Early efforts at evangelization were centered on a rich array of state rituals, passion plays, and indigenous dances and songs, adapted to convey European or Christian significances.[31] Many commentators have argued that well before the arrival of the Spanish, the indigenous societies of Mesoamerica experienced constant encounters (both violent and peaceful) with one another throughout the vast territories they occupied; these experiences led to the Indians' great capacity to inventively handle simultaneous, heterogeneous practices and codes.[32] In this view, the attitude of indigenous Mesoamericans toward other religious systems was an open one: the Aztec, for example, legitimated their domination through the incorporation of the gods of the peoples they conquered. Consequently, although the Spanish—and Europeans generally—overwhelmingly figured conversion as a rupture with the past and its practices, for the Indians, shifts or changes in the nature of the sacred were frequently matters for integration or incorporation rather than wholesale transformation.[33]

Thus, despite obvious contrasts between Christian monotheism and an indigenous pantheon of gods, many superficial similarities already existed between indigenous belief systems and Spanish Christianity, and this served to ease the apparent merging of these religious codes.[34] Mesoamericans were already familiar with rituals resembling baptism, communion, and confession; they practiced a cult of the saints, who were regarded as intercessors with miraculous healing powers akin to the traditional indigenous patronal deities or tutelary gods; and they made ready use of incense, fasting, penitential rites, and pilgrimages. The communal basis of worship, the special ritual consideration for the dead, the crucifixion (sacrifice), the importance of ritual calendars, the belief in a supernatural mother, in the immortality of the soul, and in supernatural others who dwelled in an underworld—all were important aspects of pre-Conquest Mesoamerican indigenous religion. Similarly, a richly mixed indigenous "iconographic heritage" added to the didactic value of European religious imagery, including panel paintings, murals, and wooden effigies. Spanish missionaries used such images to make abstract doctrine concrete through techniques of "enforced imitation."[35]

Attempting to characterize the nature of Mexican religion in the seventeenth century, in the early days of contact and transformation, the historian Serge Gruzinski writes,

In many situations transitory systems emerged that revealed the shifting and diffuse presence of an indeterminate symbolic and conceptual zone, where attempts at *overinterpretation* (the fire of hell and purgatory was also the god Old Fire) rubbed shoulders with *decodification*: hell was no longer the prehispanic Mictlan but not yet the Christian hell.... As there were often only personal, furtive and clandestine syntheses, this explains the precariousness of these products, their improvised, groping character, the facility with which, denied or admitted, they became undone or crumbled. Their coherence derived from a personal experience, a unique and subjective experience, rather than from a systematic and collective construction.[36]

In short, each religious practitioner made of this mixture what he or she could, engaging and imbuing communal rituals with complex emotional, moral, and aesthetic significances. We cannot, of course, ever know precisely the ways that these religious syntheses took place; we can only guess at when and where and why they happened, and imaginatively reconstruct—on the basis of what we know about the shifting practices of faith-based rituals today—how various Mesoamerican individuals and communities put together the materials of their sacred. In this space of exchange, heterogeneity, and ambiguity, the paradigmatic structure of popular religion, with its inherent creativity, plasticity, and porousness, was congealing. This popular religiosity was practiced by those on the margins of colonial society, first the indigenous in rural regions and then those who settled closer to emergent urban centers like Antequera, the city that eventually became Oaxaca.

It seems that indigenous populations opened up their own ("popular") cultural domains in the peripheral urban communities to which they were relegated, like colonial Antequera. Ultimately, despite the large number of regular and secular clergy who continued to live among the Indians after the Conquest, the spatial segregation of Indian and Spanish cultures during the colonial period fostered the development of popular-indigenous ("folk-Catholic") systems of belief and practice quite distinct from the elite or "official" Spanish system. Yet it must be remembered that neither of these religious repertoires was, itself, internally homogeneous: the religiosity of the Indian population was a polymorphous synthesis of indigenous religious traditions, African animism, and Iberian Catholicism; and Spanish Catholicism was, itself, a blend of popular and "orthodox" traditions and practices, deeply influenced by spiritualist movements in medieval Europe and—despite the Inquisition—even by Islam and Judaism. As the church scholar Enrique Marroquín writes,

[The version of Catholicism that arrived with the conquerors] had been nurtured by Cluniac spirituality, with its love of processions and romerías [pilgrimages]; its devotion to the saints brought from Byzantium, its baroque martirologies; its participation in the medieval obsession with the devil; it was contaminated by superstitions and medical concepts of the Moors; practiced Arab medicine, was fanatic about images, relics and miracles; [and] had assimilated from Ireland a strong penitential spirit and its enthusiasm for suffering and participated in the euphoria of the Counter-Reform, as expressed in the cult of the Eucharist and of the Virgin Mary.[37]

Thus the distinct threads of this new cultural synthesis took on movements of their own as they were woven into the Creole fabric of colonial Oaxaca and Mexico. The diffusion of religion as a new set of practices was enmeshed in other elements of the technology of colonization, resulting in novel forms of organizing differences among people.[38] These varying, locally determined religious syntheses were no doubt precarious, as Gruzinski suggests. Nevertheless, with an expanded symbolic reservoir, individuals and communities were able to create new spaces for the articulation or enactment of refashioned sources of power and senses of identity.

Evangelization in Oaxaca, and elsewhere in the New World, brought the façades of Catholic faith to the indigenous masses and yet was only partly successful at destroying the deepest roots or habits of conceiving the sacred of their prior belief systems. It seems that Indians frequently and successfully adapted their own religious concepts within a process of creative religious synthesis that was able to eliminate many of the visible signs of the ancient "idolatry": the physical evidences were gone, but the metaphysical remained.[39] For example, indigenous converts flocked faithfully to mass while still worshiping their old gods—albeit now more clandestinely; one religious form was resorted to when another failed to bring the desired result. Popular religion was a dynamic intermediary zone for the exchange of meanings, beliefs, and styles of faith among the practitioners of indigenous religion, members of other lay populations (for example, at the beginning of the colonial period, Spanish soldiers, and, in later centuries, Spanish peasants, artisans, and mariners), and representatives of the institutional church, whose own religiosity, as mentioned, was varied and far from monolithic. For the indigenous, popular religion was an area of autonomy and flexibility that nurtured and sheltered individuals and communities. Through a further brief historical examination, we can see how the ethical slant of contemporary Oaxacan popular religiosity and its characteristic self-sufficiency emerged.

Not every aspect of the development of popular religious rites had to do with a specifically religious history, however. After the Conquest, indigenous populations were reorganized along new territorial divisions—into villages, districts, and so on—which prevented the maintenance of their self-organization along ethnic lines.[40] To ensure the ongoing integration and subjugation of the Indians, the Spanish imposed a Castilian *municipio* model of town government on indigenous communities; this system of governance operated in tandem with some of the organizational systems of pre-Hispanic indigenous kingdoms, however, so indigenous elites filled the posts in the top echelons of the *cabildo*, the Spanish town council system. Thus the *cacique*, the native noble, was designated by the Crown viceroy to be the official municipal governor; the *cacique*, in turn, presided over local *alcaldes* (mayors) and *corregidores* (councilmen).[41] The communal infrastructure that developed from this system allowed for the strengthening of local identity and indigenous solidarity; it also served to elaborate practices that sustained these sources of indigenous power.

Yet the roots of many of these practices were not simply "indigenous." As disease had became rampant among the Indians in the early years of conquest, and tribute demands by Spanish governors grew ever more stringent, the church had begun to promote the adoption of local saint cults, or *cofradías* (confraternities or religious corporations), in indigenous communities to help defray the costs of religious worship. Supported by annual dues that covered the costs of special masses, rosaries, and other pious observances, as well as funerals and memorial services for members, the *cofradías* allowed indigenous communities, argues the anthropologist Duncan Earle, "to maintain an autonomous organization with power to tax, an inviolate treasury, and the ability to reappropriate local authority and redistribute local goods and services, all clothed in the protective garb of Catholicism."[42]

According to many anthropologists, the *cofradía* emerged as the institutional core of post-Conquest Mesoamerican indigenous communities.[43] It is widely argued that the religious regime of Mexican Indians came to be based on the veneration of the saints, maintained through the system of duties and obligations enjoined by the confraternity. Thus James Greenberg explains that a complete reworking of the imposed Spanish festival calendar may be seen in the *cofradías'* organization of elaborate fiestas associated with pre-Hispanic agrarian rituals or in honor of patron deity-saints. Nancy Farriss adds to the picture, maintaining that instead of the *cofradía* model known in Spain, where a particular group of devotees seeks individual salvation through individual contributions, indigenous *cofradías* were public institutions supported by the entire community and dedicated to promoting the overall well-being of the community through general propitiations to its sacred guardians.[44]

Within the region of Oaxaca, it seems that *cofradías* were not only responsible for staging various religious festivals and providing supplies for them, but also charged with organizing the evening prayers (vespers), processions, and masses for festivals such as Corpus Christi, Holy Week, Christmas, and *mayordomías*, as well as taking care of the selection and payment of priests. Land reserved for the maintenance of community *cofradías* was collectively owned, operated, and supervised by *mayordomos*, a rotating roster of community members who served as stewards and fund-raisers for these events.[45] The *cofradía* was therefore the communal organization par excellence, engaged in such charitable activities as providing for the sick and, sometimes, even for those who needed help to pay tribute. It also served as a safety net, for it permitted native elites to tap the collective stores of maize and beans for redistribution within the community at times of extreme need. With the advent of the *cofradía* system, survival as a collective effort was affirmed; major deities became corporate spiritual beings whose help had to be solicited through the corporate group, and the individual's personal responsibility was to contribute to the group's petitions according to his or her appointed role in the community.

Considerable debate surrounds the actual character of the *cofradía* with regard to its putative historical origins and economic (redistributive) effects.[46] However, the corporate enterprise of the *cofradía* has been seen as partly responsible for the recovery of indigenous political strength and numbers by the mid-seventeenth century, after their severe decline in the early stages of the colonial period.[47] Building and buttressing community identity through a system that was at once material and spiritual, the *cofradía* acted as an important bulwark against external influences, whether from non-Indians sharing the same territory or from members of other indigenous groups. Under the *cofradía* tradition, Greenberg argues, "indigenous belief, ritual and cosmology infused Catholicism with an indigenous content that continued to emphasize reciprocities among man, animals, and gods—reciprocities needed to maintain ecological and cosmological balance."[48] The gradual elaboration of such specific intracommunity cohesion resulted in the emergence of a marked pueblo-oriented rather than "ethnic" identity among indigenous peoples.

A gradual decline in pastoral attention to indigenous towns also developed during the colonial period, allowing for the growth of religious autonomy or self-management on the part of the native town administrators. Beginning in the mid-seventeenth century, Oaxaca's missions were transformed into parishes. This change meant that the initial agents of the missionary project, the friars who lived mostly in indigenous communities, were relieved of their duties. Many priests no longer had parishes; they became what are known as "secular priests," attending services in a parish served by someone else. Itinerant pastoral work in rural zones was abandoned, and parish priests (*párrocos*) were obligated to remain in the *cabeceras*, or head towns of their parishes. Then, in the mid-eighteenth century, the "enlightened" Bourbon kings of Spain, particularly Charles

III, enacted a number of reforms intended to modernize and centralize the state. The taxation of Spanish American colonies rose, the power and possessions of the church were significantly reduced, and, in 1812, the Inquisition was officially disbanded.[49] Many clerics were expelled, and convents and other church property appropriated for the use of secular bodies or the government. In 1813, of the 715 parishes comprising the dioceses of Mexico, Puebla, Oaxaca, and Vallodolid, only 23 remained in the hands of "regular" clergy.[50] According to a nineteenth-century bishop and historian of the Diocese of Oaxaca, the dearth of priests and the extent of the territory they were obliged to cover forced clergy to make only short stops in the towns they visited, without lingering in any of them.[51] More recent historians have calculated that in 1825 there were only 3,463 priests in the Republic of Mexico; of these, as few as 1,240 actively ministered to particular parishes. By 1830 the overall number of ordained clergy in Mexico had fallen to 3,282, while the population of the country was more than 7 million.[52]

Given the interdictions placed by the Bourbon reforms on the accumulation of wealth and property and other activities of the church, the religiosity of indigenous peoples in Oaxaca and elsewhere was left to develop almost completely independently. This was particularly the case when church–state relations worsened after independence in 1821. When the bishop of the Diocese of Oaxaca, Manuel Isidoro Pérez Suárez, died in 1827, Oaxaca was without a bishop for eight years, until 1835. One local historian has calculated that, from the end of the Inquisition in 1812 through the early years of Mexican independence, some indigenous communities in Oaxaca did not see a member of the clergy for more than forty years.[53] Such breakdowns in ecclesiastical authority and supervision permitted a number of "Christianized" communities to develop significant autonomous religious traditions—important antecedents to contemporary "folk-Catholic" practices in Mexico.

The final decades of the colonial period were characterized by a concerted rejection of elements of Spanish culture by indigenous populations; communities sometimes withdrew into isolated settlements to shield against outside influences, particularly encroachments on indigenous lands. It also appears that, more or less concurrent with the Bourbon reforms, a shift took place in the way that many local and saint's day festivals were financed. Increasingly, in Mesoamerican settlements, individuals who held specific civil offices became personally responsible for financing local festivals and celebrations of saint's days. This shift, from the collective *cofradía* to individual financial burden, or *cargo*, became known as the *cargo* system. Reportedly, some *cofradías* in Oaxaca remained strong forms of social and financial organization.[54] Throughout most of Mexico, however, social and religious organizations had become intertwined with forms of indigenous self-government, the *cabildo* system, and many indigenous communities came to be governed by a small group of men who ascended, as they aged, through a series of increasingly prestigious offices in a civil–religious hierarchy (*ayuntamiento religioso*). *Cargo* obligations thus circulated among the most privileged men in a given community; as a man ascended the civil–religious hierarchy, his *cargos* became weightier. In effect, while the *cargo* system accrued great prestige to the individuals who filled posts at the top of the hierarchy, at the same time it worked against the accumulation of wealth by these individuals. The responsibilities of office—or *cargos*—required significant sacrifices of capital and time. Thus a strong emphasis on status and hierarchy was counterbalanced by an ethic of egalitarianism and communalism. Although the three-hundred-year colonial period had disrupted indigenous idolatry-based cultural systems, indigenous peoples were able to reorganize their identity with new cultural elements that had been imposed on them.

In a similar fashion, from a status of persecuted and disparaged "idolatry," indigenous and popular syncretic religiosity in Oaxaca gradually came to inflect the character of everyday life among those who became what we call today the urban "popular" classes. Populated by fairly homogeneous ethnic blocs, "Indian" communities on the edge of the city—such as Villa de Oaxaca, Xochimilco, Trinidad de las Huertas, and Jalatlaco—were, for long stretches of time, quite closed to outsiders.[55] But by the eighteenth century, as the city of Antequera grew, each such "Indian" neighborhood, or barrio, developed its own commodity specialty. The communities established their own guilds—the weavers of Xochimilco, bakers of La Merced, pot makers (*alfareros*) of Jalatlaco, and so on. Like the indigenous towns in the Valley of Oaxaca, each barrio had its own *cabildo* and, in turn, its own community-level religious organization similar to the *cofradía*, represented by its own *estandarte* (banner).[56] Different barrios, symbolized by their *estandartes*, came together for the fiestas of the guilds' patron saints; such joint celebrations permitted assertions of distinct community identities but also of a unified, pan-ethnic Indian ("popular") identity at the same time. Thus, although the organization of such religious festivals in the urban region of colonial Oaxaca was not structured according to the dictates of the civil–religious *cargo* systems that were increasingly common in the countryside, the segregation of the Indian population in these urban guild zones helped ensure that popular religiosity in Oaxaca City maintained a basic ethical framework of communal solidarity and reciprocity. The constant inflow of migrants from rural, indigenous communities, and Oaxaca City's continuing profile as a largely agricultural, indigenous, market-based, nonindustrial economic city, allowed the normative slant of popular religiosity, and the traditions that supported it, to endure over time.[57]

The church continued to be needed by city residents to conduct the sacramental rites of baptisms and funerals—or at least last rites and marriage; indeed, marriages were legal only if sanctified by the church. But even in colonial Antequera, the religious and administrative center of the Oaxaca region, a number of popular religious expressions continued to take place outside the bounds of the official church. Documents in the archives of the Diocese of Oaxaca reflect a history in which a punitive church continually tried to discipline popular "pagan" unruliness. For example, from the 1770s to the 1780s the Diocese of Oaxaca, undoubtedly influenced by the Bourbon reforms in Spain, tried to quell the exuberance of Holy Week processions and "profane" popular festivities. Even the smallest practice smacking of nonsanctioned excess was disciplined, including numerous activities concerning death rites. A letter directed at priests in 1795 by the bishop of Antequera, José Gregorio Alonso de Ortiga, for example, insisted that clerics enforce the prohibition of the "popular" custom of placing flower crowns or palms on any gravestones; cemeteries were, of course, on church property and thus, like all aspects of burials, under the full authority of the ecclesiastical hierarchy.[58]

Later, as the Bourbon reforms and the liberal ideas and values of the Enlightenment spread, religion gradually became a less pervasive part of public life in Oaxaca, as elsewhere in Mexico. In "official" Catholicism, piety itself became more "interiorized"; that is, it shifted its focus away from the corporate group (exemplified by the cofradía tradition and the cult of the saints) to a direct, personal relationship with God.[59] Religious practices retreated into the domestic fold, and religious devotion of all sorts became increasingly viewed as the "proper" domain of women and children.[60] Nevertheless, today the round of annual fiestas predicated on the worship of the saints, and sustained largely by the labor of women, remains the core of domestic and community religious festivities in both rural and urban areas of Oaxaca. Indeed, not only does the contemporary fiesta calendar in rural Oaxaca schedule religious events that serve to entrench social, political, and economic ties among households in the community, but regional fiestas establish a network of such links among villages.[61] The annual festival calendar serves to underscore the symbol of the community's self-reproduction, the patron saint, who is the embodiment of collective identity.

Centuries have passed since the Spanish "sword and the cross" first left their mark on the populations of Mexico and Oaxaca. Yet the cultural contradictions and ruptures introduced by the colonial experience remain deeply rooted in popular cultural expressive modes, although these expressive modes may be articulated in changeable and new ways. Today popular religion in and around Oaxaca, centered on the cult of the saints and a rich array of ritual practice largely independent of the church, embodies the paradigmatic structure of a "traditional" ethical system underwritten by practical concerns. As a result, popular religious practices persist on the physical and conceptual peripheries of everyday life in Oaxaca, formidable reservoirs for the construction of local identities and the re-creation of everyday material reality as a sensuous, multi-dimensional, and meaningful collective enterprise.

The Church and "Popular" Religion Today

In Oaxaca today, the church has passed through a period of renewal and retains a strong concentration of authority as well as moral and material power. Indeed, the notion of "popular" religion has been formally acknowledged by the church, and efforts to make use of popular religious activities have been incorporated into the discourses of renovation and reform ensuing from the Second Vatican Council (Vatican II) in the 1960s. In Latin America, this renewal has spurred a variety of church movements of both conservative (Charismatic Catholicism) and liberal tendencies—the most radical being liberation theology, which explic-itly advances ideas such as the Option for the Poor and the "People's Church."

In the early 1990s, when I began my fieldwork in Oaxaca, many local clergy displayed the theological slant of the "progressive" archbishop Bartolomé Carrasco, who had led the Diocese of Oaxaca since 1975. During his time in Oaxaca, and despite the presence at the end of his term of an overtly conserva-tive archbishop, Hector González, it appeared that most priests agreed in prin-ciple with the tenets of the Option for the Poor and the notion of the "People's Church."[62] In Oaxaca, as elsewhere, this movement for pastoral reform was referred to as La Nueva Evangelización (New Evangelization)—a watered-down version of liberation theological principles, which advocate social justice and empowerment of "the people." In general terms, liberationist discourse sees "popular" religious forms as necessary to a productive dialogue, or recipro-cal evangelization, between clergy and the poor, indigenous social classes. In Oaxaca, the New Evangelization also involves various rationalizing explications of popular religion, a phenomenon that ultimately makes the movement's dis-course appear dissonant alongside local sacred practice and belief.

Padre Claudio, the local priest in the parish of Cuauhtémoc, which includes Colonia San Juan, had been in service in the community for sixteen years. Along with the parish advisory board, consisting of volunteers from all seven *colonias* comprising the parish, and the local deacon, he had implemented, or had permit-ted others to instigate, certain features of the "People's Church" in Cuauhtémoc. Members of the congregation were encouraged to participate as far as possible in reading lessons during mass, in ceremonies such as Via Crucis, and in religious groups such as Encuentros Matrimoniales (Marriage Encounters, for discussing marital problems) and Pláticas Bíblicas (Bible Discussions).[63] Participation in such groups was promoted as part of the overall consciousness-raising efforts of the New Evangelization, which worked for a closer integration of Catholic doctrine and personal practice. In addition, "evangelization" had been incorporated into aspects of ritual that require the participation of church representatives, exemplified by *pláticas*, or catechizing talks necessary for sacramental rites such as baptism, first communion, confirmation, and marriage. For all these rites, a week of attendance at such inspirational talks was required not only of those undergoing the ceremony but also usually of both parents and godparents. Parishioners could no longer arrange to have a baptism or wedding at any church they wished; these ceremonies, it was instructed, should take place in their own parish.

In addition to such activities, the church, under the rubric of New Evangelization, has increasingly embraced the efforts of groups whose aim is to foster socioreligious identification and cohesion among members of the local Catholic community. In part, such endeavors serve to incorporate energies within the fold of the church that might otherwise be directed toward less visible "popular" religious activities; further, these groups seek to involve residents in religious professions and pursuits on a frequent basis, including encouraging them to become more literate Bible readers and thus counteracting—or so the church hopes—the increasing influence and fervor of various evangelical Protestant sects.

In San Juan, two such socioreligious groups operated under the umbrella of the local Catholic parish. Probably the more active and larger was the Legión de María (Legion of Mary), an international organization dedicated, as its name suggests, to the cult of the Virgin Mary. As in other Latin American Catholic countries with a strong Marian (Virgin Mary–centered) emphasis, in Mexico, and in Oaxaca in particular, the Legión is especially important. The organization has a branch in every *colonia* of the parish of Cuauhtémoc, with a total membership of some one hundred people, almost all of them middle-aged women. Each chapter is headed by a president, who chairs weekly meetings that take place, on a rotating basis, in the members' homes; ideally, as many Legionarias attend meetings as possible. Shortly after moving to the *colonia*, at the urging of one of my neighbors, I became a member of the Legión de María.

During my stay in San Juan, the Legión worked closely with the Cuauhtémoc church, taking on such pastoral duties as visiting the ill, the elderly, and prisoners in the city jail; giving catechism instruction and encouraging children to have their first communion or confirmation ceremonies; urging couples "living in sin"—those who were never married by the church, even if they underwent the civil ceremony—to legitimize their relationship "in the eyes of God"; and helping with important religious fiestas by handling organizational details, collecting donations, and mobilizing the participation of members of the community at various church events.

The Legión was a social group as well as a religious organization. Each week, those in attendance at meetings would discuss their aches and pains, gossip about their neighbors, and complain about dogs frightening their children or spreading garbage. This exchange was far from trivial, however; on the basis of such reports and stories, the women kept one another abreast of matters affecting the *colonia* and its residents and helped position them to do something about problems as they arose.

Despite the group's considerable contribution to fiestas and other events in the parish, and its dedication to a host of pastoral tasks, the Legión was often harshly criticized by the Cuauhtémoc deacon, don Reynaldo, and others on the parish advisory board for being "too closed" and for having a "divisive effect" on the local religious community. Although membership in the Legión was technically open to anyone, certain San Juan Legionarias were frequently accused at parish council meetings of exclusivist tendencies or charged with believing themselves to have a higher religious authority than other members of the laity. There were also complaints that compulsory attendance for members at events dedicated to the Virgin often conflicted with parish events, which, some said, should be the Legionarias' priority. In addition, Cuauhtémoc's priest and deacon opposed the Legión's preoccupation with the Virgin Mary, which, they explained, caused Legionarias to lose sight of the primacy of Jesus Christ. (I am sure, too, that they objected to this focus on Mary as a particularly "old-fashioned" and "ignorant" remnant of medieval Catholicism, out of place in the modern church.)

The integration of the Legión de María into the parish was thus not complete. An organization in and through which many women in the church took power, the Legión was regularly castigated in order to keep its members in their place. We were never to forget, no matter the extent or importance of our activities, that the church was a patriarchal institution in which ultimate authority devolved from and revolved around men. Charges of "exclusivity" levied against the Legionarias ultimately, I thought, had something to do with the fact that members of the church hierarchy were not themselves closely involved with the regular functioning of the group.

For in addition to the Legión de María, there was Pláticas Bíblicas, a Bible discussion group, whose members met at least two evenings a week. Although it resembled the base communities described by others in urban Mexico and Latin America, the group in San Juan was clearly nonpoliticized.[64] The members' avowed purpose was to discuss readings from the Bible, but they also carried out pastoral tasks similar to those performed by the Legión. Like the

Legión, Pláticas Bíblicas was composed completely of women, except for the deacon, who led the talks. None of this group's meetings was ever attended by a member of San Juan's Legión de María because of long-standing personal antagonisms between their respective members; this ongoing conflict was an obstacle to solidarity between the groups and impeded their ability to join forces to catalyze increased church participation and attendance. It also meant that the two groups of women who were most active in the parish maintained tense opposition to each other, and would never, together, challenge any aspect of the authority of the church hierarchy.

A sense of renewal and revitalization saturates the program of the Nueva Evangelización, along with its exhortation to the "apostolic mission" of the true and loyal Catholic believer. One of the campaign's principal stated aims was to strengthen Catholics' faith through a more profound and enriched knowledge of church doctrine. And part of the reason for this goal involved the effort to "purify" certain components of popular religion that reflected a misinterpretation or misuse or both of Catholic symbols and tenets. Examples of such "corruptions of faith" were drunkenness during church fiestas and ceremonials, the use of confession to divulge the sins of others, and ritual overspending on *mayordomías*, baptisms, and weddings—celebrations known to be salient arenas for intense competition for prestige within the community.

Significantly, in Oaxaca City, the project of New Evangelization seems to have adopted many aspects of the charismatic proselytizing style of Evangelical sects: it stressed self-empowerment as well as spiritual rebirth involving an abrupt "change of life," and the abandonment of ideas and vices standing in the way of the individual's spiritual and social development. Indeed, David Stoll argues that post–Vatican II church reforms in Latin America used Protestantism as a model, particularly its emphasis on the Bible as a guide to faith and the forceful encouragement of lay leadership.[65] Reflecting the call to renewal, baptism in Cuauhtémoc was stressed as a rite entailing a strict obligation (*compromiso*) to follow the sacraments of the church. Don Reynaldo claimed that, once this obligation was recognized, "we cannot live as we did before. We were cleansed, purified, and reborn by means of baptism. Afterward we must not go back." A more *literal* application of formal doctrine to everyday existence was stressed: religion was represented as ideally being a conscious (*consciente*) aspect of one's everyday activity, exemplified by the encouragement of participation in Bible study groups.

Knowledge about and an understanding of faith were crucial aspects of the New Evangelization. Thus the campaign's discourse, heard particularly at the Bible discussion gatherings I attended in Cuauhtémoc and other parishes in the city, emphasized a modern, dynamic church whose members were "conscious" and aware, in both personal and sociopolitical terms. In keeping with the rational, modernist tone of the campaign, Padre Claudio told me, for example, that popular religion was "very good"; he acknowledged it as "an expression of faith, though not very clear nor profound." Popular religion, in the priest's opinion, "should be conserved but also should continue to be renewed and interpreted with more consciousness." Thus, for example, in 1990, when I took part in the Via Crucis, which is held each year during Holy Week to commemorate Christ's penitential march to Calvary, the parish of Cuauhtémoc had newly reconstituted the ceremony in an effort to harmonize its practice with the New Evangelization program and its didactic orientation toward heightening participants' consciousness of the relevance of the Bible's message to concrete problems in everyday life. As is traditional, rosaries were said at every station of the cross, but post-rosary reflections, read by a representative of the church, emphasized the relationship between Christ's penitence and death and our sins of everyday life. While this represented a fairly straightforward doctrinal interpretation, it had been given a singularly practical, realist spin, which was strongly moralizing. Holy Week, we were instructed, is about the communion between Christ and all who believe in him. The Eucharist itself, and the act of taking communion, is symbolic of a communion with God, but it also functions as an affirmation of the unity among us all. The Resurrection is about *la iglesia levantada* (raised Church), or the renewed, reinvigorated Catholic Church. "We are the living Christs" (Nosotros somos los cristos vivos), don Paco, a deacon-in-training emphasized, as he led the Via Crucis procession through the parish.

While the form of the Via Crucis was not radically altered by its incorporation into the New Evangelization activities, frequently the campaign has resulted in a patronizing assault against certain popular religious traditions, a stance not altogether distinct from colonial ecclesiastical practices and attitudes. In particular, the popular practices that the progressive church is concerned to "purify" are those that threaten its hegemony: religious activity of an independent nature that takes place outside the church's physical or discursive domain of control. The cult of the saints and other religious practices that are centered on domestic liturgies, for example, pose a strong threat to the centralization of spiritual teachings and devotions. Thus the Marian character of popular piety and the great devotion to the saints—purchasing and dressing icons for home altars, for example—are frowned on by both church officials and more orthodox or "evangelized" Catholics.

In Cuauhtémoc, certain members of the parish have been accused of being overly idolatrous, of indulging in "paganism" (a charge that carries the usual connotations of ignorance and backwardness associated with indigenous identity), and of ignoring the fact that the various Virgins and "Señores" are simply distinct refractions of single figures. As one man put it, disapprovingly—he was an "evangelized" Catholic who participated fully in church extracurricular activities—"people will travel miles to visit the Virgin of Juquila, but they forget about God."

Perhaps most important, the points of conflict between popular Catholicism and the "renewed" Catholic campaign are often translated in conceptual terms as a debate between "tradition"—in its most negative sense—and "progress."[66] The progressive church and its discourse on "modernity" are attempts at rationalizing and systematizing popular religious practice without alienating the popular masses of "the faithful" in the process. While the few overtly liberationist priests in Oaxaca City celebrate and encourage elements of popular tradition, others—although they appear, on the surface, to support a progressive pastoral praxis—place more emphasis on the drawbacks that might be found in the indigenous origins of popular religious practices; such priests often adopt a modernizing tone and suggest that associating with a "naïve," "ignorant," or "backward" lifeway is an impediment to getting ahead (seguir adelante).

It cannot be denied, however, that some aspects of the New Evangelization movement in Oaxaca, particularly the encouragement of active lay Catholic groups such as Pláticas Bíblicas in Colonia San Juan, appear to have instilled in many people a sense of self-direction as church members. Under the New Evangelization campaign, many parishioners, particularly women, were enabled to take on public leadership roles in ways that heretofore would have been impossible. A deepened knowledge of the Bible somehow conferred a sense of empowerment; participants in Bible study groups felt increasingly confident about their own abilities to understand and make sense both of readings and of the world. In addition, in Cuauhtémoc, involvement in gatherings such as the Bible discussion groups and the parish advisory board nurtured a notion of shared identity among members and a moral commitment to one another and to their immediate community, for local problems were shared and dissected in a "sacred" setting that favored altruism and reconciliation rather than antagonism and conflict.

Nevertheless, judging from my experiences in Cuauhtémoc, individual reasons for joining Bible discussion groups—the principal organizational expression of the New Evangelization campaign—varied considerably. For most participants, almost all of whom were women, as noted, meetings appear to have functioned as an important source of mutual support and advice for troubles they encountered in their daily lives. The social aspect of the gatherings that followed the Bible discussion, the singing of hymns and prayer, was particularly pronounced: those who attended took the opportunity to chat and gossip about others in the neighborhood. Leaders of these get-togethers were typically either the parish deacon or charismatic, respected women in the *colonia*. Yet attendance at the twice-weekly meetings was not consistent, nor did I note matters of wider political interest entering the discussions; the concerns talked over remained immediate and, almost literally, parochial.

At the time of my initial stage of fieldwork, representatives of the church in Oaxaca, taking their cue from Rome, were trying hard to purge religiosity of the "idolatrous" aspects popularly linked to the cult of the saints. Don Reynaldo, for example, declared it an embarrassment and waste of money that the church sacristy was full of dresses for the parish figure of the Virgen del Rosario; these sumptuous robes had been purchased at great expense over many years for the *mayordomía*. Thus don Octavio, the *mayordomo* for the festival in 1991, told me that he had spent more than 2 million old pesos (U.S.$400) on clothing for the Virgin alone, including 600,000 old pesos (U.S.$120) on jeweled earrings, although Padre Claudio told me that don Octavio later removed them from the image and took them home. Money is typically spent most profligately in such ritual contexts when individuals like don Octavio are unambiguously the financial sponsors: acting as the organizer of a saint's day festival, hosting or acting as a *padrino* for a wedding or *quinceaños*, or supplying ornate tombstone decorations for the Day of the Dead. *Colonos* frequently rationalized such conspicuous expenditures in relation to fiestas as displays of their great "love of God," but paying out great expenditures also clearly helped to raise one's stature in the community.

Thus when representatives of the church in Cuauhtémoc attempted to temper the immense devotional fervor surrounding the fiesta of the Virgin of the Rosary by promoting the feast day dedicated to the parish's patron saint, Santo Tomás (a fiesta not organized as a *mayordomía*), they were not particularly successful. They tried to respond to an evident reluctance to donate time or money to ritual activities whose costs are anonymous by setting up a board that would display the names of contributors to the Santo Tomás festival just inside the entrance to the church, but parishioners did not respond with much enthusiasm. Clearly, the church could not so easily supplant or invent "popular" religious engagement.

The apparent failure of aspects of the New Evangelization campaign to change popular religious practice in significant ways exemplifies the rift between "official" religious discourse and the everyday reality of San Juan residents; personal or individual motivations for participation in Bible discussion groups or other activities frequently do not concur with church perceptions or aspirations. Making matters more difficult for the official church, the New Evangelization movement was not the only source of spiritual and practical support for *colonos*; also actively soliciting people's participation were a wide range of associations from

Evangelical sects (Mormons, Seventh-Day Adventists, Jehovah's Witnesses) to *espirituistas* (New Age groups), Alcoholics Anonymous, and other Catholic factions such as the Charismatics. Most important, however, the "progressivist" campaign of the official church also works against the intrinsic plasticity, inclusiveness, and flexibility of popular religious praxis. Like the practice of Protestant religions, the "renovation" campaign ultimately functions to purge everyday rites of elements that do not adhere to a more strictly defined doctrine.[67]

In sum, the supposedly radical program for pastoral renewal, initially promoted by the former archbishop Bartolomé Carrasco, has often become manifest in the city in a form that has been effectively conservative. In terms of the actual religious behavior and practice of many individuals, the campaign appears to have had little influence. When I asked María, a poor, middle-aged woman in Cuauhtémoc who professed to be "very religious," about her limited participation in local church activities and her rare attendance at mass, she explained, "Donde quiera se puede encontrar a Dios" (Wherever one likes, God may be found). Such statements were echoed repeatedly during my fieldwork by those interviewed and in casual conversation.

It seemed to me that such statements of self-reliance were partly a reaction to the efforts of the local church to define "proper" Catholic practice within the New Evangelization campaign. At the same time, these statements attest to a self-defined field of meanings characteristic of popular religiosity and function as a challenge to the church's attempts to control expressions of faith through the imposition of "official" doctrinal interpretations. The independent quality of local popular Catholic belief and practice derives from a deep entrenchment of religiosity in everyday existence. Popular religious practices suffuse the most important communal gatherings and celebrations; they are found in everyday settings, such as domestic altars, and in special festivals that punctuate the cycle of seasons, or, as with the Day of the Dead, they serve as sites of memory and filial duty. These relationships are deeply personal and satisfyingly ornate; they involve anticipation, tastes, scents, and convivial associations in many sectors of daily life. Nor are these relationships linked to a clearly delimited, exclusively *Catholic* religious identity. By contrast, the discourse of the New Evangelization movement tends to privilege the officially sanctioned meanings of rituals over the plasticity of ritual performance. And although the movement has attempted to appeal to individual freedom and progress through rationality, knowledge (*conciencia*), and self-determination, such weighting of ecclesiastical discourse with "modern" concerns has been far from persuasive to many among the religious. For arguably, in Oaxaca today, as elsewhere, individuals' experiences of sociopolitical alienation, transience, and fragmentation—the accompaniments of urbanization and the embracing of "modernity"—appear to intensify interest in popular practices that articulate the desire for the reaffirmation of morally positive "traditional" forms of sociality and a firm connection to an idealized "local" past.

Charged with moral resonances, popular religiosity in Oaxaca embodies, on an ideal and intimately practical level, a distinct way of thinking, of being, and of acting. At the same time, it contains a covert social critique of dominant systems of meaning by which those very popular values and modes of interaction are devalued. Important aspects of this fundamentally material and practical popular religious sense are displayed—and revitalized—by the complex of rituals surrounding the event of death and the recollection of life in Oaxaca. If, as popular religion argues, true moral or spiritual life begins when one is baptized and enters into the community of souls, popular death rituals in Oaxaca suggest that proper treatment of a body and bodily remains function both to release the soul into eternal life and to help keep it in the orbit or memory of the community. Unlike the gestures of the orthodox Church, which unite a small material element, such as a few drops of water or oil, with great spiritual changes—the baptism into the community of believers or the release of the soul into God's grace—popular religious rituals call for extensive material preparation and both individual and communal sacrifice. Popular religious rituals require that people regularly set aside or transform aspects of their daily material life. Such extensive material investments are, as we shall see in the following chapters, not merely signs of inward change, but also important agents of transformation in their own right.

PART 2

Rites of Popular Death in Oaxaca

"And your soul? Where do you think it's gone?"

"It must be wandering up there on earth, like all those others, looking for people to pray for it. I think it hates me for the bad things I did, but that doesn't worry me anymore. I'm rid of all the pain it used to give me. It made me feel bitter about everything, even about not getting enough to eat, and it made the nights unbearable, full of terrifying thoughts. Visions of the damned and things like that. When I sat down to die, it told me to get up again and keep on living, as if it still hoped for some miracle that would come and clean away my sins. But I wouldn't. 'This is the end,' I told it. 'I can't go any further.' I opened my mouth so it could leave, and it left. I felt something fall into my hands. It was the little thread of blood that had tied it to my heart."

—JUAN RULFO, *Pedro Páramo*

CHAPTER 3

Living with Death

Vivimos y morimos, culturalmente (We live and we die, culturally).
—ENRIQUE MARROQUÍN, *La cruz mesiánica*

FOR MANY MID-TWENTIETH-CENTURY ANTHROPOLOGISTS of functionalist and symbolic bent, the biological event of death—the extinction of individual life—was understood to be the single most significant social disruption imaginable in a community. The irregular, unpredictable nature of death, the solitude and transience evoked by human mortality, posed an enormous threat, so the argument went, to the claims of unity, permanence, and continuity so necessary to the survival of a social order. Accordingly, death must be hemmed in and controlled by rituals and events that invoke its transcendence.[1] Funerals, then, might best be understood from such a perspective—as events where a necessary mediation takes place. In other words, a funeral is what bridges the existential chasm between life and death; it is the paradigmatic social act that stitches the individual—even after his or her last gasp—back into the collective fabric of the community.[2]

Recently, however, such broad, cross-cultural claims for the importance or necessity of some sort of communal bridge or "conquest" over the ruptures and unruliness of death have come under some fire. Death is not simply a matter of a loss of, or threat to, productivity or fertility; it is not everywhere and forever a perfect antonym and extinction of life. In her elegant study of mourning practices of women on the Greek island of Mani, for example, Nadia Seremetakis opposes such classical views, charging that they separate death from the sphere of the everyday by imposing a rigid, linear analytical framework, defining death ritual as a threat to the social order. Seremetakis claims that a discursive, historicizing approach allows for the treatment of death "as an arena of social contestation, a space where heterogeneous and antagonistic cultural codes and social interests meet and entangle."[3] Thus, in these terms, the meanings—both symbolic (or implicit) and explicit—of death rituals are understood as shaped in close dialogue with their social and historical contexts.

Following Seremetakis, I propose that Oaxacan death-related ritual performances can be seen as emanating organically from everyday life; they are not ritual arenas carefully cut away from other domains of living. However, Seremetakis's preoccupation with death ritual neglects the importance of the dead themselves as ever-present cultural signs with a vital social force of signification.[4] Despite identifying an absence of clear-cut, formal performative beginnings in the ritualization of death, she focuses on the agency of living social actors—particularly women—in the perpetuation of traditional cultural consciousness in Mani. Thus she implicitly underplays the significance of the ongoing practical ritual engagement and exchange between dead and living in the construction of social knowledge and historical memory.

In the course of my fieldwork in Oaxaca, I sensed a different value being accorded to death itself, leading me to ask certain questions: How does continual exchange with the dead affect "popular" senses of belonging—to a place and to a community? How does a belief in the ongoing social importance and value of the dead inform such a Oaxacan "popular" consciousness of community?

Indeed, in some places, like the communities in Oaxaca where I lived and worked, death does not threaten the social order so much as provide an occasion to revitalize it. There life and death are reciprocals, not antagonists or contraries; living is such that even the dead must pull their weight, and death is such that even the living must contribute to the welfare of the dead. Of course, a broadly Christian eschatology aids this popular view in Oaxaca: Christ's true life begins after his death and not before; it will be likewise with his believers when they are raised up on the last day. But, as I will show, while the emulation of Christ's life—indeed, at times a seeming wholesale identification with it—in aspects of individual life and death may serve to explain important features of many popular funerary practices that I observed, such recourse to theological explanation does not fully account for the variety of practices that constitute a "good death" in Oaxaca. For the dead frequently belong, even as they are dead, every bit as much to the community as the living—as the bit of dialogue from Juan Rulfo's novel *Pedro Páramo* (1955) that functions as the epigraph to part II might indicate. Those dead who can still talk, who can describe the snipping of the cord between soul and heart, are not yet without active force on the world—even if they have arrived at one sort of end.

Over the course of my years in Oaxaca, I have been surprised by the ways that death, and the dead, appeared to ease, rather than to disrupt, relations in the community. In a funerary setting, enemies often put aside their conflicts; time and energy were invested in "religious" events that bore little or no resemblance to other church-led rites; certain social roles were exaggerated and stylized. No other event called forth such eager concern with observing ritual propriety or with joining others—friends, family, even strangers—to commemorate the life of a member of the community. What seemed to matter most was not the reconstitution of the community, the closure of the gap left by the death of a fellow resident, but acting properly toward the dead, granting the dead an appropriate passage, permitting, if not a good life, then a "good death."

In Oaxaca, biological death is not coincident with the extinction of someone's life as a social actor: the dead continue to exist in the lives of their surviving relatives, and the world of the dead and that of the living are tightly linked in emotional and practical exchange and interaction. The dead are social beings every bit as much as the living—despite the physical disappearance and dissolution of their physical, bodily selves. People do not cease to relate to others after death, but continue to exist somewhere in the social universe—even if no one could say exactly *where*, geographically speaking.[5]

Thus, in Oaxaca, the soul is described as a "shadowlike" and invisible form, an "energy" with almost human qualities, and its protracted immortal journey involves movement through both time and space. The soul is thus understood to be a sort of "spiritual duplicate" of the deceased, or *el otro yo*, as one person explained it to me, an alter ego or other self.[6] In the words of another: "It does not have a form but it's something that one carries inside; it's what feels; it's what makes one feel." To make matters more confusing, it is often suggested that each person also possesses another soul-like essence, a shadow that, during life, can already become separated from the individual and go on to exist independently. As the shadowlike emanation of the soul is believed to leave the physical shell of the body at death, so, too, does this second shadow self sometimes depart during life. The sudden loss of the shadow self thus serves as the folk etiology of ailments such as *susto* (a shock or fright that produces the escape of the shadow self from the body) and *mal de ojo* (a sickness caused by a strong gaze of envy).[7] As the soul is often said to linger near its home after death, or to journey about the earth visiting the sites of its sins, so the shadow self is regarded as that entity that wanders during sleep or in dreams; it is thus vulnerable to being stolen by some *mal aire*, a lurking malevolent spirit (literally, "bad air.") In other, more colloquial senses, death is also always a semantic presence in daily verbal exchange. It is commented on, joked about; it, too, hangs in the air, never entirely absent. Above all, death serves as a touchstone for talking about and evaluating other issues of everyday life and experience.

In Oaxaca, life and death are not viewed as mutually exclusive ontological states. Death is not experienced as an event that introduces discontinuity and disruption; not only are numerous temporary "deathlike" conditions such as *susto* or *mal de ojo* or dreaming experienced by the living, but the dead are understood to return frequently to the domain of the living. Indeed, the Day of the Dead is a celebration of this return, a day dedicated by the living to the care and feeding of the dead, of waiting, in expectation of their arrival. And on this day, and every other, those who are dead retain their individual identities and maintain social relations with those they have left behind.[8]

Of course, to give such voice or presence to the dead is, in a sense, to return them to life—to bring them from offstage, from the margins of social existence, to center stage, into the current of social life, not as ancestral ghosts or spirits but as persons who linger as present memories and feelings, influencing people's actions, contributing to their sense of identity and connection. Unsurprisingly, the rites of death are quite important in such a context. They are what authorize and cement an understanding of death as a social relation; they make manifest some of the ways that relations between the ancestors and those who are not dead respect a logic other than that which imagines that this body is all there is to living.

DEATH RITUALS

When death comes, and the soul leaves the body, the material "shell" that has contained it, the soul is said to escape the body through the open mouth, "like a little dove" (*como una palomita*). Immortal existence in the afterworld, or *más allá,* begins at this point; the soul no longer resides in the mundane. Such a conceptual code, which sets out the contrast between a person's physical, natural self (*carne y hueso* [flesh and bones]) and his or her spiritual aspect ramifies into other facets of popular belief. Death is conceived as a passage from domesticated "inside" to uncertain and uncontrolled "outside." This passage, however, requires help from the living if it is to be entirely successful. Not only must the physical corpse be disposed of properly, but the dead person's soul, which has been thrust into a new, ambiguous state of limbo, is subject to the influence of those who are still alive. The instrumental goal of the series of rites surrounding death is to ensure that the soul can leave peacefully and find eventual rest in heaven with the promise of salvation.

Ritual attention begins before death has actually taken place. As soon as a person is believed to be in the throes of death, a priest is called to give absolution and to administer last rites, or the Unción de los Enfermos. In the course of these activities, or *auxilios espirituales* (spiritual aids), which are a prescribed sacrament in the Catholic Church, the priest hears a confession if the person can speak; he may bring communion to the bedside if the dying person can receive it; finally, he anoints the sick or dying person with oil and recites prayers belonging to last rites. Some *colonos* have claimed that even *evangelistas*, or members of Protestant sects, were known to call the Catholic priest so they could confess before they died. Once death occurs, someone nearby goes to notify those relatives, friends, and *compadres* who do not live in the immediate vicinity. The death is proclaimed to the rest of the local community by the tolling of the bell at the parish church; the deliberate, heavy cadence of the death knell is easily distinguishable from the joyful, enthusiastic rings that announce happy occasions such as weddings or Christ's Resurrection on Easter Sunday.

Customarily, a wake (*velorio*) is held on the night immediately following the death; the wake is attended by friends and family, who offer condolences, or *pésame* (literally, "it weighs on me"), to the grieving relatives and take part in prayers. These prayers, which plead for the salvation of the dead person's soul, last through the night. The next day, following a special mass at the church, the body is buried in the cemetery. It is believed that the deceased's soul, however, remains in a liminal state, "floating" on earth; some interviewees told me that the *difunto* (deceased) spends these first nine days of limbo in its former house, and others maintained that the soul wanders on earth, usually in the vicinity of its home, until God judges the soul worthy of admission to heaven or sends it to do a period of penitence in purgatory or to suffer in hell. On the night of the funeral, after both mass and burial have taken place, and on each of the eight subsequent nights, a group gathers in the *difunto's* home to say rosaries and to call for God's mercy. This series of prayers for the deceased culminates on the ninth night with the ceremony of the Levantada de la Cruz (Raising of the Cross); this period of nine nights is called the Novenario de los Difuntos.[9] The aim of these days of prayer is to aid the deceased person's soul in achieving salvation; by praying for God's forgiveness at the critical time when he is deciding the fate of the deceased, the living hope to help bring the soul of the dead person to a good and peaceful rest.

Death and burial are thus part of a protracted social transition guided by the imperative of proper care and treatment of the body of the dead and of the dying by the living, so as to enable a "good" death. For until the *difunto* earns a place in heaven—which cannot happen until after the end of the penitence period, at least a year—he or she cannot act as an intermediary between living persons and powerful sacred beings. Before then, a *difunto* exists in a delicate, liminal, and potentially dangerous state of unrest. In this marginal, "unsocialized" condition, a *difunto* is taken to still be impure, unsettled, uncontrolled, hazardous; hence she or he becomes the object of pity, concern, and fear. The proper accomplishment of funereal rites allows for the "resocialization" of the dead, for some form of closure and control in terms of the risks of social pollution or of unrest into which the newly dead plunge the living. For it is widely believed that the recently dead, unless sufficiently cared for at the point of death, may remain in the earthly realm to haunt certain sites or to cause general mischief. Most commonly, however, *difuntos* reappear in dreams and communicate with those who were close to them in life. Such apparitions are usually interpreted as warnings that a *difunto* is troubled and requires some sort of aid from the living in the form of intercessory prayers or a mass. For after a person dies, he or she needs the help of those who are still living to pay—pray, make offerings, keep watch—for his or her sins.

SPACES OF DEATH: *EL MÁS ALLÁ*

In Oaxaca, among the popular classes, death is viewed as a particular sort of journey; this journey is not linear in geographic or temporal terms, but is concrete and cyclical. Thus many of the Oaxacans I interviewed spoke of death not as the extinction of life, but as a *paso* (step), a spiritual transition from one state to another, whether better (heaven) or worse (hell). Indeed, popular doctrines concerning ends are quite strict: informants often spoke of heaven as the fate of baptized children (*angelitos*) and the souls of the truly saintly or good (very few adults); purgatory was described as the often lengthy but ultimately temporary destination of those (most of us) who must *penar* (serve punishment) for any venial sins committed in life, before an ascent into heaven; hell is the destiny of those whose evil deeds during life were too great for any pardon.

Such descriptions reflect a pronounced concern with "proper" fates according to widely shared ethical prescriptions. Moral valuations thus routinely accompany and preside over the decomposition of the body in the cemetery; changes in the physical condition of the body, its dissolution and dissipation, are bound, by popular eschatology, to shifts in the fate of the soul. As soon as the soul departs from the body and embarks on its penitential journey—indeed, according to some accounts, *because* the soul leaves the body—the body begins to return to the materials of the earth; frequently, the period of the soul's wandering corresponds, roughly temporally, with the period of the body's decay.[10]

Thus, with the exception of *angelitos*, who ascend immediately to heaven, most *difuntos* are believed to undergo a necessary period of penitence before achieving a final restful state in paradise. Those who have not yet gained entry to heaven are known as *almas penitentes* (penitent souls) or *almas bendigas en el purgatorio* (blessed souls in purgatory), and these souls are spoken of in this way in prayer. Limbo is another intermediate dwelling place, inhabited by *almas inocentes*, the souls of innocent children who have died without being baptized.

Frequently described to me as a place somewhere "in the sky," heaven was figured as a utopian realm where there would be plenty to eat and drink, and harmonious social relations between all who dwelled there; in many respects, this heaven stood earthly reality on its head.

Informants' descriptions of the places where a soul might journey were situated in an explanatory framework that was clearly Christian, although revised from the orthodox form. When asked for their image of purgatory or limbo, most interviewees described both domains only as *oscuro* (dark): an appropriate codification of the realm of the unknown or the uncertain. Unlike limbo, a place souls can never leave, purgatory is a transitional space, neither earthy nor heavenly. Most often, purgatory is characterized conceptually; it describes an ontological condition rather than an actual location in the world. Because the dead can remain in a perpetual state of penance—one atones for one's sins for as long as God deems fit, but who, before God, ever arrives at the end of his or her grief for wrongdoing?—it is important to ensure that those who go on living will go on praying and interceding, soliciting God's mercy on behalf of the dead. Apparently, even the sufferings of those in hell can be affected by the prayerful actions of those on earth. Although hell, like the devil, did not figure very prominently in informants' discourse—most often hell was described as a *fuego* (fire), where suffering is eternal—one person explained that, for the duration of any mass dedicated to souls in purgatory, the souls in hell were also raised above the flames. Accounts of the hereafter thus reveal the flexibility of popular eschatology and its ideas of fate, and focus, in particular, on the indeterminacy or mutability of outcomes, the possibilities of intervention by the living in the fates of the dead. Such views of the fates of the dead suggest a strong feeling of interdependence between the living and the dead—even the reversibility of states of "life" and "death."

THE DEAD

There are two general categories of the dead: adults, who are the *pecadores* (sinners), and children, who are the *angelitos* (little angels). Children who die are always considered *angelitos*; guiltless of sin, they are *criaturas*, little creatures who will go directly to heaven. An *angelito*'s baptismal godparents, usually among the first to be notified of the death, are responsible for providing the clothing in which the child will be dressed for the wake and burial, and sometimes also the casket. This clothing (usually a tunic, or *ropón*) is always white; occasionally, the child will be dressed to look like a particular saint, if a boy, or the Virgin, if a girl. Outward demonstrations of mourning at a child's funeral are said to harm the *angelito*. This is not to say, of course, that the death of a child is not an occasion of intense grief. (Many people told me that, in rural areas, it is common for an *angelito*'s death to be celebrated with a fiesta and *baile* [dance] following the funeral, rather clear efforts at keeping grief at bay, although I never witnessed or heard of this occurring in Oaxaca City.)[11]

During my first stay in Oaxaca, in 1990, I was invited to two funerals of *angelitos*: one for a six-year-old girl, and the other for a baby boy. Both times I accompanied a distant relative of the deceased child, and this bit of distance made these events more bearable. As is customary, the two children were buried in white caskets, symbolizing the purity of their souls, and a mass took place at the church. The boy's burial was much like others I had seen for adults, but the little girl's funeral was slightly different: the funeral party composed primarily of children, some carrying red and pink flowers amid the usual white. Flower petals, candy, and confetti were thrown by a few adults as the coffin was carried to the gravesite and lowered into the ground, and among the hymns we sang that afternoon was "Las mañanitas," the song normally associated with a child's birthday party.

These unusual commemorations reflected the *angelita*'s ambiguous status and untimely death. A small white wooden cross was buried at the head of the grave, although crosses marking the graves of *angelitos* are sometimes pink for girls and light blue for boys. Because they have died free of sin, the wakeful prayers of a *novenario* (nine successive evenings of prayer) are considered unnecessary for *angelitos*, although frequently masses are held on the anniversaries of their deaths.

The distinction between *angelito* (non-sinner) and *difunto* (sinner) is considered to be quite important, although not every member of the community agreed, in every case, on the grounds for the difference. Factors of differentiation, however, always involved issues of sin or, more precisely, "conscious" sin. Thus although a child would typically be thought capable of committing a sinful deed, the child would not be fully aware of the deed—and therefore would not be considered responsible for the action. A truly potential sinner was someone who consciously recognized the difference between right and wrong. Some people I spoke to cited age as the distinguishing factor between *angelito* and *difunto grande*, but they rarely concurred on the exact moment or year that would mark the change in status.[12] For example, when Sara, a twenty-four-year-old woman from San Juan, was killed in a tragic bus collision on her way to her workplace in the Isthmus of Tehuantepec, there was much debate about her moral status in the community. A large number of people in the *colonia* turned up at Sara's wake, for they were upset by the senseless death of such a young woman. Conversation turned on the question of whether Sara's relatives would choose to have a *novenario* on her behalf. In the end, because Sara "was still a *señorita*" (in short, a virgin), her relatives elected not to hold a *novenario*. But had she been male, she probably would have been buried as a "sinner"—and therefore would have been "in need" of a *novenario*. Indeed, I observed a marked tendency for the community to nominate girls or young women in their upper teens and early twenties as *angeles* (innocents), whereas boys or young men of the same age were almost always considered already to be sinners. This gender-based distinction probably stems from several reasons, among them the strong enjoinder traditionally placed on girls and women (and not on boys and men) to preserve their virginity until marriage and the general association of femininity with morality.[13]

Certainly marriage was one factor that almost always effected a change in category from innocent to sinner, undoubtedly because sexual life is so closely linked, in popular discourse and imagination, with original sin. Thus *El Pecado* ([One Big] Sin) is a euphemism for sexual intercourse. But occasionally I heard about older women who, if the community believed they had lived an especially pious life, were buried without *novenarios*, even if they were technically married women, or *señoras*. Doña Leticia, a woman in the *colonia* in her thirties, told me that her sister, who had died while giving birth, did not have a *novenario*. The priest had told the bereaved family that since she had died "while fulfilling her ultimate duty as a woman," the sister was ensured a direct path to heaven. Another man explained: "It's not important, even if she's been evil, since she died at the moment of giving life to another being." In this situation, the "sinfulness" of female sexuality disappears, and all is forgiven. The birthing mother has the same status as a young girl or an old woman, for she has accomplished the meaning of her life and is thus excused from the need to atone for any sin. Likewise, when doña Luisa, an elderly woman and grandmother in San Juan, died after a year of painful illness, a neighbor explained that doña Luisa would go straight to heaven like an *angelito*. Because Padre Claudio and Deacon Reynaldo had repeatedly visited her during the period leading up to her death, she had received "the spiritual aids" of confession and the rite of absolution, and she had suffered so long on earth, doña Luisa, in the popular view, had been sanctified. According to my neighbor: "She was like a little girl—all was forgiven."

Thus the moral encoding of popular death-related practices is fully dimensioned and concrete, demonstrating the unique qualities of popular religiosity as a vital, experiential faith, bound up with the actualization and performance of the "good death."

THE WAKE AND FUNERAL

According to Oaxacan (and Mexican) tradition, after death a cross is drawn on the floor of the dead person's home, often in the room where the death occurred.

Once typically drawn in ash, today the cross is more frequently made of pow-dered white lime. The body of the deceased is then placed on this cross for a time (half an hour is the minimum period); the cross is supposed to absorb the dead person's spirit. Sometimes bricks are set under the *difunta*'s head, to aid the deceased during the period of *penitencia* (penance). The *difunta* is dressed, usually in clean "good" clothing.[14] The person's eyes are closed, and, after the time on the cross, the body is placed in a coffin (*ataúd* or *caja* [box]) on a stand to one side of the room where the wake will be held. This often is the *difunta*'s bedroom (especially if the death occurred at home) or simply the room where guests are normally received. Typically, the coffin is of a dark shade; a gray or blue coffin signifies a *difunto grande*. In this way, a deceased sinner is distin-guished from an innocent, for *angèlitos* are always buried in pure white caskets. Flowers, symbolic of sacred blessing and purity, may be placed on the body or around the edge of the coffin; the *difunta*'s hands are crossed over the chest, and frequently a cross is placed beneath the fingers.

The rituals of death thus carefully mark the separation of those two dimen-sions or aspects understood to make up personhood: body and soul. At first, the physical, corporeal form of the person, represented by the body in the coffin, and the spirit (*espíritu*) or soul, embodied in the cross of lime (*cruz de cal*), lie side by side but separate. From this point on, their journeys will increasingly diverge: the body will be committed to the earth, and the soul will be cast on the atmosphere, to wander and seek rest. In order to orient and speed the soul, behind the coffin is usually erected a screen of crushed velvet or some other heavy drapery, from which a crucifix is hung, usually one that has been removed from the household altar. Four long white candles in tall metal candelabras stand at the four corners of the coffin; I was told that these are necessary "to light the path to glory." And below, the cross of lime—the social-material residue of the deceased, the container of the soul—is outlined in small votive candles. At its side is placed a glass of holy water, and sometimes a saucer for anyone wish-ing to contribute a few coins toward the cost of the funeral.

Once the *difunto* has been laid out in the coffin, people may begin to visit the house. A house where a *difunto* lies is usually marked by a large black rib-bon hanging above the entrance; the door is left open, for anyone is welcome at a *velorio*, even someone who did not know the deceased or the family. Indeed, strangers of one sort or another often show up with friends or relatives. As one especially religious older man in the *colonia* told me, "Any person [can attend] as if we were all brothers; it doesn't matter—race, color, language. For God we are all his sons and daughters." Such statements are consistent with the percep-tion that it is the collective community, and not just the grieving relatives, that buries the *difunto* and says good-bye to one of its members. The social separation signified by death is thus counterbalanced by an ethos of inclusiveness and openness that permeates all rites commemorating death.

Attendance at a wake is considered to be a gesture of support for the bereaved relatives; it can also function as a demonstration of respect for the person who died or for the person's family; frequently, people attend wakes to say farewell (*despedir*) to the one who has died. I was repeatedly told that the greater the number of people praying to God on the occasion of a person's death, the greater will be his forgiveness toward the deceased. A large number of people at a wake may indicate the popularity of the *difunto*. But if the family of the deceased person is believed to be well-off, then (or so it is said) some visitors will be lured to a wake by the expectation that an abundance of high-quality food and drink will be served to guests. Usually visitors are welcomed by a member of the *difunto's* family, and, in keeping with the Oaxacan *guelaguetza* tradition, it is common for anyone attending the wake, as throughout the *novenario*, to bring a token gift as a contribution—flowers, food traditionally consumed at this time (for example, tamales, a dish of *mole* [rich, spicy chocolate-flavored sauce characteristic of the Oaxaca region], bread, coffee, chocolate), *veladoras* (votive candles), or a monetary gift of any size. Typically, visitors are immediately encouraged to sit down to eat and drink. They are offered coffee, hot chocolate, and something to nibble, maybe a tamale or sweet roll. Mescal or some other kind of liquor may be served later. Such exchanges make up and cement relations of social connection and interchange; the items given and shared thus function as metonyms or extensions of the concrete, substantive links among kin, friends, and *compadres* who compose the majority of *velorio* and *novenario* participants.

Throughout the night, prayers (rosaries) are said for the salvation of the deceased's soul; the frequency of these prayers depends on the devotion, will, and dedication of those present. In my experience, most visitors arrive at a wake between 8:00 and 11:00 p.m.; an individual's stay may vary from a few minutes to several hours. During this time, there is at least one rosary session, although only a small number of those present at the house may actually choose to participate in the prayers. The praying takes place in the "sacred area" immediately in front of the open coffin and before the lime cross. Usually a core group made up almost exclusively of women performs the prayers, kneeling in the sacred area or standing if space is limited. Those who do not participate, principally men, always remain on the margins or completely outside the sacred zone; often they drink beer or mescal. Among other cultural effects, then, popular funeral rites seem to enable women to create a new social center that, by rendering the male-dominated spheres of both "street" and church peripheral, represents an inversion of customary spatial valuations. Without question, here women are the major actors, for they oversee and speed along the separation of matter and spirit; they are the leaders and gatekeepers in this liminal zone, those who know what to do and how to do it.

Everyone present is served food and drink after each prayer session; if a person remains at a wake for a long time, he or she is served repeatedly. To stay in attendance for many hours, especially after most visitors have left—especially after midnight and until dawn—is granted particular moral weight in terms of its self-sacrificial or penitential value. Those who stay thus "offer" or "pay" in some respect for the soul of the deceased, as well as their own souls. For the stated imperative during the *velorio* is to keep the *difunto* "accompanied" for the entire night. Thus although exhaustion settles in and prayer sessions and eating and drinking have ceased, a number of people must persist in keeping watch through the darkest hours of the night. Only in this way can the journey of the soul be vouchsafed.

The day following the wake, a special mass precedes the burial ceremony. Oaxaca remains one of the few places in Mexico where the old custom of the Misa del Cuerpo Presente (Mass of the Body Present) is still practiced. In this mass, the body is placed at the church door; this mass stands in contrast to what is today more widely customary, a requiem mass, said subsequent to burial, when the body is no longer present. In Oaxaca, before the body is taken to church, a final prayer session is held in the house; this prayer session ends with a special prayer of farewell, or *despedida*. Then many of the flowers decorating the "sacred zone" are removed and distributed among those assembled at the house who will attend the burial. The funeral pallbearers, always men, are typically close relatives or friends of the deceased. If the deceased was male, these pallbearers will often also be elected to act as *padrinos*, or family representatives, during the Levantada de la Cruz, nine nights hence.

On the day of the funeral, the coffin is brought before the entrance to the church; the priest receives it at the door and blesses it with holy water. Four to six pallbearers then carry the coffin, feet first, up the central aisle to the front of the church, where they place it at a right angle to the altar. Chief mourners and close relatives of the deceased sit in the pews nearest to the front of the church; others tend to seat themselves in a manner that likewise spatially corresponds, roughly, to the nearness of their relation to the family or the *difunto*. While family members closest to the deceased may dress in black, many people wear their everyday clothes.

Most of the sermons that I heard during funeral masses in Oaxaca focused on the theological significance of death and its relation to salvation and Christ's Resurrection. At the end of the funeral mass, the priest once again blesses the coffin by sprinkling it with holy water. He closes the ceremony by making the sign of the cross over the dead body with a thurible smoking with incense, and then draws another cross with earth on the head of the closed coffin.[15] The pall-bearers then reclaim the coffin and head down the aisle, followed immediately by the *difunto's* relatives or chief mourners and the rest of the congregation. In a gesture that reiterates the collective, communal spirit of the rite, white flowers are handed to the mourners from bouquets brought from the wake or supplied by individuals in the congregation. The coffin is then carried directly to the cemetery adjacent to the church, or, if the body is to be buried elsewhere, it is placed in a vehicle—sometimes even a pickup truck, van, or station wagon—that will convey it to another graveyard.

If members of the funeral party are unable to travel in one vehicle, the group gathers outside the cemetery until the casket and full entourage have arrived. Once the group has collected, the procession sets out, led by the cross bearer, who carries a wooden cross, about three feet long, inscribed with the initials of the *difunta*, the date of death, and the letters D.E.P., which stand for Descansa en Paz (Rest in Peace). The pallbearers, holding the coffin aloft, follow the cross; as they pass, the remainder of the party falls in behind them, praying and sing-ing. The procession moves slowly into the cemetery. Often someone waves an incense burner in the coffin's path; sometimes, too, music from a group of hired or volunteer musicians accompanies the procession. The tunes played may be proper funeral marches like "Dios nunca muere" (God Never Dies), a haunting melody by the Oaxacan composer Macedonio Alcalá, which is very popular all over the state, or such other popular hymns and melodies as "Las golondrinas" (The Swallows) and "La canción de la Mixteca," the unofficial Oaxaca state hymn. On occasion, if the deceased had a particular love of mariachi music, a mariachi band will be hired to accompany a coffin to its burial site.

Once the funeral party arrives at the grave (which has been prepared for the burial by cemetery employees), everyone gathers around the site. Sometimes, before the coffin is lowered into the ground, family members, *compadres*, or friends of the *difunto* open the coffin for one last farewell.[16] Often the opening of the coffin is an intensely emotional moment; frequently, someone is on hand with a bottle of rubbing alcohol or a bundle of *ruda* (rue) to revive any mourners who might faint. The casket is gradually eased into the grave by means of two ropes, which are slowly released by men in the group, often with the assistance of a cem-etery employee. Prayers continue, typically led by one person who is, ideally, an official church representative but, more frequently, has agreed to act as the *rezador* (prayer specialist) for the whole series of death rites, including wake, funeral, and *novenario*. Sometimes *rezadores* expect a fee in return for their services, although in most of the funerals I saw in Cuahtémoc the *rezador* was a volunteer.

As the coffin slides into the grave, each person present tosses a handful of dirt on top of it; some do so in the form of a cross. This gesture represents a symbolic acceptance of the *difunto*'s death and departure; it is also commonly explained as a means of gaining indulgences for the dead. At one funeral I attended, the deceased's widow refused to throw dirt into the grave. "Throw dirt to him, *comadre*," her *compadre* urged. "Throw dirt, or he will never rest!"

Flowers are also often tossed into the grave. Frequently, someone pours the contents of a bottle of holy water over the coffin—again in the form of a cross, thus giving the *difunto* a final blessing. The grave is then filled with earth, sometimes by employees of the cemetery but more often by a small group of men in the funeral party. After the burial, or as it is nearing its end, mescal may be distributed in little cups, often by a *compadre* of the *difunta* or her family; men usually are the only recipients of this libation. Once the coffin has been sufficiently covered so that it is no longer visible—or if the *difunto*'s family is having particular difficulty in dealing with the death—close relatives are led away from the gravesite and sometimes away from the cemetery altogether. Many people in the funeral cortège also leave at this point. However, prayers and hymns continue until the grave is filled, and any remaining earth is shaped into a promontory mound over the tomb. Finally, the wooden cross that led the procession to the gravesite is embedded in the earth at the *difunto*'s head, and flowers and small lighted candles are placed all along the grave (figure 3.1).[17]

FIGURE 3.1 A grave following burial.

"Raising of the Cross"

For the next nine nights, prayers are said over the lime cross in the *difunto's* house. On the ninth and final night of the *novenario* is held the ceremony of the Levantada de la Cruz (Raising of the Cross), which marks the last farewell to the soul; on this night, the soul is sent on its way to the land of the dead. Significantly, I often heard people refer to the Levantada as a "second burial"; this is perhaps because it enacts a removal and separation of the spiritual remains of the *difunto* from a prior domain of existence—the home, or the realm of the living—to the cemetery, or the realm of the dead.[18] The lime cross is thus like a "second body" of the dead; it retains some remnant of the combined physical-spiritual essence of the corpse.

Although in most parts of Mexico the *cruz de cal* or *cruz de nueve días* (cross of nine days) remains unchanged or unadorned until the Levantada, in Oaxaca, on the ninth day after burial, it is customary for a *tapete de nueve días* (carpet of nine days) to be made as an embellishment. I have seen more than two dozen *tapetes* throughout the city, the first having been made on top of the gravestone of one of his relatives by a man in the Panteón de Santo Tomás Xochimilco. Although this *tapete* was for the Day of the Dead, the man who made it, Gerardo, was an artist from a nearby *colonia* who was regularly hired by families to make *tapetes de nueve días*. The *tapetes* I have seen have been quite varied in appearance, but all were striking and shared a general form: paintings created from a base of moistened sand or sawdust that had been colored with powdered paint. Sometimes the painting is done in relief, and the *tapete* is always adorned with flower blossoms and candles. Traditionally, the design is determined by the gender of the deceased: a saint or Christ image is usually deemed appropriate for men; the figure of the Virgin, for women. Nevertheless, the tastes of the deceased person or the family are also considered; thus one *tapete* that Gerardo made in memory of a young man killed in a neighboring *colonia* consisted of a representation of the Virgen de la Soledad, for the *tapete* was made on this saint's fiesta day. Another *tapete* I saw in Colonia San Juan was copied from a *difunto's* favorite calendar illustration of Christ. Usually the letters D.E.P.—Descansa en Paz (Rest in Peace)—and the *difunto's* name are spelled out at the bottom of a *tapete* (figure 3.2). It is perhaps important to note that a colorful *tapete* functions merely as a decorative and devotional complement to the lime cross it adorns, for it is the cross that receives the *difunto's* spirit immediately after death.

On the ninth night, the cross—and the entire *tapete* that contains it—are "raised" or "taken up" following a prescribed pattern by *compadres* or godparents specially chosen for the event: *padrinos* if the deceased was male, and *mad-*

FIGURE 3.2   A newly completed *tapete de nueve días.*

rinas if female. Typically, *padrinos* or *madrinas* are selected because of a close relationship to the deceased; normally, such godparents are good friends or kin. They become what is referred to as the *compadres de la cruz* (godparents of the cross), and they function as "godparents" of the head of the *difunto's* family (the person who hosts the Levantada); thus they may be asked to help cover the extra expenses the ceremony entails. There are usually five godparents for the Levantada; this number corresponds to the five sections into which the *tapete* is typically divided, although occasionally the number may be much greater if the *tapete* is particularly large. I have seen up to ten *compadres de la cruz* at such an event.

The person directing the Levantada may be a paid *rezador*, but more frequently—above all, if the family is very poor—the ceremony is directed by an elder or a member of the clergy, experienced with its forms and sequences. (Gerardo, for example, had learned the Levantada prayers and offered his services as a ceremonial leader, along with making the *tapete*.) The Levantada de la Cruz is a popular and noncodified ritual and thus, although no formal rules dictate its procedure, follows a pattern generally agreed on. Details may vary, however, according to the previous experiences and background of the person directing it. The Levantada usually begins around 11:00 p.m.; earlier in the evening, *novenario* prayers will have been said for the last time. The ritual is usually timed so that the "taking up" is completed just before midnight—so as to end the *novenario* appropriately at the finish of the ninth day. (Formerly—and apparently in some pueblos still—the final night of the *novenario*, including the Levantada, was an all-night affair; at dawn attendees would go to the cemetery to bury the remnants of the cross and the *tapete*.)[19]

The Levantada begins like every other prayer session of the *novenario*, with a recitation of the rosary. Then, during the litany, the "taking up" process begins. First, the *compadres de la cruz* remove the flower blossoms and candles from the sand carpet. Then, when the litany is completed, the raising of the remainder of the *tapete* begins. Each godparent is given a small cardboard box (or, if the *tapete* is large, a bucket) into which he or she will put the sand, lime, and flower blossoms scraped up with a piece of cardboard and a brush. The *tapete* has been divided into sections, each corresponding to a certain part of the "body" of the cross (head, right arm, left arm, foot, and "heart"). Each godparent is in charge of "taking up" a particular section of the *tapete* and cross, and these sections are taken up in a special order, each having its own prayer (figure 3.3). The prayer is said first, and then the godparent scrapes up his or her piece of the *tapete*, accompanied by the singing of a special hymn, "Alabanzas de la Santa Cruz" (In Praise of the Holy Cross):

Alabemos y ensalcemos	Let us praise and exalt
A la Santa Cruz	The Holy Cross
Pues que en ella expiró	Since on it expired
El dulcísimo Jesús.	Sweet Jesus.
Alma, vida y Corazón	Soul, life and Heart
Te ofrecemos, Cruz preciosa	We offer you, precious Cross
En ti fue redención	In you was redemption
O bandera prodigiosa.	O, prodigious banner.
De ángeles y serafines	By angels and seraphins
En el cielo estás rodeada;	In heaven you are surrounded;
De los hombres en el suelo	By men on earth
Llegas a ser despreciada.	You are scorned.
Adoremos, pecadores	Let us adore, sinners
A la Santisima Cruz	The most Holy Cross
Y entre músicas y flores	And among music and flowers
Al corazón de Jesus.	The heart of Jesus.
O Cruz santa prodigiosa	O Cross, holy prodigious one
Es tan grande tu poder,	Your power is so great,
Que huye y tiembla de terror	That evil Lucifer flees from you

FIGURE 3.3 Levantada de la Cruz: (*a*) a *tapete de nueve días* right before the Levantada ceremony; (*b* and *c*) *padrinos* remove candles from the *tapete* in preparation for the Levantada; (*d*) the *rezador* divides the *tapete* into five sections; (*e* and *f*) *padrinos* take turns "raising" their sections of the *tapete*; (*g*) buckets with *tapete* contents are rearranged in cross formation; (*h*) "Adoration of the Holy Cross."

El maldito Lucifer.
Santa Cruz resplandeciente
En que Cristo fue esclavizado
Yo te ruego humildemente
Que me libres del pecado.
Cruz, divina, misteriosa
Eres trono del Eterno
Librame, tu generosa
De las penas del infierno.
Eres linda y sacrosanta,
Brillantísimo lucero,
La alegría del Redentor
Y la Escala para el cielo.
El que al cielo quiera entrar
Será amante de la cruz,
Porque es el ara del cielo
Y el tesoro de Jesús.
Bendita la Exaltación
Del Santo Autor de la Cruz
Pues en el nos redimió
El dulcísimo Jesús.
Alebemos sin cesar
A la madre de Jesús,
Pues sabemos que asistió

Constante al pie de la Cruz.
Los Varones te bajaron
¡O dulcísimo Cordero!
Y de reliquias quedaron
La sábana y el madero.
Por tu Cruz y tu pasión
Y por tu rostro sagrado
Te pedimos, Padre amado,
Que nos des la salvación.
En los cielos y en la tierra
El madero sea ensalzado,
Donde fue crucificado
El mansísimo Cordero.
Alabemos a la Santa Cruz,
Puesta en el Monte Calvario;

And trembles with terror.
Radiant Holy Cross
On which Christ was enslaved
I humbly beg of you
That you deliver me from sin.
Cross, divine and mysterious
You are the throne of Eternity
Deliver me, O generous one
From the sufferings of hell.
You are beautiful and sacrosanct,
Brilliant star,
The joy of the Redeemer
And the ladder to Heaven.
He who wishes to enter heaven
Will be lover of the cross,
Because it is the altar stone of heaven
And the treasure of Jesus.
Blessed be the Exaltation
Of the Holy Maker of the Cross
Since on it we were redeemed
By sweet Jesus.
Let us praise without ceasing
The Mother of Jesus,
Since we know that she held constant
    vigil
At the foot of the Cross.
The Great Men lowered you
O sweetest of Lambs!
And the shroud and the wood
Remained holy relics.
By your Cross and your suffering
And by your holy face
We beg of you, beloved Father,
That you grant us salvation.
In heaven and on earth
May the wood be exalted,
On which was crucified
The sweetest Lamb.
Let us praise the Holy Cross,
Placed on Mount Calvary;

En tí murió mi Jesús	On you my Jesus died
Para darme eterna luz	To give me eternal light
Y librarme del contrario.	And deliver me from evil.
Adios, Santísima Cruz,	Farewell, Most Holy Cross,
Adios, Madre Dolorosa,	Farewell, Suffering Mother,
Ruégale a tu hijo Jesús,	May you beg your son Jesus,
Nos de una muerte dichosa.	That he grant us a blessed death.
Quien a Dios quiera seguir	He who wishes to follow God
Y en su gloria quiera entrar	And enter into his glory
Una cosa ha de asentar,	Must affirm one thing,
Y de corazon decir:	And from his heart declare:
"Antes de morir de pecar,	"Before dying from sin,
Antes que pecar, morir."	I would rather die than sin."

The first godparent "takes up" the head of the cross; the second, its right arm; the third, its left arm; the fourth, its foot. Finally, the fifth godparent "takes up" the "heart," or center. Once the *tapete* has been completely "raised," the "Adoration of the Holy Cross" begins. Every person present, beginning with relatives of the deceased and then the godparents, takes a turn in kissing the crucifix from the household altar, which had been placed on top of the *tapete*. As each mourner kisses the cross, the assembly recites a line from a prayer called the "Adoration of the Holy Cross":

Adorote Cruz preciosa; adorote, Cruz sacrosanta; adorote, árbol santísimo entre todos los árboles; adorote, santo madero; adorote, trono de Dios; adorote, escabel de sus pies, con el cual pisará a sus enemigos los pecadores, y les hará ver y conocer como solo él es Señor y Creador de cielos y tierra, juez de los vivos y de los muertos; adorote, galardón de los justos, por el cual se salvan y justifican; adorote, deleite de los ángeles; adorote, remedio de los pecadores; adorote, tálamo de Dios, en el cual está puesta su corona real. Adoro los clavos y espinas, título de Jesús Nazareno, y los instrumentos que adornan. Adoro a mi Redentor y Salvador en tí puesto; adoro tu santo bulto; adoro tu santa faz. Bendigo, glorifico y adoro sus santos miembros, que obraron en tí mi redención. Adorote, árbol salutiferio, árbol frondoso, florido y grandioso, por tí me suba al monte de los ángeles, él que por tí me redemió en el monte de los malhechores. Por tí me de vida él que por tí venció a la muerte; por tí me conceda en este mundo gracia, él que por ti me abrió las puertas de la gloria.

Jesucristo, óyenos, Jesucristo escúchanos y has que las almas de los fieles difuntos descansen en paz. Amen.

(Praise be to You, precious Cross; praise be to You, Holy Cross; Most Holy Tree among all trees; praise be to You, holy wood; praise be to You, throne of God; praise be to You, stool of your feet, with which You will tread on your enemies the sinners, and You will make them see and know that only He is Lord and Creator of all heavens and earth, judge of the living and the dead; praise be to You, reward of the just, by which they are saved and justified; praise be to You, O delight of the angels; praise be to You, remedy of the sinners; praise be to You, bed of God, on which was placed his royal crown. Praise be to the nails and the thorns of the title of Jesus of Nazareth, and the instruments that adorn You. Praise be to my Redeemer and Savior placed in You; I adore your holy form; I adore your holy face. I bless, I glorify and I adore your holy members, who in You brought about my redemption. Praise You, tree of health, luxuriant, flowery and magnificent, by You may I be raised up the mountain of the angels, he who by You redeemed me on the mountain of the evildoers. May he who by You vanquished death, give me life; may he who by You opened to me the gates of glory, grant me grace in this world.

Jesus Christ, hear us, Jesus Christ, listen to us, and allow that the souls of the faithful dead rest in peace. Amen.)

When everyone in the room has kissed the cross, the *rezador* leads the group in a prayer called "El sudario" (The Shroud):

TODOS: Señor Dios, que nos dejaste la señal de tu Pasión y muerte santísima en la Sábana Santa, en la que fué envuelto tu Cuerpo santísimo, cuando por José fuiste bajado de la cruz; concédenos, ¡O piadosísimo Señor! que por tu muerte y sepultura santa, y por los dolores y angustias de tu Santísima Madre Sra. nuestra sean llevadas las almas del purgatorio a la gloria de tu Resurrección, donde vives y reinas con Dios Padre, en unidad del Espíritu Santo, por todos los siglos de los siglos. AMEN.

(ALL: Lord God, who left the sign of Your suffering and Holy Death on the Holy Shroud, in which your Most Holy Body was wrapped, when by Joseph you were taken down from the cross: grant us, oh merciful Lord! Through Your holy death and burial, and through the pains and sufferings of your Holy Mother, our Lady, may you bring the souls of purgatory to the glory of your resurrection, where You live and reign with God the father, in the unity of the Holy Spirit, forever and ever. AMEN.)

Then, in the order in which they had "taken up" the *tapete*, the godparents arrange the cardboard boxes filled with the remnants of *cruz* and *tapete* into the form of the cross. (Thus the godparent responsible for the first section places her box at the head of the cross, the godparent responsible for the second section places his box so as to make the "right arm" of the cross, and so on.) The arrangement complete, this new cross is surrounded by small candles and by the flowers that had been removed at the beginning of the ceremony.

At the end of the Levantada, the head of the family—or another representative, such as a "first order" *compadre*—delivers an impromptu narrative thanking the godparents and everyone present. The *compadres* take this opportunity to thank the family head for asking them to be godparents. Often godparents offer a brief eulogistic commentary reflecting on the *difunto* and his or her death; sometimes this will be an emotional account of how the dead person had suffered during life or a discussion of what this death means for those left behind. I found, as I attended funeral ceremonies, that such eulogies were apt to be especially long if the death had given rise to a crisis or rupture within the family or local community; in these cases, the eulogy appeared to be expressly designed to externalize or to calm underlying tensions by exhorting those present to subordinate their personal grievances to the honor of the memory of the *difunto*. Thus this ritual gesture integrates the memory of the deceased into the ongoing semantic stream of the world of the living and denies any erasure of the signifying power and identity of the dead.

The conclusion of the Levantada signals the end of the *novenario* cycle. During the nine days of the *novenario*, the soul of the deceased person is said to remain in the cross of lime on which the *tapete* was made. The ritual of "raising the cross" can thus be understood to dramatize the departure of the soul from the earthly realm; at the point of the Levantada, the soul leaves the mundane world and rises up to meet God's judgment.

The morning after the Levantada, another rosary session takes place; this is followed by a repetition of the prayer of farewell, first said before the *difunto* was taken to the church for the funeral mass. The godparents then take the cardboard boxes filled with the *tapete* scrapings to the cemetery; other mourners bring along the flowers and candles that adorned it. At this point, a second, more permanent cross, usually made of metal or cement, is embedded in the earth at the head of the *difunto*'s grave. Next a mourner takes a shovel and carves a depression in the form of a cross in the earth over the burial mound. While prayers and singing continue, each godparent takes a turn in pouring the contents of his or her cardboard box into this crucifix; each godparent then sprinkles the grave using a flower dipped in holy water. Finally, the earth is rearranged to cover this *tapete*-filled cross, and the flowers and candles are placed on top of the mound. After the *tapete* has been buried, the *rezador* sometimes offers an oral summation of the *novenario* and words of thanks. Another period of *convivencia* (social gathering surrounding the sharing of a meal) at the original *novenario* site usually follows the departure from the graveyard.

IN THE GRAVEYARD: THE ARCHITECTURE OF DEATH

In Oaxaca, I often heard the dead spoken of fondly, angrily, solemnly, or sadly—and always as though they were present. Significantly, those who die remain attached to the whole community in a way that is quite rare in the United States and Canada: they are figured not merely as memories but also as active players in daily life. Death shifts the place of a person's activity but does not necessarily diminish it, for, even in death, a person is still a part of the community; indeed, someone who dies passes into a broader community that consists of both the living and the dead. Deaths are always somehow commemorated in the daily life of a family or community, even if that tribute is simply a matter of the spirit of the *difunto* finding honor in the flickering flame of a candle placed on a household altar. Because the dead remain so thoroughly alive in some respects in Oaxaca, the graveyard, or the meeting place between the living and dead, is a place of particular importance and is used quite regularly for a variety of purposes.

As the physical manifestation of the realm of the dead in the landscape of the living, the graveyard is a carefully circumscribed meeting place and, therefore, a setting for the experiencing of a spectrum of intense emotions: fear, love, sadness, and joy. Cemeteries are spatially bounded, "timed spaces of grief," as one commentator has described them; funeral architecture thus particularly renders, in tangible form, a relation bound by the ties of blood, sentiment, and the sediment of shared histories.[20] Because, as places, Oaxacan cemeteries are imbued with such ultimate and emotional importance, they have also served as material stages for the projection or enactment of critical conceptions of self and community. Thus although no stricture dictates the socioeconomic status of people buried in a particular cemetery or visiting graves there, some generalizations may be made about the relations between social order inside and outside the graveyard. For example, the Panteón General (General Cemetery), on the northeastern side of the city, is known to contain the dead of Oaxaca's oldest and wealthiest families. (In official records, this cemetery is referred to by several names, including the Panteón Municipal Número 1 and Panteón San Miguel; it was the second to be established in the city and remains its largest burial ground.)

By tracing the successive construction of cemeteries in Oaxaca, one may track changes in sensibility, social order, and funerary practice. In particular, important as cemeteries continue to be in popular funeral rites, they have also been sites where the political struggles between the state and municipal governments, on the one hand, and the state and church, on the other, were conducted.[21] What happens in these spaces, then, is not merely personal, nor is it a domain where the relations between the living and the dead alone are played out. Cemeteries are also zones of civic self-representation, sites of contest between various sorts of bureaucratic rule and hygienic order. Nevertheless, in the earliest years of its establishment and throughout the colonial period, the municipal government of Antequera—as Oaxaca City was then known—was not concerned with the establishment or management of places of burial. Those who died were taken to a local church for a funeral and then buried on the church grounds (*camposantos*), in the walls, or at the foot of the altar inside the building. The poorest families—those unable to afford any donation to the church for a funeral—left their dead at the church door during the night, with the hope that "Christian charity" would aid to bury their loved ones properly.[22]

The first cemetery in Oaxaca belonged to the Chapel of San Juan de Dios and was located next to the central city market. The space occupied by the market was later converted into the hospital grounds of San Juan de Dios—an architectural linkage that responded, perhaps, to mounting "scientific" and secularist liberal sentiments in the nineteenth century.[23] Increasingly, as the century wore on, the state wrested greater and greater control from the church over the place and proper form of burials. Thus, when in 1850 Guadalupe, the two-year-old daughter of Benito Juárez—then the governor of Oaxaca and later the president of Mexico—died, despite Juárez having the legal right to bury her in a churchyard, he was adamant that she be laid to rest in the Panteón San Miguel, "to give an example of obedience of the law."[24]

Particularly fascinating are the origins and history of this cemetery, which was established as the main city cemetery in 1832 and is more widely known as the Panteón General. At the end of the eighteenth century in Oaxaca, as elsewhere in the country, the church forbade non-Catholics to be buried in the churches or church grounds in the city. At the time that this edict was issued, the faithful were buried inside the churches, beneath tombstones, or *lápidas*. (Burial sites of this sort are still visible in some churches in Oaxaca; San Felipe Neri, located in the city center, is one example of such a space.) According to the local historian Rogelio González Medina, because of this prohibition non-Catholics were buried just outside the city in the area known as Tepeaca. In 1781, after a smallpox (*viruela*) epidemic struck Oaxaca, the Tepeaca burial grounds were converted into a cemetery, which came to be known as San Miguel. Then some forty-five years later, in 1826, following another smallpox epidemic that left several dead, many of them children, the site was formally designated the general cemetery (*panteón general*) for the city. Seven years later, in 1833, a cholera epidemic caused an alarming number of deaths in Oaxaca. The bodies of these dead were sent to the Panteón San Miguel—newly renamed the Panteón General—and were incinerated, along with cemetery benches and other furniture, to prevent the spread of the epidemic, which continued into the next year.

Thus, in 1834, the graveyard was formally declared to be the municipal cemetery. Located just beyond what were then the outskirts of the city, the cemetery became, at this point, a space for the use of every citizen—although Catholics and non-Catholics were still buried separately. The removal of all bodies for burial outside the city limits was a fairly new idea. Borrowed from Europe, and modeled on Tolsá, in Mexico City, this wresting of control of the dead from the churches was justified, in legal decrees, by concerns for hygiene, then a novel science.

A government decree in 1844 finally forbade the burial of bodies in church grounds, a move that dramatically increased the use of the new municipal cemetery.[25] An 1845 description of the cemetery reveals that outside the main *camposanto*, or sacred ground, consecrated to Catholic burials, "a space was designated for the use of non-Catholics." A series of 2,355 niches was also built in order to accommodate the increasing numbers of the dead. (Of these niches, 103 were occupied by the bodies of cholera victims.) In 1870 another two sections, or *cuadros*, were added to the eastern side of the cemetery; these were designated for "the poor," who could bury their loved ones there at no cost.[26]

In 1897, when the cemetery reached what was declared "full occupancy," the municipal president of Oaxaca, Francisco Vasconcelos, initiated the construction of a new cemetery. Built in 1899, immediately adjacent to the Panteón General, the new cemetery was known officially as Panteón Número 2. It, too, was divided into four sections; initially, they apparently separated adults and children, as well as Catholics and non-Catholics.[27]

Today the Panteón General, the name under which these two nineteenth-century municipal cemeteries have been combined, is still marked by traces of the Tuscan architecture that typified its earliest construction. There is, for example, a crumbling and elegant chapel at its center that dates from 1834 but was never completed. Separated into three sections by high limestone walls with arched entryways leading from one section to another, the cemetery, like the city that has now engulfed it, shelters its oldest graves at its core, or central *cuadro*. A long wall filled with doors runs along the front of the cemetery; these are the burial niches built in the mid-nineteenth century to accommodate the expansion of the graveyard—although, for reasons of hygiene, burials in the niches have been prohibited since 1891. Today the proportion of simple earthen graves relative to finished tombs varies from section to section. On the whole, graves in the oldest middle section are more finished and permanent in appearance; frequently, in this section, the graves consist of tombs of expensive stone, embellished with an ornate headstone or statue. Very wealthy families frequently bury their *difuntos* here in a personal crypt within the family mausoleum; typically, the family surname is conspicuously displayed above a locked glass door, through which expensive objects such as brass candlesticks and religious icons, images, and portraits may be seen.

Technically, however, the old bases of distinction—age, religion, and social class—are no longer formally in operation in municipal cemeteries. And, unlike other cemeteries I have visited elsewhere in Mexico, where the graves of *angelitos* sometimes are separated from those of adults, in almost every graveyard in Oaxaca the graves are arranged in the order of the date of death—except, of course, for such "collective" graves as family crypts, tombs, mausoleums, or gravesites. This sort of temporally based disposition of cemeteries in Oaxaca permits graves of very different types to lie next to one another, in a way that houses, for example, particularly those in very wealthy zones, sometimes do not.[28]

In many respects, however, the grave represents an extension of the domestic realm or the domain of the "inside." The gravesite is often referred to as the *difunto*'s "real house," and I was frequently told that the soul does not visit its former family home for the Day of the Dead in the first year after death, since it is too busy "taking care of its new home" (*cuidando su nueva casa*).[29] The graves of rich and poor families are thus often distinguished from each other in much the same way as rich and poor residences are distinguished. Not only are gravesites purchased like other kinds of real estate, but graves are also similar to houses in terms of the manner of their construction. Those who are able to purchase a plot under an agreement of perpetuity often do so outright—frequently long before the gravesite is actually needed—and then build the whole tomb at once. Poorer families, however, have no other recourse but, in effect, to rent space from the Oaxaca City *municipio*: they pay an initial fee for the grave and then a yearly maintenance tax. (And, as with other rents, the fees for a grave, particularly in periods of population expansion or high demand, may go through periods of rapid escalation; thus an initial fee of 100,000 old pesos in 1989 jumped to 1 million old pesos in 1990.)[30] Similarly, poor people I knew often began with a simple earthen grave to which they gradually added improvements as they were able to do so. These improvements usually depended on family labor or a contract worker who could do the job inexpensively; likewise, the materials most often used to enhance the graves of the poor are the same used in the construction of their houses: *carrizo* (reed), brick, unpainted cement, and metal, including corrugated iron for roofs. In the same way that fences enclose longer-established lower-class homes, an attempt may be made to build such a barrier around older graves. By contrast, the graves of the wealthiest Oaxacans frequently resemble fortresses; set off from the surrounding community in terms of materials, structures, and styles—as are the residences of the wealthy—these graves often consist of a granite or marble crypt or mausoleum (figure 3.4). Less often, such a grave might consist of an expensive carved-out stone or cement grave or tomb adorned with a statue or sculpture. For both rich and poor, however, when possible, family members are buried together in one grave or "house" (often, for the wealthy, a mausoleum or crypt) or in neighboring "properties" or burial plots.

A cemetery thus reproduces many aspects of the physical structure of a residential community—not only in terms of its architectural forms but also with regard to its spatial organization. Relatives frequently reside together in the same "neighborhood," although rich and poor, particularly in the city's older cemeteries, may die "next door" to one another, which seems to make differences in the appearances of graves especially significant. (Such proximity between rich and poor is not always the case, however, and may be less and less frequent. For example, the expensive private cemetery Recinto de la Paz, constructed in the early 1990s just outside Oaxaca City, constitutes an economically homogenous community rather like the rising number of exclusive residential *fraccionamientos*

FIGURE 3.4 Graves of (*left*) a poor person, fenced with bricks and embellished with a simple wooden cross, and (*right*) a rich person, enclosed in a modern A-frame structure whose supports form a cross.

[or suburbs].) Similarly, just as the material dwelling places of saints, religious images, and humans are considered to be sacred sites, so are the "homes" of the dead. Graves often resemble altars and are adorned with candles, flowers, images, and religious portraits and other relics. (This sort of symbolic affinity is further accentuated during Day of the Dead celebrations, when graves are decorated so that they closely resemble domestic altars, decked out with flowers, photographs of *difuntos*, incense, and sometimes food.) According to the logic of such ritual mapping, the house of the living is allied with the resting place or grave of the dead; in turn, the model for both these "residences" is the church, which houses the faithful, the prophets, the resurrected body of Christ, and all the saints.

The iconography of graveyard architecture and decoration, like the symbolism of the funeral, is usually rife with emblems of fertility and procreation. In many ways, a graveyard also resembles a garden; in addition to the trees and bushes surrounding most graves, and the bouquets of flowers that family members regularly leave for their *difuntos*, it is quite common for flowers and herbs to be planted in the earth of a grave plot itself.

Despite the symbolic parallels the cemetery serves to map between the realm of the living and that of the dead, it is most often understood to be an intermediary zone between the domains of life, death, and the afterlife.[31] The physical remains of a dead person, contained in his or her grave, are only a metonymical sign of the *difunto*; they stand for the person without being the person; they mark out a space where the spirit may be contacted, but, for many Oaxacans, a *difunto*'s spiritual aspect is not in the graveyard but in the beyond, or *más allá*. Of course, there are many ways in which a cemetery represents the mysterious and otherworldly domain of the dead; it marks out a realm whose nature is vague, unknown, and frequently feared, a space where death and an imagined and ghostly afterlife somehow coincide. At the same time, cemeteries are profoundly human artifacts; they are zones where certain acts take on cultural significance for and among the community of the living. Thus activities by the living in the cemetery center on the care and tending of the environment surrounding the dead, and an unattended, abandoned grave is read as a sign of severed family ties, obligations, or loyalties—in other words, a social disintegration.

The social meanings that may be read into the dispositions of graves have significance both temporally and spatially. The cemetery is not only a meeting *place* of the living and the dead, but also a zone where different sorts of time intersect. Thus "the time of the living," which is temporary, and "the time of the dead," which is eternal, are brought together in a graveyard.[32] In popular communities and practices in Oaxaca, the cemetery elaborates and shelters a permanent space where living and dead may interact in an alternative temporality in which both are very much present. Other spaces and gestures, however, also mark the conjunction of such a double temporality; indeed, many of the activities that belong to funerary and *novenario* rites attempt to bridge the difference or the distance between these two time frames, to provide comfort to the *difunto* as he or she makes the transition to a new state.

Thus, in keeping with the material nature of a sacred imaginary in Oaxaca, the journey undertaken by the dead is conceptualized in rather concrete spatio-temporal terms. Families whose indigenous beliefs and traditions are still very strong may place in the coffin items thought to be of use to the *difunto* on his or her journey on the *camino muy extenso* (long path) to the otherworld; frequently, these items include clothing or money—or, more rarely, tamales, tortillas, and *huaraches* (sandals). A Mazatec family living in Colonia San Juan told me that they customarily put a turkey into the coffins of their *difuntos* before burial; this was a "rural" custom they replicated in the city in order to ensure that their dead would not become hungry on the long journey *más allá*.

Similarly, the spiritual emanation of the *difunto* is believed by many to remain for a time among the living. Some people claimed that the soul stays in or near his or her home for the nine days of the *novenario*, which explains the need for the ceremony of the Levantada de la Cruz to accomplish the final sending off of the soul to heaven. For others—usually more "evangelized" Catholics—the Levantada ceremony was only symbolic; they explained that, in line with more conventional Catholic doctrine, death signified the immediate separation of the soul from the physical body, and the soul's subsequent transmigration up to God to receive judgment.

Nevertheless, in both cases, a close conceptual identification of the journey of the soul and the putrefaction of the corpse obtains; thus whether or not the soul is understood to linger in the zone of the family home for nine days before being sent off on its second and final journey, the dissolution of the deceased's body is taken to be a metaphor for the soul's social and moral transformation. Indeed, such conceptual interdependence between the fate of the soul and that of the body helps explain why it is so important that the *difunto*'s spiritual aspect, housed in the lime cross and *novenario tapete*, be reunited with the remains of the body at the gravesite at the conclusion of the Levantada. This sort of linkage between the fate of the body and the progress of the soul also accounts for the oft-heard belief that a *difunto*'s soul does not return to earth to visit with the living until one celebration of the Day of the Dead has passed; a *difunto* is still considered to be paying for his or her sins as long as the impure flesh of the cadaver has not completely decomposed.

Many of the people I have talked to in Oaxaca suggest that after the Levantada, the *difunto* spends forty days in an uncertain transitional period, rather like the forty hours that Christ was in limbo after his death and the forty days he walked on earth following his Resurrection. It is widely believed that, during this time, the soul is sent by God to wander the earth; in such wanderings, the *difunto* visits the sites of his or her sins to be redeemed (*recoger sus penas*). Often, on the fortieth day following the ninth day of the *novenario* cycle, a special rosary gathering—or even a mass—marks the closure of this particular period of wandering, or *vagando*. Typically, between the *novenario* and the fortieth day, a *veladora* (oil candle) is left burning on the bereaved family's household altar. This candle is spoken of as a light to help illuminate the soul's path in the darkness of the otherworld. A glass of water is also often placed on the household altar, since the soul, it is believed, needs to be able to quench its thirst during its journey. (Sometimes a glass of water is placed by the lime cross during the *novenario* on the deceased's grave and on a Day of the Dead altar to refresh the soul during its stay on earth.)

On the fortieth day, it is believed, the soul will arrive at its destination: heaven, where it will receive welcome into paradise; hell, where it will be condemned; or purgatory, where it must pass time in penance. During this time, it is considered particularly important to offer aid to the *difunto*, for the deceased is, effectively, on trial for his or her sins and is awaiting God's judgment. As most *difuntos* will be sent to purgatory, the period of active penitence is often seen to last quite a bit longer than the initial forty days—often this acutely penitential period is said to last for at least a year. And until this process of guilty atonement is finished, the soul cannot rest.

As Robert Hertz argued long ago, based on his observations of death rituals in Indonesia, such journeys of contrition imply that, as long as there are fleshly remains, the soul retains its connection to the profane world. Once the body has disintegrated, spiritual purification may be considered to have taken place.[33] In Oaxaca, the decomposition of the corpse, the process of corruption itself, is frequently linked to the *difunto's* suffering in the "darkness" of purgatory. To keep a candle burning on the grave or the home altar (or both) during the first year after a death was thus considered especially important. I was repeatedly told that, because one's mortal, physical aspect is the base or sinful part, putrefaction produces an unmistakable unpleasant odor. Similarly, it was explained that the reason one's personal scent grows stronger with age has to do with the accumulation of sin—and thus the resulting "corruption" of the body. The wide use of both incense and flowers in funeral rituals, then, can be understood as an effort to mask or counterbalance the sinful odor of death with prayerful or naturally purifying means.

Women's Work: The Labor of Death

Accomplishing the organizational and practical tasks associated with death in Oaxaca, as well as participating in its ritual activities, can bring deep satisfaction to some members of the community; their actions are a part of the effort to make sure that the *difunto* has died "well." Even if a person does not take an active part in *novenario* activities, other participants accord a good deal of importance and moral weight simply to putting in an appearance, particularly for protracted periods. The sacrifice of long hours for the good of others in the context of the *novenario* pertains especially to women and is broadly consistent with cultural expectations of female "self-abnegation."[34] Although a professional male *rezador* sometimes is hired to lead the prayers, those who actively and typically participate in funereal and *novenario* prayers, and the accompanying singing of hymns, are usually women (and children). The purchase, preparation, and serving of food and drink—and the cleaning up afterward—also fall on the cooperative shoulders of the female members of the bereaved family, aided by female friends (especially *comadres*) and neighbors. If the deceased person had no female relatives or if they are incapacitated by grief, the necessary acts of service and vigilance are taken on by other women. In marked contrast with other events in Oaxacan daily life, funerals provide occasions for the striking blossoming of female virtue and leadership. On such occasions, women create new social centers and shoulder new responsibilities for the guidance and continuity of community social relations.

The Oaxacan popular symbology of space involves a sharply gendered division of labor: women look after the "inside," whereas the domain of masculine action is "outside," or in the outer world. On the surface, the rites of death do not alter this dominant cultural spatial divide. Typically, after a death, a core group of women is present each night to "host" the *novenario* and to carry out its prayers. Frequently, both young and adult men arrive at a house in time for a prayer session but never step foot inside the home; nor do they recite a single word of prayer. Instead, they tend to stand in clusters outside the house, often drinking alcohol. In my experience, men were more inclined to join women both in prayer and in the subsequent period of *convivencia* if there were few other men in attendance, whereas if many men were gathered at the house, differences in gendered modes of behavior tended to become more exaggerated. On such occasions, some men take it upon themselves to serve alcohol or distribute cigarettes; thus most of the men present are preoccupied with ritual drinking. And even if a man drinks until he is on the verge of passing out, he is never forced to leave as long as he is understood to be "accompanying" the *difunto* or other mourners or both; regardless of his state of mind, such a person's presence at the *novenario* is valued. (In this context, spending time in the place of mourning takes on the qualities of a gift, as do the typically more material items of ritual exchange.) As one woman explained, such sharing of goods is to be expected, since it is part of the necessary *convivencia* that binds the living in the face of death: "It's a custom [*costumbre*] that they [men] take their bottle of mescal and many take liquor to give out there [in the cemetery,] after which they bury the dead person. After they give it to the *panteonero* [graveyard keeper], they give it to everyone; here in the wake it's customary to give out mescal, cigarettes, supper, drinks—everything is offered."

Interestingly enough, such a clean division of gendered labor during *novenario* and funeral rites, and the emphasis on female "goodness," appear to contrast markedly with the messiness of other popular cultural representations of women and death in Oaxaca. For example, La Santa Muerte, also known as La Santísima Muerte (Most Holy Saint of Death), is a skeleton dressed in a Virgin's garb; her ghoulish image graces everything from packets of magic dust and prayer cards to candles available at any city market (figure 3.5).[35] Most of the people I spoke to were familiar with the Santísima Muerte as an image of popular culture but not as a force of popular power. Thus her image cannot be found with those of other popular religious icons; for example, she is not seen alongside the saints in the racks of portraits, electric globes, and other items for sale from the many *puestos* (or stands) in front of the Iglesia de la Soledad. Nevertheless, a couple of older female informants argued that the formidable powers of the Santísima Muerte may be summoned to protect someone against death or to use against one's enemies. And a middle-aged male owner of a grocery store in the center of town told me that people often wear the image around their necks as a kind of protection, although I never saw it used this way.

Another individual, a woman who sells the "dust" of the Santísima Muerte at a stall in Oaxaca's central city market, told me that although the Santísima's frightening image kept many people from buying the dust, the packets were often purchased by policemen, who hung them in their cars. (Hence it would seem that the Santísima has taken on qualities of a devil-like figure with whom the police—commonly perceived as agents of corrupt "official" authority—have established a kind of Faustian pact.) And later, at another *puesto*, I found a slim volume called *El libro de la Santa Muerte*. This book contains many prayers that may be said to the Santa Muerte in the form of a *novena*, as well as *hechizos* (spells) "against jealousy and the desire to dominate a spouse" ("three nights of voodoo") and prayers "so that the Man you love may Forget his current Woman" or so that you might "Conquer a Difficult Man." And a short explanation accompanies the "Prayer for the Santa Muerte": "When a person does not

FIGURE 3.5 La Santísima Muerte.

follow through with what he has promised you, you can use this prayer to oblige him to carry out his promise. Warning: this is very powerful—afterward, that person will remain dependent on you . . . until you free him! You many also use this invocation for your own protection. Until the moment of your death!" The Santa Muerte is thus a distinctly popular personage—at once saintly, beatific, and treacherous—capable of bringing about misfortune. In this way, the Santísima Muerte condenses multiple, often polarized connotations of female identity—virtuous self-abnegation, nurturing, and succor, in combination with a dangerous maleficence.

Another well-known and ubiquitous female image of death in Oaxaca—and throughout Mexico—is La Llorona (Weeper), also known as Matlaziwa, the mythical ghost of a woman who, legend has it, murdered her children before killing herself. She is especially well known for leading astray men who have been drinking. One of my neighbors explained the legend to me in this way:

> According to the legend she [La Llorona] presents herself to . . . [alcoholics], and they try to follow her. And it is said that those men always wake up at dawn the next day, in thorns, in the bushes on a hill—not in their house—and they begin to recall, and they say, "La Llorona took me away." But they always go to places where there are bushes with thorns, to ditches, places like that; there they say that they saw her.

It is said that the nocturnal spirit of La Llorona may be heard screaming in secluded and marginal—especially "natural"—sites, wandering and calling out for her children. She is regarded as particularly dangerous to men who are alone at night and have been drinking or behaving in undesirable ways; it is said that, in such states, men may be seduced into death by the beautiful ghost. The myth of La Llorona follows a common cross-cultural paradigm for female witches. In his study of folk Catholicism in central Mexico, John Ingham notes her resemblance to Old World figures such as Eve, Lilith, and Schalangenjungfrau, or the Enchanted Lady.[36] Such myths function allegorically; in the tale my neighbor related, La Llorona, like other Oaxacan cultural ideals of women, enacts the sinful ambivalence of female sexuality, the risks of being both seducer and mother. Indeed, the tale of La Llorona stands as a warning, and not simply to lonely drunken men. Besides committing the sin of suicide, La Llorona enacted the unspeakably horrific crime of murdering her own children. Consequently, she is rendered socially dead in a double sense; forever condemned to suffer for her evil deeds, she develops a sexuality that threatens men whose behavior may similarly bring them too close to the taboo-laden, excitable edges of moral society. And she is an anti-model for women; a way not to be around death—or life, for that matter.

The figures and myths of La Santísima Muerte and La Llorona both feminize and condense a number of "inner," changeable, or "dangerous" characteristics and thus serve to cement, at the level of popular culture, certain widely held associations among female identity, liminality, danger, and death; in such popular figures, childbirth, sexuality, passionate emotionality, and even virginity are linked to female violence and death. Thus the exclusion of women from the "rational," "outer" domains of public and political life is typically justified; culturally speaking, for both good and ill, women become tied to death, to its circumstances and rituals. While it is easy (and quite reasonable) to regard figures such as La Santísima Muerte and La Llorona as psychological displacements or projections of anxiety about female power, or fears about the granting and carrying of life and death that female sexuality frequently involves, the association between women and death in Oaxaca does not always deprive women of the scope to act. On the contrary, it carves out an emotional domain for female action that is essential to the identity and continuity of the community—that is, to its survival.

For, in many respects, the domain of popular religiosity provides a series of cultural resources to women and others who are, or tend to be, marginalized in the public sphere. Its character—noncodified and sensuous—requires both ritual and emotional knowledge, readily adaptable to changes in circumstance. It is not quite enough to say that the pervasive presence and leadership of women in popular death rituals simply reflect a social role in which "good" women are to be incarnated in the image of the Universal Virgin Mother as religious and moral paragons.[37] While a belief in the virtue of the self-denying and all-suffering mother, or *madre abnegada*, seems to permeate and organize women's lives in many parts of Mexico, in Oaxaca, during the course of popular funeral rituals, I observed women behaving in ways that made it plain that their concerns were not simply or overwhelmingly a matter of fulfilling the role of the good woman.[38] On the contrary, maintaining valued social links between persons both living and dead was the reason for their actions, and this political and emotional activity frequently provided the basis of women's platforms of symbolic power in the community.

In Oaxaca, as in much of the world, the feelings of sadness and pain that the living experience following a death were expected, considered to be natural, a necessary step in one's confrontation with the absence of someone loved. Death causes one "to feel an irreparable loss [sentirse la perdida irreparable]," as one man in San Juan put it. Doña Isabel described this loss more graphically:

> You feel pain because your son has died, or your mother has died; you feel as if a piece of flesh has been torn out of you: as if they took out your eye, an arm, a tooth—because it is your blood, because it hurts—if someone gave you a hard blow [*trancazo*], you'd feel it, no? Because it's your body, your blood.

But an excess of grief was spoken of as something dangerous: it left a person vulnerable and made him or her inclined to "fall" into illness. After the funeral *novenario*, grief is gradually expected to subside. This expectation does not mean that community members are intolerant of those who continue to show sadness long afterward; in my own case, my closest friends in the *colonia* were always willing to listen to me sympathetically when I felt overwhelmed by a wave of grief after the death of my father. I was repeatedly told that "mourning is carried in the heart"; thus, in popular communities in Oaxaca, the wearing of black or other prolonged outward signs of bereavement were not particularly important. Aside from the few older women who wore black clothing for months or even years after losing their spouse (as was the custom in Spain), there is no strong, clearly defined tradition of mourning customs with regard to behavior or dress, nor are there proscriptions against remarrying. Still, behavior that may not appear in such explicitly codified fashions can nevertheless be found externalized in other expressive modes; one such example is the particular way that women in Oaxaca frequently bear and absorb suffering within the rites of mourning.

Until the 1980s, it was uncommon even for ethnographers who explicitly and specifically studied death rituals and processes of collective mourning to speak of the emotional impact of death on the living. Frequently, ethnographic accounts focused on various socioeconomic functions of mourning behavior within a given culture; discussions of the way that death is experienced personally—the way it often seems to cut across the heart of one who survives, to derange one, to drop one into a space of irreparable starkness—were not taken to be a part of the subject matter of the social science of anthropology.[39] To be sure, as a number of contemporary anthropologists have noted, emotions are always expressed in particular culturally sanctioned forms; in this sense, they are not, strictly speaking, "raw" universal data. But for precisely this reason, they are important aspects to take into account when studying particular cultural forms.[40] Thus how emotion works in a particular locale—who carries which emotions and why; the kind of work particular emotions perform in specific contexts, and the responses they elicit—may help us to understand important aspects of a culture that otherwise we are likely to miss.

For example, although many contemporary North Americans schooled in feminist theory are alive to the limited (and limiting) value of associating women with emotionality, to take such an association as merely pejorative or "unenlightened" would be, in many situations, to miss some of the important ways that emotionality might be viewed as a source of women's social value.[41] In her ethnographic account of a village in the Mexican state of Morelos, Joann Martin makes such an argument about the social power that emotional work gives women. Suggesting that women's access to political power in the village stems from a widely held belief that a great and necessary experiential knowledge is rooted in women's capacity to suffer for others, Martin writes: "While [women's] . . . labour was exploited, the role of mother was demonstrably full of possibilities for gaining symbolic power. This power is derived predominantly from the tradition of Marianismo, which idealized qualities of the Virgin Mary: suffering, humility and nurturance as the model for proper mothering." [42]

Likewise, in Oaxaca, it is possible to argue that, by way of a sort of emulative exchange, women in the community take on the role of assimilating and objectifying a collectively felt grief. During popular funeral rites, women's capacity as sufferers, as privileged agents of a certain emotional repertoire, serves both as a source of self-definition and as a form of social power and influence. In this context, suffering is a kind of "emotional labor" akin to childbirth; it carries within it a morally valued, sacred resonance with Christ's self-sacrifice and the moral redemption that it brought about for all. Women's suffering in the context of the funeral rites is, then, a sensuous emulation of the Passion. As doña Amelia, a middle-aged matriarch in San Juan, put it, "As the Bible says, those who suffer with patience go to heaven—we should suffer everything with patience; we don't have to deny what we suffer." In the context of mourning, women in the community act to assume pain, which they carry in a time and manner parallel to the soul's suffering in penitence. In effect, the women who gather to pray for those who have died, and who serve other living souls in attendance, accomplish an empathetic deliverance of themselves, others, and the *difunto*.

For this reason, in the popular community where I lived, the emotional work performed by women at funerals was highly valued. It reinforced (and constituted) ties of sociality among the living and the dead; it wove—and maintained—the tissue of community life. The performance of such emotional labor may also function to grant women a certain leverage through which they may, for a variety of reasons and in a variety of settings, enlist the practical help and support of other social actors. Certainly, embodying and carrying a certain emotionality at funerals and on other occasions frequently allows women in Oaxaca to affirm their moral superiority over men in the larger social field.

CONCLUSION

Despite the absence of clear rules dictating exactly how people should commemorate the death of a loved one, paying a great deal of attention to "maintenance" practices of the cult of the dead is a characteristic component of Mexican and Oaxacan popular culture and religiosity. Many people—especially women—visit the graves of their *difuntos* regularly, especially in the first year after death. And the fortieth day after a death is often marked with a mass or a second Levantada. One friend, Beatriz, dedicated a mass to her son every thirty days after his death; close *compadres* and friends were always invited. Such frequent remembrance and prayer for the release of a soul from purgatory is not a rare custom in Oaxaca, especially during the first year after death. Beatriz, however, was emphatic that she intended to continue the practice of arranging for a mass every thirty days until she herself died. Such an intensity of ritual commitment suggests the immediacy of the emotional tie that Beatriz still feels with her son; others offer examples frequently as acute. Indeed, the entire series of popular ritual practices detailed in this chapter is concerned with enabling the living to hold on to the tangible presence of those who are dead and to go on living.

The first anniversary of a *difunto*'s death is called the *cabo de año* (end of the year) and is generally commemorated by a special mass dedicated to the deceased. Significantly, in popular opinion, the *cabo de año* coincides with the end of penitence—that is, the minimum time it might take the flesh of the corpse to decay. Often, in addition to arranging for the mass, a bereaved family hosts a gathering at someone's house in memory of the deceased. Sometimes this gathering replaces the church ceremony altogether, which might illustrate, above all, the sort of religious independence typical of the poor. At some non-church events in Cuauhtémoc, the deacon, don Reynaldo, was invited to give a simple service referred to as the Celebración de la Palabra (Celebration of the Word), a mini-sermon, followed by communion and then a period of *convivencia*. Sometimes a family chooses to mark the *cabo de año* with another Levantada de la Cruz; this ceremony involves the making of another *tapete* and may be preceded by nine nights of prayer in the family home.

Again and again, the living come together to remember the dead. Death, in effect, provides a series of occasions on which the community of the living may renew itself. In and through the "right" practice of rituals of death, certain members of the community of the living—above all, women—rise to prominence and exercise force over the moral shape and scope of the community. Thus popular rituals of death confer moral benefits and distribute social power in the realms of both the living and the dead.

CHAPTER 4

The Drama of Death

Death has only given and received meaning, that is to say, it is socialized through exchange.

—JEAN BAUDRILLARD, *Symbolic Exchange and Death*

ONE OF THE FIRST EVENTS I ATTENDED in Colonia San Juan was a wake and funeral. I begin this chapter with a rather lengthy description of this experience from my field notes of 23 February 1990:

I was at doña Filomena's house in the evening for one of the neighborhood celebrations of La Paradita del Niño Dios, one of the series of post-Christmas fiestas that continue until Ash Wednesday. Two young women arrived, breathless. They had run up the steep hill from the highway in front of the hotel; in panicked voices they reported having seen someone named Manuel (a name I didn't recognize) hit by a car. His body had been launched a good twenty feet into the air, and, as I've learned happens all too often around here, the vehicle that struck him had sped off.

Later that night I visited Manuel's home for the wake. Typical of many dwellings in the *colonia*, Manuel's home consisted of three cement-walled rooms with dirt floors. The rooms faced onto a courtyard or an open general living area outside. The furnishing was sparse, and there was no plumbing; water was brought in buckets from the collective faucet down the street. A woman showed me to the room farthest from the door from which I'd just seen three people emerge. As I passed, several people sitting in the courtyard greeted me with sleepy murmurs: "Buenas Noches."

Most of the small room that I entered was taken up by the dead man's corpse, which was lying under a white cloth in a simple wooden casket. Large bouquets of sweet-smelling white gladioli and four white candles burning in metal stands surrounded the coffin. Behind the whole assembly was a dark velvet curtain from which a crucifix hung. And immediately in front of the coffin, a powdered lime cross about three feet long had been drawn on the floor; small candles outlined this cross.

I sat down on one of the chairs ranged along the wall. Two women were already there. They paid little attention to me and continued conversing quietly. I overheard snippets of dialogue about the latest local scare—a mysterious hooded person called "El Encapuchado," who was apparently going about shooting people and stealing their bicycles. His most recent victim had been a young man from the *colonia* right next to ours.

A young woman carrying a tray full of cups brought us coffee. Time passed. Eventually both women left. I was alone then. I nursed the coffee that was too sweet for my taste and stared at the strange, amorphous lump lying there beneath the white sheet in the casket. Suddenly the abrupt entrance of about five young people—four young men and one young woman—broke the peace, and my deep absorption in somber thought. The members of the group seemed boisterous, even drunk. Two of the young men approached the coffin; brusquely uncovering Manuel's body, they gently touched his face and whispered to him. One young man crossed himself, and then the two rejoined the others who had already seated themselves next to me.

Loud laughter and joking followed. One member of the group, whose face looked vaguely familiar, said he'd seen me in the San Juan cemetery during the Day of the Dead; he asked why I had been there. As the joking continued, the same young woman who had served me before returned with more coffee and sweet rolls. She was not bothered by the raucous behavior of my companions; she even laughed along with them.

The one who had spoken to me, Alfonso, proceeded to tell me about the *difunto* Manuel. Since he and his buddy had uncovered Manuel's body, I'd been stealing glances at it; by this time I had grown accustomed to the sight of the dead man. But I was unprepared for the wave of sadness that swept over me when I realized that I'd known this man who was dead. Now, despite the gash in his head and his closed eyes, I recognized the señor that I passed occasionally at the base of the hill, down from my home. We'd never exchanged more than a few words, but he'd always given me a warm sleepy smile and sent me on my way with a very polite, "Que le vaya muy bien, señorita" (May it go well with you, Miss).

"Yeah, Manuel liked to drink," Alfonso informed me, heavy-tongued from his own recent indulgences, "but if he ever found you drunk, he'd always take care of you. But now," he added, as a wide grin spread across his face, and he tossed an arm in the direction of the coffin, "now, he's not going to be doing anything!" That broke everyone up into great guffaws of laughter.

Manuel's wake and funeral were the first such events I attended in Colonia San Juan. I remember that the wake went on until the early morning, and visitors came by the house, singly or in small groups, to pay their respects to the deceased and to his family. At first, I was quite surprised that behavior like that of Alfonso and his friends was tolerated at such mournful events; my own culturally formed sense of the awful seriousness of death was slightly shocked, yet also fascinated by such laughter and tenderness and horseplay with or around a corpse. Precisely the familiarity that Alfonso and his friends had had with Manuel dictated their ease with his dead body and his reputation: their laughter, their drinking, their boisterous behavior, their jokes.

Death happens to all of us, sure, but the way it is greeted and what it is taken to mean differ radically from place to place. Indeed, because they bridge attitudes toward, and relations between, the living and the dead, funeral rites have often been taken to offer a particularly telling view of core aspects of a given culture. In this case, in Oaxaca, funeral rites are the space where the popular ethical system and its related customs and social relations are dramatized in their most vital form. Taken in the broadest and most ideal of terms, in popular communities in Oaxaca, funeral rites operate as one of the most important means available to create the image of a collective whole. This collective whole—even if it is an ephemeral projection—involves establishing a unity of purpose between the living and the dead, as well as establishing or reinforcing a strong sense of local identity and social memory.

Death Performances

In Oaxaca, death raises the curtain on a social stage for the practical construction and dramatization of a moral community to which many of the living demonstrate a resolute commitment. Both *novenario* and Levantada de la Cruz followed most deaths I witnessed in Colonia San Juan, and although there were differences of detail in the ways these rites were practiced, that it was necessary to follow them was not in question. Some families could not in any way afford to bury deceased relatives, let alone host a *novenario* and Levantada, but they frequently appeared to defeat all odds by finding the necessary funds in the end. The emergence of the necessary resources time and again demonstrated many important features of the informal economy of the neighborhood; it also suggested that holding a *novenario* was widely seen as the "good" and "proper" way to mark the end of a person's mundane existence. When I asked about these rites, many people explained that the Raising of the Cross ceremony was a *buena manera* (nice way) to finish the *novenario*; it is also clearly considered a "nice way" to commemorate the anniversary of someone's death.

The testimony that something is "nice" or "right," however, does not begin to convey the force or importance that participation in such ceremonies often had in people's lives. What could compel so many community members to carry through with a full ten days of ritual activity, a period often requiring considerable economic expenditure and even sleepless nights of preparation, before hosting throngs of guests or spending several hours in prayer or other ritual activity? For a long while, the apparent urgency of such participation puzzled me. In time, however, I began to see that, in addition to the religious ends served by the *novenario* (the prayer for penance, the remembrance of the deceased as "one of the community of saints," and so on), these rites served to conjure up a context of heightened customary "traditional" ideal Oaxacan social interaction. Ritual had an ontological role; it was bound up with the very possibility of being, both individually and collectively. Special ritual language, highly coded modes of behavior, and many other nondiscursive ritual contents served to provide a context within which a collective narrative of experience could accumulate around the death event. Ultimately, this narrative served to organize individual perceptions; it conferred a sense of communal belonging on participants that overrode—if only for a limited time—personal interests and instrumental goals.

There were many striking cases of voluntary—and often spontaneous—neighborhood cooperation in the context of funerals in Colonia San Juan that contradicted the realities of conflict and tension prevailing in other spaces of social interaction. For example, when Manuel was killed, many people in the neighborhood joined resources and forces to ensure that, despite the tragic accident that had killed him, he met a "good" end. At the time that he was hit, Manuel was fifty-nine, half-blind, and an unemployed widower with four grown children. Manuel's married daughter, Concepción, her husband, and their two children, as well as one of Concepción's brothers—Manuel's younger son—lived with him in the *colonia*. Although he was known to be an alcoholic—rumor had it that he had been drunk when he was struck—Manuel had been well liked; he spent much of his time strolling up and down the steep streets of Colonia San Juan, where he frequently stopped to chat with neighbors and *compadres*. *Colonia* residents appeared to be very sad that Manuel had been killed, although they seemed to accept the death rather matter-of-factly; more disturbing than his death appeared to be the violent manner in which he had died.

Two days after the accident, a short article, accompanied by a photographic close-up of Manuel's dead body, complete with head injury, appeared in the local paper, *El Observador*. This was not unusual, for such yellow (*amarillista*) journalism or sensational *Policiaca* sections of the city newspapers regularly report on the latest crimes and accidents in the region, in as much grisly detail as possible. Entitled "Dramática muerte de un padre de familia al ser atropellado" (Dramatic death of a father upon being hit), the article reported that Manuel had sustained massive injuries to the head, as well as numerous fractures elsewhere. As is customary for all persons who die in a violent manner in Oaxaca, Manuel's body was taken by ambulance to the Red Cross amphitheater in the center of town for an examination (*necropsia de rigor*); while there, his body was formally identified by his daughter, Concepción. The article announced that because of the violence of Manuel's death, the case had been officially adopted by the state Procuraduría General de Justicia; as far as I know, however, nothing ever came of the investigation.

A neighbor, doña Isabel, told me that Manuel's immediate family did not have the means to cover all the expenses of the funeral and other related events—an amount equal to about U.S.$200, or forty times the minimum daily wage. Although Manuel's brother-in-law, another *colonia* resident who ran a successful contracting business, could have afforded to foot the cost of the funeral, as a Jehovah's Witness he was not willing to sponsor a Catholic ceremony. (Over the course of my time in Oaxaca, however, I did see that Jehovah's Witnesses and other non-Catholics were quite willing to attend—and demonstrably participate in—certain aspects of Catholic funerals.)[1] Consequently, doña Isabel and others in San Juan, particularly members of the the Legión de María, a Catholic women's group, assumed financial and practical responsibility for the organization of this funeral for "a soul in need." A collection to gather the necessary funds was taken up the day after Manuel's death; his immediate family contributed what they were able. Doña Isabel, who was also one of Manuel's "first-order" *comadres*, paid for the funeral mass, while money collected from the neighborhood was enough to cover the remaining costs: the coffin, the cemetery plot, the hiring of a bus to transport bearers and body to and from the graveyard, the rental of enough chairs from the local Club de Leones (Lions Club) to accommodate guests who arrived at the house during the *novenario*, as well as flowers, candles, and the food, drink, and cigarettes offered after the burial and after every nightly prayer session, and the special *tapete* made for the Levantada ceremony. A core group of women, composed for the most part of Legión members, were regularly present during the *novenario*: these women took turns leading the prayers; they shared the labor of preparing and serving the food, coffee, and hot chocolate, and took care not only of the cemetery arrangements but of the hiring of the *tapete* maker. Members of this group also asked Cuauhtémoc's deacon, don Reynaldo, to give a special mass on the ninth night of the *novenario* before the Levantada ceremony. The job of *rezador* fell to doña Carolina, an older woman known to be well experienced in such prayers.

Every evening during the *novenario*, doña Carolina led prayers in the family house; members of the neighborhood chapter of the Legión de María, including me—for I had recently joined the organization—accompanied her. The prayers took place in the room where Manuel's body had lain during the wake. We stood before the cross of lime and the candles on the dirt floor and read Scriptures, recited the rosary, and sang. After each session of prayer and song, the group of those in attendance broke up; those who remained in the room were invited to gather on the patio for coffee, hot chocolate, and bread. Occasionally doña Carolina, who was involved in don Reynaldo's re-catechizing efforts within the New Evangelization campaign, used this brief interim period to initiate a conversation among those who stayed in the room. We were urged to reflect on the content of the passage of the Bible read during the prayer session. There were never any objections to such initiatives. The people who participated in these discussions were usually the older members of the group at the night's prayer session, often women in the Legión de María or Pláticas Bíblicas, the *colonia's* Bible study group. In these conversations, Manuel's death was related, in a direct and simple way, to God's teachings on death and sacrifice. It was obvious that these reflections served to layer the goings-on with an aura of sacredness and a sense of respectful solemnity; for this reason, despite the departure from what were more clearly "popular" rites represented by these discussions, they served to underline, rather than to work against, important aspects of the social drama going on throughout the *novenario*.

I soon observed that Manuel's death was the occasion for a compelling enactment of idealized interpersonal relations, relations that were at odds with the expressions of envy, bad feeling, and self-interest often in evidence in San Juan in any situation of social interaction—whether sacred or secular, formal or quotidian. It was as though a funeral provided an occasion for community members to be swept up in a drama of their own making, a mise-en-scène whose plot and ending appeared to be understood by all participants. Thus, despite the fashion in which individual roles seemed to involve spontaneous and contingent behavior, the whole scenario was strongly structured by tacit consensus and expectation. In the case of Manuel's funeral rites, the occasion of his death allowed for a variety of interpersonal relations to be "resolved" and idealized emotions to be exhibited; thus one could witness enactments of fidelity to a father, "proper" neighborliness, the carrying out of *compadrazgo* obligations, demonstrations of self-sacrifice, and so on. Although outside the ritual context of this funeral neighbors could be seen to interact in a variety of other, less "desirable" ways—fighting, not speaking, backstabbing—it was clear that death provided the occasion for community members to dramatize for one another the script of moral ideals to which they aspired, despite their inability, in other spaces and on other occasions, to measure up to these ideals.

Not long afterward, another death—that of an elderly man—provided, more clearly still, a view of the broad stage on which community members enacted their "best selves." Well known in the parish as a *huesero* (bone setter, a specialization of local healers, or *curanderos*), don Wilfrido was the third person to die in the *colonia* during my fieldwork. I had first heard his name at one of the weekly Legión de María meetings, when someone had mentioned that a solitary old man who lived just up the street was very ill; he was refusing to eat and "waiting to die." He had no known family members. For twenty-five years, don Wilfrido had lived alone in the same tiny shack, which was constructed of rough sheets of tin on a skeletal wooden frame on property borrowed from another San Juan resident. When he fell ill, a number of women who lived on the same street began to share the task of bringing him food and monitoring his condition.

It was agreed at the Legión meeting that three of us should speak to Padre Claudio and ask him to visit Wilfrido to administer the last rites, which apparently the old man had requested. We hoped that the padre would be able to come the next day, since Wilfrido's condition was noticeably worsening. The women who had been taking care of Wilfrido agreed to share the job of getting him cleaned up the next morning for the padre's visit. When I arrived at the tiny *cabaña* the next day at the arranged hour, Wilfrido had been bathed in preparation for the priest's visit. The belongings in his home were very few—bundles of clothes and, as were customary in rural Oaxacan dwellings, odds and ends hanging on the wall and from the ceiling. Wilfrido was lying on the floor on a *petate* and covered by a dirty blanket. As the priest gave him his last rites, Wilfrido appeared to be very grateful: he prepared for absolution, and propped his frail, trembling hands on his sunken chest in a position of prayer.

Early the next day, as I descended the hill from the *colonia* into town, I was told that one of the women of the Legión had discovered that Wilfrido was dead when she brought him breakfast. When I went by Wilfrido's place that afternoon, preparations had already begun for the funeral rites. His body was laid out in a casket and surrounded by flowers; the owner of the lot where his shack stood had offered space in a partially constructed house on the same property for the wake and *novenario*. The Velatorio Popular of Oaxaca City had donated Wilfrido's coffin and, as was customary, had lent all the necessary wake accoutrements, such as candle stands, a crushed velvet screen, and the crucifix that hung from it.

María Zarate Aquino founded, in 1980, the Velatorio Popular, the only formal organization in the state that supports "popular" wakes. Sponsored by the government social welfare program Desarollo Integral de la Familia (DIF, Integral Family Development Program), the mission of the Velatorio Popular is to aid city residents who lack the necessary financial resources to bury their relatives. To this end, the Velatorio first surveys the family that is applying for aid; this enables the organization to determine the size of the subsidy required, a grant that may range from a small portion to the entire cost of the burial and the *novenario*—if the family is Catholic and wishes to hold one. (According to one Velatorio employee whom I interviewed, the Velatorio often helps poor families pay to transport their *difuntos* to their places of origin, where they will be buried "according to local rituals and ceremonies.") In the case of don Wilfrido, although the Velatorio Popular supplied some of the necessary props, the costs of the funeral rites were covered in a variety of other ways.

When I arrived for don Wilfrido's wake, my neighbors were just counting the hundreds of coins that had been discovered in a container buried beneath the dirt floor of Wilfrido's simple dwelling. Although many of the coins were worthless, thanks to the radical devaluation of the peso over the years, the stash still amounted to some 250,000 old pesos, which at the time, in 1990, was equivalent to about U.S.$60. This money was put toward the cost of Wilfrido's funeral, and the rest of the expenses were covered by contributions from the neighborhood. Every night, neighbors and acquaintances gathered at the site where Wilfrido had died to offer their time, their accompaniment in prayers, in *convivencia*, in preparing food, in serving *novenario* guests, or in washing dishes and cleaning up. We prayed, ate, and drank; we sat around and joked or gossiped; sometimes we said nothing at all. Each *novenario* session for this lonely old man lasted for several hours, and sometimes the *novenario* organizers did not leave for home until the early morning.

What immediately impressed me about the first death rituals I witnessed was how willingly neighbors organized themselves to help a member of the community meet a "good" death. Apart from the fact that funerals were financed through collective means, an extraordinary amount of energy and time were expended in preparing and attending the long series of funeral rites. This enthusiastic cooperative effort was usually undertaken by a core group of *colonos*—many of them *compadres* of the *difunto*. But others, too, went out of their way, sacrificing long exhausting hours to the funeral *novenarios* of both Manuel and Wilfrido. Wilfrido's case was particularly impressive, when one considered his relatively anonymous status within the *colonia*. Unlike Manuel, Wilfrido lacked both family and *compadres* who would otherwise be obligated to come to his aid. I wondered why people in the *colonia* were so readily prepared to organize a *novenario*—nine long nights of intense ritual prayer and *convivencia*—for an old man whom they barely knew and to whom apparently no one owed anything in terms of *compadrazgo* or other social obligations. It seemed ironic to me that Wilfrido had become a more integral member of the community once he was dead than he had been when he was alive. His highly marginal social status as a poor, elderly, "indigenous" man without family—one in extreme "need"—meant that his death allowed my neighbors to demonstrate an extravagance of altruistic sentiment and generosity. I saw women, especially, competing with one another to play martyr-like roles—making coffee, chocolate, or mounds of tamales; attending to participants; cleaning the site of the *novenario*; or staying up until the wee hours, often long after their husbands had left.

The spontaneous and pronounced manifestations of generosity and idealistic cooperation that I witnessed during the course of these funerals and in other similar ritual occasions might be regarded as a display of self-interest in that such acts of giving imply certain acts of reciprocity. Those who give shall also receive—in an appropriate and commensurate manner. But to reduce the meaning of these gestures of charitable extravagance to calculated moves in a series of strictly "economic" exchanges could lead us to miss other significant aspects of these rituals. For again and again, the sacrifices demanded at funerals served to illustrate how, during moments of crisis, residents in San Juan felt called on to pull together, and disagreements and disputes—if merely for the moment—were either forgotten or put aside.

In time, as I attended many more such events, I came to recognize that these ritual occasions were integral to the production and maintenance of an ideal, shared social space; while such ritually created spaces were clearly liminal in many respects, they continually reinforced the delicate web of relations among people by allowing favors to be repaid, and new links and new debts to be incurred. The particular ritual content and quality of the *novenario* also enabled the regular revitalization of "traditional" values, norms, and practices commonly considered to be important to collective welfare. Often such customs take on a uniquely material social force and weight.

The "Good" Death

The imperatives of social closure, harmony, and integrity that order the treatment of a *difunto* immediately after death continue through time, informing the content of subsequent ritual events that compose the funeral cycle. But these imperatives also pertain to the mourners. Thus on the final night of the *novenario*, the closing eulogy or commentary functions as explanatory narrative, which works, overtly, to smooth over conflicts that may exist among people closest to the *difunto*. The metaphors of sociality that surround the treatment of the dead have to do with principles of ongoing exchange between the community of the living and that of the dead; these are part of processes that work to ground a sense of local belonging.

People I interviewed frequently spoke about the *novenario* as a critical aid to the *difunto* at a time of special need. One does not simply pray in honor of the *difunto* at a *novenario*; the prayers of the community at this point are also believed to affect the fate of the deceased's soul by mitigating the severity of God's punishment of a person's sins. Thus many believe that the more people who pray at a *novenario*, the greater God's pardon. Similarly, my fellow Legion-árias instructed me that the proper and most effective way of reciting a rosary is slowly and "sincerely"; also, the potency of the prayers is accentuated if one kneels as one prays.

According to popular belief, not only can one beneficially affect God's treatment of the *difunto* in the afterlife with proper *novenario* prayer, but one's own punishment in the afterlife can also be mitigated. Accordingly, because I went so often to *novenarios* in the parish, I was told by a woman in San Juan, "God is going to love you very much." Attending a funeral and participating in prayer sessions—even merely visiting a *difunto*'s home—are among the good and noble (and not necessarily religious) deeds regarded as holding penitential value or benefit for a person in the eyes of God. In this context, one's behavior is believed to have a direct effect on the treatment that one will receive from God—whether one's fate is punishment in hell, atonement in purgatory, or the ascent to celestial reward in heaven.

Although largely abandoned or downplayed in modern official Catholic theology, a certain notion of indulgences is alive and well in popular Oaxacan religious ideology. Indulgences are regarded as something akin to merit points—actual days of remission—that one may earn to reduce the length of one's eventual period of penitence in purgatory. An example of an important divergence between popular religious beliefs and "official" Catholic doctrine, the idea that indulgences may be gained by or for the *difunto* contradicts the orthodox belief that a person's fate cannot be altered after death. Thus, in popular circles, the penitential period is commonly conceptualized in terms of a series of temporally circumscribed stages—nine days, then forty days, then a year. Each phase represents a new stage on the path to achieving final rest in heaven. Such popular notions of penitential progress follow rather systematic conceptions of a quid pro quo payment for evil deeds according to their severity. "Purgatory," one woman explained to me, "is like here in life when a person kills someone. He is put in jail for five or six years and then freed; it means he's then paid his sentence . . . one goes to purgatory to pay for his sins, and then the day arrives when he is released." Such comments suggest a vision of an afterlife that is an existential mirror of this one, in which one must "settle accounts" (*entregar cuentas*) for one's deeds.

On the face of it, the most "orthodox" and literal form of this account of inevitable sin and retribution through sacrificial "payment" defines life as one long preparation for death. One enters the world a sinner, stained by an original sin that has been passed from parent to child since the day that Adam and Eve were ejected from the Garden of Eden. Baptism is sometimes seen to wipe away this inherited legacy of sin, but then, once one's childhood innocence comes to an end, a life of unavoidable sin follows. As a consequence, anyone concerned about his or her own eternal life may attempt to "balance the scale" by various penitential means. These means include confession and *buenas obras* (good works), as well as practices or behaviors involving some sort of self-abnegation or sacrifice: going on a long pilgrimage, taking part in a devotional procession or prayer on one's knees, staying awake all night in a sacred context, and so on. (The custom of resting a cadaver's head on a brick is also designed to gain indulgences for the *difunto*; forbearance and physical duress, even after death, evidently "count.")

After a while, I realized that, in addition to counting, something else very important was going on in these ritual penitential activities; they were not merely a sort of spiritual "savings plan" for the next life. For these sacrificial, penitential practices testified to a widespread insistence on the reality and gravity of a moral economy in which actors, both mortal and supernatural, may change one another's fates. What one person does has an impact on other members of the community, whether living or dead.

When a person dies, the point in life at which death occurs is also an important counter in popular views of a "good" death. Structured by metaphors that tie the span of a life to social completion and closure, the "timing" of a person's death often has everything to do with how it is marked or commemorated. Thus when death seizes children or young adults—*angelitos* or those viewed as "unfinished" social beings—very often the funeral rites appear to be more like other, age-appropriate life-cycle rites, such as a birthday party or a wedding, than a funeral observation. A "good" death is thus defined not strictly by the form of the rites that attend it, but by the moral state of the person who has died. Death is "good" if a *difunto* has arrived at death in a state of moral harmony—that is, both "cleansed" of sin in the eyes of God (a precondition for salvation) and in good standing with family, friends, and others who go on living. If a person dies in some state of deficit, whether financial or relational, it is the duty of those who live to make up this lack, one way or another.

Thus although official Catholic teachings divide sins of thought and deed into categories—mortal (severe, deadly) or venial (minor, excusable)—according to popular religious views, what matters are not internal spiritual states or motivations but *deeds* or *acts*, particularly for others. Above all in the popular view, a person is called to the fulfillment of his or her responsibilities and obligations to family and an immediate social circle. Such fulfillment is spoken of using the verb *cumplir*, a word that comes to bear in a variety of important and, for the most part, *active* moral contexts: to do one's duty, to keep a promise, to observe a law, to serve a prison sentence, to reach a certain age. Leading a good "Christian" life in the popular sense means not only striving to keep oneself from sin or atoning for one's sins but, in the interests of maintaining healthy kin and social relations, helping to ensure that, through one's actions, others also have the opportunity to be absolved from sin.

For this reason, it is especially important that members of the family or community ensure that a *difunto* has received requisite spiritual aids (last rites, proper bodily care) and a proper funeral conforming to the general prescriptions of Catholic ("moral") doctrine. I was repeatedly told how important it was that the deceased receive a proper burial—"in the earth." If the body—and its subsequent treatment—spell out the *difunto*'s social identity and place in the community, then a death without a burial creates a contradiction, a disturbing void, a conspicuous lack of appropriate social closure. Thus although cremation is now approved by the Catholic Church in certain circumstances and it has become progressively less expensive than burial since the building of a crematorium in Oaxaca in 1992, in Colonia San Juan, turning bodies so quickly to ash is generally opposed quite vehemently.[2] One man's protest is typical: "After the resurrection the spirit has to find the body, and if there is no body, what can it return to?"[3] Burning the body is taken to contradict the divine and perceived "natural" model of an earthly burial set by Christ's burial in a tomb, as well as the cyclical model represented by the biblical axiom "ashes to ashes, dust to dust." Perhaps, in a context in which the metaphoric linkage of the soul's penitential journey with the process of decomposition is so strong, an act such as cremation, which accomplishes the sudden destruction of the *difunto*'s body—above all by human, rather than divine, agency—appears to be sacrilegious. Such speedy destruction of the material of the body could only bypass or circumvent the necessary periods of penitence, marked as they are by the withering of bodily remains and material connection to the earth.

When a *difunto* is cremated, however, the scattering of the ashes sometimes follows. One woman told me that when her non-Catholic brother died, the family complied with his desire to be cremated. But on the advice of a priest, they did not scatter his ashes over the ocean, as he had requested; instead, the family buried them in the graveyard. The woman explained that this placing of her brother's remains would help him find his body again "on Resurrection Day."

Although Catholic doctrine declares that from birth, one begins to prepare for death, such preparatory activity is taken to be particularly important in

Oaxaca as a person nears death. This is because dying "well" requires that one be morally and spiritually prepared for the event. As don Hugo put it: "A good death is when the person goes *en gracia de Dios* [with God's grace]." The manner in which a person dies is therefore critical in determining the well-being of the *difunto's* spirit. A "bad" death occurs in untoward circumstances such as a traffic accident or a murder, since the abruptness of the event would not have allowed the *difunto* to prepare spiritually by cleansing his soul of sin through confession or by ensuring that her relations with kin or friends are left in a good state. Such deaths are also considered "bad" for another reason: because they occur in the sphere of the "outside," far from the moral center of daily existence, they add extra suffering to the labors of the dead. As one informant explained, "A good death is when you die in your home [*en su lecho*]; a bad death is to go out [*salir a la calle*] and never return." As a result, the souls of those *difuntos* who meet death in a sudden or violent manner are thought to need special attention and aid from the living. One neighbor told me about the murder of the son of another woman in San Juan: somewhere outside Oaxaca, beside a river, the young man had been killed by his best friend. When the *tapete* was made, mourners returned to the site of the murder to collect earth for burial with the body, for the soul had to be retrieved and brought "home."

Such examples uncover a widespread belief that a "scattered" or fragmented soul marks a being that exists in a morally dangerous state. Typical of such a view was a commentary on organ transplants delivered by one middle-aged woman in San Juan: "It's not good because it leaves a person incomplete . . . if God sent us here as we are—complete—then complete we should remain." Her commentary reflects not only a particular set of rather orthodox religious views but also an insistence on the integrity of the social person; this is a sense of personhood that extends beyond the autonomous, biophysical individual, beyond the bounds of life or death.

To hold a *novenario*, to ensure that the proper rites are carried out for a "soul in need," is an obligation that the living owe the dead if the souls of the dead are to leave the earthly realm in a tranquil and "properly" oriented state. These rites help guarantee that the soul will eventually achieve peace and salvation or entrance to heaven. Friends and relatives repeatedly told me that they performed the funeral rites for reasons of respect—because of their emotional ties to the *difunto*, and because they wanted to carry out those duties expected of them in the community—as well as from a sort of concern for "preventive" social maintenance. Many of those I interviewed believed that a soul that does not or cannot "leave peacefully" is likely to bring mischief or real ill on those who have been left behind. Although it is impossible to measure the seriousness with which such ideas are entertained (after all, I was an interested and probably, often, a gullible listener), I occasionally heard mention of souls straining in purgatory or of malignant ghosts who came back to haunt the living. "Here for example," an elderly woman told me, "if you don't make someone his *novenario*, it's thought that he will come back to frighten people [*asustar*]. That's what a lot of people think . . . it's something really important, you see. Because that can happen." Many of these beliefs draw on a rich oral tradition in Oaxacan popular culture, including the legend of La Llorona. For this reason, Cuautémoc's priest, Padre Claudio, dismissed such stories as "superstitions." But *panteoneros* (grave-yard workers), whom I interviewed related a variety of stories of "witchcraft" (*hechicería*) that took place on the cemetery grounds and spoke of the little bundles of needles and cloth, the bodies of small birds in jars, and other oddities they had unearthed. "Superstitious" or not, such practices and stories attest to the continued belief in the potency of the dead.

On the whole, however, the bad luck brought about by the dead was not spoken of in such dramatic or colorful terms. The "bad" of a "bad death" appears more like a pall over the community of the living, a general sense of unease, a feeling that something is not quite right; certain relationships are out of order. The importance of the proper closure of interpersonal relations before death also explains why the ritual context is used for the resolution of social frictions or ruptures.

Some interviewees claimed that because they will (eventually) dwell in the realm of the sacred, *difuntos*, like saints, particularly after the first year of penance, may act as intermediaries, linking the living with higher supernatural beings like Christ and the Virgin Mary. And many Oaxacans with whom I spoke believed that the dead were aware of deeds performed by the living on their behalf. Not only could the dead affect the well-being of the living, but, reciprocally, the actions of the living could influence the fate or well-being of *difuntos* in the afterworld.

Throughout the entire series of rituals associated with the cult of the dead, the realm of the living is linked to the realm of the dead by reciprocal interactions. But equally important, in this context, is the reciprocity that takes place among the living, in which items exchanged include money, food, and other material goods, as well as the gift of one's participation in terms of praying, helping with the various practical tasks, or simply being present, "accompanying" both the living and the dead.

As a social passage that fuses the "here and now" of the living with the threads of experience and knowledge of past generations, death is implicated intimately in the constitution of social memory. During the *novenario* ritual cycle, an ideal, "traditional" Oaxacan setting is brought into existence and transforms the remembrance of the dead from an individual, private memory to a communal space of recollection. This memory is incorporated in tacitly registered relationships of place and is mediated by bodily metaphors of social connection and balance.

For each of the *novenarios* I attended, the circumstances surrounding the death were somewhat different, as was the ceremony, for how it unfolds depends on the age of the deceased, the relative wealth of the *difunto's* family, the composition of participants, and so on. Such differences are marked in the simplicity or elaborateness of the ceremony, the number of people in attendance, their clothing, the relative solemnity or emotional tone of the events, and the like. My own connection with and engagement in these events also varied, depending on my closeness to the family. But every event had this in common: an overarching ritual script allowed mourners to display to one another their personal commitment to a given set of ideals, and to reconfirm a moral vision of the social environment they were immersed in.

Despite the differences among various rites and ritual occasions, I observed that at each *novenario* mourners re-created a unique ritual "order," an ideal affirmation of authenticity and rootedness that stood at odds with many of the instabilities and flux in their social milieu. In and through their death rituals, *colonia* residents were able to project their desires for an enduring and traditional "community," an ideal space of belonging and relatedness.

The "Resolution" of Death

The experience of death in Oaxaca entails a drama of loss and reintegration involving a range of social actors in the *difunto's* immediate community of kin, *compadres*, friends, and acquaintances. Over the course of the nine days of the *novenario*, a particular texture of community is consensually created and reinforced. Everyone who enters the inclusive, highly symbolically elaborated, "popular" ritual frame is enfolded into the sacred space of the imaginary community by certain shared social and aesthetic practices. Ultimately, the values invoked in and by this sacred space serve to frame everyday reality for many residents. Thus the ritual strengthening of idealized community ties, the sharing of time and resources, and the acting out of beliefs that ensure the "correct" ordering of the world (including the proper treatment of the dead, their separation from and ongoing relationships with the living, and the orientation of the entire community toward a better future life) serve to construct important parameters in individual and group self-understanding.[4]

For example, I observed that the emotional behavior of community members at funerals varied, but in quite predictable ways. Of course, as is true anywhere, the feelings an individual experiences in relation to a death undoubtedly depends largely on the nature of his or her particular connection with the person who has died. Such individual feelings, however, are also always framed by certain community values and expectations, which prescribe (or circumscribe) appropriate emotions and behavior. In Oaxaca, typical and appropriate funereal behavior by those closest to the *difunto* was marked by a dramatic emotional tone that others read off and responded to in an equally predictable and more or less scripted manner. The ability to gauge and to participate in the emotional texture of the *novenario* was a critical dimension of the integration of participants into the overall ritual performance.

Thus, for the first few days of the *novenario*, death still hangs heavily in the air. The ambience at the deceased's home is typically hushed and solemn. Conversation during *convivencia* gatherings following the nightly prayer sessions is almost always centered on the deceased. Those present share reflections on the circumstances surrounding the person's death; they mull over the days leading up to the death and discuss the repercussions of the event for surviving family members and friends. Memories are revisited, stories traded, histories dissected. All this discourse contributes to the elaboration of a common reservoir of memory and interpretation; what had been individual, interior memories and intimate events now become exterior, social events. While individual accounts differ in nuance and meaning, and while tales about the *difunto* are sometimes contradictory, ultimately these conversations contribute to a work of collective interpretation and assimilation of the death event.

During the stressful period immediately following the death, *novenario* participants who were less close to the *difunto* focus their attention and care on the grieving relatives. This care provides the space for emotional release, as well as an exhibition of socially sanctioned "weak" and dependent behavior on the part of immediate family members (particularly women); during this time, the family becomes the object of intense affection and attention. Often members of the grieving family (both male and female) appeared to collapse emotionally: weeping and fainting, they compelled others to comfort them. To my Canadian eyes, such intense cathartic emotional outpourings seemed almost staged; where I grew up, reserve and stoicism were the norm, (mis)taken as signs of "inner strength." In Oaxaca, by contrast, emotionalism served to qualify and cement relationships. The need for others so readily exhibited by relatives of the *difunto* served to test and reaffirm the strength and reliability of their ties with those closest to them: kin, *compadres*, and friends. Such pronounced need, in turn, allowed others—typically women who were close to the chief mourners—to take on ideal caring and maternal roles.

A tone of exaggerated altruism thus presided over many interactions throughout the ten-day ritual period; mourners went out of their way to demonstrate solidarity and concern for one another through a particularly pronounced politeness. I was periodically caught off guard in such situations, for now and then unexpected truces were declared. Women who were not fond of each other might strive to treat each other with special sweetness, or a funeral would be taken as the occasion for an enmity to be set aside. One aspect of the "softening" of relations during the *novenario* period was marked by a unique speech pattern, which involved transforming several words into their diminutive forms, as well as the frequent use of *compadrazgo* terms and name diminutives—common discursive signs for respect and affection. Thus one woman would say to another, "Have yourself a coffee, *hermanita* [little sister]," or a man might be told, "Please have a seat over there, *compadrito* [buddy]." Such gentled discourse set these days aside; the emotional dimension of funeral rituals evidently required a different "affective register" than that found in most social situations. The language evoked by the drama of mourning was an "interior," domestic language; often used with children, such speech contrasted sharply with the crass sexual or scatological language play I often heard—especially among men—in the street.

But, like "street talk," the gentled speech of the *novenario* period represents a popular discursive form, quite distinct from the highly formalized and anonymous text typical of contemporary official or public speech. Such affect-laden ritual forms of speech contribute to the "setting aside" of the *novenario* time and space; within this space, a collective reality is organized and shared. Individuals are integrated into the space and partake of its softening, its rituals, its language. Gradually, over the course of the series of rites, the accentuated or extraordinary quality of mourners' speech and behavior dissipates, until, once again, ordinary concerns and reality intrude.

Thus as the *novenarios* I participated in moved toward their final days, the ambience at the *difunto*'s home notably relaxed; participants fell into different rhythms. Patterns of conversation became more casual and quotidian, less formulaic, more improvised. Mundane matters began to infiltrate the dialogue as neighbors discussed the weather, the latest illness to befall a nearby resident (health was always an especially popular topic of discussion), and so on. The focal center of the narrative—originally devoted exclusively to the *difunto*—diffused outward and became thematically heterogeneous. During the final days of the ritual, I often heard jokes and laughter as mourners conversed; although just a few days earlier, such joyful emotions would have been considered improper, exterior to the carefully crafted "interior" ritual space. Sometimes this late-arriving levity seemed a contrivance, an effort to relieve and reassure those of us gathered around a death that life, after all, does go on. As the *novenario* neared its end, even the *difunto's* relatives frequently behaved in a manner suggesting that they had recovered some emotional equilibrium. As the ceremonies drew to a close, the *novenario* resembled many other social get-togethers—so much so that I often had to remind myself that death had been the precipitating event for this particular gathering.

Attending *novenarios* also afforded me the opportunity for intense social interactions, which abated my own sorrow, as well as the feelings of loneliness and anxiety that especially accompanied my first months of fieldwork. Night after night, for a period of nine days, neighbors and acquaintances gathered in a *difunto's* home to pay their last respects. The crowd inevitably changed from night to night, or from event to event, but over time I encountered many of the same people. Consequently, the very special liminal space of funeral rituals allowed me to get to know certain *colonia* residents much better than I might have; my participation in these intimate rituals served to integrate me into the community in some important ways. I still recall certain nights vividly: how the heady scent of copal incense filled my nostrils, mixing with the perfume of the flowers; how my legs ached from kneeling on the hard floor and hypnotically reciting the prayers along with the other women; how my heart leaped to my throat each time I was asked to lead one of the mysteries in the rosaries.

Many of the activities of the *novenario* cycle's ten-day series of ritual events illustrate how a pronounced collective, communal spirit is actualized by ritual practices throughout the entire cycle: there are the gifts brought to the *difunto's* home by friends and neighbors, including money, flowers, candles, and items of food or drink; there is a cooperative organization of required tasks, a collective participation in the performance of religious rites, and a general accent on accompaniment and commensalisms—all symbolically adorned by the sharing of mescal, food, and flowers. A highly stylized but deeply felt "community of sentiment" is thus formulated that holds fast throughout the ritual period and dissolves only in the *novenario's* final days.[5] In this context, the way that repeated discussion of the *difunto* and his or her death is woven into the narratives of the participant's lives and of events in the neighborhood in general serves to articulate the ritually constructed world of the sacred with the world of everyday experience and understanding.

Such ritual practices thus serve as cultural mnemonics for the conservation of a certain aesthetic sensibility, part of a shared experience of life and death. Ritual words, senses, actions, and symbolic metaphors help ensure that participants will be able to muster certain "proper" ways of behaving toward one another. Arguably, these ritual practices operate on several levels—through the special tastes and odors, the particular modes of speech and prayer called for by the event, the timing, the intensity, the lateness of the hour, and the unusual activities. Such sensuous profusion, such out-of-the-ordinary experiences, help crystallize a certain configuration of feeling within the "popular" social environment: emotionalism, altruism, and communal affect are thus valued and consolidated.

But it would be a mistake to view such highly "moral" behavior as simply or unequivocally motivated by a unilateral altruism. For the details of the funeral events—what one contributed and where, who attended which evenings and for how long—were subject to careful scrutiny by participants; the strength of the network of tacit exchange obligation that ties certain community members to one another is thus always tested and measured in such events. For, to be sure, the nine days of ritual prayer are for the bereaved relatives as much as for the deceased person: the relatives receive emotional and practical support from the community; the *difunto* is "helped" by the petitional prayers of the participants. To offer such aid—indeed, more generally, to attend the *novenario*—is regarded as an important statement of friendship or esteem for the *difunto* or the bereaved. Such a sacrifice of time and resources in honor of the deceased and his or her family tacitly commits them to a reciprocal sacrifice. When Beatriz's neighbor lost her husband, Beatriz spent the next three days in succession at the widow's house. When I asked her the reason for this gesture of friendship—for the widow was neither a *comadre* nor a close friend, Beatriz explained that she felt obligated because the previous year, when her son had died, the newly widowed woman had made a similar gesture of support.

At first it was difficult for me to understand such fervent preoccupation with an exact and commensurate reciprocity. But when I began to think about this concern with "balance" in relation to other local beliefs surrounding death, I began to understand its importance. Nadia Seremetakis states that in funerals in the "traditional" Greek communities of Inner Mani, the unaccompanied death is a "bad" death, a silent and asocial death.[6] Similarly, one of the greatest fears that many of those I interviewed in San Juan confessed to me was to be forgotten, unaccompanied, not to have enough people to attend one's own wake or *novenario*; such impoverishment of company at the point of death would mean, I was told, that one would pass from life without the intercessions of the living, without their prayers for clemency on one's behalf. Many also suggested that observing strict reciprocity in the attendance of *novenarios* was a good thing— even in situations where there are no strong ties of kinship or affection. Thus, for example, the presence of a particular woman in San Juan, notorious for her rude treatment of her neighbors, at several *novenarios* and other religious gatherings in the parish, was interpreted by some of those neighbors as her way of ensuring that others would attend her *novenario* when she or a member of her family died. "According to our beliefs," insisted doña Perla, when I asked her about this woman, "if we don't go to accompany a wake or a *difunto*, when it's our turn, no one will accompany us."

People's manifest concern for conspicuous participation in death-related occasions appeared, in the end, to be inseparable from a larger set of ideas about reciprocal exchange within the local moral and aesthetic economy, where personal and symbolic sacrifice is part of a broader ritual system working toward a kind of social equilibrium or the maintenance of values and practices that prioritize the interests of the socially idealized, unified collectivity. Participation in popular ritual settings thus enabled an invocation of certain "authentic" feelings and behaviors of communalism and social harmony, values widely associated with the poor social classes and popular culture in general.

For this reason, death rituals in Oaxaca—loaded as they are with critical moral overtones—are implicated in important processes of identity construction, in which adherence to certain ritual practices becomes a reference point for the assertion of the ethical superiority of the poor (*los pobres*). In Colonia San Juan, residents participated in popular death rites for both collective and individual reassessment of their circumstances. Sometimes participation in death rites served to both project and cement group feelings of strong community loyalty and sentiment—an archetypal example of what Emile Durkheim called "conscience collective." At other moments, acting to enable a *difunto's* "good death" might offer a reference point against which a participant might assess his or her own moral worth or that of others. Funeral rites also offered the occasion for individuals or families to distinguish themselves from others; sometimes a relative or a family lavishly "splashed out" on food, flowers, or funeral decorations, or a particular individual energetically "martyred" herself by sacrificing significant resources or time in a given ritual setting.

Ritual and Formulations of the "Popular Community"

Typically, social boundaries are reflected or constructed by the selective participation in or observation of particular customs or ritual events. For example, having one's child baptized is a statement of affiliation with the Catholic Church or with moral, Christian society in a very general sense; it is a rite observed by almost all urban Catholic Oaxacans of all classes. However, holding a (supposedly Catholic) *quinceaños*, a coming-out party celebrating a girl's fifteenth birthday, is traditionally the privilege of only middle-class or wealthy families, who use this festival ritual to launch their daughters in society. The *quinceaños* ceremony therefore serves as a kind of declaration of real (or pretended) wealth or of a desired affiliation with mestizo society (with all its positive connotations). But these days, many people of elevated status forgo the *quinceaños* celebration, viewing it as a "traditional" custom that does not fit with their actual—or desired—social status.[7]

In a similar fashion, I saw Oaxacans sometimes compete with one another in terms of the lavishness of the funerals they sponsored. As elsewhere in the world, the expenses involved in funeral events can vary considerably—the cost of just the coffin can be highly variable. Although families who elect to have a funeral parlor take care of the arrangements for the wake and *novenario* are typically among the better off, it remains the case that some people simply lack sufficient space to accommodate the large number of mourners who may arrive at the family home. In these cases where the family is poor, the municipal Velatorio Popular (which supplied Wilfrido's coffin) can be called on to help. The Velatorio Popular supplies the requisite space and equipment at a cost that is much lower than that charged by most funeral parlors. And a special Instituto Mexicano del Seguro Social (IMSS, Mexican Institute of Social Security) *velatorio* for municipal workers and their relatives, where I attended three wakes, provides the same facilities. In my experience, although, in form and matter, wakes, regardless of location, were the same in almost every aspect, the atmosphere of *velatorios* or of funeral homes contrasted strongly with the intimate ambience of family homes. And opting for services such as embalming for the wake or cremation instead of burial is not an alternative open to members of the poor, popular classes. "Almost all those who are cremated here [in Oaxaca] are the rich [*los ricos*]," I was told by a young man I met in the cemetery of San Martín Mexicapan. "The poor person [*el pobre*] always prefers to bury his dead."

Accordingly, although the funerals of upper-class Oaxacan Catholics are broadly similar to Manuel's or Wilfrido's, they typically differ from a popular funeral in the elaboration of details. For example, the event may be orchestrated by a prestigious funeral agency such as Nuñez Banuet, which, in addition to housing and servicing the wake (or, if the family prefers holding the wake at home, providing all the necessary supplies: curtains, candle holders, flower vases, and candles), often arranges for an announcement of the funeral to be broadcast over the radio or published in the newspaper, and sends out *esquelas* (invitations) to selected mourners. Funeral parlors keep their doors open for public inspection and are often fronted by glass windows, through which coffins for sale are displayed. Thus it is not difficult to distinguish which establishments are the more expensive and therefore likely to be patronized by wealthier families (figure 4.1). When a well-off person dies, an expensive wooden or metal coffin is typically selected and displayed at the funeral mass, which may be held

FIGURE 4.1 An (*above*) upper-class and a (*below*) "popular" funeral parlor in Oaxaca City.

at one of the more prestigious churches in the city—San Felipe Neri, Sangre de Cristo, or Santo Domingo, where the cost of such private masses is considerably higher than elsewhere, and not available to just anyone.[8] Special church decorations or a choir may embellish such a service. A real hearse may be hired for the burial (a luxury unheard of in Colonia San Juan); also, many people are likely to be present because of the *difunto*'s typically more extensive circle of social and personal influence, and more of the mourners will be dressed in black. The behavior of those in attendance also tends to be more restrained than that of members of the popular classes at funerals. A priest rather than a *rezador* customarily accompanies the cortège to lead prayers, and an ensemble of musicians at the gravesite is a more probable feature. Large expensive floral wreaths, each bearing a ribbon with the name of its donor, are likely to be among the flowers carried by mourners; these may be left standing, ostentatiously, over the grave after the burial.

Where a person is buried is also typically intrinsic to one's social class. The oldest families in Oaxaca, which are also some of the wealthiest, are buried in the Panteón General (also known as the Panteón San Miguel), which therefore has the reputation of being the cemetery "for the rich," even though members of very poor families are also buried there (figure 4.2). Indeed, the northwestern corner of the cemetery has a small, barren section, about the size of a tennis court, called the Fosa Común (Common Grave), where unidentified or "unclaimed" dead are buried.

The Panteón General and many of the other older city cemeteries no longer have space for new graves. Families can usually overcome this constraint by burying their dead in plots already occupied by other relatives. Officially, cemeteries allow this practice only if at least seven years have passed since the burial of the previous *difunto*. In such circumstances, the grave is reopened; the bones of the last *difunto*, once exhumed, are disposed of or placed in the new casket; and the grave is covered once more. This practice is made easier if the family owns an underground crypt—not an uncommon sight in any graveyard, and especially typical of wealthier families. Often these crypts quite literally contain the bodies of members of one family several generations deep. Otherwise, if the members of a given family have one or more desirable gravesites in a cemetery, they are usually able, even when they do not posses such a crypt, to keep all their dead together. I have seen, in the Panteón General, for example, five to eight members of one family next to one another. There, remains of *difuntos* are sometimes removed from tombs and then "reburied" in one of the *nichos* found in the walls of the cemetery; the Panteón General is the only graveyard to have such wall crypts. This may be because an earthquake struck Oaxaca on 14 January 1931, resulting in considerable damage to the graveyard. Many of the

FIGURE 4.2 The Pan-
teón General: (*above*) an
overview of the cemetery
and (*below*) a tombstone
from the older section of
the cemetery.

niches were broken, and human remains spilled out into the cemetery, causing a cholera scare. Since that disaster, burying someone directly in the niches has been prohibited, but after seven years bones may be removed from the earth and stored there.

In addition to such differences in the place, style, and expense of funeral rites, most "upper-class" mestizo Catholics dispense altogether with the *novenario*, including the Levantada, for these are rites with strong folk or popular associations. If wealthy families do observe the *novenario*, it is usually in the form of special paid masses, dedicated to the deceased at one of the more prestigious city churches. As with funerals, notification of these special masses may be made in the newspaper or on the radio.

Most of the funerals I participated in had to do with people connected in some way with the residents of the parish of Cuauhtémoc. As a result, those attending the funerals tended to belong to similar socioeconomic backgrounds. Although it is not unusual for a poor person to attend the wake or funeral of a wealthy individual, in my experience the opposite is rarely seen, reflecting the fairly closed social circles in which Oaxacans of different classes customarily move. The poor people I interviewed on this subject typically had quite a lot to say about the ways that wealth mapped onto distinct funereal practices and moralities. For the poor, morality became a way to describe and make sense of socioeconomic differences. Their value system, which associated wealth with insincere faith and lack of a moral, communitarian spirit, turned the relative weight of being rich or poor on its head and plainly articulated the boundaries of the popular moral community. This distinction between the rich and the poor was revealed in informants' explanations of the differences between their funerals. I was told, for example, that the rich never hold *novenario* prayers in the home because they do not know how to *convivir* (live together, socialize, or get along) and that the wealthy—considered incapable of expressing "authentic" grief—sometimes hire professional *llorones* (weepers) for their funerals. One individual explained the distinction in stark terms: "Those who are cremated are usually the rich. The poor always prefer to bury their dead... rich people have fewer beliefs." Several especially resonant ideas associating material wealth with a depraved ethical sense are elaborated in the words of another San Juan resident, don Oliverio:

> The *humilde* [poor] class will always go with their candles, with a little *cooperación* [bit of money], perhaps a few flowers, but they always go with an open heart, they go in fulfillment of a debt to the person who goes to the *más allá*. Those in the middle or the bourgeois classes give their presence only a little while—one or two hours and then they just leave those who are mourning.

The poor, no. The poor remain, they stay awake the whole night and are still there when dawn arrives, and the next day are still present with the same feelings and sentiments. . . . Usually for a rich person, people go to see him for his money—Mr. So-and-So died—look what he had! One, two, three wives can be attributed to a wealthy man. Meanwhile, for the poor person, no—just one wife. It will always be just like that—people will go to see a rich man for his money and his possessions. That's the difference between a rich and poor person's funeral. But there'll always be more people at a poor man's funeral.

Don Oliverio's words speak clearly of the moral impoverishment of material wealth—a popular rhetoric that might be viewed as a fair balancing of personal resources. Also apparent is the view that being wealthy connotes an absence of compassion; to be wealthy means to lack an affective sensitivity or the capacity to *feel* as the poor do. Such distinctions between self and other were also commonly extended to categories of religious affiliation. For example, when asked about her sense of obligation in attending a neighbor's funeral, doña Isabel stated, "At least in the Catholic faith one feels obligated to go and *cumplir*, to go and accompany the bereaved as much as the *difunto*." Doña Isabel also offered an extended and somewhat ambivalent commentary on the moral superiority that may be claimed by members of the popular classes:

It's like I told you, these are the customs of our ancestors. With you [meaning the United States and Canada], it's more civilized. There's a lot of difference in that sense; you're not going to waste your time going to the graveyard because the person's already dead, you feel sad but you don't go to the graveyard to see him, you don't express your pain in those civilized places, as you say—"now he's dead, he's not coming back"—and you leave him. But us, no, we still hold on to that memory for years on. Yes, there is my great-great-grandfather who used to speak to me; now I go to see him. And there is my grandfather. And in this way you remember your family; that remembrance [*recordatorio*] is now years old. But over there [in the United States or Canada], no; because over there when something is finished, it's finished—it's just like the new songs; when the new one comes, the old ones are just as quickly left.

Doña Isabel's rhetorical characterization of "civilized" society reveals a critical, and common, perception of her social milieu as one that lacks refinement. Yet her apparent self-effacement is tinged with a hint of sarcasm. Death was not part of the everyday experience of people living in such "civilized," "modern" places as my home; death was something that was truly *felt* only in a place like Oaxaca, where the luxuries of modern life that buffer the painful blows of death are in short supply. Life "over there" (outside Oaxaca) was a frightening, morally wanting world of rabid consumption, where connections to people, and the preservation of their memories, are likened to the latest fashionable commodities in their superficial transience and disposability. Isabel's statement declares her awareness of both realities and implies an anxiety about some of the ways that her own life and modes of memory might be changing.

Her statement of her views is important, for it represents a claim to the moral value of "tradition" in the social field as embodied by the dead; the invocation of the memory of the dead is the particular concern of those, like doña Isabel, who are able to appreciate their value in the fullest sense. According to Isabel, the dead are not symbols of past experience in the sense of things forgotten that can have no influence or bearing on the present ("now he's dead, he's not coming back"); instead, those who have died are called back onto the stage of everyday exchange and interaction, and take part in the construction of shared remembrances and a profoundly registered sense of social connection and belonging. The behavior of Alfonso at Manuel's wake suggests that he felt the impact of the death of someone he had known all his life, someone beside whom he had grown up. But he said good-bye to Manuel in a manner consistent with the teasing, playful manner with which he would have addressed the old man if he were still alive. Manuel's death for Alfonso was not unthinkable, fearful, something to be repudiated at all costs. Death had happened, as it inevitably would happen again to someone else, or to him—perhaps even arriving when it was least expected. It had to be faced, greeted, and treated with respect, and the person who died appropriately greeted and remembered.

If I compare the Oaxaca of today (2002) with the Oaxaca of the first years of my fieldwork (1989, 1990), it is clear that, on the whole, fewer resources and less time are devoted to holding a "proper" *novenario* now than ten or twelve years ago; relatives are also more and more frequently widely separated geographically from one another. Some may work or study in other cities or in the United States for months at a time. Nevertheless, what is taken to constitute a "good" death by the people I lived among remains, overall, the same. Oaxacans of the popular classes, despite greater urbanization and increasing migration and other pressures of globalization, remain concerned to remember and send off their dead in ways that suggest love, deep honor, and respect.

CABO DE AÑO

The first year after a death is often commemorated by another ceremony; at this point the soul of the *difunto* is usually considered to have completed its earthly wandering. From now on, the *difunto's* soul may be called on, like the saints, to intercede occasionally in earthly affairs. And from this point forward, on every Day of the Dead, family members will be expected to observe the appropriate ritual offerings and commemorations. Like the Day of the Dead celebrations, and unlike the funeral, the *cabo de año* is not, typically, a terribly somber occasion, although it may be a time when friends and relatives do feel some grief.

For several months in the spring and early summer of 2002 I was in Oaxaca conducting new fieldwork and finishing a draft of this book, when I heard about a *cabo de año* ceremony for a young woman I had known. I stayed in Oaxaca long enough to attend this second Levantada. The following is from my field notes:

It was a beautiful way to end my time in Oaxaca this summer, if a sad one. Not long after arriving in the spring, I made a point of visiting my *compadres*, Lulu and Samuel, in Cuauhtémoc; they had lost their adult daughter, Gisela, a young mother of three, the year before. When I saw them, they told me about the Levantada ceremony they were planning to commemorate Gisela's *cabo de año*—right around the time I planned to return to Montreal. I postponed my departure so that I would be able to attend the ceremony.

The night of the Levantada I arrived at the mass at Xochimilco late, just as people were coming out of the church. We walked along Azucena Street, then straight up the hill to the family house. The evening was cool, crisp. I was struck by how much cleaner the air is in San Juan than in other parts of Oaxaca. As we passed by Isabel's house, I popped in to visit. She was in fine form, although she insisted, as always, that appearances deceive; inside, she told me, she is worn out; from time to time she feels that her heart leaps into her mouth, and it is as if she's on the brink of death. I tried to be sympathetic, but eventually I had to laugh at her serious face, and she broke into a smile.

Around nine o'clock I accompanied Isabel up the hill to Gisela's family's house, just a minute away. Tables had been set up outside on the street, and a provisional kitchen—fire, pots, and cooking utensils—in the neighbor's yard. I saw many people that I knew or recognized—doña Victoria, Judith, Candelaria, those strange, very pious sisters, the son of one of them, that woman with the thick, dark shiny braid that always hangs neatly down to the small of her back.... Cars were parked perpendicularly so that they blocked off the street; here kids played. The scene was peaceful and soothing; I suddenly recalled neighborhood gatherings of years ago.

As soon as I arrived, I climbed the steep stairs and went into the house to look at the *tapete*, made earlier that day by two brothers in the neighboring *colonia*. I stayed for the end of one of the rosary sessions. Afterward we went outside to sit at the long table there and to have chocolate and bread. Javier,

Gisela's brother, was serving, and came by to say hello. He told me about his little boy, his new job doing something for a cable company, and that his wife is pregnant—around seven months from the look of it—with their second child.

While we were sitting there talking, a group of youth arrived with guitars. They entered the house to sing "Las mañanitas" in front of the *tapete*. Neighbors came and went. Tomás's wife, now an *abuelita* [grandmother]—her son married Marisol, Gisela's little sister—carried her sleeping grandson in her arms. She came over to say hello and told me how nice it was I'd come. I told her how much the gathering reminded me of times ten years earlier: how all the neighbors and their *compadres* got together—Tomás, Uriel, Raymundo, Lázaro, Juan. . . . We talked about Lázaro and his jokes, the *mezcales*, how the men all just sat there and talked and laughed while the women labored hard getting all the food ready, and then served it long into the night.

Was it she, or was it I, who started talking about don Wilfrido's death, how we'd all pitched in to give the old man the death he merited? I realized suddenly how extraordinary such gestures were: the outpouring of generosity and genuine good will that seemed to deny pain and divisions among *colonia* residents. As we talked and I mused on the changes that death and the passage of time had wrought in the community, it occurred to me that such pulling together around don Wilfrido's funeral also denied the obvious signs that people's lives were changing in fundamental ways, that, increasingly, *colonos* were tied up with other things, with goals and desires that were frequently at odds with such communal ritual observance.

Tomás's wife filled me in on all the details. Lázaro was now on the "Other Side," in Chicago; having escaped his debts, he would certainly never return to San Juan. Her husband, Tomás, the mechanic, was apparently well, although his back bothered him—"all that heavy lifting," she reported. But Uriel, Laura's husband, who was also a mechanic, has become so crippled with arthritis that he can hardly walk. Juan became a teetotaler, and has been heavily involved with Alcoholics Anonymous; only Raymundo, from all reports, was pretty much the same as he used to be.

Yet not one of them was there that night; the crowd was conspicuously female. Why? I wondered. Where had the others gone? Were these *convivencias*, these gatherings of generosity, mutual caring, and support, also passing away?

We went inside to watch the Levantada ceremony. It was nearly 11:00 p.m. I perched on the rough cement steps, observing, while a middle-aged woman—she seemed familiar, but I couldn't place her—orchestrated the goings-on, her Levantada guidebook in hand.

I was taken back a decade. We sang the hymns I remembered: "La Muerte, dónde está la Muerte," "Resuscitó, resuscitó, resucitó, hallelujah." Many people held hymnbooks, although just about everyone seemed to know the words anyway. Those of us gathered there in Gisela's memory were almost all women—except for one of her sister's sons, Samuel, and Paco, doña Saturnina's son, who was directing the praying along with Valeriana, Isabel's unmarried daughter.

The *tapete* was extraordinary, a beautiful representation of the Virgin of Solitude; the filigree pattern on her robes had been done in glittery gold paint, the head done *en bulto* (three-dimensional form), the face rendered delicately: alabaster white skin with fine features.

Susana and another woman scraped up the head first; it seemed a pity to watch all that laborious effort suddenly vanish. The right arm was collected by one *comadre*; the left arm by another; then the feet were scraped into the box, and finally, the heart. There were enough *madrinas* to collect the whole thing; they included Marisol and Xóchitl, Gisela's sister and her younger aunt. Marisol still looked quite young to me, maybe just twenty or so, but I noted that she had already assumed that true *ama de casa* look— rolls of fat along the sides of her stomach, the pained yet serenely placid pose that many women assume after they've married and had a child.

Gisela had had that look, too, when I last saw her alive—was that three or four years ago? Her picture was there on the altar. It showed her in full health, smiling; maybe it was taken before she had had the three kids. It was as I remembered her: vivacious, coquettish, conscious of her prettiness, her face fairly made-up. She was seventeen when I had first met her in San Juan. And then she had died in a hospital in Mexico City on her twenty-eighth birthday. It made no sense to me, such a flickering guttering of life.

How did everyone else make sense of Gisela's death? When I first heard from Javier in the market last summer, he had delivered the news matter-of-factly. I was dumbfounded, could only respond thickly—"What do you mean, she's *dead*?" I had gone up to Francisca's house the following Sunday; the black cloud that hung over the family was palpable. Samuel had moved so slowly, so heavily. Yet Lulu had taken her daughter's death even harder: her face had fallen inward from grief, black rings circled her eyes; her sorrow was a dark weight on her shoulders.

This year, not long after my arrival in January, I had spotted Samuel in his car, driving through the *centro*, and promised to come up for a visit. Not long afterward I'd seen Samuel's sister, Katia, and Xóchitl and Davíd on the street. Katia told me that they were going to the cemetery that Sunday, and so I arranged to go along. We had cleaned and tidied up Gisela's grave; we cleared the weeds growing among the plants that were Gisela's favorites, and lit the candles. The mood had been light, peaceful. Katia told me that the flowers we had brought were in Gisela's favorite colors. She and Samuel talked over changes that they wanted to make to Gisela's grave, including a bench to sit on right beside it—"like that other grave close to Gisela." I was struck by their pattern of speech: they were not talking about Gisela's grave really, but about her, about where she was. Gisela remained unmistakably alive, present; in important ways she was not really gone.

Now here we were, half a year later. Samuel remarked, out of the blue, as we were standing on the street just outside the Levantada, "The thing is, Kristina, you remember the one who's gone, with sadness, but with joy, too." I asked him how he was feeling. He said okay, "almost recuperated. Although one never recovers from something like that completely." "But Lulu," he said, was still sad, "still carried that *tristeza* around her heart," her eyes.

Compared to ceremonies I remembered from the old days, the Levantada proceeded fairly quickly; there were no long prayers, although we did sing the standard hymn about the Santa Cruz: "Alabemos y enzalcemos, a la Santísima Cruz." The mood wasn't too heavy; it seemed less thickly sacred than other events I remembered, the air was less intoxicating, the sweet scent of flowers milder somehow. Copal incense had been burned but only briefly. Stark fluorescent strips shone above, lighting up the entire room.

Although much had changed in ten years, much was also the same—there was the same spirit of support, caring, love, respect among those present: almost all of whom were women, young, old. The understanding of what this event was about was tacit, unambiguous. Children rambled around, weaving in and out of the seated adults. Everyone sang, knew the prayers. They focused on the commemoration of Gisela's death. But the event was not about Gisela, so much as it was about the community of those present—those who had known one another for years and years, had seen one another through marriages, infidelities, children, tragedies, joys, celebrations, births and deaths. . . . What we communicated with our presences there was unsaid, but it felt clear, palpable. And I was a part of their lives, too, a part of their memories—maybe not a particularly important part but present nonetheless.

When the *tapete* was completely scraped up into the buckets, these were placed at the edge of the place where the sand carpet had been. Small candles were moved to the center of the space and arranged in the form of a thick cross. The crucifix was brought out. Xóchitl held it while family members stepped forward to cross themselves before it, and then to kiss the feet of the Christ figure. Lulu went up, then Samuel, Javier, Rebeca. . . . The crucifix was taken to Teresa, Gisela's grandmother, who was seated in her wheelchair off to the side of the room. Then Lulu's sister crossed herself, followed by the *comadres de la cruz*, and then the rest of the neighbors, until everyone present had participated.

And then it was over. The *rezadora* made some final touchups to the placement of the cross, while I said good-bye to those who were still in the room—Laura's daughter (who looked sad, worn down), my goddaughter Veronica. Then we moved outside, where I bid farewell to those who were seated at the table, drinking hot chocolate and coffee. Finally, I said good-bye to Samuel, Lulu, Katia, Pepe, and his wife, the kids—all of them. As I looked around, a wave of nostalgia—which was not a sense of sentimental detachment but a deep missing of being in the community—washed over me. So much had changed in all our lives, yet nothing had.

I started down the street toward the *centro*.

CONCLUSION

Not only do Oaxacan death rituals display the sensuous, mimetic, and performative character of popular religiosity, but, like other popular ritual practices, they also allow participants to construct a moral identity that is largely independent of the church. To be sure, the discourse of the New Evangelization did penetrate local ritual contexts in the form of church agents and "evangelized" Catholics such as doña Carolina, who led various prayer sessions and other funeral rituals. Nevertheless such interventions are a far cry from an imposition on or usurpation of the popular significance of death. Participants in these popular rites make use of certain Catholic ritual customs, including confession, the last rites (Unción de los Enfermos), the funeral mass, and other aspects of the funeral and burial, but in ways that specifically harmonize with the orientations of popular eschatology. In particular, this popular theology of death endowed the account of Christ's Passion and Resurrection, as well as a host of associated ideas of penitence and salvation, with a special collective social significance. These rites demonstrate an underlying "experiential script" that defines and organizes the ritual contents into a logical, progressively unfolding form, a narrative that imitates and makes concrete the ongoing pertinence of Christ's death, suffering, and resurrection to the community of believers. Death thus contributes to an ongoing social life; it reaffirms and extends local social memory, and renews and builds new networks of exchange and interdependence among neighbors, family, friends, and generations. Popular death rituals as I observed them also involve a solidifying of rural–urban ties, for it was customary, even for migrants, for family members to make a strong effort to return home for the funeral of a loved one.

It could be argued, then, that Oaxacan death rituals help build and perpetuate an awareness of the "local" and, further, that the ritualization of death in Oaxaca involves residents not only in the enactment of "popular selves," but in an entire popular "imaginary community" whose values enable them to deal meaningfully with the contradictions and ambivalences of contemporary urban, individualist, and, for many Oaxacans, increasingly migrant global life. Popular rites thus enact a redemptive scenario; idealized aspects of the self and the community are reasserted within ritual contexts that permit them to live on, for the moment at least, along with the personal ties and obligations they demand—despite a host of pressures toward change.

The most significant and elaborate of the cult of the dead rituals in Oaxaca is the Day of the Dead. The celebration of El Día de los Muertos may be seen as an extension of the series of funeral rites, for these rites necessarily precede those of the Day of the Dead. It is widely believed, for example, that the soul of a particular *difunto* cannot return to visit for the festival until its "immortal journey" is complete—that is, until at least a year has elapsed since the *difunto*'s death. On the Day of the Dead, the mournful atmosphere that surrounded the first funeral rites is replaced by gaiety, loud noise, games, *convivencia*, and the enjoyment of food and drink—pleasures that are to be shared among the living as well as with the dead. El Día de los Muertos is celebrated annually by Oaxacans in order to honor the dead of their particular households as well as the entire "community" of the dead. Specific dead are remembered and celebrated by each family, but the celebrations are done so concurrently that, in a sense, the dead are remembered collectively. The Day of the Dead thus represents the culmination of a process of socialization of the dead that is constituted concomitantly by ritual performances during the full funeral cycle. In this way, the finiteness and sterility of an individual mortality are denied—even, in Oaxaca, rendered nonsensical. On this day, the living join together to celebrate not just the community of the living but also the size and force of the community of the dead.

PART 3

Living the Day of the Dead

Todos iguales en este lugar; contemporaneous en la eternidad (Everyone is equal in this place; contemporaries in eternity).
—INSCRIPTION ABOVE THE MAIN ENTRANCE TO THE
PANTEÓN GENERAL, OAXACA DE JUÁREZ

I like this cemetery because it is free land. It doesn't have locks on any side. If I want to leave, I can leave at any hour, and go drinking with a friend, and then we can come back again. No problem. Here it's free, everything is free. . . . In the United States everyone belongs to the government, but here we aren't subject to anyone.
—RAFAEL F., PANTEÓN DE SAN MARTÍN, 13 NOVEMBER 1990

CHAPTER 5

Days of the Dead in Oaxaca

La Muerte es la salsa de la vida (Death is the sauce of life).
—COMPARSA PARTICIPANT, SAN AGUSTÍN ETLA, 8 NOVEMBER 1995

EVERY YEAR IN SEPTEMBER, posters advertising the *comparsa* of the Noche de Muertos, a masquerade associated with the celebration of the Day of the Dead, begin to appear in the city (figure 5.1). And before long, *pan de muertos*, bread that is shaped into human or skeletal forms, can be found for sale in city markets. At this time of the year, thrifty, forethoughtful urban residents begin to purchase and put aside candlesticks, chocolate, and other festival necessities in order to avoid the sharp rise in cost of these items as November approaches. Soon the tiny, intensely bright yellow flowers that proliferate in the Valleys of Oaxaca, especially in October and November, may be seen blooming at the edges of the city; these flowers are part of many popular *ofrendas* (offerings) placed on the altars for the dead. "Ah, ya vienen los Muertos," people will say to one another with a wry smile. By happy coincidence, mention of "los Muertos" does double service in such utterances, for los Muertos are both the dead and shorthand for the Day of the Dead. "The Dead are coming," indeed, and so, too, is the Day of the Dead, and it would be well, so the stories warn, for all to be ready.

For example, one day when I encountered an elderly woman in a cemetery, tending a grave, this is what she told me:

The day of Los Muertos was approaching, and a woman said to her husband, "What are we going to put out for your mother? Soon it is going to be the time to put out her *ofrenda*."

The husband replied, "Go and get a *mojada* of beef, and put it there on the table. And a glass of water, too. If she wants some water, fine, and if not, well that's fine too." He left the house then, to go and get drunk.

FIGURE 5.1 Posters advertising a "Tradicional Comparsa de Muertos" and a Halloween costume party, to be held in a local discotheque, in Oaxaca City.

The Day of the Dead came and went. That night, the man went out to get drunk and in the middle of the night he headed back to his house. On his way, he turned into a big wide street, where he saw a procession. He realized that this was the procession of the dead. They were all talking to one another, singing and laughing, very happy because they were carrying their *ofrendas*—their fruit, their *mole*, bread—they were carrying everything that had been put out for them, even their candles. And right at the very end of the procession came the man's mother, carrying her *mojada* of beef and nothing else. She was weeping because her son hadn't put out anything for her. He saw this from the doorway where he had hidden himself. When she passed him, he called out to her. "Mother," he said. "Mother, I promise you here and now that I will stop drinking so that I have enough money to put out an altar for you next year."

When the next year came, he made a proper altar. He sent for two turkeys, and he killed one, and he put them on the table, with a tray. He said to his wife, "Put one of the turkeys there on the altar and make the other into a turkey *mole*. Put lots of *mole* there on the altar, and plenty of fruit too." And so she did.

They put out a huge amount of food on their altar, and he went out into the street—not to drink this time, but so that he could find the procession of the dead. He hid himself in the same doorway.

Finally, he saw the procession. His mother was right there among all the *difuntos*. He saw how she was walking proudly, carrying her *ofrendas* of turkey, her *mole*, her tortillas, bread, flowers, and everything that they had put out for her because he had made a vow to his mother the year before, when he had seen her shadow. Everything that previously he had wasted in drink was now spent in making the altar. And he never drank again.

We used to live close to this man, and we saw that during the week leading up to the arrival of the *difuntos*, he went to the hill to gather the flowers that he was going to put on his altar for his mother.

Like most such stories, this one has a clear moral: failure to look after your *difuntos* causes them pain. Casting them into disarray, or forgetting them, is a clear sign that all is not well in your own life. But in addition to the moral, which plainly instructs *how* one ought to commemorate one's ancestors on the Day of the Dead—not only should you build an altar, but you would be wise to fill it with good, beautiful, and expensive things, signs of thoughtfulness, sacrifice, and respect on the part of the living—just about every such story contains some sort of eyewitness testimony. "We used to live close to this man"—that is, "I really saw this. The return of the dead truly happens. Woe unto you if you do not believe it!"

Day of the Dead stories are thus told for a variety of reasons.[1] People told *me* such tales in the context of interviews, to impress on me the seriousness with which certain cherished traditions are followed "here in Oaxaca." More generally, such stories instruct, chide, warn, entertain, and reaffirm, resoundingly, the values of the "popular community." They are cautionary ghost tales, where the actions of the living are more to be feared than those of the dead, for, on the Day of the Dead, *difuntos* are utterly at the mercy of their more vital relations. For example, another elderly woman recounted the following fable about a disbelieving—and consequently unwittingly cruel—son.

There was a son who did not believe that his father returned for Día de Muertos. A friend of the young man said to him, "Aren't you going to put anything out for your father?"

"No," the young man replied. "Why on earth would the dead come?!"

His friend advised him to put out some fruit for his father.

"No," said the young man. "No, I'm not going to do that because none of it is true. I'm going to put a pile of stones on the altar just to prove it to you."

And so he did. The night of the fiesta, around midnight, he began to dream. He dreamed about his father, and in this dream, his father said to him, "Son, how ungrateful you are to put stones out for me; I'm not going to be able to carry them, and so I will suffer."

The young man woke up suddenly, and said, "I just dreamed about my father; he reminded me of the stones I left out for him." And then he fell asleep again. Again he began to dream of his father.

This time his father said to him, "Son, go to the door at twelve midnight. From there you will be able to see me pass carrying my sack full of stones."

So the young man got up and went out. By this time he had started to think about what he had done, but he said to himself, "I'm going to go just to see if what I have dreamed is true."

He went to the doorway of his house, where he could see the street, and suddenly he saw a huge glow of light. Walking within the light were the dead. He saw them walking along singing and happily carrying their full sacks and baskets. They walked with candles of all kinds: that was the glow of light that they walked within. The young man said to himself, "So it must be true!"

Then he heard a voice cry out to him: "Ay, son, I cannot bear the weight of these stones that you left out for me!"

The young man was frozen with fright. When the glow of light had passed, the young man saw, trailing the light, a dark image that had no light (for he had not put any candles on his altar). When he saw that it was his father stumbling beneath the weight of a sack of stones that he could hardly carry, the young man cried out, "My father!"

When his father passed close to him, he said, "How ungrateful you are, son. Even if you had not wanted to leave an *ofrenda* for me, you shouldn't have given me this punishment."

The father went on, and the son remained there, in a state of shock. It took a week for the effects of the *susto,* the *mal aire,* that had touched him, to start to go away. Seeing his father carrying that huge pile of stones that he had left on the altar for him filled the son with sadness. The young man carried his sadness here, heavy in his heart, the way his father had carried those stones. He could hardly move. The least he could have done was to put out a candle, a bit of food, a piece of fruit, but no.

Proper observation of the Day of the Dead is extremely important, according to such tales, not only for the well-being of the dead and the emotional health of their family members but also for the memory and conscience of the community. Uriel, a middle-aged teacher, told me the following instructive tale about the importance of respecting customs and helping your neighbors. Told as though it were a true story—"and from that moment on," he concluded—the story follows the familiar pattern, moralizing the sorrows of those who fail to provide for their relatives. Interestingly enough, however, and unlike many others who related such stories, within the frame of his story Uriel interpreted its meaning for me: "Here in Oaxaca," he said, "we 'solidarize' ourselves in times like these [during a festival, on the Day of the Dead]." He went on to proclaim the importance of the "moment" he recounted for all "Oaxacan[s who have] a conscience." No one can be rescued from the obligation to care well for departed relatives:

There was once a person who went away to work outside his pueblo, when all of a sudden he realized that he had forgotten to leave money for his wife to make the Day of the Dead altar. At home, the man's wife said to herself, "What will I do? What will I do, my husband didn't leave me any money for the altar expenses! Oh no! I know, I'll go ask the neighbor if she will help me." And so she went to speak to her neighbor.

Here in Oaxaca, we "solidarize" ourselves in times like these. No matter where you are—a cup of chocolate, some coffee, some *pan de yema*, or a little bit of *mole*. Anywhere in Oaxaca there is something to eat, and during those days of the festival especially, nothing is ever denied you.

And that woman, what does she do? She goes to ask for help from her *comadre*, from her cousin, from this person and this person and that person, in order to make her little altar. But she was only able to collect a little bit of money. When the *Dia de los Grandes* [adults] arrived—what we call the second of November—the woman had hardly anything. And she was left with a great sadness, her heart in her hand.

"I want to offer them something more, something, something! Especially for my mother-in-law." But she was not able to satisfy her wish. Then suddenly she saw those people [the dead], the relatives, loaded up with big baskets, bags full of fruit, of bread, of chocolate—so many, many things. And she saw her mother-in-law, but she was without anything but an *adobe* in her hands—a brick of earth.

Then all of a sudden in that procession, on the path, the *difunta* found her son passing by. The son came across all the dead, and admired the abundance of food that they had with them, baskets and buckets full of it. But then he saw his mother, with tears in her eyes, carrying nothing except a brick of adobe.

"Mamá," said the man. "What is wrong?"

"Ay, my son," she replied. "There was nothing left for me at your house."

The son went straight home. When he arrived at his house, he said to his wife, "Listen, wife, didn't you put anything on the altar?"

His wife answered, "Yes I put food out, but very little. You didn't leave me any money to cover the expense."

"My mother just passed me," the man told her. "And instead of carrying food and fruit, she had an adobe in her arms."

And from that moment on, people have taken this story to heart—and there is no Oaxacan who has a conscience, who, more than anything, is of a religious character—who does not put out at least something to eat on their altar.

ON THE ORIGINS OF THE DAY OF THE DEAD

Todos Santos (All Saints), or Día de los Fieles Difuntos (Day of the Faithful Departed), and Día de [los] Muertos (Day of the Dead), are the Mexican forms of two Catholic feast days, All Saints' Day and All Souls' Day, celebrated on November 1 and 2, respectively. According to the church, Todos Santos is held in honor of all canonized saints, as well as all those who attained saintly status during life but were never recognized. But in Mexico, the significance of the festival runs far deeper, for folk Catholicism defined Todos Santos long ago as the time when the spirits of the dead return to the earth to visit the homes of their living relatives. According to this folk wisdom, most of those who die are *pecadores* (sinners) and must therefore begin their supernatural lives in purgatory. Only *angelitos*, children or the exceedingly pure of heart, may ascend to heaven immediately, without serving time in purgatory. For those dead who must do penance for their sins, however, the Day of the Dead represents a certain freedom: on this day, God grants those souls undergoing their period of penance temporary respite, or a *día de descanso* (day of rest), as many people I spoke to explained it. According to popular belief, on this day *pecadores* serving time in purgatory are released so that they might voyage to earth to see those who have survived them. Only those souls condemned to suffer eternal damnation in hell are excluded from the opportunity to commune with the living during the course of the festival; they are beyond sorrow, respite, or retrieval.

For a variety of reasons, including long periods of alternating disapproval and suppression by the state and the church, there is not much significant local documentation of the historical forms of popular celebrations like the Day of the Dead.[2] Nevertheless, surveys of materials found in the municipal archives of Oaxaca and in the archives of the Diocese of Oaxaca, read in tandem with other historical accounts, help draw a picture of the evolution of this colorful macabre festival.

The present form of the celebration of the Day of the Dead in Mexico has come about through a lengthy and circuitous historical development, which has resulted in the fusion of certain southern European folk practices, medieval and Renaissance Catholic rituals, and indigenous Mesoamerican customs. The feast of All Saints' Day and the liturgical celebration of All Souls' Day have long existed in the European Christian world. Thus, although there is some debate about the accuracy of the claim, according to some sources, All Saints' Day was introduced into the festival cycle by Pope Boniface IV (ca. 550–615) in the seventh century, usurping a pagan festival for the dead. Originally celebrated in May, it was moved to November 1 by Pope Gregory III (731–741) in the eighth century. By the beginning of the ninth century, November 1 was set aside as a day to commemorate all saints and martyrs in Western Christendom. Toward the end of the eleventh century, Pope Gregory VII (1073–1085) established All Saints' Day in its contemporary form, and by the early fourteenth century, this feast had become quite popular in southern Europe, especially in Spain.

As for All Souls' Day, in about 1030, Saint Odilo Abad, the bishop of Cluny in France, decreed that on November 2 all Christian Cluniac monasteries must follow him in commemorating the "faithful dead" by means of requiem masses and prayers. Despite the bishop's decree, this feast was not a routinely accepted part of the church calendar until the end of the thirteenth century. By that time, despite the reluctance of the church to officially establish a specific day for propitiating and honoring its dead, November 2 was widely accepted as the day set aside to celebrate the "faithful departed"—those who had died within the fold of the church.

According to official church doctrine, November 2, All Souls' Day, is intended as a day of communion with those who are in heaven; on this day, the church also offers prayers for those who are in purgatory, so they may be cleansed of sin and enter the kingdom of heaven. In effect, the day marks a moment of collusion between the living and the dead; the dead are recalled, thanked, appeased, and appealed to, so they might watch over the living. Unlike All Saints' Day, All Souls' Day never truly attained official liturgical status, which suggests that the church was loath to give official recognition to a feast so apparently pagan in character, with its shades of ancestor worship, pre-Christian rites, and ceremonies of the cult of the dead.

In his work *Todos Santos in Tlaxcala*, a richly detailed monograph on the development of the cult of the dead in the central Mexican state of Tlaxcala, Hugo Nutini argues that—in contrast to an increasingly rationalist, scientific, and de-ritualized Protestant Europe—in Catholic New Spain the rites, ceremonies, and significance of All Saints' Day and All Souls' Day, brought by the conquering Spanish, became progressively elaborated and have persisted as important elements of indigenous culture. By the sixteenth century, the feasts of All Saints and All Souls had been combined and were known in Spain as Todos Santos. These feast days, which had been widely celebrated in southern Europe, according to various medieval Mediterranean folk practices—which included the offering of food to and feasting with the dead, the use of special bread and sweets, the offering of food at cemeteries to honor the dead, the widespread use of skulls and skeleton imagery, the invention of playful sayings about mortality, and the emergence of rather theatrical groups that wandered from house to house serenading and begging for food for the dead—were transferred to the New World, where they took on new life and importance.

No doubt, part of the success of the practices of Todos Santos in the New World had to do with the fact that these new, semi-Christian observances already coincided, roughly, with the time of year when Mesoamerican indigenous peoples celebrated the harvest and made elaborate ritual feastings of the dead. How Todos Santos was affected and altered by such Mesoamerican practices, and how these calendar dates became the Day of the Dead, a uniquely *Mexican* festival, remain a matter of great historical interest, for clearly the Day of the Dead as any of us may know it today is the result of great cultural upheaval, collusion, confusion, betrayal, and fusion.[3] It is, as folk festivals frequently are, a feast in a state of constant evolution. Consequently, although the practices outlined and described in this chapter call on "tradition" and cultural memory, they can be taken as only meaningful tendencies, snapshots of practices typical in a part of Oaxaca in the 1990s. Already as I write, and as I discuss in the next chapter, some of these practices are changing, under pressure from tourism, government intervention and organization, secularization, globalization, and the growing popularity of North American commercial holidays such as Halloween. Nevertheless, as the stories recounted earlier testify, the Day of the Dead in Oaxaca, I argue, continues to gather into itself powerfully organizing communal and moral forces that remain important bulwarks against the centrifugal influences of the global marketplace.

PRACTICING LOS MUERTOS

The Day of the Dead in Oaxaca—commonly known as Los Muertos—is a time for family, both living and dead. In most homes in Oaxaca, especially in poorer city neighborhoods like San Juan, in honor of the visit of the dead, family members build altars for their offerings of food and drink, candles, flowers, incense, and even toys for *angelitos*. The faithful visit the cemeteries to clean, repaint, and adorn the graves of their loved ones. These graves will soon become sites of family gatherings or, less frequently, of solitary vigils (*la velada*, or *la velación*, from the verb *velar* [to stay awake]). Many city residents also use El Día de los Muertos as a chance to visit and spend time with relatives, *compadres*, and other friends.

But not all the preparations for the Day of the Dead are private or conducted within the shelter of the family or home. In the days that lead up to the festival, death becomes an omnipresent and oddly celebratory theme; it or, more properly speaking, its icons make appearances in shop window displays, at discos, at parties, in catering establishments and food displays, and in the market. Everywhere you look, there is the grimace of death; it spares no one, neither rich nor poor, neither tourists nor locals. Altars for the Day of the Dead appear in hotel lobbies and in the offices of other businesses around town. In some quarters, costumes are prepared, dance steps tried out, and theatrical parts rehearsed; soon various Comparsas de Muertos (Masquerades of the Dead) will take place in various barrios just outside the city limits or, on designated Días de Panteón (Cemetery Days) throughout the month, in particular city cemeteries (figure 5.2).

For a visitor arriving from elsewhere for the first time, such playfulness and joy lavished on the specters of death can be surprising, shocking, and quite unnerving. It all seems sacrilegious, dangerous, as if to joke with death might

FIGURE 5.2 A Comparsa de Muertos outside the Panteón del Marquesado.

unwittingly call it down. Can this festival really be about death? How can so many people gamble so freely with grand sorrow in this way?

One man I met in the Panteón General during the Day of the Dead celebrations in November 1990 explained the paradox in this way:

> Funerals are sad because you know that you're not going to see the *difunto*, and so you feel his absence. You feel the sadness because, physically, he isn't there. He's in the coffin; he is still, now, unmoving. But you still see him. When you go to the cemetery you know that when you put him in the ground, you aren't going to see him anymore. In contrast, during this festival [the Day of the Dead], well, you go to visit him, you go to eat. It is as if he were with you spiritually, no? You go to the cemetery, you go to leave, now, for example [indicating grave at his side]—this is my mother's grave; she died around five months ago. You feel it because, well, yesterday we still had her, today we don't; yesterday we spoke to her, now we don't: She's dead. We're not going to see her. That is the sadness.
>
> Now in this celebration [the Day of the Dead] we know we are going to be with her, that she's going to be coming here. The first beer I opened, I poured it out there [on top of the grave]—there's the bottle.

The Day of the Dead may be joyful because it is the one day of the year when the living get to cheat death a bit of the souls it has taken. On this day, so it is said, the dead come back to walk the earth, to see their loved ones, and to feast on the offerings left out for them. Whereas during a funeral, as the man I spoke to explained, you see the inert body of the deceased for the last time, before it is buried, on the Day of the Dead, the living may not *see* the dead, but, as legend has it, we who are living are all *seen by* the dead. Once a year, until a soul passes from purgatory to heaven, the Day of the Dead affords the opportunity for those souls serving penance to gather with their living relatives, to partake of the same food and drink and light and scents and music and *convivencia*. The Day of the Dead is thus a profoundly sensual celebration; during this festival, both the living and the dead are treated to all sorts of earthly pleasures that, after death, can no longer be common fare.

In Oaxaca, the focus of the Day of the Dead festival spans both the first and second days of November. November 1 is known as the Día de los Angelitos, when the spirits of babies and children are said to pay their visit to their earthly relatives; November 2 is known as the Día de los Grandes, when the souls of sinners, those who died when they were adults, return to earth. Opinions vary regarding times for the arrival and departure of the souls of the *angelitos* and the *grandes*. Some claim that the *angelitos* arrive on October 30 or 31, at midday;

according to these authorities, if *angelitos* arrive on October 30 at noon, then they leave on October 31 at about the same time. According to this calendar, the adult souls come on October 31 at midnight and depart on November 1 at midday. But others in Oaxaca maintain that the adults arrive on November 1 at around midday and stay until either November 3 at midday or the afternoon of November 2. Regardless of the details of such debates—which, among other things, appear to prolong the period during which the souls of the dead walk the earth—November 2, All Souls' Day in the Catholic liturgical calendar, is usually considered the principal festival day.

In Oaxaca, however, unlike in much of the rest of Mexico, the festival is not limited to this stretch of time from October 30 or 31 to November 2. November 2 remains the principal Día de los Muertos, on which those families who have relatives buried in the Panteón General, or in the relatively new Panteón Jardín, decorate and visit their graves. But on the following Monday—and then on consecutive Mondays until the end of the month—other graveyards around the city are opened on a rotating basis for the preparation and visitation of graves. These Mondays in November are no longer considered part of the Day of the Dead itself; they are, instead, referred to as Días de Panteón or Días de Responsos (Responsory Days), set aside for special prayers (*plegárias*) that beg heaven for clemency toward the dead.

Indeed, in Oaxaca, November is known as the Month of the Souls; throughout the month, special attention is given to the souls of the dead in the form of prayers and other commemorations. On November 14, for example, a special mass dedicated to the deceased members of the Legión de María, or *difuntas legionárias*, was held in the parish of Cuauhtémoc. Likewise, as is common on the anniversary of someone's death, during the month of November relatives may pay for masses in which the names of their *difuntos* are mentioned and God's mercy is requested.

Six city graveyards form part of the Cemetery Day cycle, which begins in the Panteón General (also known as the Panteón San Miguel) and the Panteón Jardín on November 2. On subsequent Mondays, the following graveyards hold Responsory Days: Panteones del Marquesado, San Martín Mexicapan (also known as San Martín), San Juan de Chapultepec (also known as San Juanito), and, finally, at the end of the month, Santo Tomás Xochimilco, which is the graveyard where many people in Colonia San Juan had buried their relatives.[4]

I was unable to discover a clear reason for this pattern of celebrations in Oaxaca. It is possible that, because all these cemeteries are located in neighborhoods of the city that began as separate towns—indeed, San Martín is still an independent municipality—each town independently elected a day in which to honor its dead.[5] In Santa Cruz Xoxocotlán, for example, the all-night graveside vigil takes place on October 31, whereas in Tlacolula, another town outside Oaxaca, the celebration takes place over three days in the third week of November. Given the regularity of the calendar governing Oaxaca's Cemetery Days, however, a more plausible explanation suggests that the month-long rotation of Cemetery Days allows families with *difuntos* in more than one cemetery to pay a full and proper visit to all their dead relations instead of trying to fit all their visits into one day.

In addition to preparing and visiting the graves of one's deceased relatives, an especially important activity on the Day of the Dead involves constructing and supplying altars for the dead. Preparation for Day of the Dead altars frequently starts long before the beginning of November. Because setting out a proper altar may represent a great expense for some families, many neighbors or other *colonos* I met in the course of my research begin preparations for the festival altar weeks or even months ahead, collecting and putting items aside in anticipation of the celebration. That October is one of the busiest months for owners of local pawnshops suggests that the sacrifices that preparations entail are considerable. Likewise, the last two weeks of October are typically the most bustling market days of the year. Oaxaca's main market, the Mercado de Abastos (Basic Provisions Market), on the northern edge of the city, becomes a zone filled with rich aromas and bright colors: mills grind cocoa beans, sugar, and cinnamon together and press them into blocks for making hot chocolate or *moles*, while the bakery churns out an endless supply of *pan de muertos* (bread of the dead) in a variety of shapes and sizes. Most common are round loaves adorned with faces made of colored dough, which is then baked right into the bread. A special area of the market, referred to as the *tianguis*, or Plaza de Muertos, is set aside for stalls that sell specialty items for the Day of the Dead, including candles, religious portraits, bright mounds of flowers, *pan de muertos*, candied fruit (including *nísperos* [loquat] and squash), humorous skeletal figures, and skulls called *calaveras* (figure 5.3). These are made of colored sugar, and may be adorned with anyone's name and put on an altar or given as a gift.

An enormous amount of time and energy is invested in preparations for the Day of the Dead. Special dishes are concocted as *ofrendas* and placed on the altar; in addition, the numerous guests that can be expected to pass through one's home throughout the festival must be well fed. Meals are also prepared for consumption in the graveyard. It is also customary to send cooked dishes, *pan de muertos*, and fruit to the homes of relatives, *compadres*, neighbors, and friends. This exchange of offerings between friends and relations is referred to as *mandando muertos* (sending the dead). In this context, the *muertos* are not only the *difuntos* who will be returning to their former homes, but also, by metonymic association, the *ofrendas*. (Indeed, after El Día de los Muertos is over, some households exchange altar contents with other households, in a practice

FIGURE 5.3 Mercado de Abastos: (*above*) loaves of *pan de muertos* and (*below*) *calavaras*, adorned with names, for sale in the *tianguis* area of the market.

also called *mandar muertos* [sending the dead], or children go from door to door collecting *ofrendas*, a practice called *pedir muertos* [begging for the dead]).

Altars

Typically, a household Day of the Dead altar is built over the course of the last couple of days in October, just in time for the arrival of the *angelitos*. The altar for the dead usually represents an embellishment of the home altar already in place; often an extra table or two is added for the *ofrendas*, and the whole house is far more elaborately and expensively decorated than usual. Both form and content of any given altar are determined by individual aesthetic choices, limited, of course, by very real constraints on a family's finances and time. Altars and *ofrendas* vary considerably in size and general appearance, as well as in terms of the hours and attention lavished on their decoration. Certain staple elements are common to virtually all Day of the Dead altars, however, including

- An *arco* (arch), which is erected over the altar. Most often, it is made from two stalks of sugarcane, which are fastened together at one end. Flowers and fruit are attached to and adorn the arch.
- Numerous flowers, including the marigold known locally as *flor de muerto* (flower of the dead) or *sempazúchil* (a colloquial variant of the Nahuatl *cempoalxuchitl* or *zempaxuchítl*) and the crimson *cresto de gallo* (cockscomb) (figure 5.4).
- *Velas* (wax candles) or *veladoras* (oil candles).
- Copal incense, made from a pine resin, which was known across Mesoamerica before the Conquest.
- *Ofrendas* of food and drink, typically including *pan de muertos*, tamales, plates of *mole*, chicken soup, *atole* (gruel made from ground corn), tortillas, mescal, *aguardiente* (sugarcane liquor), *tepache* (flavored fermented maguey juice), blocks or balls of chocolate, coffee, tea, water, bottles of soft drinks, fruit (bananas, oranges, mandarins, apples, pears, *nísperos*, melons, *tecojotes* [sloe fruit], guavas, *anonas* [custard apple], limes, *jícamas* [yam bean], and plums), squash, peanuts, nuts, novelty sweets (such as figures made of colored sugar like *calaveras*, coffins, or animals), candied fruit, and fruit conserve (*nísperos*, miniature apples [*manzanitas*], or squash in *almíbar* [sugar syrup]).
- Other non-comestible offerings such as cigarettes or toys for *angelitos*.
- Photos of family *difuntos*.
- Religious portraits or images.

FIGURE 5.4   Flowers for the Day of the Dead, for sale at the Mercado de Abastos.

Day of the Dead activities frequently impart a sense of continuous move-ment, re-creation, and renewal, in addition to the social, affective, and sensu-ously rich efforts at interaction with the dead. Thus in many households, the *ofrendas* are changed and renewed between the hours when the *angelitos* are thought to leave and the adult souls arrive. Miniature bread of the dead, blocks of chocolate, *tortillitas*, toys, and small candles are replaced by normal-size ver-sions of these items or offerings more appropriate to adult tastes, such as spicier food or symbols of vice like mescal and cigarettes. In addition, many women I know—for these domestic activities fall overwhelmingly within the sphere of women's expected responsibilities—change the dishes on the altar at each mealtime. As one woman told me, "At three in the afternoon I serve the food, after heating it as if it were ready to eat. I put it on the altar with hot tortillas and everything." According to an ordinary mealtime schedule, then, bread and cups of chocolate are often put on the altar early in the morning, and then removed later in the day and replaced by a warm plate of chicken or turkey *mole* and tor-tillas. Coffee and more sweet breads, the customary late-night meal, may then be placed on the altar at night. Once removed from the altar, these "meals" are usually thrown out; occasionally, however, they may be put back into the pot for someone else's consumption.

The next day—for as long as the spirits of the dead are said to remain in the

household—this renewal of offerings is repeated. In general, there is a prohibition against consuming items from the altar until all the spirits have departed,
but, in practice, families seem to adhere to these restrictions to differing
degrees. Many people told me jokes about the warnings that children typically
receive: if they have stolen anything from the altar, *los muertos* will come and
pull their feet while they are asleep. I did not see anyone take this sort of threat
very seriously. After November 2, some householders leave the altar up for a
number of days so that even the marginal of the spirit world—*las limosneros*
(the beggars), *los olvidados* (the forgotten ones, or souls with no family to
return to), *los matados* (those who were murdered or died a violent death and
are consequently not at rest), and *ánimas en pena* or *almas malas* (those with
the largest number of sins to purge, and believed by some to be released later
than others from purgatory for the trip back to the world of the living)—may
still have a share in the *ofrendas*.

In the days following the festival—or, in some households, during it—food
on the altar that has not spoiled is shared within the home or sent as a gift to
another household. On the night of November 2, many children dress up in
costumes and go from house to house *pedir muertos*—to ask for contributions
from the household altar. A well-established tradition, in its present form, *pedir
muertos* appeared to me to resemble a fusion of the *comparsa* (masquerade)
that forms a part of many Day of the Dead celebrations, and the American
and Canadian practice of sending costumed children to ask for treats from the
neighbors on Halloween.

Day of the Dead altars are constructed to honor the dead of one's family as
well as the community of the dead in general (figure 5.5). The altar's content is
typically determined by the tastes of the *difuntos* to whom the altar is dedicated,
and it is believed that the dead arrive first at the homes of their relatives to enjoy
the familiar *ofrendas* set out on the altars there. Subsequently, after visiting their
former homes, the dead are believed to move on to the cemetery, where they
visit their own graves before departing from the land of the living. After visiting
one another's homes, and trading *ofrendas*, the living, too, gather at the cemetery to celebrate the return of their deceased relatives on the Day of the Dead.

THE CEMETERY VISIT

It is early morning on November 2, 1990, at the Panteón Jardín, which is situated on the northern edge of Oaxaca City. Unable to get to the cemetery the
day before, as she had planned, Lucía crouches on her knees and begins the
task of clearing her son's gravesite of weeds, noticing with sad exasperation

FIGURE 5.5
An altar for the Day of the Dead.

that the flowers she had planted on the edge of the grave the week before are gone. The morning light is bright and hazy; clouds of dust from her energetic sweeping are still hanging in the air. Across the way, Lucía sees a family—mother, father, and several children—arrive to tidy and decorate their relative's grave. She goes to fetch water from the nearby public faucet, commiserating with a woman waiting there about the high cost of flowers at the Mercado de Abastos that morning. As she speaks about the flowers, Lucía feels even more grateful to her *comadre* Elena for giving her a beautiful bunch of red *crestos de gallo* for her son Alejandro's grave the night before.

The stone on Alejandro's grave is new; Lucía had waited until the date of Los Muertos was near before paying the cemetery worker to construct a cement tomb and erect a metal fence around the grave. She had wanted the gravesite to look its best for this special day, the first Día de Muertos since Alejandro's untimely death the previous December. She busies herself with washing the tombstone with water and a rag that she brought for the task. After emptying dead flowers and a bit of water from the large tin cans that serve as vases flanking the headstone, she refills them with new water, readying them for the fresh flowers that she has brought with her. Finally, Lucía replaces the candles on the grave, which have burned out. She relights them, ready to welcome Alejandro again.

A visit to the graveyard where one's relatives are buried on the Day of the Dead is a part of the public cult of the dead that forms a vital complement to activities centered on the household. The ritual visit is made easier for people like Lucía whose *difuntos* are buried in the Panteón General or the Panteón Jardín, for November 2 is a public holiday. Getting time off later in the month to devote to particular Cemetery Days at other cemeteries can be more difficult to manage. Perhaps this is why, on November 2, the graveside atmosphere often takes on the character of a family outing or a Sunday picnic, whereas, later in the month, Cemetery Days tend to be quiet affairs, attended mostly by women.

One particularity of all these cemetery visits in Oaxaca, regardless of the day of the month when they occur, is that most take place during daylight hours. (Exceptions to this daytime rule include the nighttime *velada* in the cemetery in Xoxocotlán and in San Felipe de Agua, towns on the city's southwestern and northern edges, respectively.) Such daytime graveside Day of the Dead vigils or celebrations are not typically the case elsewhere in the country—not in or around Mexico City, not in the state of Tlaxcala, not during the well-publicized Day of the Dead festivities in Michoacán, where the all-night vigils held in many areas of the state, including on the picturesque island of Janitzio, are internationally famous tourist attractions. It seems, however, that in Oaxaca, graveyard visits have, for as long as anyone can remember, always occurred during the daytime. Indeed, even on the Day of the Dead, most cemeteries are locked at 7:00 or 8:00 p.m. In the Panteón General, for example, a bell gongs in the evening, signifying the closing of the cemetery. And although the General Cemetery is open until midnight on November 2, few people remain there after dark. Even in places such as the Panteón San Martín, which is open and accessible at all times, almost no one stays—or goes—after sundown.

Typically, graves are cleaned on November 1 (or the day before the relevant Cemetery Day), if not early on the festival day itself. Sometimes one family member assumes responsibility for cleaning a grave, but more often this is an activity collectively carried out by family members. Flowers and candles are arranged on or around the grave, and often a photograph or portrait of the *difunto* is propped against the headstone or cross. More personal touches such as a radio for a *difunto* who was fond of music may be added, and offerings of a glass of water or mescal, and occasionally pieces of fruit or even whole plates of food, are placed on the grave. It is widely believed that the dead are particularly thirsty after their long journey home. Beverages quench their thirst; water, too, on the analogue of holy water, is often believed to act as a purifying substance for returning souls.

Specific *ofrendas* suggest a tangible and immediate relationship between *difuntos* and their loved ones left behind. In affirmation of this sort of relationship, graves are adorned and tended just as people would ready their homes for the arrival of a family member or any other special visitor.

Some family members and visitors stay for the whole day in the graveyard, eating, drinking, and socializing; others stay for just half an hour or less—time enough to place flowers on the grave, spend a few thoughtful moments with their *difuntos*, and then leave. Often one or two family members arrive in the morning and set up a sort of base camp or picnic; then, throughout the afternoon, the group gradually fills out. At midday, a Catholic mass takes place in all the cemeteries visited; in many graveyards, the service is repeated later in the afternoon. Although the church allows three masses to be held on Sundays, El Día de los Muertos is the only other day on which it is officially permissible to hold three masses, even if the festival falls on a weekday.[6] Priests or deacons may be seen moving from grave to grave at the request of family members; they recite responsory prayers for the souls of *difuntos* and bless each grave that they stop at with holy water. In a similar manner, small musical groups of four or five members sometimes circulate through the graveyards, stopping at particular graves to perform popular songs that a family has requested be dedicated to their dear departed. Visiting goes on between graves, for the holiday affords many neighbors the opportunity to see one another. Food and drink are widely shared; mescal, in particular, is in ready supply. Indeed, on more than a few occasions, I witnessed celebrants who got so drunk that they passed out—on a grave!

Adjacent to the cemetery, a thick cluster of stalls sell a range of food and other items normally associated with the Day of the Dead—flowers, candles, incense, and *calaveras* of various kinds. These are typically cardboard or wooden skeleton toys held together and manipulated by strings, but *calaveras* may also take the form of sugar skulls or coffins, or of tiny scenes made humorous because they are peopled by only skeletons, such as a funeral procession, a bar, a soccer game, or a beauty salon (figure 5.6). Other nearby vendors sell the board games traditionally played at this time of year—Coyote, Lotería, and Snakes and Ladders (figure 5.7)—and every year there are more and more Halloween items, such as plastic pumpkins, witch masks, and various costumes. All sorts of other items are for sale at these stalls as well: neon-colored stuffed animals, key chains, music cassettes, posters of rock or *telenovela* stars, pictures of the pope, and

FIGURE 5.6 *Calaveras* in the form of (*left*) toys and (*right*) coffins, for sale in the *tianguis* area of the Mercado de Abastos.

hair ornaments or clothing. The Day of the Dead market stalls that proliferate around the Panteón General on November 2 are so numerous that the streets immediately outside the cemetery have the carnivalesque appearance of a fair and include the usual features of every large religious or secular fiesta—rides, games of chance, and a variety of *comida típica*: tacos, popcorn, potato chips, *nieve* (ice cream or sherbet), candied fruit and other sweets, *empanadas*, hot cakes, *licuados* (fruit blender drinks), soft drinks, *tepache*, and beer.

Vivid symbols of this fair travel fluidly back and forth between the outside of the cemetery (the world of the living) and the inside (the world of the dead). In a few cemeteries I visited, games of chance—shooting ranges, wheels of fortune—are erected right alongside the graves; the excited cries of the small crowds that gather to cheer players on mingle with the animated chatter of people mov-

FIGURE 5.7 The board game Snakes and Ladders, for sale in the *tianguis* area of the
Mercado de Abastos.

ing through the graveyard. As families gather, peddlers, too, wander among the
graves, hawking their wares in high-pitched nasal wails. They sell food and drink,
as well as varied novelties, balloons, and occasionally *calavera* newspapers (figures 5.8 and 5.9). Called *calaveras* after the skull imagery that adorns them, these
papers, remnants of pre-independence satirical broadsheets critical of the government, tend to be irreverent; frequently, the verses that fill them are mocking
obituaries of the living, written ostensibly by the dead. In Oaxaca, some *calaveras*
appear as special newspapers; others are included as a broadsheet or insertion in
other, more regular newspapers and magazines. Happily, for *calavera* satirists, the
demand for *calaveras* coincides opportunistically with the Informe, the annual
address of both the state governor of Oaxaca and the president of Mexico; these
events provide *calavera* writers with much of their material.[7]

SALINAS.
En México todo es posible
que me crean que estoy loco
diciendo a quién se le ocurre
nombrar Presidente a un loco?

MAQUI [PAN]
EL LIDER PARA EL CAMBIO

Núm. 21   Noviembre de 1990   Dir. Lic. Ernesto Cruz Ramos

Calaveras del Terror!!

REGIDORES DE OAXACA.
Fué una burla, una bufonada
de estos seres de engorda
gente ignorante y sorda
que no sirve para nada.
Ni por equivocación trabajaron
estos comodinos golfos
más parecían gordolfos
sus "dietas" puntual cobraron
Reunioncita tras reunioncita
sin proyectos ni planteamientos
en juntas de aburrimiento
se fueron al esquermento.
Ya murieron, ya se han ido
estas lacras chupadoras
del pueblo fueron vividoras
dejándolo triste y en cueros.

SANITARIOS DEL MERCADO
En un caso extraordinario
no hay aquí equivocación
esos no son sanitarios
sino focos de infección.

Sólo sirven pa garantía
del municipal en turno
al que desearía con ansia
que hubiera horario nocturno.

JAVIER ALCAZAR
(disque comentarigleta)
Quiso ser muy "pico"
se creyó genio sesudo
y por boca de un embudo
siempre
habló como perico.
Nunca pasó al Trío "Fantasía"
insultando a los maestros
fué rastrero y arrastrado
sus traumas siempre escupía.
Odiaba a Jiménez Ruiz
y también a Sandoval
a la Universidad trato mal
este hijo del comal.
Cuando murió este bocon
Oaxaca si se alegró
su yerto nadie cargó
por hablador y sangron.

D. LUIS H. ALVAREZ.
(Presidente Nal. del PAN)
Este señor bonachon
no me lo ván a creer
al PRI LE HECHO A perder
toda su corrupción.

**BARUC ALAVEZ
MENDOZA**
Ex-presidente Mpal. de Huahua-
pan
comparado con Durazo
con Serrano o con la Quina
dejó al pueblo en vil ruína
este carbon raterazo
Compro una gasolinera
a su mamita diez locales
con movidas muy venales
este hijo del gobierno.
En el panteón ya reposa
el que en vida nos robara
las arcas vacías dejara
y el mismo cavó su fosa.

**LIC. HELADIO
RAMIREZ LOPEZ**
Soy chapurrito, no soy norteño,
soy de Oaxaca tierra nuestra,
me gustan todas las muestras
me hace mucho las comparsas

PUEBLO HUAJUAPEÑO.
Bajo tanta martingala
valió el pobre puro cuerno
si no del moco de un ala
lo trajo siempre el gobierno.
Lleno de tribulaciones
pasó toda su existencia
soportando vejaciones
con ovejuna paciencia
Al hoyo bajó el canijo
y aunque este dicho no cuadre
revirando a cada hijjal
sendas mentadas de madre.

LOPEZ PORTILLO
Este gacmaplın sintético
en Madrid se refugió
y de un ataque apoplético
dicen que se petateó.

Como había de suceder,
murió podrido en millones,
y junto con su mujer
dejó al pueblo sin calzones.

As jumbled and carnivalesque as such scenes may be, at the same time the cemetery visit on November 2 (or throughout the month) involves flagrant displays of class distinction. Not only are disparities of wealth manifestly visible in terms of the architecture and other sorts of expenditure devoted to particular gravesites, but wealth also seems to mean that family members are not required to clean or maintain their graves—workers are hired to do so—nor do they spend so much time at the cemetery celebrating and socializing; for example, it is unlikely that they will eat there. Thus although a carnival atmosphere pervades the streets outside the Panteón General on November 2, whole areas in the cemetery, those with graves belonging to the wealthiest and most influential residents of the city, are sparsely visited and are not at all a part of the general hubbub.

Three weeks later, the scene on the Día de Responsos in the graveyard in San Martín Mexicapan, situated on the city's western edge, is remarkably different. San Martín, whose history as an officially independent settlement dates from the Conquest, is a poor, "popular" neighborhood of some twenty thousand people, with a strong community identity. Unlike the Panteón General, where great limestone walls surround the graveyard, San Martín, a considerably smaller cemetery, is not enclosed. As soon as I arrived in San Martín, I had the distinct impression that almost everyone in the cemetery knew one another; enthusiastic socializing carried on throughout the day. Many visitors stayed until sundown, sharing food and drinking mescal together until some of them were quite inebriated. Part of the exuberance of the Cemetery Day at San Martín is surely owing to the fact that it coincides with the *mayordomía* (annual festival) of the local patron saint: St. Martin. Nevertheless, the difference between the way death is greeted and celebrated here, and the way it is greeted and celebrated in the Panteón General on November 2, is instructive.

Most of the graves in San Martín, for example, reflect the generally more humble socioeconomic situation of members of the local community; many, in fact, are simple stark earthen graves marked by only a headstone or a cross. Such graves, however, unlike stone monuments, allow for a great deal of innovation in terms of adornment; the earthen graves of San Martín are often far more elaborately decorated than are finished or expensive graves. Some residents

FIGURE 5.8 (*opposite page, above*) A balloon seller in the Panteón del Marquesado.

FIGURE 5.9 (*opposite page, below*) A *calavera* newspaper.

spend hours painstakingly laying flower blossoms in careful patterns; often such works of art are embellished with an epitaph or a phrase such as Descansa en Paz (Rest in Peace) and the initials of the beloved *difunto* (figure 5.10).

Not infrequently, residents of popular communities such as San Martín articulate the relationship between the care they lavish on their dead and the moral superiority of the poor. Such commentaries may implicitly or explicitly also condemn the lax practices of the wealthy. For example, on November 2, 1990, one older woman and her adult granddaughter, spending the day in the cemetery with their family, walked me through such contrasts at the Panteón General:

FIGURE 5.10
Graves decorated
for the Day of
the Dead.

OLDER WOMAN: Go and look over there [she points to the western, newer part of the graveyard] at that side of the cemetery. Over there are many poor people, so over there all day long they sit there beside their graves, their little chapels, whatever, taking care of them. And there they eat, like we do. But a rich person—look, there is the chapel of a rich person. [She points.] The family came early to leave flowers and then left. Their dead relative [*su muerto*] is not important for them. This one over here, the same thing. [She points again.] It's not important for "society people" [*gente de sociedad*] to come here and be in the cemetery with their relatives. The poor person [*el pobre*]—this is who is with his relatives, his *difuntos*.

K.N. (objecting): But it's the poor person who can't afford the things for the altar—

GRANDDAUGHTER: No, the poor person will almost always have an altar in his or her home. Like us. Look, the poor make their *ofrendas* in their house—they make their altar, a big altar, and then they keep on adding things on little by little . . . and then they put on fruit, like *jícama*, nuts, peanuts, apples, mandarin oranges, bananas. And it's a pleasure to put on flowers, many flowers, and little lights [*lámparas*]. And on the first day, as they say is the custom here, come the little dead ones [*los angelitos*]—*difuntos*, but children. They come on the 31st at noon. And then they leave at noon the next day, the 1st [of November], and at one o'clock the adult dead [*los grandes*] arrive. So you put their chocolate out early, their bread, their gelatin, their sweet apples [*manzanitas en dulce*], and then you light up their copal, their incense, and their candle. My grandmother came yesterday to leave flowers, to clean up a bit, and to leave a candle.

According to such popular accounts, "the poor" are those who know the sacrifice of love, time, and effort that is required to honor the dead as they deserve; the poor are those who have not lost the cherished connection with those who have gone before them, who are not lost themselves—unlike "society people"— in the transient, material things of the here and now. They are those who have remembered their *difuntos* well, generously and lovingly. (Such a collective ethic is also symbolized by a monument in the Panteón General dedicated to El Muerto Olvidado [Forgotten Dead One], which, during the Day of the Dead, is covered with flowers and candles left by passersby [figure 5.11].) It is clear that the enactment of various caring and social ritual forms operate, for those in popular communities, as a kind of dynamic allegory; here social contradictions and tensions are addressed, articulated, manipulated, and resolved in ways that appear to have some rather significant long-term effects.

FIGURE 5.11 The monument to El Muerto Olvidado in the Panteón General.

THE MEANINGS OF DEATH

The Day of the Dead is the festival during which relations with supernatural beings, in this case the dead, are most fully domesticated and most ritually amplified. The returning dead are fed, welcomed into the home, and celebrated. The living, in turn, send their hospitality out into the cemetery, to the gravesides of their loved ones; they become, in effect, both hosts and guests of the dead in this "house" of the dead. Annually, the fiesta presents numerous opportunities for the living to fulfill their obligations to the dead; their obligations to the dead involve both public and private acts, and encompass both the dead of their own families and the community of the dead as a whole. Indeed, many participants in Day of the Dead activities believe that the living secure their own interests as well as the interests of the community through proper behavior toward and maintenance of relations with the dead. As one man explained:

> Here it is thought that if you don't put out an altar for the *difuntos*, they go off sad, nothing more. . . . They don't do anything, but they go off sad and something bad can happen to the person who didn't make the altar, for example, an accident, she or he may trip or fall—that is the belief here.

Or in the words of another man, a faithful skeptic who believes in hedging his bets:

> We keep following the customs, and we keep hanging on to our beliefs. In reality I've never felt the physical presence of my ancestors, no? But I believe if I don't follow through with this obligation of making them their *ofrenda*, I won't have a bad nightmare, but something can happen to me. So always, every year I try to make it better for those who may come, they feed themselves with what we put out for them, and they may see that we are following through with what they taught us, following through with this custom.

To show care and respect to the dead implies that you show care and respect for yourself as well as for your living friends and relatives. These are ideals not limited to Catholics, but are part of a realm of culture shared by most Oaxacans. As two Pentecostal sisters remarked, while explaining their reasons for participating in this folk-Catholic festival, "This day, well, one tries to come *a convivir*, to be with one's relatives, so that they are happy, no?" Or as another *colonia* resident put it: "In part [the Day of the Dead] is sad because one remembers one's loved ones. And me, well, my mother died a year and some months ago. For me it is sad but at the same time I remember the good things about her, everything that she liked and all that. . . . I feel calm, yes?"

In the end, as I was repeatedly told, death is unavoidable for us all, and so it is best that we prepare ourselves. If you live well, then you are likely to die well, and can take comfort in the hope that death itself—or its aftermath, purgatory—will not be so onerous; you may also hope that your loved ones who remain on earth will remember you and offer your soul consolation and nourishment. Such popular religious sentiments provide the residents of Colonia San Juan and other such communities with a moral language for talking about the world and articulating its injustices and, in doing so, perhaps gaining some measure of control over them. People plot their experience within the dynamic framework of physical and moral transformation, a movement that is both forward and upward. The journey that is life is a journey of suffering, hard work, marginality, and struggle but is of implicit redemption. Death is reckoned simply as a step, a movement into another life: "Death is something that has to happen, no?" stated don Pancho, an older man in San Juan who was training to become a deacon. "The bottom line is that we have to die. Because we're not of this world, we're only passengers, pilgrims. We go on walking toward the eternal life, to the beyond [el más allá]."

In this view, death is a step into another, better, life and thus should not be regarded as a terrible tragedy. Nor should it be feared. Death is eminently natural, inevitable. "Death is a moment that cuts off one's life. It's a natural moment," one woman told me. Another reflected, "We should never fear death because we carry it in the palm of the hand . . . it's something so simple." Such statements are characteristic of "popular" claims about death; they are declarations of intimate knowledge and profound understanding that come from experience and a sober, if not resigned, outlook on human nature and society itself. I was repeatedly told that those who fear death are stuck on the things of the world, or las cosas del mundo. Such people, doña Amelia said, are those "whose God is power, is pleasure. The worldly life is their God and for that reason they don't want to die, they want to be eternal." According to such accounts, the end point of the moral narrative of death is always judgment, whether spoken of in literal biblical terms—El Día del Juicio Final—or simply in terms of death's unavoidable reality. Ultimately all scales are balanced by death.

Being ready for death is thus a question of preparedness; it involves consciousness of the thin line separating the living and the dead: "No one knows the moment of one's death. You have to be prepared, not to be unprepared, you have to think about that, about death always," warned don Pancho, echoing the Bible. In Oaxaca, I found a down-to-earth readiness to encounter death and to know it. There was also an acceptance of the fickle nature of death, its continuously haunting presence, its uncertain yet final arrival. As one woman put it:

From when they're little we have to instill in the child that he awaits death, because it's natural and there's no need to fear it. Because sooner or later it has to come. There are babies who, recently born, die; and other people who at a hundred years die, or twenty years, forty years. . . . I mean, death is equal, no? And we have to explain that to the child so that he goes with the conscience that the moment has to arrive, that he doesn't have horror because, well, it's a natural thing of life that no one escapes and we have to confront it.

Death is an inevitable, transcendent force, part of a natural, organic exchange; it is an equalizer, a leveler, of imbalances and inequities. Indeed, death may well be regarded as the source of reverence for life and sociality itself. Consciousness of death—and thus of the meaning of life—is sustained through the maintenance of memories of the dead.

But memories depend on an acceptable narrative frame for their telling and a physical site for their enactment. Thus although the ashes of my father were thrown to the ocean around the island where he lived before he died, and the island embodies his memory, the absence of a specific physical site of commemoration leaves his memory, to an extent, still floating in my feelings, unspoken, unspeakable, frozen—and private. By contrast, in Oaxaca, the cemetery functions as a place where the localization or mapping of memory occurs; it is the site where individual and collective histories are merged, both literally and figuratively. The cemetery becomes the ground for common memory; all rites of the dead begin and end there. The dead, their bodies, the memories and evidence of their lives are all vehicles of social memory and artifacts for remembrance. They are regularly invoked, enhanced, and cared for by funerary rituals and festival occasions such as the Day of the Dead. Mourning in Oaxaca does not remain merely a private affair, but is always, and repeatedly, an activity that calls for, and calls out to, an entire community.

At various death rituals in Oaxaca, and during the festivities of the Day of the Dead, stories are told about the dead; the dead are spoken of and remembered. These informally recounted narrative histories, like gossip, are a feature of communal memory. They are both physical and temporal. It seems, however, that other kinds of souvenirs or receptacles of memory are also necessary, especially if a memory is to be continuous. Epitaphs on the headstones in cemeteries write a history of individual, family, and community. The grave itself functions as a tangible memory, made into a home, a place both familiar and intimate. The graveyard itself is a theater of memory where another sense of time and space is created, where food and lives are shared. In this sense, then, remembering is about re-collecting the pieces of the social body; it involves encoding ways of feeling or knowing that are held in the recesses of bodily memory. But it is also true that images of the past, and recalled knowledge, are conveyed and sustained by ritual performances.[8]

On the Day of the Dead, for example, many Oaxacans turn the cemetery into a sacred field for the seamless reconnecting of the dimensions of the living and the dead; on that day, the notion of time is exempt from the rules that govern more mundane social spaces. Memories of the dead are not retrieved so much as they are invoked; they are reawakened in the present. The image of the dead fostered by such ritual communal activity renders them both strong and vital;

they are sung to, feasted, loved, and remembered as temporal, finite, desiring, hungry beings.

The Importance of Food

Food is especially significant during the Day of the Dead festival. Not only does it function as an offering, a gesture of respect, and an invitation to the dead souls who come to wander the earth in early November, but it also serves to distinguish between the living and the dead. Offerings are left for the dead while food is made, shared, and consumed by the living. Indeed, food offerings is the feature that distinguishes All Souls' Day celebrations in Mexico from the official Catholic form of the festival. Food is almost always mentioned first in local newspaper accounts of the festival and in other written accounts. And whenever someone is asked how the festival is celebrated, the topic inevitably is food.[9]

Above all, in Oaxaca, *mole* is a requirement of virtually every fiesta occasion, especially the Day of the Dead. A thick, chocolate-based sauce with a multi-layered, subtle, protean, rich flavor, every *mole* recipe is complex, and many are household, generational secrets. Making a *mole* is a laborious process. Dozens of ingredients must be gathered—a range of chili peppers, cacao beans, and spices; these may include black pepper, bread crumbs, sesame seeds, sugar, salt, banana, cloves, cumin, peanuts, oregano, *chile huajillo*, almonds, raisins, toma-toes, garlic, onions, green tomatoes, thyme, and *chile ancho*. Then, if one is to make a traditional *mole*, the old way (for now prepared packages of the sauce in paste form may be bought easily at the market), one must spend hours grind-ing the ingredients together by hand on a grinding stone, or *metate*. Once the ingredients have been prepared, long hours of cooking follow.

Indeed, throughout the fiesta cycle in Oaxaca, food establishes a complex web of reciprocal interactions, both actual (it is what it is) and metaphoric. Food and drink are used to facilitate and symbolize social interactions; they also stand as markers of special occasions. The question—which is also a joke—"Should we make *mole*?" is, for example, synonymous with asking if someone plans to be married. Certain foods and drinks are common to all special occasions—*mole*, tamales, and chocolate or mescal, for example; frequently, however, a particular festival is associated with a specific type of food or dish. Often this association has to do with a seasonal abundance of one food or another, but not always. Sometimes it is the shape or form of the food that is important. The fiesta of the Virgin of Juquila, celebrated on December 13, for example, is characterized by the sale of distinctive sweets, and Epiphany, the celebration of the arrival of the Wise Men in Bethlehem on January 6, is associated with a crown-shaped cake called *la rosca* or *la rosca de reyes* (wreath of the kings). A meal of barbecued goat and beer is identified with the Day of the Holy Cross on May 3, and the famous Día de los Rábanos (Festival of the Radishes), held in December, involves the consumption of a special maize-based stew called *pozole* and *buñuelos* (donuts), followed by the ritual smashing of one's clay bowl against the wall of the central city cathedral in the *zócalo*. During the Christmas Posadas, a period that begins on December 16 and culminates at Epiphany on January 6, gelatin, tostadas, sandwiches, and candies are always served to guests; these foods are also distributed at La Candelaria (Candlemas) or "elevation" of the Child Jesus on February 2, a festival commemorating the day on which the Infant Jesus was first presented at the Temple in Jerusalem. Bread and hot chocolate are served on Good Friday for the "wake of Christ," just as they would be served at any other wake.

Many Oaxacans I know describe a given festival by listing in lavish detail the foods that are typically prepared for the celebration. For the Day of the Dead, this sort of description is particularly rich; frequently speakers use diminutives and describe the feast in highly nostalgic, sentimental terms. Often past practices are idealized, or the festival being described is set in the past, in a rural space—for, as one funeral director told me in the midst of a particularly extravagant description, "Oh no, we don't do that here in the city." Such recollections are not infrequently spoken of in conjunction with memories of "Mi mamá" and the joys of nourishment in the intimate bosom of one's first family. The Day of the Dead appears to allow people to articulate, in an especially intense way, the reality of a fantasy of plenitude on earth, rooted in a concrete place, time, and set of relationships.

The exchange and treatment of food and drink enacts, represents, and mirrors certain crucial relationships within the community. The making and offering of food is at once allegorical, metaphorical, and actual; it is the sign and evidence of the community's welcome and well-being, the mark of its sensuous attachment to this life, and its respect for death. Food propitiates visitors and ghosts, functioning as a sort of communion between the sacred and the profane, among friend, family member, and neighbor. It remains the practice in both urban and rural regions of Oaxaca to offer food and drink to any guest as soon as the person arrives at your home. This refreshment is typically offered *con confianza* (with trust). To refuse this offering amounts to a repudiation of the social tie between guest and host; it is a gesture of the utmost disrespect, an utter refusal to offer or to receive trust or any other social good. Thus when food and drink are offered to the dead during Day of the Dead festivities, this offering is made *con confianza* and establishes a set of important commonalities between the living and the dead. The offering of food reaffirms that both the living and the dead belong to a single existential and moral universe, as supernatural and mortal beings are both sharing from the same pot.

Another dimension of the exchange of food and drink during the celebration of El Día de los Muertos relates to the quality of the *ofrendas*; many people I interviewed told me about the great pains they took to put "the best of everything" on their altar for their *difuntos*, "so that they will be happy and enjoy themselves." It is said that the dead do not actually consume the *ofrendas* left for them, as those who are alive would. Indeed, who sees this happen? Rather, it is the ephemeral "essences" of the food set out for them—the flavor and the aroma—that the dead take from their offerings.

One knows that the dead have come and sampled the *ofrendas* on the altar, I was told, because both smell and taste disappear from what has been left. Such material evidence for supernatural events is characteristic of popular religion, which demands more than mere signs. Concrete manifestations are necessary, and are apparent everywhere to those who know how and where to listen or look. Thus some people I spoke to maintained that *los muertos* come back to earth "like the breeze"; odd noises, the barking of dogs, or a moment when a piece of fruit rolled off an altar are all taken to be proofs of the arrival of the dead. Similarly the meaning of a drop in the level of a drink placed on the altar has nothing to do with evaporation: *los muertos* have come; you can see that they stopped and sipped the offerings left for them.

The collective meal in the cemetery takes place immediately before the dead are supposed to return to the supernatural realm; this event, therefore, is an appropriate culmination of the fiesta: reciprocation and dramatization of ideal relations between the living and the dead. The graveyard is embellished by a profusion of signs of the living—food, flowers, and brightly colored decorations, as well as the music, chatter, and laughter of *convivencia*. Young and old, kin and non-kin, friends and strangers gather together, with the dead and their memories of the dead, in this place of the dead, and, at least for a few hours, the sacred theater of the cemetery becomes, for all those present, a resonant simulacrum of paradise on earth, a rejoicing in a sensuous universe of plenty.

THE CHURCH AND THE DAY OF THE DEAD

For many years, the Catholic Church and various ruling bodies objected frequently and vociferously to the "disorder" brought about by the popular celebration of the Day of the Dead; many aspects of the festival were prohibited by civic authorities in the 1780s, and, until quite late in the twentieth century, the church often actively discouraged participation in the festival, sometimes by trying to co-opt or shift popular religious activities toward official ecclesiastical practices.[10]

Today the confrontation between "official" and popular religiosities in the Oaxacan Day of the Dead is a subtle one, but it remains significant. The private, domestic-oriented aspect of the celebration of the fiesta, represented by the building of household altars and the making of *ofrendas*, clearly contradicts orthodox Catholic theology, which in almost all significant ritual contexts emphasizes the need for an official representative like a priest to act as a kind of broker with the sacred domain. Representatives of the church in Cuauhtémoc attempt to pull the faithful away from popular, domestic religious activities by focusing the celebration of El Día de los Muertos on the veneration of the total corpus of souls. The church holds special masses and proclaims the significance of Christ's death to all people. A small handout distributed to those of us gathered at one mass on November 2 to commemorate *los fieles difuntos* (the faithful dead) referred to the date as the Fiesta de Resurrección (Feast of Resurrection). Another handout in a different parish contained the text of a responsory prayer to be recited by family members for a particular *difunto*; on the back of the handout, however, a more general creed was printed "Creemos en la resurrección de los Muertos, creemos en la resurrección de la Humanidad, creemos en la resurrección de Nuestra comunidad" (We believe in the resurrection of the dead, we believe in the resurrection of humanity, we believe in the resurrection of our community).

Many church-sponsored Day of the Dead activities bore a strong relationship, in both medium and message, to the funeral masses preceding most funerals. Despite the explicit New Evangelization framework at work in the organization of such alternative activities—goals that the progressive New Evangelization campaign sets for itself involve rooting out various "ignorant" aspects of popular culture, and bringing members of the popular classes more fully within the fold of the church—in Oaxaca I have never observed any attempt to discourage or expunge popular aspects of the Day of the Dead celebrations on the part of representatives of the church. Instead, the church increasingly tries to make itself present among the people; if the people will not come to the church, then the church will come to the people.

Thus, in the Panteón de Santo Tomás Xochimilco (where most of the *difuntos* of San Juan residents were buried), placards with biblical citations referencing the promise of the resurrection of the dead at Christ's Second Coming were pinned to the trees. These signs announced the time of the mass to be held that afternoon in the cemetery. For example, one informed visitors of a "Solemn

Eucharist at 5:00 P.M. here in the cemetery." This useful information was followed by several verses from John 11, the story of the raising of Lazarus. In the verses cited, Jesus promises Martha, the sister of Lazarus, that although her brother is dead, he will live again, thanks to his faith. In one of the most frequently cited passages of the New Testament, Jesus then goes on to make a promise of salvation to all the faithful:

> Jesus said, "Your brother will rise again."
> Martha replied, "I know that he will rise again on the last day, in the resurrection of the dead."
> Jesus told her, "I am the resurrection and the life; whoever believes in me, though he should die, will come to life; and whoever is alive and believes in me will never die."

Another church placard, suggestive of the progressive tone of the New Evangelization movement, made use of the language of St. Paul to proclaim: "While there is injustice, while there is suffering, we are dead to God—to Jesus!"

The mass took place that afternoon in the middle of the festive popular space of the graveyard, outdoors, among the individuated "homes" of the dead. And throughout the day, the church representatives don Reynaldo and Padre Claudio tried to maintain as conspicuous an official presence as possible. Thus they agreed to offer responsory prayers at particular gravesites throughout the afternoon, although, as they conceded, their presence was not necessary to the efficacy of such private prayers. On other occasions at celebrations of the Day of the Dead, I saw other church groups mingling in cemeteries and offering prayers; in 1990, for example, in Xoxocotlán, a Catholic youth group was invited by the municipality to say prayers with and for the families of the dead.

Such activities are not only about recentering the church in the lives of the faithful or displacing popular religious activities. Part of the New Evangelization movement has also been aimed at cleaning up the conduct of both clergy and laity. Such a widespread official presence at popular festivals also helps root out impostors and stop various kinds of bribery or graft. For instance, the assurance offered to me by Father Daniel Quiroga, parish priest of the city barrio El Marquesado, that he had not given *responsos* in his parish since 1972 was surely in response to the rumors, which were rampant, of priests who were earning handsome sums by arguing for the necessity of their paid presence at graveside responsory prayers. Indeed, when I showed Father Quiroga a photograph that I had taken of a priest performing *responsos* on Cemetery Day in the Panteón del Marquesado in 1990, he told me that the man was not a priest, but a con artist in costume.

To be sure, the message of the church is not entirely at odds with the overall themes of the festival; indeed, at its most basic, the orthodox church seeks to engage beliefs that are congruent with a crucial aspect of "popular" theology. Such a convergence is perhaps most clearly expressed in relation to the celebration of Easter and Holy Week (Semana Santa), the most important feast days on the official religious calendar. Although popular religious preoccupation during the Easter season tends to be with the martyrdom and death of Christ, and with the church's emphasis on his Resurrection and symbolic victory over mortality, these two positions are not always very far apart, as evidenced by other events such as funerals and the Day of the Dead. Indeed, the Day of the Dead might be seen to mediate between the high holy day of Easter (a regular, annual festival) and the funeral (a sporadic event) by honoring the representatives of erratic mortal death on a fixed annual occasion. (Local variations in popular practice sometimes serve to underline such confluences even further: in the Isthmus region of Oaxaca, Easter is the time for honoring all dead ancestors, and Todos Santos stands as the date when households that have lost members in the previous year may make cemetery offerings.)[11] If the church emphasizes the link between mortal death and Christ's Passion during the Day of the Dead, popular religion focuses on recognizing both individual *difuntos* and the entire community of dead souls.

At the beginning of the 1990s, when the New Evangelization campaign was in full swing, church representatives in Cuauhtémoc and elsewhere made efforts to temper or sway the singular popular fixation on death and its travails by promoting Easter as a time for the spiritual rejuvenation of all members of the church community. Numerous sacraments—baptisms, weddings, first communions, and confirmations—were scheduled to take place during this sacred period; in addition, a day was set aside especially for confessions and the blessing of the sick. The intention was to identify Christ's Passion and self-sacrifice with the regeneration of the community as a social and moral whole. The additional effort by the church to add a reflection on the entire community of souls of the dead and of the saints to Easter activities was an attempt to enlarge the scope of this official holiday and to defuse the intensity of the popular, household-centered focus of Day of the Dead devotions. It is hard to say whether this effort was successful, for regardless of the date of the celebration the linkage between communal renewal and the remembrance of the dead is already present in popular discussions of the meaning of death. For members of the popular classes, such attitudes and reflections seem to remain most closely tied to the Day of the Dead, with its sensuous, family- and community-centered material practices. Unlike Easter, the Day of the Dead makes concrete demands on individuals; it compels particular acts of respect to known relatives and ancestors;

these acts involve specific objects and stories exchanged or recounted within the framework of close community ties. It draws on personal experiences, histories, and relations for its meaning, which Easter, strictly speaking, does not. For while the church calls on the commitment of its members, and helps them develop a personal faith within its fold, the faithful are often asked to respond to histories and ideas that can seem immaterial and far more remote than those put in play by celebrations of the Day of the Dead.

The church's wish to shift the activities of the Day of the Dead away from the personal is quite profound. The church no longer directly opposes these activities, but it continues to try to wrestle the individual material concerns of popular religiosity into a larger and more transcendent frame. The words of one priest I interviewed about the attitude of the church toward the Day of the Dead in Oaxaca make this effort plain: "In many places there are exchanges of food, *ofrendas*. With this, they demonstrate the memory of the *difuntos*; they also demonstrate the communion among the living, among themselves. These are great human values, cultural values of indigenous peoples that fall within the framework of Christian faith. All is valued and in fact is presently defended by the church."

The secret of the survival of the Catholic Church is its remarkable adaptive powers. As the influence of the church waned in Mexico and other parts of Latin America over the course of the twentieth century, some church sectors became far more adaptive and tolerant, even adopting some of the persuasive, evangelical tactics of its Protestant rivals in the search for souls. Such easygoing interaction with the popular concerns of the faithful represents a dramatic shift from the overtly oppressive practices and social policies of the church (with the exception of a few of its representatives) in Mexico and elsewhere in Latin America. As those in the ecclesiastical hierarchy recognize, the moral and social authority of the church, and its worldly power, depend in no small part on its capacity to maintain the faith of its congregation in the value of its specialized knowledge and powers. The apparent diminishing of this social potency in Mexico as a whole, exemplified in part by the ascendance of Protestant religious organizations, means that any effort the church makes to alter or shape the Day of the Dead is not likely to have far-reaching effects.

For although the Day of the Dead is a festival that forms part of a complex of unofficial rituals related to or derived in part from the practices of the Catholic Church, its practice is not really a sign of the power of the church. Indeed, apparently it never was. Rather, despite certain indications of its commercialization, this festival, as it is celebrated by Oaxacans of popular social sectors, embodies a distinct and sensuous social vision, with strong familial and communal ties and a sacrificial, reciprocal economics greatly at odds with the values of consumer capitalism. How long such traditions and alternative economic activities—rooted as they often are in rural, indigenous, village life—may last is an open question, especially given the rapid growth of Oaxaca City, the rise of consumer capitalism, and the globalization of the labor market. While such communal traditions may not be as old or as unbroken as many of us practitioners and anthropologists have wanted to believe—John Chance and William Taylor, for example, make a fairly convincing case for the post-independence roots of many of the economic and communal activities of such popular religious developments—the risk that they may now be passing away seems lamentable, like the loss of a zone where an idealized community might, now and then, flicker into being.[12] Perhaps such melancholy reflections on the part of an anthropologist are unwarranted, even disingenuous. After all, if history is not entirely a record of progress, and traditions are invented and reinvented, utopian tradition may yet metamorphose into another unstable and transient model of paradise. All the same, I have my doubts, uncritical and nostalgic as they may be.

CHAPTER 6

Spectacular Death and Cultural Change

Allí viene el agua	Here the rain comes
por la ladera	down the hillside
y se me moja	and it is getting wet,
mi calavera	my skeleton,
la muerte calaca	the skull-and-bones dead one
ni gorda, ni flaca	not fat, nor skinny
la muerte casera	the familiar dead one
pegada con cera.	stuck together with wax.

—"La calavera," anonymous popular Mexican *corrido*

OMNIPRESENT AT THE BEGINNING of November in Oaxaca, the *calavera* is the skull with your name scrawled across its forehead, made of a crusty sugar paste and decorated in bright colors; the *calavera* is the dancing skeleton found in Day of the Dead advertisements in the newspapers or in store windows; it is a cartoon caricature of a celebrity or local politician who, undressed of his (or her) flesh, is reduced to a pathetic and laughable skeleton, lampooned in witty and sardonic verse; it is a tiny papier-mâché skeleton with spindly limbs that jumps out of a cardboard coffin with the pull of a string; it appears in a tiny diorama of a beauty salon along with other *calaveritas* doing one another's hair, or singing in a rock band on a tiny stage; "Calavera!, mi calavera!" is the chant of schoolchildren as they wander in costume from house to house, hoping for candy, fruit, or another treat; the *calavera* is also the personage of Death who accompanies the Day of the Dead *comparsa*, dancing and shaking his scythe with a gleeful grimace; the *calavera* is the heart of a popular sensibility that, in looking on death, sees there a friend who can help one laugh at the pretenses of the rich and powerful or the capriciousness of the fickle twists and turns of fate, the very precariousness of life itself. For, as the poor so often recognize, death is the great equalizer, and no quantity of money or earthly power can hold it off forever. The *calavera*, then, is the laughing figure of the Day of the Dead who turns the world upside down and, for many, at least for a moment, rights it.

Indeed, the entire Day of the Dead festival may be seen as a beautiful example of ritual reversal; it demonstrates an inversion of the usual, virtually universal associations with death—sterility, darkness, uncertainty, danger, disorder, finiteness. Family visits to the cemetery, in particular, exemplify a ritual usurping of the figures of customary or everyday symbolic order. In addition to the heightened conviviality created by practices of reciprocity such as food sharing and visiting within the cemetery, many elements combine to add life, dynamism, and vitality to this setting of death: there are the vibrant orange and red hues of the flowers of the dead, colors that contrast with the stark white of funeral flowers; cacophonies of music obliterate the monotonous silence that usually pervades the cemetery; brightly colored balloons are seen everywhere, and children play with toys on the graves; highly spiced foods are in profusion—in short, this chaotic eruption of sensory stimuli and communal activity serves to oppose the stillness and solitude of death and the places of death.

The dramatic negation of the everyday represented by the Day of the Dead also involves what might be interpreted as a popular subversion of dominant symbolic categories as well as moral and aesthetic notions of "high" (mestizo) culture. Examples of "grotesque realism" can be seen throughout the Day of the Dead: the festival's invocation of "ignorant" indigenous ("pagan") beliefs and practices, "rude" sociability (including dancing, eating, and drinking—sometimes to the point of inebriation—in the graveyard), even the brash colors and loud music—all transgress the bounds of restrained decorum, hygiene, and the refined sensibilities of the dominant social order.[1]

Today, however, in a city undergoing rapid transformation, where cultural forms often subsume both traditional and modern worlds, and local and global significances, in what the cultural theorist Nestor García Canclini calls a "diverse and unequal" multi-temporal "hybridization," the practices and meanings of celebrations such as the Day of the Dead are also undergoing significant changes.[2] While other kinds of performances of death—funeral rites, *levantadas,* and private acts of devotion that are tucked safely away in the intimate corners of popular domestic spaces—are less vulnerable to the direct onslaught of forces of commercialization and tourism, the Day of the Dead, as an attractive "folkloric" fiesta, has come to be increasingly important as a stage on which "Oaxacan culture" may be showcased and sold for profit.

The performance of the Day of the Dead in Oaxaca today puts into play certain powerful and consequential debates about culture, including struggles over what culture is, where it comes from, how it is transmitted, who it belongs to, and who has the right to gain from the exploitation or sale of various of its elements. Who is really "in control" of popular culture in Oaxaca? What happens when state and municipal authorities extract and package previously "free" or "unconscious" expressions of collective celebration, aspects of popular lifeways, for the consumption of tourists? Indeed, what is the nature of "tradition" itself? Around the Day of the Dead and other important festivals in Oaxaca, contesting visions of community circle one another and sometimes clash.

"Give me Halowín!"

In Oaxaca, the economic "crisis" that citizens have endured for much of the last couple of decades has not abated; lately, the situation feels as though it bears more relation to low-intensity warfare than to a one-time climactic event. Talking about *el crisis* in Mexico is a bit like talking about the weather: sometimes it is a little better, sometimes a little worse, but it is always there. Since 1990, the year I began my research, the standard of living of most Oaxacans has diminished as inflation has increased. The crisis is the fallout of an economic process that failed, a protectionist economic strategy, initiated by the national government headed by Miguel de la Madrid, that favored industrialization along import-substitution lines. The result was the debt crisis of 1982 and subsequent economic reforms favoring austerity measures.[3] The height of the crisis occurred when the peso tumbled at the end of 1994 owing to the low reserves in foreign exchange and growing trade deficits. The Mexican government tried to resolve the situation by tightening the belt further, raising bank interest rates, and elevating the cost of basic services such as electricity and gasoline by 35 to 50 percent, while capping wage increases to an average of 12 percent annually. The result was that, in Oaxaca, for example, while the official minimum wage in the state grew from 12 pesos a day in 1993 to 22.5 pesos a day in 1997 (the national average is 24.3 pesos), in the same period purchasing power dropped by 50 percent, thereby offsetting any gains made by the increase in wages.[4]

When I asked city residents about changes that have occurred in the celebration of the Day of the Dead, they most often cite the economic situation, which has hit poor Oaxacans the hardest, as a major cause of the "decline in tradition." Many Oaxacans I met went on at great length about the altars they used to build for the Day of the Dead and the abundance of food that used to be placed on their household altars for the arrival of the *muertos*. The expenses of making an altar and other aspects of the Day of the Dead are more difficult every year for many to afford; small adjustments are made—for example, paper or plastic flowers are often substituted for more expensive cut flowers on altars and in grave decorations. Many Oaxacans have told me that, for the same reason, food exchanges between homes are diminishing. In addition, the increasing exigencies involved in juggling the demands of work outside the home, and tending children and aging relatives, actively limit the time that individuals have for preparing for El Día de los Muertos or for visiting friends and family. Such time constraints are becoming more acute for women in particular, for, over the last decade, women have entered the paid work force in unprecedented numbers: their participation in work outside the home grew from 14.9 percent in 1970 to 30.7 percent in 1995 and is still rising.[5]

But such perceived threats to the Day of the Dead are not new. In a survey of local newspaper stories on the festival dating back as far as the 1920s and 1930s, shortages of water and problems with security in the cemeteries were chronic and seemed to escalate, particularly from the 1950s on. One article from 1 November 1961, in fact, reported that some Oaxacans were capitalizing on the scarcity of water by bringing it into the graveyards and charging for it. That year, the "economic crisis" was held responsible for a perceived loss in the intensity and elaborateness of the celebration. It would seem that the Day of the Dead offers an especially heightened stage for the public airing of issues that affect many people throughout the year; when focused on this particularly resonant ritual frame, however, such difficulties suddenly appear in a different light.

Reasons for changes in "traditional" cultural practices are often complex, and to gloss these reasons as "economic" is both overly reductive and deceptive. Today, although many Oaxacans I know make special efforts to return to their home communities for the celebration of Los Muertos—this is especially the case for people who come from rural pueblos— many of those who migrate to work in other parts of the country or to the United States are simply unable to participate in the family reunions that the festival traditionally demands. In Oaxaca City, momentous social, cultural, political, and economic changes are imbricated in complex ways with structural changes that affect all of Mexico and beyond—shifts in the organization of labor, including an escalation of migration; gradual industrialization; and the mounting incursion of a global communications network and capitalist consumer ideology. These changes cannot help but have a genuine impact on social relations and people's lives. In Oaxaca, such processes often have a fracturing effect on communities and family integration, and, by extension, shape perceptions of the social role of the dead.

Among the signs of change in the Day of the Dead is the way that the symbols of the American celebration of Halloween have seeped into the commercial sphere (figures 6.1 and 6.2). Numerous material signs of Halloween—masks, costumes, and so forth—have also been brought back by the many Oaxacans who migrate for several months of the year to work *al otro lado* (on the other side of the border) or who now live there permanently. They are also conveyed homeward by wealthier Oaxacans who travel to the United States and by the perpetual inundation of residents via American television shows and films. In 1990 I watched as schoolchildren, dressed as witches, vampires, and mummies, were led by their teachers through the city center to collect *muertos*—mostly money and candy—from passers-by. And these days, costume parties to celebrate the so-called Noche de Brujas (Night of the Witches) are held at discos and private homes around town. More and more frequently, the *comparsa*—a carnivalesque "popular" masquerade that incorporates dancing, music, and the recitation of verses—is confused with Halloween (or Jalogüín or Halowín, as I have seen it spelled in various advertisements); over the past decade, some *comparsas* have ceased to be like playacting and have become more like a simple parade or procession from house to house—in short, more like Halloween. Even in the outlying satellite towns of Oaxaca City such as San Agustín Etla, Nazareno Etla, and San Sebastián Etla—where I accompanied the *comparsa* in 1991—where older customs still hold sway, I saw Winnie the Pooh and Ninja Turtles among the traditional *comparsa* costumes. (This phenomenon undoubtedly can be explained by the fact that many residents of Etla are seasonal migrants to California.) Indeed, today, when children march along the streets of Oaxaca to collect *muertos* from household altars, they may often be heard screaming, "Dame Halowín!" (Give me Halloween!).[6]

"Those are not Mexican customs, and even less are they Oaxacan customs," a man in the Panteón de San Martín told me in 1990, referring to the signs of Halloween that surrounded us. His statement made me curious about how Oaxacans as a whole were making sense of such transformations in Day of the Dead celebrations. Surprisingly, I found that many informants expressed their belief that in terms of its "moral principles" (*principios morales*) and sentiments, the festival remains the same. "It's a cult of *el más allá* [the beyond]," one woman explained, which was her way of saying that it is a space of the ancestors, the grounding of tradition, and the solid interlacing of the social relations of "community."

A War of Tradition

In Oaxaca, cobblestones that were laid over the past decade now cover nearly all the streets in the historic center of the city; these streets are lined with

FIGURE 6.1 Halloween paper pumpkins in the window of a store in the *centro* of Oaxaca City.

FIGURE 6.2 Halloween and *comparsa* masks, for sale in the *tianguis* area of the Mercado de Abastos.

video parlors, ATM machines, Internet cafés, and a plethora of Mexican- and foreign-owned three- to five-star hotels. The remarkably similar décor of the bed-and-breakfasts springing up everywhere features a palette of warm, earth-toned "indigenous" colors, refractions of the folkloric paintings and easily recognizable *artesanía* of the region—black pottery from San Bartolo Coyotepec, *tapetes* from Teotitlán del Valle, wooden animals from San Martín Tilcajete, and so on. Such evocations of a "traditional" Oaxacan aesthetic reflect a nostalgia for a time and place that perhaps never existed, an idealized and invented past. For visitors to the city, such unifying gestures serve to establish continuities between the "traditional" and the "modern"; in many tourist sites, past and present appear to shade into each other "naturally." The archaeological site of Monte Albán and the Santo Domingo Church, for example, serve as equivalent repositories of valuable Oaxacan culture; so, too, do fine art galleries like the Quetzalli (conveniently located right next to Santo Domingo Church), which features the work of such internationally renowned Oaxacan artists as Francisco Toledo and Rodolfo Morales.

The state, tourism, and the discipline of anthropology itself are all players in this invention of the past. As Quetzil Castañeda points out, the notion of "culture" as "the spiritual expression of people" was a product of German Romantic thinking. Arguing that, over time, culture came to be understood as a "totalizing frame of reference through which much of all social life is experienced and constituted," Castañeda discusses the elaboration of culture as a key term of anthropological enquiry, tracing its evolution from the work of Franz Boas, Margaret Mead, and Ruth Benedict to Clifford Geertz. In the process, he shows how "the culture of a people" has come to be figured as a kind of inherent gestalt, a pattern or an ethos that is distinctive and that "belongs" to a particular group as a sort of innate property held by members of the group. Consequently, differences in dress, food, and artisanry ("material culture"), as well as in less tangible expressions such as language, dance, and so on, are taken to embody essential aspects of particular geographic or ethnic groups.[7] Thus, according to such ideas, despite the fact that such cultural markers (dress, dance, language) are eminently transferable—they may be taught and learned, and even cultural "insiders" must learn them as children—the essence of a people that they represent cannot be transferred but inheres, as a necessary and distinctive property, in specific bodies.

Although, within the discipline of anthropology, such a conception of culture has been subject to extensive critique in the past twenty-five years, its Romantic premises still permeate much of the basic reasoning that informs studies, anthropological and otherwise, in the humanities and social sciences, as well as a good deal of public policy.[8] Such terms have also become part of the received idiom through which many people perceive, think about, and understand their own ways of life. For these reasons, Castañeda suggests that references to "culture" must always be understood as forms of argument rather than transparently descriptive systems. Whenever "culture" is invoked, then, what we might hear is not the ring of indisputable truth but the sound of a dialogue moving back and forth between the understandings and images that saturate mass culture, and individual fantasies, appropriations, reflections, and conceptions.

INVENTING TRADITIONS

Oaxaca holds a special place in the national Mexican imagination: its population is predominantly rural and Indian, with "a" culture that is diverse and, to the eye of the tourist, eminently picturesque. This distinctive profile is maximized in the rhetoric of tourism promotion, which reiterates the Mexican nationalist myth that subsumes the specificities of Oaxaca into a monolithic "ancient," eternal, powerful mestizo whole (figure 6.3). Oaxaca thus has a unique role to play in this nationalist imaginary drama as a kind of anachronistic pastiche or projection of Mexico's roots, the present and living image of its "former" self. Such a model requires a peculiar double stance: if it is to be visited or viewed, the traditional (indigenous) world of Oaxaca must be part of—while remaining at the same time separate from—the "modern" world. Aspects of Oaxacan culture must thus be placed, "for all time," in a sort of waxworks or museum diorama, a timeless "elsewhere" where viewers may, nevertheless, stroll in and out.

Such unquestioned paradoxes are crucial to the successful staging of highly publicized Oaxacan festivals such as the Guelaguetza, a fiesta of folkloric dance that glorifies the pre-Hispanic past in the guise of timeless yet contemporary folkloric tradition. Brochures advertising the Guelaguetza that were distributed among the public in 2000 by the city's Secretariat of Tourism Development waxed poetically about the festival's ethos of fraternal harmony:

> More important than this Folkloric gathering is the spirit that animates men and women from distinct places, distinct languages and distinct races to sing together in brotherly love with a sense of unity and fraternity with a great lady, OAXACA.

Running over two consecutive Mondays in late July and early August, the festival brings together indigenous groups from all over the state to present their *guelaguetzas* of regional dances and music—so-called after the "ancient" Zapotec tradition of reciprocal gift giving and mutual aid, tied especially to life-

FIGURE 6.3 The cover of a tourist magazine, with an image from the Guelaguetza.

cycle rituals.[9] According to both popular and scholarly accounts, the festival is described as having begun as a celebration called Lunes del Cerro (Monday of the Hill), when people from the seven regions of Oaxaca state converged on the Cerro Fortín (Fortin Hill), on the northern edge of the city, to perform dances and socialize, and to celebrate the harvest. Apparently, it was a popular celebration that coincided with the annual festival of the nearby Iglesia del Carmen Alto—the Carmelites having initiated their own fiesta in order to dilute the pagan tone of the popular celebrations on the hill. For many years, despite attempts by the church in the late nineteenth century to control or to ban it, the festival persisted as an annual event, albeit somewhat underground. By the early twentieth century, the event had resumed in the open and took place on an outdoor stage erected anew each year on the Cerro. Then, in the 1970s, the state government took control of the event and, in 1975, built a huge stadium that seats eleven thousand near the original festival site on the Cerro Fortín.[10] Today, the Guelaguetza is a massive affair, attracting visitors from all over Mexico and the rest of the world.

Described as a "celebration of folkloric dance," the Guelaguetza is the star tourist attraction of the year in Oaxaca; it receives widespread national and international state-sponsored promotion, and is highlighted in guidebooks and on hotel and tourist agency calendars. Since the 1970s, the Guelaguetza has spawned a wide variety of adjunct events and activities, designed to entertain the deluge of tourists who descend on Oaxaca during this season; these include a light-and-sound show performance of the "Legend of Donají" (a Zapotec princess); a contest to select a young woman worthy of representing Centeotl, the Zapotec goddess of corn; the presentation of *Bani Stui Gulal* (Zapotec, repetition of antiquity), a representation of the history of the Lunes del Cerro festival; and, since 1996, a Festival of Mescal. Publicity material for the festival dwelling on its ancestral indigenous roots and authentic communal spirit advertises it as the "Fiesta de Amigos," a copyrighted brand. And as the content of the Guelaguetza has expanded and diversified, "Guelaguetzas," or miniature versions of the dance festival, are now performed regularly throughout the year at major hotels in the city, such as the five-star Camino Real, housed in a sixteenth-century convent in the heart of the historic district.

Despite the claims of its promotional rhetoric, the Guelaguetza is clearly no longer the truly "popular" festival it supposedly once was. It is a slick and polished spectacle, a package of "authentic" indigenous culture tied up with a big red bow. And no longer is participation in the festival within everyone's reach. Tickets for seats close to the stage are too costly for most Oaxacans: in the decade between 1990 and 2000, the cost in pesos for the most expensive seats has held steadily at roughly U.S.$35, which is the equivalent of more than six times the minimum daily wage in the region. Even the least expensive tickets are still about U.S.$20. Without a ticket, one waits in line for hours for free admission to the auditorium's higher, "nosebleed" sections, where many watch the festival through periscopes made from mirrors and milk cartons. Just outside the stadium walls and farther up the Cerro, a competing adjunct festival goes on; a loud spectacle of American and Mexican pop music and commercial activity, the adjunct festival is, in many ways, far closer to the brash "popular" aesthetic than the Guelaguetza, that quintessential *fiesta del pueblo oaxaqueño*, could ever be now.

Just what is at stake in the Guelaguetza cultural performance? Without a doubt, the festival is a boon to all those employed in the tourist industry; every bed-and-breakfast and hotel in the city fills to capacity, restaurants do

a brisk business, and tour guides are busier than ever. Some festival promot-
ers argue that the state-sponsored Guelaguetza actively benefits Oaxacan
indigenous communities, for it encourages and celebrates their "native"
dances—although it is widely known that some of these "traditional" dances
(such as the popular Flor de Piña [Dance of the Pineapples] from Tuxtepec)
are of quite recent vintage.[11]

There is no point in arguing that the Guelaguetza is no longer "authentic"—perhaps it has never been "authentic" if by that word we mean constant,
the same as itself, unchanging, a singular (if repeatable) expression of an
immutable essence—these are the terms of the bill of goods being sold to
tourists along with the spectacle. More interesting, in my view, would be an
examination of the way the state government has used its "production" of
the Guelaguetza as an *indigenous* festival as a catalyst for tourism—for today
it is the government that very much shapes the evolution of the festival's
content. The Guelaguetza is an extreme example of a certain kind of "framing" of Oaxacan indigenous culture: its reproduction as a beautiful commodity, a frozen and sanitized artifact. Such a framing is particularly ironic,
for many aspects of the lifeways of the living, breathing exemplars of "this
rich Oaxacan cultural spectrum" are looked on with disdain by many other
Oaxacans, and—until the indigenous rebellion of the Ejército Zapatista de
Liberación Nacional (EZLN, Zapatista Army of National Liberation) in 1994
at least—any attempt to address the acute poverty and social problems faced
by indigenous communities in southern Mexico has been quite far from the
top of the government's political agenda. It is therefore quite important to see
that the positive, idealized image of indigenous culture in the Guelaguetza
depends on this hidden history as a precondition and the dismissal of the
political claims of indigenous peoples as primitive, underdeveloped others.[12]
Happy official celebrations of "indigenous culture" today frequently serve to
paper over intransigent social and economic problems and political differences. In a peculiar sleight of hand, the government lifts "a culture," all the
while making it look as if this exclusive bit of "borrowing" from a community
were an inclusive gift.

DEATH AS SHOW

Like the Guelaguetza, the Day of the Dead has become a quintessentially *Mexican* festival, a celebration that mirrors the cosmic marriage of European and
indigenous peoples and cultures that is Mexico. For this reason, the festival,
a national holiday, is regarded by many educated or middle-class profession-

als—artists, intellectuals, politicians, and so on—as an important marker of national Mexican identity, even if they do not personally observe its rites. El Día de los Muertos condenses the romantic associations of effervescent *mexicanidad* that stem from the postrevolutionary cultural explosion better than perhaps any other festival; in the Day of the Dead one sees both the roots and the replication of the art of José Guadelupe Posada and its popularization in the images of Diego Rivera and Frida Kahlo, the surreal homage to death in the writings of Juan Rulfo and Carlos Fuentes, and so on. The festival helps sustain a highly idealized and powerful image of a distinct, exuberant, and powerful Mexican culture: a hybrid European–mestizo shell that contains, at its heart, an indigenous metaphysics.[13] Such a sensibility is more aggressively asserted in the country's mestizo capital, Mexico City, but signs of such thinking are likewise present in Oaxaca.

Despite the increasingly enthusiastic claims made for the vibrancy of these national cultural practices, such "quintessential cultural expressions" are also figured as fragile entities, constantly in danger of extinction. Threats to the Day of the Dead include "foreign" encroachment or, worse still, as the Oaxacan daily *Noticias* put it in 1989, the "deculturalization and depersonalization [*deculturalización y depersonalización*]" of Oaxacan society instigated by "foreigners." The very mobility of cultural elements and the labile and saleable nature of cultural sentiments—encouraged by national cultural policies—also leads to the yearly laments published in newspapers about the "state" of the Day of the Dead.

In response, various authorities and culture ministers have developed strategies for combating such losses. In Oaxaca in the 1980s, for example, the Departamento de la Difusión Cultural (Department of Cultural Diffusion) from the Universidad Autónoma Benito Juárez de Oaxaca (UABJO, Autonomous University of Benito Juárez) began to organize an annual altar competition for students at one of the largest city high schools (Preparatoria Número 1). This competition took place in a park in the center of town at the end of October and was promoted on local radio stations. Altars were judged for their "beauty," the "authenticity" of their style, and the "content" of their decoration, as well as by the students' knowledge of the festival. I first witnessed this competition in 1989, which was the fourth year the event had been held. Above all an educational event, the competition was designed to consolidate a particular account of Day of the Dead traditions. Pamphlets distributed among students and passers-by made an explicit link between the festival and pre-Hispanic traditions: "El culto a los muertos, en Oaxaca, tiene el antecedente bien definido de la formidable herencia prehispánica" (The Oaxacan cult of the dead has a definite antecedent in the formidable pre-Hispanic civilization).

Also in 1989, an independent civic organization called the Asociación Folklórica (Folkloric Association)—whose members were mostly educated and middle-class—helped coordinate a series of public lectures given by academics in the Museum of Oaxaca on various aspects of the Day of the Dead. Topics included "Día de Muertos y Fieles Difuntos," "Culto a los Muertos," and "Leyendas de Oaxaca." The Folkloric Association also organized a self-proclaimed "authentic *comparsa*," or playacting masquerade. This *comparsa* visited homes around the *centro*, and, as if to dispel any possible doubts about its status, the costumed participant dressed as La Muerte (Death) and held a cardboard scythe bearing the neatly printed announcement "Comparsa Tradicional de los Muertos" (Traditional Masquerade of the Dead).

In addition to these activities and events, commercial and public art galleries around town organized exhibitions centered on the Day of the Dead. Performances of *Don Juan Tenorio*, written by the Spaniard José Zorrilla y Moral in 1844, a play often associated with the festival in other parts of Mexico, were also organized in Oaxaca City by members of the intellectual and artistic community and performed by a local theater group, Compañía Escénica de Oaxaca, at a moderate cost. (In 1990, the price of admission was 10,000 old pesos, or about U.S.$2.) Audience members consisted largely of artists, intellectuals, and tourists.[14]

Local writings on the Day of the Dead that appear in newspapers or other public printed sources wax romantic about the festival; they describe in fastidious detail various aspects of the festival, including the food prepared and the customs followed. The words "traditional" and "authentic" appear often in such texts, and a relationship between the festival and pre-Hispanic practices is frequently invoked. For example, an article entitled "La Muerte, compañera inseparable [Death, inseparable companion]," written by Raciel Martínez, which appeared in the Oaxacan daily *Noticias* on 1 November 1995, is typical of such commentaries:

> For all peoples, birth and death are most transcendent.
> The cult of death arose long ago.
> For example: among the jewels found in Tomb 7 of a Monte Albán notable
> is a gold breast shield bearing the image of a figure wearing a skeletal mask.
> In the Mixtec codices, many gods were associated with death.
> The poems of the Mexicas sum it up:
>
>> We've only come to dream, we've only come to sleep
>> It's not true, it's not true
>> that we've come to live on the earth.

Where will we go?
We come to be born
Our home is there
in the place of the fleshless.

Is it true that one lives on earth?
Not forever, not on the earth; we are only here for a little while.

Perhaps death is a sort of waking from the present dream.

During the colonial epoch, death was represented by a skeleton, bearing a scepter in his left hand.

At the beginning of the 20th century, that master of engravings, José Guadalupe Posada, reanimated death with a humorous touch.

And today, in this age of scientific and technical revolution, the majority of Mexicans, especially those in the southeast, continue the custom of making offerings to death and to the dead.

Who would not be anguished to know the arrival of his own death?

Many hope to see their names raised high in the streets; in this way, death cannot erase them completely.

Altars for the Faithful Dead, filled with *ofrendas,* are made in countless homes and in the most isolated locales. Drinking is not what is important at this moment; there is no glory in getting drunk. What is most important is that one fulfills one's obligation [*cumplir*]; for belief in the return of the souls of the dead remains firm with us.

Although this day is called the Day of the Dead, the living wait with joy, with music, and with all the little things that the dead [*los difuntos*] have loved.

The odors of *cempazúchitl* and incense fill the air, mixing with fragrance of fruits, *moles* and conserves, chocolate and peanuts.

And those houses in rural communities that were closed down and silent suddenly come back to life everywhere.

Today, the cemeteries are cleaned and cleared of weeds, graves are painted, and containers of food, new hats, cigars, fruit, a bottle of *mescal,* and burning candle are placed on them.

These customs and traditions change from town to town. But what is essential is that respect for death is offered and maintained.

It does not matter if you put up a cross of oak or pine. It could be of plate, pure silver, or of forged iron.

The important thing is to love and respect death, that inseparable companion.

The verse-like format of the text, accompanied by photographs of an altar, the Comparsa de Muertos, and a candlelit graveside vigil—including shadowy images of simply dressed people and a *campesino*'s hat hung on a grave cross—serve to evoke the mystic aura that surrounds the Day of the Dead. Particularly noteworthy in this article is its rhetorical use of a pre-Hispanic past (by including the "authentic" poems of the ancient Mexica or Nahua) and its fusion of urban life and a pristine rural zone, which is "closed" and "silent"— ironically "dead"—to talk about what is happening in the city and to declare what the festival "really" means. It is those Mexicans "especially those in the southeast"—that is, Oaxaca—the article claims, who most carefully maintain the festival's authentic meaning.

The invocation of an indigenous rural (past) culture in order to represent a unified Oaxacan aesthetic may also be seen in other public Day of the Dead texts. Claims made in a small book written by Luz María Gonzáles Esperón and sponsored by the Oaxacan Institute for Culture and the State Fund for Arts and Culture are typical of many publications that I have found over the years:

> In our view, there will always be a world in which room will be given to the life, color, and magic of Oaxaca. Art has been known to Oaxacans since ancient times; from the time man first began to populate the region's valleys, mountains, and littorals, artisans, thanks to their indigenous roots, have been imbuing their works of art with interpretations of death that have unique characteristics.
>
> And so it is that in Oaxaca, during the month of November, the month of the dead, we celebrate traditions that contribute to deepening the links between the living and their past. These traditions have come to form an essential part of the daily life of Oaxacans.[15]

While exalting "the authentic indigenous traditional essence" of the Day of the Dead, this little book also bitterly bemoans the present loss of tradition, a result of insidious foreign cultural invasion:

> Nevertheless, since the celebration of its traditional festivals is something that has come to distinguish Oaxaca as much within as outside the country, one has to underline that urban zones are suffering the penetration of foreign customs, whose only end is to commercialize a number of elements that have nothing to do with the festivities, altars, and *ofrendas* that for long years have allowed us to find ourselves in the past, to honor our loved ones who are no longer present but who we still keep alive in our memories.[16]

The familiar refrain, it seems, may be found everywhere—even in promotional material. Nestor García Canclini offers some useful insights into the logic of such appropriative utterances. Writing of the famous Día de los Muertos celebrations on Janitzio, a picturesque tourist island in the state of Michoacán, where the traditional fiesta has taken on spectacular dimensions of a "photogenic culture," García Canclini argues that today the Day of the Dead on Janitzio is "a giant make-believe venture." He goes on to say that "the light from the candles is by now as much a customary part of the ceremony as the brightness of flashlights; mourning songs blend continuously with whispers in English, French, and German." The celebration of the Day of the Dead in Janitzio, in his view, exemplifies a capitalist modernizing tendency to secularize traditional events while retaining their symbolic content, if that content can be exploited for profit. Such elite manipulations of Mexican popular culture, he argues, constitute rather violent "relocating" practices, complicit in a hijacking and sanitization of popular/indigenous identity as part of the nationalist project of cultural centralization.[17]

In my efforts to learn more about various aspects of the tourist promotion of the Day of the Dead, in 1990 I spoke with the man who was then acting director of the Bureau of Tourism Development in Oaxaca, Juan Arturo López Ramos. López Ramos hailed from the Mixteca region of Oaxaca and had studied in the United States and Spain. He was, in many respects, a cosmopolitan figure, but his responses to my questions emphasized the culture of Oaxaca as a unique spirit of place that makes for something like a genetic or instinctive spiritual inheritance—not at all, as he repeated several times, a matter of education.

Q: How do you see your role with respect to Oaxacan indigenous culture?

A: As far as my own vocation goes, I love the culture of my ancestors. . . . What makes us different from other countries is precisely what makes us more attractive to tourists. Consequently the more we deepen our own culture, the more we preserve it and conserve it.

Q: But if you don't yet truly know what you're trying to preserve, doesn't that complicate your work quite a bit?

A: No, because we are all Oaxacans, and, as Oaxacans, we are immersed in the same cultural context. . . . You as an anthropologist can learn something about the Fiesta de los Muertos, but we live it on a daily basis. So, we well know what it is; we don't have to go to school in order to learn that which we live every day.

Q: But you live it in a different way depending on your family, no?

A: There are certain universalities, like mankind itself. Each human being is different, but since all of us live in the same time and the same cultural context here, we have a common basis with which to appreciate our form and model of life. It's important to point out that Oaxaca's culture is not transmitted through a formal process of education in the schoolroom. It's an informal process that takes place through life itself.

Many of my interviews with such official "gatekeepers" of culture reiterated similar themes. Culture in Oaxaca is something that "belongs" to the people as a layer of their very being. It is internalized or absorbed by them through a process akin to osmosis ("[W]e are immersed in the same cultural context. . . . [W]e live it on a daily basis," López Ramos insisted). As such, it is something that can be understood only from the inside. Like an endangered animal caught in the sights of a hunter, this culture is something that must be shielded from external threats. It is the job of the gatekeepers, of course, to be sure that such protections are maintained.

One of the great logical peculiarities of such arguments is that a major vehicle of the "preservation" of tradition, from the point of view of the municipal and state departments of tourism, is tourist promotion. Thus, although "authentic culture" must be protected from the encroachments of *extranjeras* (foreigners), people like me, it also appears to depend—at least in terms of levels of official involvement—quite a bit on us: foreigners and Mexicans from elsewhere. The system of state appropriation (protection) of culture depends, then, quite stringently, on locating both a danger to culture and a market for it. And if both can be found to reside in the same bodies, so much the better. The danger to culture becomes precisely the *reason* why it must be brought to the marketplace—thus preserved, it may be shared with everyone, as long as we are all clear about who is an "insider" and who is an "outsider." Selling the fantasy of being an insider increases the profits of tourism, but in order to preserve those profits (culture), the distinction must hold fast.

Such a scenario sets up other logical conundrums as well. For despite the minister's repeated insistence that Oaxacan culture did not have to be taught in the schools, various bodies, involving all levels of government, have dedicated considerable effort to educate the populace regarding the properly authentic and traditional way to celebrate the festival. In part, such "educational" efforts are part of the relocation, hijacking, and sanitation of popular practices discussed by García Canclini. Designed to turn heretofore unconscious, somewhat casual undertakings into spruced-up, conscientious practices, these educational efforts produce small museum displays, dioramas of "traditional" life. Clearly, too, even if its scope is widening, not every such effort to "teach the culture" falls under the aegis of the Bureau of Tourism Development. Contrary to the naturalizing rhetoric of officials like López Ramos, as every parent or teacher or immigrant knows, there is more to learning cultural practices than simply breathing the air. Thus education of some sort creeps in, with the very everyday existence of "life itself." Of course, this is where the "dangerous" transferability of culture, its mutability, liveliness, and inventiveness, also shows up: the very thing the Bureau of Tourism Development, and other guardians of renovated "tradition," try to stand so strongly against.

Since I began studying the Day of the Dead in Oaxaca, the promotion of the festival has become more lavish and more complex. In 1989 and 1990, for example, a series of simple mimeographed publicity pamphlets, printed on plain white paper, were distributed throughout the city. At the time, promotion of the Day of the Dead by the municipal Bureau of Tourism Development was conducted in coordination with other federal, state, and municipal government agencies, such as the Secretaría de Desarollo Económico y Social (Ministry of Economic and Social Development), the Dirección de Educacion, Cultura y Bienestar Social (Department of Education, Culture, and Social Welfare), the local Universidad Autónoma Benito Juárez, and the Instituto Nacional de Antropología e Historia (INAH, National Institute of Anthropology and History). The focus was on multifaceted cultural undertakings involving a wide range of city groups and organizations (state public civil institutions were involved in the activities: entities such as secondary schools and *preparatorias* [high schools], the Instituto Mexicano de Seguro Social [IMSS, Mexican Institute of Social Security], and the Instituto de Seguridad y Servicios Sociales de los Trabajadores del Estado [ISSSTE, Institute of Security and Social Services for State Workers], as well as the INAH). Tourism and activities that would generate profit were secondary considerations. Altar exhibitions and competitions were organized for *preparatoria* students, as well as for civil servants and public workers; these took place in the building of the Department of Public Education, in museums, and in public parks. A list of cemeteries around the city, or even in towns around the state, was distributed, but few details were provided. Clearly some forms of local knowledge were presumed.

I have translated one brochure from that period, a schedule of events issued by the municipal Bureau of Tourism Development, in 1990 (figure 6.4).

Within ten years, the focus of official or government-sponsored festival organization had changed considerably. Beginning in 1996 the orchestration of the Day of the Dead in Oaxaca took place under the aegis of the reconstituted

FIGURE 6.4 (*opposite page*) A schedule of events for the Day of the Dead in 1990, on a poster issued by the Bureau of Tourism Development.

FIESTA DE MUERTOS

1 and 2 November 1990

PROGRAM OF EXHIBITION OF ALTARS OF THE DEAD
Sunday, October 28, at 10:00 A.M.

Altar of the Dead   Preparatory School No. 1
(Antonio Labastida Garden)

Wednesday, October 31, at 10:00 A.M.

Altar of the Dead   Workers of Coordinated Services
(Ministry of Public Education Building)

Altar of the Dead   Secondary School No. 6
(Blvd. Eduardo Vasconcelos No. 300)

Thursday, November 1, and Friday, November 2
Museum of Oaxaca (Andador Turístico)

Altar of the Dead   Population of the Villa of Mitla

Altar of the Dead   Mitla Cultural Center

Traditional Tapete de   State Tourist Bureau
Levantada de Cruz

INAH Regional Museum
(annex of the Church of Santo Domingo)

Altar of the Dead   IMSS (Mexican Institute of Social Security)
ISSSTE (Institute of Security and Social
Services for State Workers)

Altar of the Dead   Secondary School No. 6
(Blvd. Eduardo Vasconcelos No. 300)

Traditional Tapete de   State Tourist Bureau
Levantada de Cruz

"El TOPIL"
(Antonio Labastida Garden No. 2)

Altar of the Dead   Oaxacan Folkloric Association

Altar of the Dead   Folkloric Cultural Institute of Oaxaca

Coordinators: Oaxaca State Government
Department of Economic and Social Development
Bureau of Education, Culture, and Social Welfare
Bureau of Tourist Development
Institute of Anthropology and History
Autonomous University Benito Juárez of Oaxaca

Secretaría de Desarollo Turístico (SEDETUR, Secretariat of Tourism Development). The simple paper pamphlets I had collected in 1989 and 1990 had evolved into proper brochures—shiny, slick, and colorful. The schedule of events listed in the brochure featured only a few activities in the center of town, but most of these events were located in "traditional" towns and barrios on the edge of the city's core or outside it: Xochimilco, Xoxocotlán, and San Juanito. An explanatory text offers a now familiar account of a mystical and timeless "Mexican" death: "In Mexico, people play with death; the great majority of Mexicans feel they have a moral obligation to make offerings [*ofrendar*] to the dead, whether in their homes or in the cemetery. Many people take advantage of these holidays in order to spend time with the dead, to share food with them, to decorate their graves, to burn incense [*copal*], and—Why not?—to toast with and to them."

A bilingual poster listing the festival's "program of activities" was also issued in 2000 by SEDETUR and pasted all over town. The English-language text from the poster is shown in figure 6.5.

When compared with the mimeographed schedule of events available in 1989, this detailed poster suggests that over the decade the activities and events included in the promotion of the Day of the Dead specifically for tourist consumption had been both diversified and streamlined. By 2000 activities for tourists had become quite numerous and included not only various altar displays and competitions but also a number of *comparsas*, exhibitions of Levantada *tapetes*, and an event called the "Offerings of the Children" in Xoxocotlán. The last, another "invented tradition" inspired by the supposedly pre-Hispanic origins of the Day of the Dead, relies on a poetic image for its effect: children, the young of today, are sent to take flower offerings to Monte Albán, the site of an ancient city, to pay their respects to the "ancestors." Along with the *comparsa* and the Levantada de la Cruz (explained in bare-bones fashion as "a tradition in Oaxaca . . . a painting of religious images using colored sand"), such events, listed in a blurry, nonspecific, and unskilled manner, strip the Day of the Dead of any symbolic potency or threat. The festival is tamed and, just like the colorful objects of Oaxacan *artesanía*, turned into a quaint, picturesque display of Oaxacan "folklore" to be experienced, photographed, and consumed.

A map at the back of the brochure shows the location of the cemeteries it mentions, gives directions on how to get to them, and lists the price of admission (usually 2.50 pesos, or roughly 25 cents, although admission to the Xoxocotlán cemetery was 5 pesos, or 50 cents). Even though anyone was always able

FIGURE 6.5 A "Program of Activities" for the Day of the Dead in 2000, on a bilingual poster issued by the Secretariat of Tourism Development.

DAYS OF THE DEAD IN OAXACA / PROGRAM OF ACTIVITIES

Panteón San Miguel (Panteón General)

During the Days of the Dead, the Panteón San Miguel undergoes a marvelous and spectacular transformation. This is the main cemetery in Oaxaca City, and it is a must for you, the visitor to Oaxaca, to witness the care and love that the people demonstrate in the decoration of the tombs of their relatives. As well, you will see the magnificent Altares de Muertos (Altars of the Dead), which compete for the authenticity, originality, and traditional displays. Families decorate the tombs with many beautiful flowers, including marigolds (*cempasúchil*) and cockscomb. Marigolds are a symbol of truth, wisdom, beauty, and eternity and were traditionally used by ancient pre-Hispanic cultures in Mexico. On top of the tomb, crosses are formed using many types of flowers, and skulls made of sugar or clay are included in the decoration. The pleasant aromatic smell of burning copal is also part of the ritual to attract and satisfy the returning souls. From early morning outside the cemeteries, stalls are set up selling regional foods and drinks. Bands play, and the scene becomes more like a fair. At dusk and far into the night, the sacred grounds of the Panteón glow with the light of thousands of votive candles in homage to the departed souls, lighting the way for them to return to visit their families and friends.

On October 31 and November 1 and 2, the Panteón San Miguel (General Cemetery) opens its gates to public visits from 10:00 A.M. to 1:00 A.M. (10h–01h). By choosing to visit the Panteón San Miguel during this celebration, you will witness and share some [of] the deep-rooted traditions and customs of the people of Oaxaca. Many activities have been organized by the municipal Bureau of Tourism of the City of Oaxaca.

Tuesday, October 31

9:00 A.M.	Installation of the Municipal Altar Main entrance
	Installation of the Altars of the Dead (for competition) Grounds of Panteón San Miguel
	Installation of the Carpet of Sand* and the Altars of the Dead Main entrance: Panteón San Miguel
Noon	Exhibition of the Municipal Altar, the Carpet of Sand, and the Altars of the Dead Main entrance and the grounds: Panteón San Miguel

* Carpet of Sand (Tapete de Levantada de la Cruz) is a tradition in Oaxaca. It is a painting of religious images using colored sand.

(*continued*)

8:00 P.M.–midnight	Illumination of thousands [Spanish version said 2,400] of votive candles Panteón San Miguel

Wednesday, November 1

9:00 A.M.	Judging of the Altars of the Dead (for competition) Panteón San Miguel
Noon	Exhibition of the Municipal Altar, the Carpet of Sand, and the Altars of the Dead Main entrance and the grounds: Panteón San Miguel
8:00 P.M.–midnight	Illumination of thousands of votive candles Panteón San Miguel

Thursday, November 2

1:00 P.M.	Presentation of prizes in the competition of the Altars of the Dead The ceremony will be held outside the gates of Panteón San Miguel.

PANTEÓN DEL MARQUESADO

November 1 and 2, Marquesado Cemetery opens its gates from 7:00 A.M. to 9:00 P.M. (07h–21h) for public visits. In addition to the decorated tombs, visitors may enjoy music in the afternoon.

PANTEÓN DE SANTA CRUZ XOXOCOTLÁN

There are two cemeteries in Xoxocotlán, the "old one" (Panteón de San Sebastián) and the "new one." In both cemeteries, people can go during the day and stay during the night.

November 1 and 2, the cemetery is open for public visits from 10:00 A.M. to 9:00 P.M. (10h–21h).

Tuesday, October 31

7:00 P.M.	Exhibition of Altars of the Dead in the main street of the city
8:00 P.M.	Visit the cemetery. This occasion is noteworthy for the excellent decoration of the tombs and the guitar music played by many of the relatives of the deceased. Exhibition of the Carpet of Sand (Tapete de Levantada de la Cruz) inside the grounds of the

cemetery. The cemetery glows with candlelight until 5:00 A.M. (05h) the next morning

Wednesday, November 1

11:00 A.M.

Offerings of the Children. This begins from the Central Park in Xoxocotlán. Children take their floral offerings to the archeological site at Monte Albán, where they are dedicated to the deceased.

5:00 P.M.

Costume parade (*comparsa*) of children in the central park in Xoxocotlán. Children parade in the main streets of Xoxocotlán dressed in masks and costumes they have made. They are accompanied by a band.

Thursday, November 2

1:00 P.M.

Costume parade (*comparsa*) of adults in the central park in Xoxocotlán. A competition is held for the most original and traditional costumes of the *comparsa*. Also enjoy music of the local band.

PANTEÓN DE SAN FELIPE

Early in the morning on November 2, the people start to decorate the tombs and prepare everything in readiness for the visit of the deceased. The cemetery is open until approximately 5:00 A.M. (05h) the next day (November 3). There are stalls outside the cemetery selling regional foods.

PANTEÓN DE SAN MARTÍN MEXICAPAN

This cemetery opens its gates for public visits on November 1 and 2 from 8:00 A.M. to 8:00 P.M. (08–20h).

PANTEÓN DE SAN JUAN CHAPULTEPEC

This cemetery opens its gates for public visits on November 1 and 2 from 8:00 A.M. to 7:00 P.M. (08–19h). A mass (Los Fieles Difuntos) is celebrated in the cemetery chapel on November 2 at noon (12h).

PANTEÓN DE SANTO TOMÁS XOCHIMILCO

On November 2 the people decorate the Altars of the Dead. A mass is held at 5:00 P.M. (17h). After the mass, follow the costume parade (*comparsa*) as it wanders through the streets of the village accompanied by a band. Regional foods can also be enjoyed.

to visit the cemeteries, because of the brochure the graveyards were converted more obviously, at least for the first few days in November, into tourist sites. The Day of the Dead had become "spectacular" theater; more organized (the brochure offered specific times for activities, although events rarely begin at the appointed hour), this version of the festival was also obviously directed at tourists. Visitors were warned not to leave valuables in their car; they were told how they might obtain information at each cemetery (from the Ángeles Verdes [Green Angels]) or reach emergency services from "strategically arranged" "rescue teams" (*cuerpos de rescate*). In addition, by 2000, other organizations in the city concerned with Oaxacan culture (the Asociación Folklórica and the Universidad Autónoma Benito Juárez) had all but disappeared from the picture, as had any mention of the activities that these institutions may have been organizing. Instead, similar to what had happened with the Gueleguetza, SEDETUR's promotional activity was concentrated on events deemed to be the most "show-like" and appealing to tourists. Many other activities did—and do—go on, like the Cemetery Days throughout the month, but only in the margins. Fortunately, perhaps, not every Day of the Dead activity registered on the tourist map.

A photograph of the nightime *velada* (the only one in the city) at Xoxocotlán—a cemetery that receives a great deal of promotion in Oaxaca for its "authenticity"—appears on the front of the colorful tourist brochure. For the purposes of such official representations, "authenticity" appears to be measured in terms of practices that more closely resemble the Day of the Dead in its most "standard" or familiar form—that is, according to widely publicized photographs of the Day of the Dead celebration in famous locales such as Mixquic and Janitzio and in the region of Patzcuaro (Michoacán). That the *velada* in the cemetery of Xoxocotlán lasted until 1:00 A.M. in 1996, until 2:00 A.M. in 1997, until 3:00 A.M. in 1998, and until 4:00 A.M. in 2000 suggests that such a generalized "authentic" pattern is the source of several of these more specifically tourist activities. Visitors are brought to Xoxocotlán graveyard by bus (in 1996, seventy-eight tour buses went to the cemetery) to see the *velada* and to take as many photos as they please. The trip there is to be an adventure, but not too much of one. Jose Gil Calzadias, a representative of SEDETUR, told me that the extension of the cemetery's closing hour and other such alterations to the celebration of the Day of the Dead were made "with the intention of returning to ancestral traditions and in doing so present to the visitor a vision of how the festival was celebrated in former times. . . . We don't try to invent anything new."[18]

What these former times were, I suspect, no one knows.

Within just a few years, certain of the most public celebrations of the Day of the Dead in Oaxaca have become simulacra, spectacles, ironically, of their most "authentic" selves. As the poster for the year 2000 suggests, the visitor is encouraged to see Oaxacan culture in "participatory" fashion, through *witnessing*—"it is a must for you, the visitor to Oaxaca, to *witness* the care and love that the people demonstrate in the decoration of the tombs of their relatives"—and *sharing*—"you will *witness* and *share* some [of] the deep-rooted traditions and customs of the people of Oaxaca." Implicit in such rhetoric is the idea that culture, these deep-rooted customs, may be "enjoyed" by the visitor but that they still belong to the authentic bearers of that culture, the generic collective individual: the "people of Oaxaca." At the same time, more and more Oaxacans are learning that aspects of "their" culture previously taken for granted can, and do, have a price. Authenticity sells. By the turn of the twenty-first century an increasing number of private citizens in Oaxaca were seeking to capitalize directly on the growing general interest in the Day of the Dead.

CULTURE IN AND ON THE NET

In Oaxaca today, the Internet is a key interface mediating the desires of buyers (tourists) and sellers. Oaxacan entrepreneurs have been quick to recognize the benefits of setting up informational Web sites, particularly if they are in the transportation or accommodations business. One Web site I encountered during my first surfing session appeared under the rubric "Oaxaca Tours." Entirely in English, the site is titled "The Day of the Dead in Oaxaca, Mexico" and was created by a family that runs one of the pricier bed-and-breakfasts in the center of town. The site provides the visitor with an explanation of the Day of the Dead that makes use of the same evocative language we have encountered before in such descriptions: "In preparation for this day, the last days of October are spent *preparing* special loaves of bread ... and desserts; *harvesting* special flowers, including marigolds; *creating* altars in the home; and *decorating* gravesites [with d]ecorations in the form of macabre but whimsical skeletons and candy skulls [my emphasis]."

The dynamism that imbues this description of activities is part of the ploy of seduction at work here: the active "authentic" Oaxacan ("preparing," "harvesting," "decorating") invites the passive tourist "to participate in this *magical* time by taking advantage of one or more of the workshops or tours listed. . . . Workshops are *small* and *personal*, and take place in a *family* atmosphere. Tours are respectful of local traditions and *sacred* rites [my emphasis]." In this very self-conscious and contrived elaboration of authenticity authored by Oaxacans, the Oaxacan is actively inside his or her culture, engaged in all sorts of "traditional" handiwork, yet, in the context of a workshop, he or she is, at the same time, able to step outside it and view it "objectively."

The activities in this particular Day of the Dead tour include a *mole* cooking class, a visit to the Xoxocotlán cemetery on the October 31, and a "Spiritual Ritual with *Curanderos* (Healers)." The purposes of this last activity are to learn "about rituals and beliefs that date back to pre-Hispanic times" and to experience "aromatherapy and the cleansing of aura and energy." Like the Buddha statuettes and crystal pyramids I saw for sale in the *curandero* stalls in the market, the description reflects the peculiar mélange of New Age discourses and trends, and romanticized indigenous or traditional practices, that today seems to be showing up more and more often in Oaxaca.[19] The text of the tour, like the colorful Day of the Dead brochure, reflects a sense of culture as an objective entity that is "owned"; such culture is a kind of extension of the (Oaxacan) self, but it can be shared—for a price. The Web site ends with an appropriate exhortation: "We hope that these activities will increase your knowledge of *our customs & culture* [my emphasis]."

With its gracious and welcoming tone, the Web site's overall message is an inclusive one. Nevertheless, in a subtle but clear manner, its rhetoric seals off any real opening to the inner secrets of Oaxacan culture. It also precludes any objections to such closure by rejecting a priori the grounds for any—and hence, one might argue, the possibility of "true"—transcultural dialogue or understanding. The only space available for exchange requires maintenance of a clear opposition between "Mexican" or "Oaxacan" and "other" cultures. Yes, the visitor (who is, implicitly, "one without authentic culture") may often wield economic power over Oaxacans, but they have other means at their disposal to raise themselves symbolically, for they possess "authentic" culture. Adding to the complexity is that such an argument is made as a part of a self-conscious self-presentation by Oaxacans.

Such presentations and interpretations of Oaxacan culture, created by Oaxacans themselves, suggest a displacement of self-awareness that amounts to a peculiar sort of self-objectification. A separation has been made between ideologically self-conscious discourses and more unconscious everyday perceptions.[20] Dominant "official" notions of tradition and cultural identity have become a part of people's self-image and of their understanding of what is appropriate and acceptable festival practice. The dialogue between Oaxacan and tourist, insider and outsider, is based on the tacit assumption that "one's culture" is valuable; yet the reasons why these traditions should be preserved are taken for granted—hence they remain utterly ambiguous, perhaps even to Oaxacans themselves. Consequently, the intrinsic "value" of a culture may be rather quickly conflated with a kind of value measured in dollars—preferably American dollars.

Unsurprisingly, perhaps, many Oaxacans I interviewed spoke about the cultural richness and diversity of their state and city as a source of pride, and they appeared to enjoy the foreign interest and attention. When I asked if tourism was changing the Day of the Dead, one man responded in a manner that, over the course of the interviews, I found to be typical: "No, tourism has no influence. On the contrary, how great that tourism comes so that we can show people the custom [of El Día de los Muertos]!" It is notable that this was the same kind of attitude I encountered when I asked people their feelings about the Guelaguetza; many of them could not understand my objections to the prohibitive cost of tickets or to the highly sensational, hyperbolic promotion of this celebration of "authentic" indigenous Oaxacan culture. I had to ask myself if I was conducting my own romantic resuscitation of "authentic" Oaxacan culture. How much did commodification change the nature of the relationships and interactions that composed such festival events? Was I witnessing the piecemeal shifts and reinventions of any living traditions, or were there altogether significant changes in the character of the event and the relationships it fostered thanks to the intervention of state organized tourist displays? I am still not sure.

There do seem to be signs in Oaxaca, however, that attitudes are changing with regard to how people choose to spend their money on traditional ritual practices like the Day of the Dead. Profligate spending in the context of all kinds of religious fiestas—from *quinceaños* and *mayordomías* to weddings and funerals—is sanctioned partly because these are sacred events: lavish expenditure reflects a positively viewed intensity of devotion. Yet one trend I have observed in Oaxaca suggests that nowadays people are more inclined to contribute financially to religious festivals when they are distinguished as its financial sponsors. Increasingly, if their names are prominently displayed, benefactors are contributing to the costs of church renovations or to certain festivals with no tradition of sponsorship, such as the *mayordomía*. An anthropologist friend working in a Zapotec town in the environs of Oaxaca City found that new saint festivals had been added to the annual festival calendar in order to accommodate the number of individuals—especially those who had made money as migrant workers in California—with newfound wealth that they were eager to show off.[21] It is difficult to pinpoint the precise reasons for the emergence of these practices, but I believe that they demonstrate an increasing sense of individuation in people's attitudes in Oaxaca City, part of a set of attitudes characteristic of contemporary, "modern" Oaxaca that, as in much of the rest of the world, is increasingly driven by a money economy, with the erosion of economies of community exchange. For these new forms of sponsorship appear to be less about obligations or duties to a community than about direct means of acquiring status by purchasing it.

The Day of the Dead and the "Popular Community"

For some residents of Oaxaca, the Day of the Dead is an ongoing expression of the sacred significance of the cult of the dead, a rite performed to reduce the chance of bad fortune and the discontent of dead souls. For many, the placing of *ofrendas* on the household altar is a strong indication of the real and persistent, mysterious reality of the visit of the dead. Nonbelievers in this sort of thing, Jehovah's Witnesses in Colonia San Juan, for example, rarely set up household altars or set out *ofrendas*. But the distinctions between the activities of believers and those of nonbelievers were not always so evident or so characteristic. Some families do build simple altars in their homes, although they do not believe that the dead return to visit; like the proliferation of Christmas trees elsewhere in North America (and increasingly in Oaxaca!), the setting out of an altar can function as a generic expression of seasonal sentiments.[22] In this case, the altar represents a loose social commitment to the basic ideals surrounding the festival, ideals that—regardless of people's avowed institutional religious affiliation—are as much a part of popular culture as they are of Catholicism.

There are still other households where the families do not construct an altar, yet they do visit the graves of their relatives on November 2 or on the designated Cemetery Day. This phenomenon may be explained by the fact that the domestic aspect of the celebration—that is, the building of the household altar and the placing of *ofrendas* for the dead—have folk-Catholic or indigenous (even *pagano* [pagan], as some put it) origins and associations, whereas the visit to the graveyard forms part of the conventional, official Catholic celebration of Todos Santos. The construction and maintenance of a household altar, and the setting out of offerings, are private expressions of devotion to the dead, whereas the visit to the cemetery is obviously more public. (Exceptions that should be mentioned include "showcase altars," on display in homes around the city that are open for public viewing, or altar displays erected in hotels. The addresses of these places are advertised on posters put up by the Secretariat of Tourism Development.)

The public cemetery visit is not strictly Catholic, however. It, too, is a cultural event in a wider sense, and incorporates a variety of "folk" aspects. Hence I met some Pentecostals and even a few self-proclaimed atheists in the cemeteries, visiting the graves of their dead. Above all, particularly among members of the popular classes, Oaxacans used aspects of the Day of the Dead to express a common membership in a moral community; at the same time, their personal practices were subject to personal interpretations or desires for expression. Among other functions, such "folk-Catholic" festivals offer ample opportunity for members of a ritually and rhetorically invoked "popular community" to assert an identity over and against the general thrust of Mexican national culture.

Newspapers published during the first half of the twentieth century often adopted a particularly patronizing tone in their stories about the Day of the Dead. Consider, for example, the following quote from an article published in the Oaxacan daily *La Voz* in 1948:

> The celebration of the deceased, in which our dearly beloved who have been transported forever beyond the borders of this world, attracts the attention of all social sectors, but especially our indigenous classes, interrupting all ordinary activities for active expressions, more profane than religious, in order to have a kind of sentimental bridge between this world and the beyond [*el más allá*], and to bring themselves closer to the memory of the departed.

In an effort to shape tasteful literate opinion, the papers of the 1930s and 1940s expressed many of the attitudes and values of the state and its official culture, which put down and distanced itself from various "backward" indigenous sources in order to elevate a "forward-looking" and paradigmatic generalized mestizo body as the "modern Mexican way." Control of carnivalesque irruptions of "popular" bodies was paramount and was conducted through a variety of more or less violent practical and rhetorical means: legal restrictions; physical containment of particular groups; economic, social, political, and geographic marginalization; the elaboration of hygiene campaigns, which suggested that popular bodies were "dirty" or "dangerous"; and so on. Practices of indigenous people and other members of the popular classes—particularly those involving various kinds of emotional public assembly and outpouring—were to be disrupted and discouraged as much as possible. The "unofficial" or unimportant should be left no quarter from which they might get out of control or gain power.

Detailing such widely held "general" attitudes, one article published in *El Oaxaqueño*, on 1 November 1934, for example, describes the prohibition by the municipal government of the sale of medals, rosaries, and images and portraits of saints. Aimed at the *defanatización* (de-fanaticism) of the festivities, the prohibition was levied against stands selling these items. Vendors of Day of the Dead objects were charged with "exploiting people's incredulity and ignorance." Another piece from the same newspaper, published on 2 November 1937, condemned a whole litany of "popular" foods for sale during the festival; *nicuatole*, *mole*, sweetened squash or *calabaza*, chocolate, and even *pan de muertos* (bread of the dead) were described as vehicles of insidious "intestinal guests" that threatened the health of anyone partaking of or passing around such food in the graveyard.

Having "cleaned up" the festival—or at least public opinion—official policy in later decades could gradually begin to revalue these "unruly" practices. Beginning in the 1950s, press coverage of the Day of the Dead in Oaxaca suggests that there was a gradual recognition of the festival. The Day of the Dead (or Todos Santos) emerged as a more acceptable part of traditional, yet mestizo Mexican culture; appropriated into the mainstream, the holiday, in official purview at least, began to shed some its "folk-Catholic"—that is, indigenous—associations. Today the festival is widely viewed, at least by official organs, as a productive (and thus particularly *Mexican)* blend of indigenous culture and Catholic (European) heritage. But views on the street vary. One twenty-year-old man explained the motivations of the festival in this way: "According to the Bible, the dead relatives come back from heaven to socialize [*convivir*] with us again, but for just a short time." The majority of people I spoke to, however—many with strong indigenous roots themselves—put the accent of the festival on its indigenous associations while acknowledging its syncretic aspects. As one man put it, "Es católica, y tiene algo de tradición también de nuestros antepasados" (It's Catholic, and it also has something of the tradition of our ancestors). But another man from Xochimilco explained, at far greater length:

The Day of the Dead is outside of what is Catholic religion. Because this commemoration of our ancestors is not only the date on which we know that Christ came back to the world, but also, if we look for example, at the ancestors like the *zapotecos*, the *mixtecos*, we see that there were offerings to the dead even without them knowing the existence of Catholicism. So it's a celebration for the dead, a *recuerdo* for the dead that is almost outside the context of what can be Catholic religion.

Despite their growing emphasis on the indigenous identity or roots of the festival, the efforts of the representatives of "high culture" to regiment the celebration of the Day of the Dead and fix its significance, suppressing many of its more "popular" meanings, are still very evident. In the contemporary context, official regulations continue to pivot around concerns about hygiene and safety in the cemetery—above all, in relation to the consumption of food there. And some people I interviewed, for example, turned up their noses in disgust at the idea of eating in the graveyard or deplored the drunkenness and "debauched" behavior of certain individuals, who, in their view, contributed to "bringing the community down."

How one celebrates the festival today, then, involves critical factors of social distinction. While various "popular" practices are disdained by the guardians of order—various officials, tour operators, and "elevated" members of the popular community—the festival also provides a clear platform from which some of the poorest members of the community can express their moral superiority. As a thirty-eight-year-old man in the Panteón de San Martín put it: "Among the poorest people are those who have the most joy, the most sense of *convivio* [communal spirit] in remembering their faithful dead [*fieles difuntos*]." Another man nearby had this to say: "The poor lack many things. Many of us will sell the little that we have—often we have to borrow, and then we pay back our debts later—so as not to lose the tradition we have. That's how it is. But definitely with inflation, the way of life is changing." A sixty-year-old woman from Colonia San Juan echoed these sentiments about the moral importance of the festival and the challenges and changes that it faces:

There are many rich people who now do not make an altar . . . because they feel that it's not of any interest to them; they say that the tradition of *los difuntos* belongs more to the poorest people [*la gente más humilde*] . . . because [the rich] believe the dead are gone and so there is no reason to make an altar for them. Strange, because there are many rich who still know the tradition, but although they know it, they don't practice it. . . . But if they have money they should be going to the cemetery. The poor person there has to sell his hens or borrow money, and, well, [the rich] should be making a better altar, no? . . . Because they, of course, are good businessmen, very important, in offices, and their wives, too, are walking around looking very nice, because they are important men, or *comerciantes*, they forget all that. . . . The only thing that interests them is money. The only thing they do is go to the cemetery; yes, they arrive there where they have huge gravestones [*lápidas*], and they pay the cemetery workers to clean them. . . . It's like they have houses there, chapels. . . . What happens is that they say to themselves, why are we going to make an altar if we don't have time?

These were, I found, quite common reactions among the popular classes, who viewed themselves as the true bearers of moral sentiment and values. Another man I met in the Panteón de San Martín argued that heaven, and not riches on earth, was the greater reward reserved for the poor:

On the Day of the Dead there is true sentiment from the heart . . . those of us who have faith, that's how we celebrate this fiesta. The rich who have money . . . have never followed the law of God. The rich never pay any attention to the *humildes*. This means that they are not kind. They don't know the Day of the Dead. We, in contrast, although we are *humildes*, we are kind and generous with everyone else. That is how God wishes it—that we may love one another as brothers on this material earth. But the rich are rejected according to the law of our Lord God. There above [pointing to the sky] is the reward for everything we do here on earth.

Such comments demonstrate the ways that the festival allows an apparently disadvantaged group—in this case, the politically weaker social sectors, a category that embraces most city residents—to point to concrete reasons for rejecting the dominant codes by which they are disadvantaged. The celebration of the Day of the Dead by the poorest residents of the city allows them to point to their own acts of generosity and profligacy not as signs of wastefulness or false consciousness, but as the indications of their great faithfulness and concern for others. These testimonies turn the world and its values upside down, and lay claim to larger and more permanent truths. Thus, when in the graveyard of the "peripheral" neighborhood of San Martín Mexicapan on its Cemetery Day, a man said to me, "Here in San Martín, we are the poorest people"—his was a statement of apparent pride. In his statement the stigma of poverty is revalued and transformed into a badge of honor. Thus the poor fight back, their words separating the goats and the sheep, the people "in the city"—those corrupted by worldly, materialistic values—and those "in the pueblo," where core communal values of sharing and concern for others hold sway. In the pueblo, I was told repeatedly, household Day of the Dead altars are enormous; likewise, the devotion of pueblo residents to their dead is stronger. One man who is now a resident of Oaxaca, although he came originally from Tlacolula, a town not far outside the city, explained: "[In Tlacolula] there is more of a fiesta, a lot of expenditure. There a lot of people want to follow through [cumplir] with the custom even though they are poor. But they still fulfill this obligation."

When I asked about the future of the Day of the Dead, many people responded by invoking similar distinctions between rich and poor or town and city. As one man from Xochimilco, a barrio near the center of Oaxaca City, put it:

The celebration in the towns is very different; there they go on to the cemetery with their food, their drinks, beers, even their mescal, and there they are. They're singing, they're praying. But it's another form of feeling there, not like in the city. In the city you go to the General Cemetery or some other cemetery in the city, it's the same everywhere; the people are seated there, they are accompanying [acompañando] the dead there by the grave, and then they just leave and that's it. But in Xoxo[cotlán] or in San Martín it's another ambience. I think it depends on the [class] level of the people. . . . In some way, [in the towns,] I think, people want to express their solitude because a person is not with them any longer. So [they do that] precisely by being there, by eating with them, as if they were eating in that moment with them. They have their mescal right there because, I believe, it's as if the spirit of the other were there, too, having a drink with them, a beer, or some food. That is the form in which I think they feel it. In contrast, we here [in Xochimilco], are getting closer to the city, and things change. I know that here is my father-in-law, that my parents are here, that we buried them here, but that's it.

The city is represented as a place of money, distractions, and forgetfulness. But when I asked if this urban forgetfulness was the future, not everyone agreed. For although a moral universe is mapped onto the spatial distinctions between city and pueblo, rich and poor, for members of the popular social sectors, these distinctions do not also involve sharply demarcated temporal shifts. City and town are different, and that is all. Unlike official or tourist discourses, which argue that the city is the future, a move away from the towns is progressive, and the practices found in the towns are ancient, "traditional," and therefore quite possibly "endangered," in popular discussions temporal distinctions are not quite as spatialized (or at least not on this earth). There is the present—in which there are places of iniquity, where one's moral universe may fall apart (the city)—and the *más allá*, the beyond, which, for the faithful, ultimately leads to a reward in heaven.

When I asked one man from San Martín Mexicapan, "Do you think that the custom of the Day of the Dead will disappear?" this was his answer:

I think that in the towns the tradition will never die. Here in the city, maybe. But in the towns the custom is still strong. . . . In Oaxaca there isn't the same respect that there used to be. In a pueblo there is more respect—people are more *humilde*. . . . The rich have fewer beliefs . . . those rich people in the Panteón General, almost everyone is from the *centro*. They don't have the same customs that we in the pueblo have, for example. . . . The customs here are richer, more beautiful. In the city the traditions are fading now. . . . I don't know why, but the people of the pueblo put more enthusiasm and effort into them than those in the city.

This man hedges his bets. Is the city the future? Perhaps not, but it is a space of the "fading" or loss of traditions.

Sometimes the state of Oaxaca itself was figured in terms of such oppositions between pueblo and city, tradition and modernity: "Those in Oaxaca are the ones who attend to the dead the most. In other states, no. . . . Oaxaca is the state that conserves everything most all of its traditions." In 1989 the director of Difusión Cultural (Cultural Diffusion) at the Universidad Autónoma Benito

Juárez argued that while "in the North" the *sentido* (feeling) of the festival had been lost, "in the south of Mexico, there is more of an *apego* [tenacity], more *cariño*, more faith in fiestas."

It is hard to know how or why such statements might be true, if they are, given the conflation between "traditions" and "indigenous" populations that has become typical in many institutions that keep an eye on the growth of tourism and marketable "culture." It is difficult not to believe that, having exhausted the celebration—not to mention the useful marketability to Europeans and North Americans—of "traditions" derived from the conquerors, many official bodies simply turned to "indigenous" spaces as a new site of cultural expropriation and exploitation. Thus the lifeways of the popular classes may function as a new gem to be mined, polished, and redisplayed in sanitized set pieces for tourists who, wearied by the unchanging aspects of their own cultural dominance, are desperately in search of exotic chips, representations of another life, to carry home. In the absence of careful historical work in such contexts, ongoing and largely undocumented practices of the popular classes are seized on as unchanging dioramas of an "authentic" past or as perfectly preserved little costume dramas. Suddenly, even the very "backwardness" of the popular classes is a worthy source. Here, "exquisitely preserved," as if by formaldehyde, is the past of the nation; that Mother who has been cast down will be lifted up, rhetorically at least, and sold, again and again, to the highest bidder.

"Tradition" is a remarkably slippery word, for it is equally at home in a variety of settings. If it means one thing to the purveyors and consumers of "authentic" culture, it might mean something quite different to the community-based practitioners of a set of popular rites. Often, when the members of the "popular" classes speak of tradition, they do so in order to invoke a community and a sense of identity, rooted in a past that is peopled with familiar and well-loved ghosts and intimate memories. As a twenty-year-old man in Colonia San Juan put it: "Tradition is a custom that the Spanish taught us and that is passed from generation to generation." "Tradition" in this sense also involves bodily memories—ways of doing things, gestures of propriety, love, and respect, handed down from mother to daughter, from father to son.

"Tradition" is thus imbued with positive morality—even sacredness—having to do with loyalty, respect, and the reaffirmation of communal ties. Those who do not keep such "traditions" have digressed in ethical terms; they have lost not only their own memories but a certain history for the community. The Day of the Dead is surrounded by a sacred aura; it is a place where past and present are bound together and revivified in the repetition of certain ritual gestures. Many people told me, from within the midst of their "meals with the dead," why the practices of the Day of the Dead would never die. A thirty-five-year-old man in the Panteón General said that it was "because it's a tradition that our ancestors left us. A tradition that parents teach to their children, and their children to their own children, and so it will continue." A forty-three-year-old woman, in the Panteón del Marquesado, reaffirmed these generational ties: "I come here every week. I come to the cemetery to leave my *difunto* his . . . it may be only a flower, but I still come to leave it. Because it's a custom that I grew up with, and I have fulfilled my obligation [*cumplido*]."

In my interviews, I found that many people made a clear conceptual distinction between those sacred aspects of El Día de los Muertos related to the cult of the dead (particularly the graveyard visit) and its more public and secular aspects. For example, according to most, to make a distinction between Halloween or "Night of the Witches" and the *comparsa* was irrelevant. The fiesta of Los Muertos or Todos Santos, however, was regarded as a distinct and far more important event. "Halloween," one young man I met in the General Cemetery explained to me, "or Noche de Brujas, consists of dancing, fun, nothing more." Perhaps the fact that Cemetery Days take place throughout the month of November aids this conceptual division, emphasizing its importance. For most of my interviewees were quite insistent about the differences between various festival activities at the beginning of the month; they tended to separate rather sharply in importance those activities organized by businesses and the government for tourist consumption (altar displays, Day of the Dead/Halloween costume parties) and those that were domestically oriented (the building of the home altar and the graveyard visit).

Reminiscences about past ways of celebrating the Day of the Dead, particularly enthusiastic memories of the former abundance of flowers and food placed on household altars, were common topics in my interviews. Over time, I came to see that memories of a better, more faithful past functioned in significant ways. They served as an important means of retaining a past in the present; they also allowed a speaker to critique the present situation. Thus such recollections of past abundance, whether true or false, anchored the speakers firmly within the community of the dead and the living, and allowed them to call others (youths, children, lax neighbors, and relatives) to order in the fallen and sinful present. Such appeals to the past permitted those I interviewed to speak prophetically and to call for change in many sectors—in the government, schools, and other bodies. An appeal to tradition serves, then, as a kind of jeremiad; it is a lament, a moral castigation of the present in the name of the more faithful past.

For example, one woman, whom I interviewed in the Panteón de San Martín, tied an economic critique of the government to her lament about the expense and "loss of tradition" in Day of the Dead rituals in Oaxaca:

Now we can't celebrate the way that we used to. Why? Because now with fifty, sixty thousand pesos one can't do anything. How much does bread cost? Five thousand, six thousand pesos. How much is a bunch of flowers? So people just don't have the same enthusiasm anymore. The tradition is going to be lost here in Oaxaca, and before it happens we need a special kind of government, a government that is going to help us out economically.

A fifty-five-year-old man in the Panteón del Marquesado in 1990 echoed similar frustrations with the government's laxity in helping to protect Oaxacan traditions like the Day of the Dead:

The organizers of some fiestas are from the government. And because the municipal government is changing every three years, the state government every six years, every person has his own ideas of what folklore is. That's why some fiestas have changed so much. But fiestas like Día de los Muertos, the government doesn't organize them, the people do. The people of the pueblo never forget their tradition. In times of change, the government forgets its traditions because the authorities don't put the same interest into conserving them. For tourism, yes. Those who work for tourism sometimes seem to care more about the tourist trade than about those of us who live here. And it shouldn't be that way. It should be something more balanced, with both the government and the people benefiting from tourism equally.

Another woman, seventy-three years old, whom I interviewed in the Panteón General, used the occasion to launch a scathing critique of the schools and the "youth of today": "Even in school they can teach them another kind of custom. That's how it starts to be lost. And the youth of today, well, it's not like before; the way we were still taken by the image of past times, no? And still today many follow the tradition in that way." When I asked her if the youths of families in other cemeteries were still following the traditions, she replied:

Yes, because, for example, in other cemeteries it's almost all "market people" [*gente del mercado*], poorer people [*más humilde*]. So generally those people still give that custom to their kids. . . . But these modern kids [*chavos modernos*] of today now have more modern ideas. Now it's not the same. Maybe the young women, yes, but now among the young men, it's becoming lost—the customs, the traditions.

Others I interviewed did not always agree with such assessments. Yes, the Day of the Dead was under threat, some said, but others maintained that, although the festival was under pressure from various "modern views," it would never die, for what mattered was the coming together of the group, the family, the marginal community and its values:

Many poor people, we will sell the little that we may have so that the tradition won't be lost. Often we'll borrow money and pay later. But the tradition we have will not be lost.   Saúl L., age thirty-five, Panteón General

It's what they say, that we should conserve this festival because it is our culture, no? It's what identifies us really from the people who don't really believe in all that and who don't make altars, so we identify ourselves in some manner with other people.   Manuel, age fifty-seven, Xochimilco

It's a lie [that El Día de los Muertos is dying]. It can't be. Because in one way or another, people will make sacrifices so they can carry out the tradition that is already theirs. It is very deeply entrenched, something that has come down through the generations, and even if the economic situation becomes more difficult, people will keep on with the tradition, because no one can just drop customs like this all of a sudden.
                                   Susana P., age forty-six, Panteón de San Martín

The dead are with us spiritually, nothing more. But yes, this tradition will continue, because you can't just suddenly forget your *difunto*, and abandon this family reunion [*convivio*].
                                   Guillermo R., age fifty-five, Panteón del Marquesado

Look, it's important you understand something. Here [in the graveyard] we all come together, and everyone here is part of a family. And a family is understanding, and talking together and communicating with each other. I'm John Smith, I've been coming here for years, there's Joe Smith, he's been coming here for years. . . . What we have here is union. Union and strength. . . . It's a *convivencia* of the family we have here.
                                   Rafael F., age forty-two, Panteón de San Martín

"Tradition," for most of those I interviewed from the popular classes, means a coming together within the bosom of family and community. It is these relationships that appear to anchor the popular rites of the Day of the Dead and give them their meanings, not the commodities and objects that represent the festival in a national or an international imagination. In this sense, although, in truth, certain activities may change rather constantly, "tradition" holds fast—as long as these relationships do, relationships that for many in the community hold the meaning of life. Thus when I asked seventy-eight-year-old doña Calixta in the Panteón del Marquesado whether the form of the Fiesta de los Muertos had changed, she replied:

No, it hasn't at all. We here, we don't change, our religion, nor our faith, nor our beliefs, for anything in the world; for all the treasure in the world we won't change, because those are ancient, ancient traditions, and we can't just change now. They want us to change, they want us to spend a lot of money. But us, no. We won't change. People are free to spend money in their own way—although here we have only a little, here in this country we are free to spend our money in whatever way we wish. . . .

Yes, I am *humilde*, I am poor, alone. I have no husband, my children are married, no one supports me, and I buy flowers. And I buy candles, and I buy fruit, everything in the *ofrenda*. I make my altar, little though it may be, but I make one. There is never any problem in that.

The dedication of this woman defines the constancy behind her insistence that nothing changes. As another woman commented:

We all believe the same deep down. We all have a *difunto* and we all have to pray for that person when death comes in some way or another. . . . Everyone is going to die, we are all in the same situation. . . . We are all there in the cemetery—rich, poor, Catholics, Protestants, Mormons—whatever we are, we are all there. Here in life is where we are opposed or arguing, but everything ends here in this place. This is why the tradition will never die. The festival of Todos Santos will never die because in some way we all carry a flower and a candle, because a light represents the path of God, that which tells us that he's always there, is the light. For that reason, when they baptize a baby in the church, they grab the candle [*la luz*] first, the light.

Susana P., age forty-six, Panteón de San Martín

The relationships the people share with one another, the inevitability of death, and the love of God for his people hold the community together to ensure the perpetual importance of the Day of the Dead. As another man said:

In Mexico, the people of the countryside believe that it's of no importance being rich, because we are all the same, we are all going to arrive eventually in a grave, and there the worms will eat us all.

Mario M., age fifty-three, Panteón del Marquesado

CONCLUSION

Death is in life and life is in death; one day all of us will meet the same fate, regardless of our earthly stations. The Day of the Dead, for many members of the popular classes, invokes a sense of time that bears little resemblance to the monological linear unfolding that characterizes the modern life of "facts" and institutions; rather, for celebrants of popular festivals, time has the character of something that folds back on itself, a snake biting its tail. Thus movement, transformation, and renewal are all important themes and concepts; "tradition," in this popular sense, is something one lives within, rather like a house. Although filled with new inhabitants, and put to new uses, it remains an overarching and containing structure, a shelter for the living, one of many preserves where the community discovers and reaffirms itself. Similarly, ideas of the popular do not belong to a distinct group in the city who reproduce themselves from one generation to the next, but are formed out of complex transactions of meaning and value that come from diverse sources. Thus the community is somewhat open-ended. A person does not, strictly speaking, have to be born into it to be a part of it, but one cannot buy one's way in. For what matters is to know where the heart is. No culture is static, especially popular culture, which, despite its moral anchor in "tradition," remains relatively uncodified—that is, open, absorbent, and dynamic.

Is the Day of the Dead changing? Undoubtedly. But, then, what is its future?

I believe that the festival will have two deeply intertwined futures. One of them will be polished, public, official, and increasingly rooted in tourism: a package ready for leisured consumption. The other will continue to be private and intimate: a communal devotion of various members of the popular classes. And while I feel uneasy about many of the strategies of expropriation and commodification involved in the former kind of celebration, I cannot say definitively that these public strategies will displace the actual practices of those who now celebrate the Day of the Dead more or less privately. No doubt, one aspect of the celebration will serve to reinforce the other, perhaps even happily.

I remain skeptical, however, of a thoroughly positive outcome. For all too often, when public celebrations aimed at tourists take over a landscape or a set of practices and reformulate them for moneyed consumption, they also quite carefully scrub those landscapes or practices or both of any elements deemed too messy or unsavory for visitors. Consequently, members of the popular classes are frequently neatly blotted out of such "official" pictures, their poverty and unruliness hidden, controlled, forced even farther into the margins or underground. Nevertheless, even in such situations, for members of popular communities, "traditional" celebrations go on as they can, even if against ever larger, noisier, and more extravagant "official" backdrops; difficulty of access to "traditional" festival grounds; or the rising costs of festival goods. For, as I have shown in my examination here of certain aspects of the history of the Day of the Dead in Oaxaca, popular practices have survived such threats and hardships before.

Such a conclusion feels somewhat anticlimactic, for it does not sit well with my own romantic fantasies about "tradition," "the people," and the importance of the communal ethical sensibility invoked by festivals such as the Day of the Dead. Yet a significant moment in my ethnographic training came when I realized that my own ideas about "how things should be" were getting in the way of my ability to see things how they were. I describe this moment in my field notes of 18 June 1994:

I'll never forget the scene in Lucía's house tonight. The two rooms; tin siding; noises of the burro, Florindo, outside; the snorting of the pig echoing sharply off the metal walls; the kitchen utensils and pots hanging from the ceiling, as is the custom in the Sierra. In come a couple of *paisanos*, as she refers to the visitors who constantly flow through her house from the sierra towns of San Pedro Yaneri or Santa María Zoogochi. The TV is left on while we eat the tortillas and beans brought from the Sierra. We watch a blurry black and white image from Mexico City on the screen. There are *telenovelas* and game shows—a reality so disjunctive with this one—full of pale, thin, curvy women in tight clothing, with lacquered nails and shrill voices, lives of leisure, romantic vertigo, and way too much money. The advertisements portray similar images: one, for the station itself, features a slender, obviously *mestizo* "*indígena*" strolling among beautiful pre-Hispanic ruins, through ancient colonial churches and carefully strewn shards of clay pottery; then another follows, for a cereal, showing a white suburban family eating breakfast to the theme song of *The Flintstones*. In that moment I had to remind myself: this was Mexico, too.

Epilogue:
Life in Death

Be kind, Oh be kind to your dead
And give them a little encouragement
And help them to build their little ship of death.

For the soul has a long, long journey after death
To the sweet home of pure oblivion.
Each needs a little ship, a little ship
And the proper store of meal for the longest journey.

D. H. LAWRENCE, "ALL SOULS' DAY"

IN IDEAL SPACES, IDEAL WORKS—religious and philosophical systems, works of art, books, critiques—we try to make all sorts of coherent, consistent systems of ethics, to extract the bad from the good, to remove those elements that are unlike or clash. These are often quite laudable enterprises, ways to seek knowledge of what to do or how to live, paths on which we search for wisdom. We do this because life is not clear; it is jumbled, complex; several value systems coexist, different worlds clash, struggle, and recombine. It is often hard to tell what is going on. And so we select certain elements, pick them up and hold them to the light, letting others fall.

For me, in the writing of this book, learning something about how a community handled death—how its members pulled together, sought and offered aid and comfort, and joined forces to keep certain memories, certain pasts, and relationships alive—has been remarkably important. Death, which is sometimes the end of all things, was not an end but a change, a site of transformation, a moment when relationships among the living, and between the living and the dead, were reaffirmed. Death became a gathering, then, rather than a scattering, as it so often is in Canada and the United States. But in order to become this gathering place, death had to be faced directly and contemplated repeatedly. Death in Oaxaca, I learned, was a familiar.

And it was more familiar there than it had been in most places where I had lived. Marginal people are not shielded from death in the ways that wealthier people are; they die from preventable diseases, accidents, and childbirth more frequently, more violently, and more often at home. Death not only is more frequent in marginal communities, but also is visible right in front of you. You cannot help but contemplate it. It is not spectacular, but intimate, achingly, awfully so.

The community gathers around so that no one is alone in this moment; no one goes into the beyond unattended; no one loses a family member and then must carry on, as though nothing happened. Grieving is never a solitary act. Nor is it a singularly sorrowful act. The dead remain with the living for as long as they, too, are alive.

In this work I have tried to listen carefully to Oaxacans' accounts of their experiences of and thoughts about death and to reflect on what light this may shed on how they see themselves and the world around them. Yet interpreting the significances that "others" attach to death is not merely a matter of careful listening. My own attempt to understand death "anthropologically" was inseparable from my own personal encounter with death. Thus I could fool myself that my fieldwork journey was essentially an academic enterprise, but, in truth, it turned out to be far more. For my experience of death opened a door within me that allowed a new kind of understanding to enter; at stake was my own quite immediate need to learn how to mourn. Ethnography, which for many researchers involves an intense immersion in the almost wholly unfamiliar, is not the only way that such rare, even protracted epiphanies can happen; but it is certainly one of the ways and, I believe, an important one. In certain circumstances, for those who are open to it (or those desiring it), such intense involvement enables a liberating shift of consciousness, a displacement of that which we take for granted, a lesson—even several lessons—in humility. For me, "fieldwork" has allowed the gradual sedimentation of a fertile, life-giving ground of connection: despite my repeated comings and goings, the "other" place has become part of a process of reciprocity, a sharing, even a merging, of spaces. Death, indeed, is part of an ongoing exchange and a shared memory of belonging.

Thus a more complete understanding of Oaxacan life is enabled through an understanding of Oaxacan death. I have suggested that this experience of death in Oaxaca has been produced necessarily in dialogue with national formulations of what death "is" for an illusory archetypal "Mexican." The rhetorical image of "Death in Mexico" is an ideological projection that subsumes a complex layering of voices—and the stifling of some. This Romantic image is a refraction of a national identity that was created in the postrevolutionary period and has crystallized over time. This rhetorical projection is the showcased death, part of sensational international imaginings of Mexico and, indeed, of Mexico's own self-image. Like other nationalist projections concerted in the interests of coherence and homogeneity, it is a façade masking a great and important diversity, one of languages, worldviews, and ways of living and dying.

Such awareness of a "politics of culture" offers an appropriate window for making sense of the subtleties of social interaction in urban Mexican communities such as Oaxaca, where highly charged elements of "traditional" and "modern" culture jostle together in interesting and telling ways. Within such contexts, popular culture offers a rich arena for observing the struggle among social groups over particularly potent cultural signs; this perspective defines the "popular" not as a fixed, clearly circumscribed cultural domain, but as the product of ongoing processes of confrontation and negotiation. Current anthropology in Mexico must attend to popular culture not as a vestige of past, "folk" culture or as a uniform expression of resistance or opposition to dominant culture and society; instead, popular culture should be seen as an array of often ambivalent, hybrid expressions fully integrated with the cultural dynamics of modernity. In this sense, "modernity" does not refer to an actual state of "progress" and development; it refers to an ideal that is firmly embedded in the ideological cornerstone of the postrevolutionary Mexican State.[1] Folded into the mountainous southeastern corner of the country, and largely indigenous in population, the state and city of Oaxaca developed on the geographic, social, and political margins of the Mexican nation, acting as repositories for the values, meanings, and identities expelled from the heart of "official," national, mestizo cultural and political life. And, by virtue of this fact, Oaxaca has always been symbolically central to national Mexican identity, creating it almost by contrast or default. Oaxaca, in turn, is a microcosm of the larger Mexican society, a social field on whose edges exist the popular classes, persons who share a subordinate status based on criteria of social differentiation that are formed from history but are continually both affirmed and contested every day. Thus marginality, like popular culture itself, is relational and does not reflect any specific, inherent characteristics.

One of my principal aims in this book has been to highlight the undeniable centrality of "religion" in popular culture. The affective and physical contours of the "popular sacred" mold all corners of the social landscape, composing a multidimensional moral geography that furnishes a meaningful framework for Oaxacans' everyday social interaction. I have tried to push the scope of our understanding of Mexican religion by means of a close reading of the texture of popular religious practice. Such a reading requires that we recognize popular religiosity in contemporary urban Oaxaca not primarily as the exotic, backward activity and belief of the unschooled indigenous, the unreflective following of the tradition of "cultural Catholics," or the conscious, purposeful practice of Protestant converts; instead, we must recognize it as a vital dimension of down-to-earth, everyday reality of poor social groups. With its roots deeply embedded in indigenous culture, Oaxacan popular religion bore shoots that grew in new directions in colonial Catholic soil; in its present expressions, popular religion embodies elements from many sources, whether they are folk, official, rural, urban, modern, or traditional. Fixing the exact trajectory of change of particular religious elements is a task that lies beyond my own interests here. Nevertheless, I contend that a certain local, kinetic experience of the sacred was sustained in Oaxacan popular religiosity throughout its history of development. This is the ethical foundation of traditionalism, key to popular religion's self-sufficiency from the church. I have suggested that this sensibility, part of a religiosity that is an integral dimension of daily existence, is inclusive, extending far deeper than surface religious affiliations such as Protestant, Catholic, and so on.

Life in "modern" Oaxaca is shot through with sharp tensions, seeming paradoxes, discordance, and fragmentation. These tensions and contradictions are, in part, inevitable symptoms of significant social flux and change. The terrain of popular culture is not a neatly delimited area of practices and beliefs; it is constantly sifting and shifting, shaped from ongoing, daily struggles over resources both material and symbolic. Members of the popular classes do not share a single mind-set or set of affinities or loyalties, and any popular neighborhood embraces a wide spectrum of persons with diverse interests and experiences. Within such a setting the social idiom of community expresses a social vision that allows the maintenance of an image of wholeness, integrity, and permanence. Whenever it is invoked, the "popular community" proclaims a resonant traditionalism, local memories, and a sense of belonging over and above the normalizing thrust of national culture and many alienating forces of modernity, commodification, and globalization. This throws into relief the importance of the traditional not as a space of backward, "past," "folk" practices that may be read as life signs of purity and authenticity, but as a cultural resource crucial in the making of (post)modern Mexican identities.

The survival of the community itself, however, is never certain. It depends on those who are driven to cherish it, to nurture it and the practices that hold it together. Its survival also depends on sites and monuments of remembrance, whether they are altars, graves, or any other places vested with such profoundly felt, sacred import. The popular Oaxacan rites surrounding death are not aspects of a cultural strategy of denial or rejection; rather, they work to bring the stark reality of death directly to the bosom of life. Death is part of an ongoing dialogue, a symbolic and concrete exchange between the living and the dead, the vital and the sensual, embracing the body of the dead closely, even tenderly, into the body of the living. Reflected here is not a stoic indifference toward death or a view born of naïve fatalism and melancholy; in an array of forms, death in Oaxaca is felt, known, and remembered, deeply.

The death rituals I encountered in Oaxaca showed me the wisdom of regular acts of remembrance and devotion; such acts help the living stay alive by keeping the dead alive inside them. For this reason, perhaps, despite tourism and the scourges of global capitalism, structural readjustment, and all sorts of other threats, the intimate ritual communal practices that I have tried to write about in this book will survive and renew themselves, along with the shifting members of the marginal communities of Oaxaca. Here is a version of life and death worth keeping, a set of practices and obligations that recollect and reaffirm our relationships to one another. I am forever in debt to those who have taught me how essential such acts and beliefs truly are.

It is November 1, and the ground outside is a sea of crisp maple leaves in all shades of red, yellow, and brown. I make an altar by clearing a small table of my books and covering it with the bright embroidered place mats I got years ago in Chiapas. I begin to gather my *calaveras*— the one I bought in the market my first year in Oaxaca with my name across the forehead, the sugar paste around the eye sockets crumbling more with each Day of the Dead; the *calavera* candleholder made of shiny brown ceramic that someone gave me as a present; the colorful tin one with the moving limbs—they all go on the altar. I find bananas, oranges, apples, a package of peanuts, and add them, too. Then a black-and-white photograph of my grandparents, facing each other across their breakfast table; another small color snapshot of my father, canoe paddle in hand, with his dog. On either side of the altar I place two vases filled with flowers; I add candles and light them.

I boil water and make tea, placing on the altar cups and saucers for my father and grandparents (remembering three heaping spoonfuls of sugar for my grandfather). I find a tin of Portuguese sardines a friend gave me, and add it for my father, who used to eat sardines when he watched football on the television on Saturdays. I take a bottle of beer for him from the fridge and add a package of slightly stale Mexican cigarettes (my grandfather was a chain smoker; my dad smoked them surreptitiously). I place cookies on a chipped plate that Dorothy (my best friend during my graduate fieldwork, now dead) bought years ago in Mexico City; they will all like those . . .

My altar is not nearly as elaborate or beautiful as many I have seen. But it is mine. And through it, I remember my dead.

The ritual becomes more important to me with time.

NOTES

INTRODUCTION

1. For an important consideration of this theme, see, for example, Rosaldo 1989: esp. 55–67. For a groundbreaking ethnography on local meanings and attitudes toward death among cattle herders in the mountains of Asturias in Spain, see also Cátedra 1992.

2. For more on this matter, see Lomnitz-Adler 1992:9.

3. Brandes (2003) offers a critical commentary on the homogenizing effect of the stereotypical image of a singular "Mexican view of death," although he does not relate it to the question of the politics of culture in Mexico.

4. Bartra 1992:2. See also Brandes 1998b.

5. Bartra 1992:138.

6. Navarrete, quoted in Ortiz 1985:8 (my translation).

7. Lomnitz-Adler 1992:3.

8. Bartra 1992:62.

9. Wade 2000.

10. González Crussi 1993:63–64.

11. Paz 1961:48.

12. Bartra 1992:140–142. See also Lomnitz-Adler 1992:10

13. For a discussion of such representations as part of the "myth of marginality"—made by Mexicans as much as by others—see Vélez-Ibañez 1983. For further reflections on the ways that invocations of this schizoid and romantic character of "the Mexican" function as a hegemonic tool in the hands of dominant social sectors or the state, see Margolies 1975; Lomnitz-Adler 1992; and Limón 1994.

14. Or Samuel Ramos, author of the classic *Profile of Man and Culture in Mexico* (1934) or even José Revueltas, author of *El luto humano* (1980).

15. Classic examples include Redfield's (1930) peasant stereotype and Lewis's (1959, 1961) elaboration of an inescapable urban "culture of poverty." Perhaps also worth mentioning, as part of a theoretical trend common in the United States in the 1940s, 1950s, and 1960s, are Kearney's (1972) essentializing psychological descriptions of Zapotec peasants in a rural sierra Oaxacan community.

Likewise, Kelly's "Death in Mexican Folk Culture" (1975) might be taken to exemplify a whole genre of writings, which all relate in careful detail the Aztec obsession with death as being fundamental to contemporary Mexican attitudes and customs. See also Aho 1981.

16. Brandes 1997:293, 2003. This view has also been argued by various Mexican scholars, including Arturo Warman (Herrasti and Aguirre 1985), Carlos Navarrete (Ortiz 1985), and Bartra 1992.

17. Nutini 1988. Here I should note Ochoa Zazueta's (1974) interesting holistic study of beliefs and practices surrounding the "cult of the dead" in the Mexico City barrio of Mixquic. Ochoa Zazueta emphasizes the emergence of religious diversity and other influences that, he contends, are working to transform death-related beliefs and practices, especially the Day of the Dead.

18. The revival of the Day of the Dead in migrant Mexican American communities in East Los Angeles and in Chicago also attests, I would argue, to the festival's power to mobilize such distinct community-building invocations of the past, the present, and the future. For the well-researched reflections of a Mexican American on the meaning of the Day of the Dead—sown through with accounts of its celebration in various parts of Mexico—see Garcíagodoy 1998.

19. In formulating my views on popular culture I am indebted to the following theorists: Gramsci 1971; Williams 1976; Hall 1981; Rowe and Schelling 1991; García Canclini 1993, 1995; Joseph and Nugent 1994; Mallon 1995; and Franco 1999. Particularly useful is Franco's (1999) definition of popular culture: "a spectrum of signifying practices and pleasurable activities most of which fall outside the controlling discipline of official schooling" (179). For an invaluable collection of essays reflecting a rigorous theorization of themes related to covering various aspects of popular culture and state formation in Mexico, see Joseph and Nugent 1994. See also Beezley and Curcio-Nagy 2000.

20. Lancaster 1988:31.

21. Candelaria's (1990) definition of Latin American popular Catholicism comes close to capturing the unique qualities of Oaxacan popular religiosity: "a system of values and ideals, and a complex of symbolic practices, discursive and non-discursive, enacted in ritual drama and materialized in visual images, all relating the human being to the sacred, originated and maintained by the poor and the oppressed" (13). Candelaria's association of popular religion with "the poor and the oppressed" follows essentialist views of the popular that may be problematic. However, he identifies the special character of popular religion as creative oral and performative interaction with the sacred that differs significantly from the more strict and text-based thrust of "official" institutional religion.

1. ANTHROPOLOGY IN A MEXICAN CITY

1. Examples of such rural-based ethnographies, wherein a community was often portrayed as representing an indigenous "people," include Redfield 1930; Parsons 1936; Beals 1945b; Foster 1948; De la Fuente 1977 [1949]; and Redfield and Villa Rojas 1990 [1934].

2. Butterworth (1962), for example, defines "urbanization" as "the modification of human behavior imposed by the urban way of life" (259). See also Lewis 1965.

3. Lewis 1959, 1966, 1968, 1969.

4. Butterworth 1962; Foster 1971; Logan 1984.

5. It should be pointed out that Lewis's model contradicts that favored by Redfield and the Chicago school; Lewis (1951, 1965) argued that urbanization did not necessarily entail a breakdown of the community-oriented practices and values associated with the rural way of life. See also Butterworth 1962, 1975; and Kemper 1977. More recently, the Mexican anthropologists Larissa Lomnitz (1977) and Carlos Vélez-Ibañez (1983) offered studies based on research conducted in the 1970s on poor urban neighborhoods in Mexico City; these studies focused on the political and economic mechanisms and dynamics of survival for marginal urban residents. While more illuminating than earlier studies in terms of the negotiation of everyday power relations of poor urbanites, the primary concern in both works remains economic and material aspects of life, rather than "culture" per se.

6. In a recent ethnography, Higgins and Coen (2000), for example, offer a portrayal of lives of "marginal" Oaxacans, emphasizing the diversity and complexity of the hybrid social spaces of today's urban Oaxaca. García Canclini (1995) has greatly influenced contemporary Mexican—and Latin American—anthropology with his notion of the "cultural hybridization" that underlines the heterogeneity that characterizes contemporary Mexico; he argues that the cultural space of Mexico is "multi-temporal" and "a . . . complex articulation of traditions and modernities (diverse and unequal)" (9). For a sensitive and innovative recent ethnography on the central Mexican city of Guadalajara, see Napolitano 2002.

7. See, for example, Napolitano 2002. See also García Canclini 1995.

8. Bernal 2001. Estimates of Oaxaca's indigenous population range from 39 percent (from the Instituto Nacional de Estadística Geografía e Informática [INEGI, National Institute of Geography and Statistics]) to perhaps 80 percent (popular perceptions); the number depends on the criteria used to determine "indigenous" identity. INEGI uses language as the main criterion.

9. According to the Consejo Nacional de Población (CONAPO, National Council of Population), Oaxaca is in third place nationally (after Chiapas and Guerrero, in that order) in levels of marginalization (CONAPO 2000a). Of Oaxaca's economically active population, 71 percent earns less than two minimum salaries (76.6 pesos, or roughly U.S.$9 daily). Oaxaca stands in second place in relation to the highest infant mortality rates (IMR) in the country (37.1 per 1,000 live births, just after Chiapas at 31.9; the national average is 24.9) (CONAPO 2000b). The illiteracy rate in the state for the population aged fifteen and older is 21.49 percent; 45.3 percent of Oaxacans aged fifteen and older did not complete primary school (the national rate is 9.45 percent, and 28.46 percent are without primary school education); more than 26.95 percent of Oaxacans have no access to potable water in their homes (the national figure is 11.23 percent); 12.54 percent of households do not have electricity (the national average is 4.79); 41.6 percent of homes have a dirt floor (the national average is 14.79 percent) (CONAPO 2000b; INEGI 2001). On average, the sector of the population in Oaxaca that is economically active has only 5.3 years of education (a figure similar to that for Nicaragua, the country with the lowest levels of schooling in all of Latin America; the average for Mexico City is 10.5 years) (Székely 2000).

10. Joseph and Nugent 1994:17.

11. Parsons 1936.

12. Bonfil Batalla 1973.

13. Taylor 1972:18.

14. Chance 1978.

15. Gruzinski 1993:177.

16. Taylor 1996.

17. See, for example, Martínez Vásquez 1990:127–133.

18. See, for example, Higgins 1983; Bartolomé and Barabas 1990; and Murphy and Rees 1991.

19. Of the population regarded as economically active in the state, 37.51 percent are employed in activities in sectors devoted to commerce, transportation, government, and other services; 19.36 percent are employed in mining, construction, and industry; and the majority—41 percent—work in the agricultural sector (INEGI 2001).

20. For an analysis of the evolution of social inequality in Oaxaca within a historical, political economic framework, see Murphy and Stepick 1991.

21. In 2001, for example, Oaxaca received 1.44 million domestic and almost 300,000 international tourists. According to the Secretaría de Desarollo Turístico (SEDETUR, Secretariat of Tourism Development) of Oaxaca, tourism generated some U.S.$530 million that year alone, amounting to roughly 6 percent of the state's GDP and about twenty-seven thousand direct jobs (Fernando Flores Kato, "Tourism—A Development Tool for the Southern States," wbln0018.worldbank.org/ . . . /$File/Mexico%20SouthSt ates%20Synthesis%20revised.pdf. Accessed 23 May 23 2005).

22. INEGI 1991; Murphy and Stepick 1991:46–47.

23. CONAPO 2000b.

24. Kearney 1986; Kearney and Nagengast 1989. Exact figures of migration are made difficult by the fact that the grand majority of Oaxacan migrants to the United States are illegal. According to the Dirección General de Población de Oaxaca (DIGEPO), the state of Oaxaca is in fourth place nationally regarding migration within the state, to another state, or to another country (usually the United States) (DIGEPO 2000). Oaxaca attracts few migrants from other states. The proportion of non-native Oaxacans living in the state is one of the lowest in the country, at 5.57 percent in 1990 and 5.85 percent in 2000 (INEGI 2001).

25. See, for example, Murphy 1991.

26. Murphy and Stepick 1989:47.

27. Selby, Murphy, and Lorensen 1990:16. Clarke (2000:153) concurs with the estimate that *colonias populares* take up 50 percent of Oaxaca's metropolitan zone, adding that such neighborhoods embrace just over 58 percent of city residents.

28. This agrees with the findings of Morris 1991; Murphy 1991; and Pacheco Vásquez et al. 1991. In addition, Pacheco Vásquez et al. (1991:42) estimate that approximately 15 percent of households in poor *colonias populares* obtain land by squatting for the requisite ten years, which, according to the Mexican constitution, gives them legal entitlement.

Exact figures of the number of *colonias* in the city are hard to obtain because new *colonias* are constantly being incorporated into the city register. According to the Oaxacan daily *Noticias* (8 March 1990), in 1986 there were 55 *colonias* registered in the municipality of Oaxaca (the central core); in 1990 the number within the city and environs rose to 145, with another 35 in the process of being officially recognized. In 1999 the city embraced a total of 255 formally recognized *colonias* (INEGI 1999).

29. Pacheco Vásquez et al. 1991.

30. Basañez 1987; Murphy and Stepick 1991. More recent work on Oaxaca's urban population reveals that this picture is growing more complex: Higgins and Coen (2000), for example, explain that Oaxaca is made up of "a very small, upper-class elite, a large and diverse middle class (ranging from local merchants to the professional classes, who are primarily in the areas of academics, the arts, government agencies and medicine) and the popular classes" (23).

Although there is no official source tracking exact numbers in the past decade, a significant portion of new immigrants to the city are educated, middle- and upper-class Mexicans from Mexico City; many of them have made a particular impact on the artistic community (including gallery owners and artists) and on businesses related to the tourist industry.

31. A *colonia* elsewhere in Oaxaca similar to San Juan provides the focus of Higgins's (1974, 1983) ethnographic account of a "settlement of the urban poor." The analytical isolation of a neighborhood, as evidenced by Higgins's study, echoes earlier works by Butterworth 1962; Lewis 1966; and others.

32. Murphy and Stepick 1991.

33. For examples of communities that did, see Higgins 1974; and Prince and Murphy 1988.

34. The source of this information was a resident of the *colonia* who had lived there since its beginnings. It is likely, however, that there was some sort of irregular occupancy of San Juan's territory at this time, and the exact nature of initial development of the *colonia* is difficult to determine conclusively.

35. As Napolitano (2002) has commented for the city of Guadalajara, places attached to ideas of the rural versus urban lifeways are associated with particular moral identities.

36. For example, out of seventy households I surveyed in the *colonia* in 1991, only three were being rented.

37. Out of seventy households sampled in a *colonia* survey I conducted, the average adult woman (aged twenty-one and older) had completed only four years of primary school; men, on average, had completed five years. "Household" here is defined arbitrarily as a group of kin or extended kin residing in the same residential unit who are more economically interdependent than they are independent.

38. Bourdieu 1977. For an interesting application of Bourdieu's model to an analysis of a Oaxacan *colonia popular*, see Mahar 1992. See also Lomnitz-Adler 1992.

39. Margolies 1975.

40. Vélez-Ibañez 1983.

41. The notion of the "double ethic" has been elaborated by Scheper-Hughes 1992.

42. Margolies 1975:141.

43. Lomnitz-Adler 1992.

44. Margolies 1975:140.

45. Todorov 1997. As the historian Florencia Mallon (1995) explains regarding post-colonial Mexico, "ethnicity is the social construction of differences in color, culture, language and dress; and in the context of specific class and gender systems, people historically define ethnic boundaries and identities in a three-way struggle: within and between ethnicities, and between the state and ethnic groups" (10).

46. Murphy and Stepick 1991:25

47. Knight 1990:73.

48. Scheper-Hughes 1992.

49. Cohen 1985.

50. See, for example, Beals 1970; Arriaga 1990 [1954]; Lipp 1991; Stephen 1991; Monaghan 1994; and Cohen 1999.

51. Foster 1971:168–169.

52. Other discussions of the *guelaguetza* in Oaxaca may be found in Whitecotton 1977:240; Williams 1979; Stephen 1991; and Monaghan 1994.

53. Monaghan 1987.

54. See, for example, Higgins 1974, 1983; Selby, Murphy, and Lorenzen 1990; and Murphy and Stepick 1991.

55. Higgins 1983:101–102 (my translation).

56. According to INEGI (2001), out of the total municipal population aged fifteen and older of 182,817, the number of Oaxacans claiming to be Catholic was 156,156, or roughly 85.4 percent; Protestants and Evangelicals accounted for 13,798, or approximately 7 percent; and the number in other categories were Jewish, 76; "other," 474; "no religion," 6,495; and "not specified," 693.

57. On divisions within the Catholic Church, see Norget 1997a, 1997b, 2004.

58. Montes García 1997.

59. Pastrana 2001.

60. In reference to the religiosity in a *colonia popular* in the Mexican city of Guadalajara, Napolitano (2002:10) explains that different ideological orientations within the Catholic Church are represented by metaphors of "new" and "traditional," thus reflecting the tensions of modernity.

61. See, for example, Gijsbers 1996; and Gross 2003. Often conversion becomes just another layer on divisions already existing between families within indigenous communities. The Protestant presence, then, can cause significant tension since many (although not all) Evangelicals refuse to participate in *tequio* or other aspects of the civil-religious *cargo* system—the *vida comunitaria* so fundamental to the discourse of the indigenous movement and indigenous identity.

62. For more on this topic and related themes, see Napolitano 1995 and, especially, 2002.

63. Lancaster (1988:215) has argued this point in relationship to Nicaragua. In a recent ethnography focusing on religion in a town in the central Mexican state of Michoacán, Cahn (2003) observed harmonious relations and cooperation between Catholics and Protestants, and attributes these to the way followers of both religious faiths incorporate elements of the other into their religious beliefs and practices, prioritizing community stability above other affiliations. The spirit of flexible accommodation that Cahn identifies is, as I argue, an aspect of a popular religious identity

and an area outside the control of the institutional churches and their representatives and of official religious discourses.

2. Practicing Popular Religion in Oaxaca

1. Norget 1991. I want to emphasize that I am speaking here of a pervasive ideal image of womanhood that I found commonly discussed and referred to among Oaxacans, both male and female, young and old. Undoubtedly, this ideal stereotype belies the actual diversity and complexity of Oaxacan women's lives, although it remains as a referent by which many women I know still make sense of and moralize their own or another woman's experience and comportment. For a recent article arguing against the relevance of this stereotype, see Navarro 2002.

2. Greenberg 1981.

3. DaMatta 1984b:234.

4. See, for example, Marroquín 1989a; Stephen and Dow 1990; and Barabas 1997. Sometimes these "saints" are not really distinct personages but consist of certain manifestations of the Virgin Mary (Virgen de Juquila, Virgen de la Soledad) or Jesus (Señor de los Rayos, Señor de los Milagros, Señor de las Tres Caídas).

5. It has been argued that the popularity of the Virgin of Guadalupe is owing to her status as a syncretic fusion of the Aztec goddess Tonantzin and the Virgin of Spanish Roman Catholicism (Lafaye 1974; Ricard 1966:188–191). According to Gruzinski (1993), the dissemination of this Marian cult in Mexico is what best exemplifies the first stages of the Christianization of the "indigenous *imaginaire*" (190). Pope Benedict XIV made the Virgin the patron of Mexico and the Americas in 1910 (Warner 1976:303). Among the most worthwhile of other writings on the Virgin of Guadalupe in Mexico are Wolf 1979; O'Gorman 1986; Taylor 1987; and Nebel 1995. Taylor (1985) argues that the view of the cult of the Virgin as a universal syncretic Indian cult synonymous with worship of the Virgin Mary is "fundamentally ahistorical, serving a providential patriotism that validates a powerful Mexican tradition by making it appear older, more popular, and more closely connected to a message of Indian liberation than it was" (156). See also Clendinnen 1990.

6. The tiny, dark Virgin of Juquila is known for being especially miraculous. The annual pilgrimage to her shrine, located in the southern sierra region of the state of Oaxaca, is one of the most important of the year (Greenberg 1989; Marroquín 1989:164).

7. At the beginning of the 1990s, the value of the Mexican peso was pegged to that of the U.S. dollar. In January 1993, in the context of a declining value of the Mexican currency and climbing value of the U.S. dollar, the Mexican government decided to revalue the peso. Three zeroes were simply dropped off the old peso value, so that 1,000 *old* pesos became equal to 1 *new* peso. To avoid confusion, when peso amounts cited in the text refer to pre-1993 (that is, pre-revaluation) values, I have specified these as old pesos, and have provided their approximate U.S. dollar equivalent.

8. Lomnitz-Adler 1991:208.

9. Taylor 1985:148–149.

10. Greenberg 1981:120–121, 125–126; Marroquín 1989:172.

11. Ramona Pérez, personal communication.

12. See, for example, Barabas 1977; and Barabas and Bartolomé 1984.

13. For a similar description of popular devotion to the saints in Oaxaca City, see Higgins 1990.

14. My use of this term follows the coinage of the historian Inga Clendinnen (1990:190), who encourages us to be aware of a range of sensory, emotional, and kinesthetic experiences that may characterize encounters with the sacred. "Experiential script" refers to the continuation of "habits of conceiving the sacred"—including strongly performative elements such as dance, drink, "sacred play," and invocation by manipulation of regalias—through which post-Conquest indigenous populations were able to retain their local religiosity, despite changes to various aspects of belief and practice. Clendinnen's argument is meant to apply to the Yucatán Peninsula in southern Mexico, yet I feel it is applicable to indigenous religiosity in Mexico more broadly. Such a physical, multidimensional character to sacred philosophy and practice is seen, for example, in the historical accounts of Carmagnani 1988; Gruzinski 1993; and Taylor 1996.

15. This emphasis on balance and communal well-being in local popular religious rites has been noted and commented on by historians of religion in Oaxaca, as well as by other contemporary anthropologists. See, for example, the historical observation by Taylor (1996): "Where Catholicism stressed the individual soul, native religions put almost no value on the individual as such, emphasizing instead the preservation of the cosmic order and the well-being of the collectivity" (551n.15). See also Christian 1981; Greenberg 1981; and Behar 1987.

16. Uzzell 1974; Rubel, O'Neill, and Collado-Ardon 1984.

17. For an interesting discussion of popular medicine and healing practices in a *colonia popular* in the Mexican city of Guadalajara, see Napolitano 2002:107–127.

18. Mahar 1974:32–33.

19. Hunt 1992.

20. For more on some of the anthropological consequences of such biophysical and communal links, see Comaroff 1985.

21. Lancaster 1988:38.

22. Whitecotton 1977:240; Williams 1979; Stephen 1991; Monaghan 1994.

23. See, for example, Brandes 1988.

24. Taylor 1996:59.

25. Taylor (1996) prefers the term "local" to "folk" or "popular," for, as he explains, following Christian (1981), "local" religion allows one to address a specificity derived from looking beyond religious institutions and objects, without overlooking broad common sociopolitical determinants.

26. Taylor 1996:59.

27. For figures on central Mexico, see Borah and Cook 1963:1; for figures on Oaxaca, see Murphy and Stepick 1991:18.

28. Prominent exceptions include, for example, the renowned sixteenth-century bishop Bartolomé de Las Casas of Chiapas, the ardent defender of the well-being of the Indians against the acute cruelty of the Spanish conquistadors.

29. Katz 1988:84.

30. Both systems resulted in appalling abuses: the unjust conditions of the *repartimiento*, for example, incited considerable protest throughout the Oaxaca region, including a rebellion in the Isthmus of Tehuantepec in 1660, and the population of the town of Cuilapan declined in short order from sixty thousand to twelve hundred as a result of the poor treatment that *encomienda* workers suffered in the fields and mines. The institution of *repartimiento* took various forms across colonial Mexico. A version in Oaxaca, known as the *repartimiento de comercios*, saw Spanish administrators forcing on Indians credit or goods at elevated prices before the harvest; in return, the Spanish would agree to purchase a stipulated amount of cochineal from indigenous producers at fixed prices. For an alternative interpretation of the *repartimiento* in Oaxaca, see Baskes 2000.

31. Ricard 1966:176–206; Clendinnen 1980:378, 1990:114; Beezley, Martin, and French 1995:xiii.

32. See, for example, De Certeau 1984; and Rowe and Schelling 1991:64.

33. For an elaboration of this sort of argument, see Marroquín 1989a.

34. Taylor (1996), for example, has argued that "monotheism was not a radically new idea to Mesoamerica although it had a more prominent place in Christian orthodoxy" (550n.8).

35. Descriptions of various aspects of religiosity among indigenous populations during the colonial period may be found in Madsen 1957; Ricard 1966; Lafaye 1974; Mullen 1975; Nutini 1976; Whitecotton 1977; Turner and Turner 1978; Clendinnen 1980, 1990; Farriss 1984; Taylor 1985, 1996; Berlin 1988.

36. Gruzinski 1993:226.

37. Marroquín 1989a:16 (my translation). For other accounts of the rich content of "local religion" in colonial Spain, see Christian 1981; Farriss 1984; and Taylor 1996.

38. Mannheim 1991.

39. Church officials were well aware of such "diabolical" and frequently "invisible" syntheses and frequently sought to expose them. For example, Jacinto de la Serna, the interlocutor of the well-known Dominican friar Diego Durán, issued a warning to fellow Catholic proselytizers in his *Manual de ministros de indios* (1656): "[The Indians] are strongly attached to the things of our holy faith, vowing great veneration to them. [They want] most of the time in their invocations, their cures and their superstitions to imitate the ministers of the Church and usurp their functions" (quoted in Gruzinski 1993:178).

Likewise, in his *Apuntos históricos*, the former archbishop of Oaxaca Eulagio Gillow (1978 [1880]) described the visit of Dominican Benito Fernández, parish priest of Achiutla, to a local clandestine altar at the top of a local mountain, where he beheld idols of all sizes arranged in niches on blood-stained rocks: "Indignation overcame him, and, fearlessly before the entire town, he began to knock them over and trample them underfoot while screaming, in the Mixtec language, that those spirits who were able could defend themselves: 'Fakes!' he said to them, 'liars and cheats! Leave these stones and pieces of wood and show your strength before me who shames you.' And he attacked them furiously [my translation]" (61).

40. For a general account of such reorientations, see Taylor 1979.

41. Mullen 1975:224–225; Greenberg 1989:179.

42. Earle 1990:120.

43. See, for example, Foster 1960; Whitecotton 1977; and Farriss 1984.

44. Farriss 1984:329.

45. Carmagnani 1988:95.

46. See, for example, the important article by the historians Chance and Taylor 1985.

47. By 1802 there were about eight hundred confraternities, many with large holdings in cattle and cochineal (Clarke 2000:24–25). "Shared poverty" in the community became an adaptive strategy and a cultural tradition passed on through the civil-religious hierarchy, or *cargo* (Whitecotton 1977:217–218). Many scholars have seen *cofradía*-sponsored religious rituals as reflecting indigenous responses to colonization in terms of self-protection encouraged by the system (Greenberg 1981; Farriss 1984; Earle 1990). Cook and Diskin (1976) argued, for example, that *cofradías* have operated to resist the social transformations brought about by acculturation into a capitalist economy in that they preserved local "traditional" systems of reciprocity, redistribution, and communitarian economic interdependence (cited in Earle 1990:133).

48. Greenberg 1989:178.

49. In Oaxaca, as elsewhere, the violence of the Conquest was rehearsed in the extraction of testimony by imprisonment and torture of the indigenous population. According to Gruzinski (1993), in the Oaxacan indigenous town of Sola (de Vega), for example, where native beliefs and practices had persisted, Indian priests, or *letrares*, were accused of idolatry and sentenced to death in ecclesiastical and criminal courts. In Oaxaca, important accusations of idolatry occurred in the districts of Villa Alta, Sola de Vega, Teposcolula, and Teutila (Taylor 1996:557n.95). Serious cases of large-scale "idolatry" in Mexico reported after 1570 happened in the southern dioceses of Oaxaca, Chiapas, and Yucatán. The Spanish officially established a tribunal of the Inquisition in Mexico City in 1570, fifty years after the Conquest (Lafaye 1974:19). Yet many clergy did not regard "naïve" idolatrous practices such as worship of natural sites as a challenge to monotheism and therefore exempted Indians from the Inquisition's jurisdiction (Taylor 1996:63).

50. Gruzinski 1993:265.

51. Gillow 1978 [1880].

52. Hamnett 1986:76.

53. Marroquín 1989a.

54. Gruzinski 1993:265. Note, too, that in Oaxaca, even after the application of the Reform Laws in 1856, liberal authorities, dependent on powerful local *caciques*, did not follow through with the appropriation of rural communal lands. See Hamnett 1986:82.

55. Chance 1986:388.

56. Marroquín 1989.

57. Chance 1986:374.

58. Archivo Histórico del Arcobispado de Oaxaca/Diocesano/Gobierno/Mandatos/ 2 July 1795.

59. See Voekel's (2002) fascinating historical research on Catholicism and "modernity" in Mexico.

60. Behar 1987.

61. Greenberg 1981:129; Monaghan 1994.

62. The Option for the Poor is a praxis based on the conviction that the true obligation of the church is with the poor and oppressed classes; this "option" rests on a reading which suggests that the poor are represented in the Bible as God's "chosen people." The option was formally accepted into the official ecclesiastical plan at the meeting of Latin American bishops in Puebla in 1978. For more on the option and related concept of the "People's Church," see Levine 1980; and Berryman 1987. For more on the liberation theology movement in Oaxaca, which was considerably stronger in rural regions of the state than in Oaxaca City, see Norget 1997a, 2004.

63. Via Crucis, or "The Way of the Cross," is an enactment of Christ's march to Calvary. Participants typically accompany a man, representing Jesus, who carried a large wooden cross. At each of fourteen stopping points or stations of the cross, an altar may be set up. A Bible passage will be read, often followed by an excerpt from a guide used for the Via Crucis. These readings typically draw explicit parallels between Jesus's suffering and the problems plaguing contemporary life.

64. For ethnographic discussions of Christian Base Communities (CEBs), see Burdick 1992; MacNabb and Rees 1993; Napolitano 1995, 2002; and Norget 1997b.

65. Stoll 1990:27.

66. Napolitano 1998, 2002.

67. For a discussion of this aspect of the New Evangelization, see Norget 1997b.

3. Living with Death

1. See, for example, Malinowski 1948; Warner 1959:285; Hertz 1960 [1907]; Van Gennep 1960 [1909]; Choron 1963; Radcliffe-Brown 1964 [1922]; Berger and Luckmann 1966:118; Obeyesekere 1968; Berger 1969:3–28; Durkheim 1971 [1915]; Goody 1975; and Blauner 1977:174. This classic anthropological view has been contested by Baudrillard 1976.

2. Confirming this repudiation of individual mortality as a virtually universal cultural dilemma, Bloch and Parry (1982:9), for example, claim that "almost everywhere" religious thought denigrates the irreversible and terminal nature of death by proclaiming it as a new beginning. See also Humphreys and King 1981. Themes of social regeneration underlie Bloch and Parrys' edited collection of essays, which focus on the ubiquitous symbolism of fertility and rebirth in funeral rites; these themes are also the main preoccupation of Huntington and Metcalf's (1979) cross-cultural comparison of mortuary rites.

3. Seremetakis 1991:15. The functionalist domination of anthropological interpretations of death has meant that most ethnographies use a framework of ordered duration, which Seremetakis contends is a metaphor for anthropology's mistaken understanding of culture as a totality, part of the "myth of holism." Seremetakis prefers instead to draw from the work of the historian Philippe Ariès (1974) on the evolution of conceptions of and reactions to death—*mentalités*—from the early medieval period until contemporary times. See also Thomas 1975; and Baudrillard 1976.

4. Baudrillard 1976.

5. Indigenous/folk ideology identifies a physical entrance to the underworld, a town named Mitla (Aztec, Mictlan [place of the dead, the Aztec underworld]), some thirty miles southwest of Oaxaca (Parsons 1936; Leslie 1960:21–22). The *difunto's* journey is envisaged as a difficult trek over a landscape pitted with natural obstacles and dangers. Sometimes a black dog was put in the coffin to help the *difunto* cross a river (identified by some as the Jordan); for this reason, folk superstition recommends that one should be kind to black dogs. See also Parsons 1936:152; Beals 1945a:62; De la Fuente 1977 [1949]:203; Cordero 1982:98; and Nutini 1988:321, 323.

6. The phrase "spiritual duplicate" comes from Hertz 1960:47.

7. During a *susto* cure, the victim's spirit (represented by the person's reflection in a basin of water) is retrieved by shouting the person's name, to which he or she replies, "I'm coming!" (Voy!). Kearney (1972:55) claims that *mala muerte* (sudden death) is the prototype of all *sustos*, since the two conditions share associated symptoms. See, for example, Leslie 1960:46.

8. The dead are also seen in many traditional areas of Mexico to pose a threat to the living (Merrill 1988:187–188), a belief that attests to the continued social force of the dead. However, this is not a strong belief in Oaxaca.

9. The custom of holding nine days of prayer for the dead originated in Spain, where it is called a *novena* (Foster 1960:150). For the purpose of simplification, in this book the word *novenario* always refers specifically to the Novenario de los Difuntos (including the wake and funeral preceding it), although the *novena* tradition in Mexico is not exclusive to funerals, since people often set aside nine days of worship before many religious celebrations, especially before a *mayordomía* (saint's day fiesta).

10. Of course, such an account of the relationship between soul and body is not unique to Oaxaca. As Emile Durkheim's student Robert Hertz (1960 [1907]), observed in "La Représentation collective de la mort" (The Collective Representation of Death), his foundational account of the order and significance of Christian death rituals, "the dissolution of the former body conditions and prepares the formation of the new body which the soul will thenceforth inhabit" (48).

11. Beals 1945a:59; Augur 1954:78; Foster 1960:147; Cordero 1982:96; Nutini 1988:135; Marroquín 1989a:189. This sort of ritual can even be accompanied by fireworks (Greenberg 1981:216; Sault 1985:189). Commenting on the relatively simple form of children's funerals cross-culturally, Hertz (1960) explains: "Since the children have not yet entered the visible society, there is no reason to exclude them from it slowly and painfully. As they have not really been separated from the world of the spirits, they return there directly" (84). Also see Nutini 1988:135.

12. In much ethnographic literature, the difference between these two statuses is, it is understood, determined by the age of the deceased (Beals 1945:59; Higgins 1974; Nutini 1988:144). Elsewhere, loss of virginity is the deciding factor; for example, Brandes (1988) defines an *angelito* as "anyone who is known to die in sexual innocence" (90). See also Whitecotton 1977:267; and Greenberg 1981:107. Still others (El Guindi 1977; Sault 1985) view marriage as the marker effecting a change in status between *angelitos* and *difuntos*. Gallinier (1989) also regards marriage as the determinant of post-death status but maintains that because of unmarried men's infertility (non-productivity of children), they will often be buried as *angelitos*.

13. Norget 1991; Howell 1997. See also Napolitano 1997, 2002.

14. Burial clothing is called *mortaja*. Sometimes the cadaver is wrapped in a sheet before burial; this is how the burial of Christ, who was wrapped in the Sábana Santa (Holy Shroud), is emulated. Other families may place all the *difunto*'s clothing in the coffin, often stuffed in a sack as a pillow. Unmarried men are dressed in dark blue, and unmarried women in a white gown similar to that worn by a *novia* (bride). Once I heard about an unmarried teenage couple who had been killed together, dressed in wedding clothes for their wake (also described by Cordero 1982:96). The relation between funerals and weddings was identified by Hertz 1960:80–81; Van Gennep 1960 [1909]:152; and Leach 1976:27. More recently, it has been examined extensively in ethnography by Danforth 1982:74–115; and Kligman 1988.

15. Since the revolution, the Mexican constitution has formally forbidden priests from celebrating mass or any other sort of religious rite outdoors in the cemetery; these laws have become considerably more relaxed over the past decades, however. In 1992 President Carlos Salinas de Gortari spearheaded a series of constitutional reforms that reestablished diplomatic relations with the Vatican after a 125-year break, permitted religious education, and once again allowed priests to say mass in public. During El Día de los Muertos, although masses take place in the graveyard, the drawing of a cross of earth on the coffin has replaced the custom of the priest blessing the grave.

16. I once witnessed this custom at the funeral of an *angelito* in San Agustín Etla, a town just outside Oaxaca. The burial took place in the early evening, and, for the final farewell, those in attendance seemed concerned that the coffin be opened facing the setting sun. This practice may relate to the tradition (rarely seen anymore in the city) of burying the *difunto* with his or her head toward the west. Greenberg (1981) says that the custom is done so that the *difunto* will go "straight to heaven" (102). See also Marroquín 1989:190.

17. Although this first cross is normally made of wood, a second, more permanent cross of metal or stone is added to the first at the head of the grave when the Levantada de la Cruz has ended. One informant told me that the wooden cross is the essential one, since Christ himself died on a wooden cross. Nutini (1988:180) describes similar practices in rural Tlaxcala, where *difuntos* are buried with *cruces de ataúd* (coffin crosses) set up on the grave at the funeral, and *cruces de parada* (erection crosses) erected during the octava of burial.

18. The Levantada ceremony formed part of the post-funeral rituals I observed in almost every case of death except that of *angelitos* and a Pentecostalist. It is mentioned in the literature but without analysis. See Parsons 1936:141–142; De la Fuente 1949:203–207; Lewis 1951:415–416; Leslie 1960:54; Romney and Romney 1966:54, 81; Harvey and Kelly 1969:669; Ingham 1970:283; Sepúlveda 1973:7; Higgins 1974, 1979:157; Lomnitz 1977:170; Nutini and Bell 1980:90–96; Greenberg 1981:105–107; Cordero 1982:101; Sault 1985:197–200; El Guindi 1986:99, 115–120; Ingham 1986:168; Marroquín 1989:190–191; and Redfield and Villa Rojas 1990 [1934]:202–204.

19. For a description of the ceremony in Tlacolula, Oaxaca, see Cordero (1982:101).

20. Graziano, quoted in Schirmer 1994.

21. Voekel (2000, 2002) explains that cemeteries were also the site where struggles

within the Catholic Church were made evident—specifically between a new religious sensibility of enlightened, Reformist Catholicism during the Bourbon period, and old corporate Catholicism.

22. Portillo 1910:160.

23. These concerns were arguably founded. Voekel (2002) points out, for example, that this was a time of epidemics, such as the cholera epidemic that struck Mexico City (and Oaxaca) in 1833.

24. Vásquez 1999.

25. In 1859 a law issued by President Benito Juárez prohibited the involvement of clergy in burials, which could no longer take place without the prior notification of civic authorities. In the "modern" ecumenical spirit of the day, ministers of any faith were supposed to have access to all burial sites and were permitted to carry out grave-side services (Berry 1981:66; see also Voekel 2002:217).

26. Portillo 1910:160; González Medina 1993.

27. Portillo 1910:160.

28. Such broadly "democratic" apportionment of cemetery space should not, how-ever, be taken to suggest that significant differences do not obtain between cemeteries.

29. Greenberg (1981) has emphasized the house as a zone fundamental to Oaxacan Chatino indigenous spatial conceptions. See also Danforth (1982:15), who describes a similar case for rural Greece.

30. In 2002, an article in an Oaxacan daily newspaper observed that "at the moment, there are no graves available into perpetuity for new cadavers in any of the city's graveyards—unless the *difunto* or his relatives made their request for a grave years ago and have kept their payments up to date. [Until new cemeteries are con-structed,] only places available for lease remain" ("Prohibido morirse" [The High Cost of Dying], *El Imparcial*, 24 May 2002). This article also detailed some of the costs of burial in Oaxaca in 2002, provided, of course, that new spaces were made available by adding onto cemetery grounds or disinterring old corpses, particularly from graves for which payments were in arrears: in the Panteón General, burial in perpetuity cost 4,596 pesos (almost U.S.$500); in the Panteón Jardín, a seven-year lease of a grave cost 766 pesos (U.S.$90), and perpetuity, 2,298 pesos (around U.S.$250); in Santo Tomás Xochimilco and the Marquesado, perpetuity cost 3,064 pesos (around U.S.$330). By contrast, "the cost of cremation is estimated at approximately six minimum daily sala-ries, or 229.80 pesos—about U.S.$25."

31. El Guindi and Selby (1976) offer a structural argument, wherein the cemetery is discussed as "a linking point between the two worlds" (82)—that is, of humans and of supernaturals. Warner (1959) also observes that the cemetery is "a symbolic meet-ing place for the dead and the living, for the realms of the sacred and the profane, for the natural and the supernatural" (286). Warner also suggests that the cemetery is a "symbolic replica of the living community" (287). In Warner's view, the graveyard is a collective representation expressing "many of the community's basic beliefs and values about . . . what the persons of men are and where each fits into the secular world of the living and the spiritual society of the dead" (280).

32. For some useful further elaboration on the meanings of such temporal intersec-tions, see Warner 1959.

33. Hertz 1960. For other accounts of similar beliefs, see also Bloch and Parry 1982:22; and Seremetakis 1991.

34. For more on this matter, see Norget 1991.

35. It is significant that, in this quintessentially "popular" incarnation, La Santa Muerte, which in Spanish may mean simply "Holy Death," has been anthropomorphized.

36. Ingham 1986:111.

37. This model of the Universal Virgin Mother is so far-reaching that the cover of one wedding invitation I saw read, "Yesterday, girl; today, bride; tomorrow, mother" (Ayer, niña; hoy, novia, mañana, madre).

38. For more on the collective conviction that it is women's destiny to suffer, see Finkler 1994. And for additional consideration of the ambivalent role of suffering in the construction of women's identity, see Napolitano 2002:166.

39. See, for example, Durkheim 1915; Hertz 1960; Van Gennep 1960; and Radcliffe-Brown 1964.

40. For some novel insights and important discussions about the cultural significance of emotions in ethnographic work, see Rosaldo 1984, 1989; Lutz and Abu-Lughod 1990; and Napolitano 2002.

41. Lutz 1982.

42. Martin 1990.

4. THE DRAMA OF DEATH

1. Often these "Protestants" would take part in the singing of funeral hymns and in Day of the Dead rituals, such as decorating and visiting the graves of loved ones.

2. According to one funeral home director I interviewed, before the construction of this crematorium in Oaxaca, those wishing to have relatives cremated had to transport the bodies to Mexico City at considerable expense—approximately 3.5 million old pesos (U.S.$840). In 2002 cremation cost 229.80 pesos (around U.S.$25), and burial costs were considerably steeper. Beginning at approximately 766 pesos (U.S.$90)—if leases on funeral plots were available at all—the least expensive lease of cemetery grounds did not include the cost of a coffin, nor did it ensure that one's beloved *difunto* could not be dug up and removed after seven years.

3. Such statements also reflect the survival of old, orthodox views. According to one priest I consulted, until 1963 cremation was considered an act of aggression against church dogma and against the Catholic doctrine of salvation. With the encouragement of Pope John Paul II, however, in 1983 the canonical laws of 1917 were amended to accept the practice of cremation, provided that the practice was not accompanied by a denial of church teaching that believers' bodies will be resurrected on the last day.

4. For an elaboration of the importance of this notion of a "social aesthetics," see Brenneis 1987, 1990.

5. For more on the notion of "a community of sentiment," see Appadurai 1990.

6. Seremetakis 1991:101.

7. See, for example, Napolitano 1997.

8. In 1990, a student *coro* (musical group) of four musicians to accompany masses at Cuauhtémoc Church cost 125,000 old pesos (roughly U.S.$20). In 1999, coffins at Nuñez Banuet ranged in price from 1,200 to 3,000 new pesos (about U.S.$120 to $300; in 1990, they had ranged from 225,000 to 650,000 old pesos, or approximately U.S.$37 to $100). In 1999, an embalming cost 3,000 new pesos (U.S.$300). To hold a wake in any of the chapels available at the funeral parlor would cost 2,500 to 3,750 new pesos (U.S.$250 to $375; in 1990, 110,000 to 515,000 old pesos), depending on the number of mourners expected and the desired decor. For an interesting article comparing the "costs of dying" in Mexico's Federal District, see Velasco 1989. See also, more recently, for Oaxaca City, "Prohibido morirse" (The High Cost of Dying), *El Imparcial*, 24 May 2002.

5. Days of the Dead in Oaxaca

1. For similar Day of the Dead tales, see Garcíagodoy 1998:3–4.

2. The Day of the Dead has, of course, been the subject of much attention by scholars both inside and outside Mexico. Although the festival has already been discussed by some historians and by anthropologists, most of them (apart from Ochoa Zazueta 1974; Brandes 1988, 1997, 1998a, 1998b; Nutini 1988; and a more recent interpretive study by Garcíagodoy 1998) have produced only brief descriptions of El Día de los Muertos, rather than full treatments of the festival itself. Many such descriptions are not qualitatively distinct from the several published accounts of the festival that have been produced in conjunction with cultural or art museum exhibitions taking place worldwide.

3. See, for example, Brandes 1997, 1998a, 1998b; and Garciagodoy 1998.

4. Carmichael and Sayer (1991:61) have noted that in Totonac communities in the northern part of the state of Veracruz, Day of the Dead celebrations also last considerably longer than is usual elsewhere in Mexico, from October 18 through the end of November.

5. For example, other, locally distinct celebrations in Oaxaca are mentioned by Berry (1981:19), for example, in his account of the Reform period in Oaxaca: the town of San Felipe de Agua (now effectively incorporated into Oaxaca City) was the site of a day's celebration marking the final day of the octave of the Feast of All Souls; in the town of Santa Lucía del Camino, celebrations during the first two weeks following All Souls' Day apparently attracted visitors from Mexico City.

6. The government interdiction against masses held in public spaces was part of postrevolutionary anti-clerical attitudes. It was removed in 1992, when President Carlos Salinas Gortari, in an effort to modernize church–state relations, amended five articles of the Constitution granting the church legal recognition and extending its public role.

7. *Calavera* broadsheets were widely popularized through the work of José Guadelupe Posada (1852–1913), who adorned them with etchings and woodcuts showing *calaveras* in a variety of humorous positions and situations. Brandes (1998:205) points out that in the 1930s, in the great artistic and intellectual *indigenista* movement that developed in the wake of the Mexican Revolution, Posada's artwork, including the

irreverent *calaveras*, became icons of Mexican nationalist ideology. See also Westheim 1953; Childs and Altman 1982; García Canclini 1993; and Garcíagodoy 1998.

8. For a rigorous scholarly work on this theme, see Connerton 1989.

9. See, for example, González Esperón 1997.

10. For a discussion of attempts in the eighteenth and nineteenth centuries by both church and government officials in Mexico City to curtail the aspects of the Day of the Dead celebrations that contrasted with the somber commemoration they were trying to promote, see Voekel 2002:214–219. The aim was to dampen the enthusiasm of revelers who filled the cemetery, disturbing solemnity with their "raucous cult of the dead," which included eating, drinking, and other "profane diversions." Cemetery visits enraged health authorities to the extent that, in 1848, cemeteries were closed to visitors on the Day of the Dead.

11. Chiñas 1973:66.

12. Chance and Taylor 1985:1–26.

6. Spectacular Death and Cultural Change

1. Grotesque realism is one of the aspects of the carnivalesque or ritual inversion of the world discussed by Bakhtin (1968). While many aspects of Bakhtin's analysis of the phenomenon of the carnivalesque are useful in the discussion of popular festivals, subsuming every such festival under the rubric of Bakhtin's work does not help elaborate the *particular* social, political, and ethical negotiations that given festivals make in or for communities and individuals.

2. García Canclini 1995:9, 27.

3. From 1970 to the early 1980s, Mexico's foreign debt rose from U.S.$3.2 million to more than U.S.$100 billion.

4. Otero 1996:7–9; INEGI 1998.

5. INEGI 1997.

6. The incursion of Halloween into Day of the Dead celebrations has been discussed by Brandes (1998a) and Garcíagodoy (1998).

7. Castañeda 1996.

8. For examples of anthropological critiques of such notions, see Wagner 1975; Strathern 1992; and Amselle 1998. On "the institutionalization of cultural objectification," see also Handler 1988; and Mitchell 1988.

9. Exactly how ancient the practices of Guelaguetza are is, of course, a matter of some debate. For instructive cautions around assuming the particular agedness of certain ostensible indigenous traditions, see Chance and Taylor 1985.

10. This popular description, which attests to the pre-Columbian origins of the Gueleguetza, has been challenged more recently by the Mexican anthropologist Jesús Lizama Quijano (2002). According to Lizama Quijano, the Guelaguetza actually began in 1932, when a group of local intellectuals and government institutions organized a program of festivities intended as a Homenaje Racial (Homage to the Races) in the context of the four hundredth anniversary celebration of the establishment of Oaxaca as a city.

11. Lizama Quijano (2002:12), for example, traces the Flor de Piña and the Jarabe Mixteco, another popular "showcase" dance, from their origins—in 1958 and 1929, respectively—through the rest of the twentieth century.

12. For a more extended analysis of the logic of various forms of cultural collection, exploitation, and commodification, see Clifford 1988:215–251; Handler 1988; Nagengast and Kearney 1990:63–64; and García Canclini 1995.

13. This sort of nationalist sentiment, which began as a leftist, antigovernment critique, is now quite fully harmonized with the nationalist project of the Mexican state. Such a conflation of aims has been made possible, I would argue, because both mid-twentieth-century leftists and contemporary government officials share the same romantic account of culture as the expression of the essence of a people.

14. *Don Juan Tenorio* is often performed in urban settings in Mexico at the time of the Day of the Dead and also in Spain on the eve of All Souls' Day. This fantastical melodrama is an adaptation of a Spanish popular legend that recounts the licentious Don Juan's seduction of a pious village woman, his murder of her father, and his eventual downfall. The second part of the sentimental and humorous drama, rife with wordplay and Catholic allegory, shows a cemetery scene involving Don Juan's mocking attitude toward death; he is invited by a ghost for dinner and then later dragged into hell through the ghost's grave.

15. Gonzáles Esperón 1997:45–46 (my translation).

16. Gonzáles Esperón 1997:14 (my translation).

17. García Canclini 1993:96, 97, 1995. Brandes (1988:88–109) discusses the influence of tourism on the Day of the Dead celebration in the town of Tzintzuntzan, also in the central state of Michoacán. For other discussions of Day of the Dead tourism, see Ochoa Zazueta 1974; and Garciagodoy 1998.

18. From an interview on 9 August 2000. It is interesting that Garciagodoy (1998:77) describes in a very positive light her experience in a tour to the Xoxocotlán graveyard in 1992, saying that all participants in the tour were given a short speech on the significance of the Day of the Dead and were encouraged to place their flowers on unclaimed graves. Although such efforts at cultural sensitization and contextualizing are not unheard of, I found from my observations of Day of the Dead tourism in Oaxaca that they are the exception rather than the rule.

19. For more reflections on these paradigmatically "postmodern" phenomena, see Castañeda 1996; and Higgins 2000.

20. In his analysis of the politics of culture surrounding the patrimony of the French Canadian province of Québec, Handler (1988) explains "cultural objectification" as the gradual emergence among members of a local population of a static, "commonsense" perception of culture as a bounded entity that is somehow separate from them, an entity that can be possessed and acted on—even lost. Thus Handler argues that people who talk about certain of their customs as "traditional" and "folkloric" have made a critical transition of objectification, creating a separation between such practices and the rest of their lives.

21. Ramona Pérez, personal communication, 1995. See also Pérez 2000.

22. In Oaxaca, unlike in Canada or the United States, setting up a Christmas tree or

making a *nacimiento* scene in December—a miniature re-creation of the manger scene resembling a whole landscape—is largely a middle- and upper-class phenomenon. The poor remain committed to popular festivals that follow a rather different calendar.

EPILOGUE

1. See, for example, Napolitano 2002:12.

REFERENCES

Aho, J. 1981. *Religious Mythology and the Art of War: Comparative Religious Symbolisms of Military Violence*. London: Aldwych.

Amselle, Jean-Loup. 1998. *Mestizo Logics*. Stanford, Calif.: Stanford University Press.

Anderson, Benedict. 1983. *Imagined Communities: Reflections on the Origin and Spread of Nationalism*. New York: Verso.

Appadurai, Arjun. 1990. "Topographies of the Self: Praise and Emotion in Hindu India." In *Language and the Politics of Emotion*, edited by Catherine Lutz and Lila Abu-Lughod, 92–112. Cambridge: Cambridge University Press.

Ariès, Phillippe. 1974. *Western Attitudes Toward Death*. Baltimore: Johns Hopkins University Press.

Arriaga, David. 1990 [1954]. "El tequio." *México indígena*, no. 6.

Augur, Helen. 1954. *Zapotec*. Garden City, N.Y.: Doubleday.

Bakhtin, Mikhail. 1968. *Rabelais and His World*. Berkeley: University of California Press.

Barabas, Alicia Mabel. 1977. "Chinantec Messianism: The Mediator of the Divine." In *Western Expansion and Indigenous Peoples*, edited by Elias Sevilla-Casas, 221–253. The Hague: Mouton.

Barabas, Alicia, and Miguel Bartolomé, eds. 1984. *El rey cono hoy: Tradición mesiánica y privación social entre los Mixes de Oaxaca*. Oaxaca: Instituto Nacional de Antropología e Historia.

———. 1990. *Etnicidad y pluralismo cultural: La dinámica étnica en Oaxaca*. Mexico City: Instituto Nacional de Antropología e Historia.

Bartolomé, Miguel, and Alicia Barabas. 1990. "La pluridad desigual en Oaxaca." In *Etnicidad y pluralismo cultural: La dinémica étnica en Oaxaca*, edited by Alicia Barabas and Miguel Bartolomé, 15–95. Mexico City: Instituto Nacional de Antropología e Historia.

Bartra, Roger. 1992. *The Cage of Melancholy: Identity and Metamorphosis in the Mexican Character*. New Brunswick, N.J.: Rutgers University Press.

Basáñez, Miguel. 1987. *La composición de poder: Oaxaca, 1968–84*. Mexico City: Universidad Nacional Autónoma de México.

Baskes, Jeremy. 2000. *Indians, Merchants, and Markets: A Reinterpretation of the Repartimento and Spanish–Indian Economic Relations in Colonial Oaxaca, 1750–1821.* Stanford, Calif.: Stanford University Press.

Baudrillard, Jean. 1976. *Symbolic Exchange and Death.* New York: Sage.

Beals, Ralph L. 1945a. *Ethnology of the Western Mixe.* University of California Publications in American Archaeology and Ethnology, vol. 42. Berkeley: University of California Press.

———. 1945b. *Cheran: A Sierra Tarascan Village.* Westport, Conn.: Greenwood Press.

———. 1970. "Gifting, Reciprocity, Savings and Credit in Peasant Oaxaca." *Southwest Journal of Anthropology* 26:231–241.

Beezley, William, and Linda A. Curcio-Nagy. 2000. *Latin American Popular Culture: An Introduction.* Wilmington, Del.: Scholarly Resources.

Beezley, William, Cheryl E. Martin, and William E. French, eds. 1995. *Rituals of Rule, Rituals of Resistance.* Wilmington, Del.: Scholarly Imprint.

Behar, Ruth. 1987. "Sex and Sin: Witchcraft and the Devil in Late-Colonial Mexico." *American Ethnologist* 14:34–54.

Berger, Peter. 1969. *The Sacred Canopy.* Garden City, N.Y.: Doubleday.

Berger, Peter, and Thomas Luckmann. 1966. *The Social Construction of Reality.* London: Cox and Wyman.

Berlin, Heinrich. 1988. "Las antiguas creencias en San Miguel Sola, Oaxaca, México." In *Idolatría y superstición entre los indios de Oaxaca,* 9–89. Mexico City: Ediciones Toledo.

Bernal, Ignacio. 2001. "La población indígena y su proceso salud-enfermedad-atención y ecosistema en el nuevo milenio." In *Oaxaca: Población en el siglo 21* 1:3. Oaxaca: Dirección General de Población de Oaxaca.

Berry, Charles R. 1981. *The Reform in Oaxaca, 1856–1876.* Lincoln: University of Nebraska Press.

Berryman, Philip. 1987. *Liberation Theology.* London: Pantheon.

Blauner, Robert. 1977. "Death and Social Structure." In *Passing: The Vision of Death in America,* edited by Charles O. Jackson, 174–209. London: Greenwood Press.

Bloch, Maurice, and Jonathan Parry. 1982. *Death and the Regeneration of Life.* Cambridge: Cambridge University Press.

Bonfil Batalla, Guillermo. 1973. *Cholula: La ciudad sagrada en la era industrial.* Mexico City: Universidad Nacional Autónoma de México, Instituto de Investigaciones Históricas.

Borah, Woodrow, and Sherburne F. Cook. 1963. "The Aboriginal Population of Mexico on the Eve of the Spanish Conquest." *Ibero-Americana* 45:226–258.

Bourdieu, Pierre. 1977. *Outline of a Theory of Practice.* Cambridge: Cambridge University Press.

Brandes, Stanley. 1988. *Power and Persuasion: Fiestas and Social Control in Rural Mexico.* Philadelphia: University of Pennsylvania Press.

———. 1997. "Sugar, Colonialism, and Death: On the Origins of Mexico's Day of the Dead." *Comparative Study of Society and History* 39:266–295.

———. 1998a. "Iconography in Mexico's Day of the Dead: Origins and Meaning." *Ethnohistory* 45:181–218.

_____. 1998b. "The Day of the Dead, and the Quest for Mexican National Identity." *Journal of American Folklore* 111:359–380.

_____. 2003. "Is There a Mexican View of Death?" *Ethos* 31:127–144.

Brenneis, Donald. 1987. "Performing Passions: Aesthetics and Politics in an Occasionally Egalitarian Community." *American Ethnologist* 14:236–250.

_____. 1990. "Shared and Solitary Sentiments: The Discourse of Friendship, Play, and Anger in Bhatgaon." In *Language and the Politics of Emotion*, edited by Catherine Lutz and Lila Abu-Lughod, 113–125. Cambridge: Cambridge University Press.

Brenner, Anita. 1929. *Idols Behind Altars: The Story of the Mexican Spirit*. New York: Payson and Clarke.

Burdick, John. 1992. "Rethinking the Study of Social Movements: The Case of Christian Base Communities in Urban Brazil." In *The Making of Social Movements in Latin America*, edited by Arturo Escobar and Sonia Alvarez, 171–184. San Francisco: Westview Press.

Butterworth, Douglas. 1962. "A Study of the Urbanization Process Among Mixtec Migrants from Tilantongo in Mexico City." *América indígena* 22:257–274.

_____. 1975. *Tilantongo: Comunidad mixteca en transición*. Mexico City: Instituto Nacional Indígenista.

Butterworth, Douglas, and John K. Chance. 1981. *Latin American Urbanization*. Cambridge: Cambridge University Press.

Cahn, Peter. 2003. *All Religions Are Good in Tzintzuntzan: Evangelicals in Catholic Mexico*. Austin: University of Texas Press.

Candelaria, Miguel. 1990. *Popular Religion and Liberation*. Albany: State University of New York Press.

Carmagnani, Marcello. 1988. *El regreso de los dioses*. Mexico City: Fondo de Cultura Económica.

Carmichael, Elizabeth, and Chloë Sayer. 1991. *The Skeleton at the Feast: The Day of the Dead in Mexico*. London: British Museum.

Castañeda, Quetzil E. 1996. *In the Museum of Maya Culture*. Minneapolis: University of Minnesota Press.

Cátedra, María. 1992. *This World, Other Worlds*. Chicago: University of Chicago Press.

Chance, John K. 1978. *Race and Class in Colonial Oaxaca*. Stanford, Calif.: Stanford University Press.

_____. 1986. "Raza y clase en Oaxaca." In *Lecturas históricas del estado de Oaxaca*, edited by María de los Angeles Romero Frizzi, 2:369–417. Mexico City: Instituto Nacional de Antropología e Historia and Government of the State of Oaxaca.

Chance, John K., and William B. Taylor. 1985. "*Cofradías* and *Cargos*: An Historical Perspective on the Meso-American Civil–Religious Hierarchy." *American Ethnologist* 12:1–26.

Childs, Robert V., and Patricia B. Altman. 1982. *Vive tu recuerdo: Living Tradition in the Mexican Days of the Dead*. Los Angeles: Museum of Cultural History, University of California at Los Angeles.

Chiñas, Beverley. 1973. *The Isthmus Zapotecs*. Prospect Heights, Ill.: Waveland Press.

Choron, Jacques. 1963. *Death in Western Thought*. New York: Colker.

Christian, William. 1972. *Person and God in a Spanish Valley*. London: Seminar.

_____. 1981. *Local Religion in Sixteenth-Century Spain*. Princeton, N.J.: Princeton University Press.

Clarke, Colin. 2000. *Class, Ethnicity, and Community in Southern Mexico: Oaxaca's Peasantries*. Oxford: Oxford University Press.

Clendinnen, Inga. 1980. "Landscape and World View: The Survival of Yucatec Maya Culture Under Spanish Conquest." *Comparative Studies in Society and History* 22:374–393.

_____. 1990. "Ways to the Sacred: Reconstructing Religion in 16th-Century Mexico." *History and Anthropology* 5:105–141.

Clifford James. 1988. *The Predicament of Culture*. Cambridge, Mass.: Harvard University Press.

Cohen, Anthony. 1985. *The Symbolic Construction of Community*. London: Routledge.

Cohen, Jeffrey H. 1999. *Cooperation and Community: Economy and Society in Oaxaca*. Austin: University of Texas Press.

Comaroff, Jean. 1985. *Body of Power, Spirit of Resistance*. Chicago: University of Chicago Press.

CONAPO (Consejo Nacional de Población). 2000a. *Indices de marginación*. Mexico City: CONAPO.

_____. 2000b. *Indices de desarollo humano y social*. Mexico City: CONAPO.

Connerton, Paul. 1989. *How Societies Remember*. Cambridge: Cambridge University Press.

Cook, Scott, and Martin Diskin. 1976. *Markets in Oaxaca*. Austin: University of Texas Press.

Cordero, Carmen. 1982. *Supervivencia de un derecho consuetudianario en un valle de Tlacolula*. Oaxaca: Fondo Nacional para Actividades Sociales.

DaMatta, Robert. 1984a. "On Carnival, Informality, and Magic: A Point of View from Brazil." In *Text, Play, and Story: The Construction and Reconstruction of Self and Society*, edited by Edward M. Bruner, 230–246. Washington, D.C.: American Ethnological Society.

_____. 1984b. "Carnival in Multiple Planes." In *Rite, Drama, Festival, Spectacle*, edited by John MacAloon, 208–241. Philadelphia: Institute for the Study of Human Issues.

Danforth, Loring M. 1982. *The Death Ritual of Rural Greece*. Princeton, N.J.: Princeton University Press.

De Certeau, Michel. 1984. *The Practice of Everyday Life*. Berkeley: University of California Press.

De la Fuente, Julio. 1977 [1949]. *Yalalag, una villa zapoteca serrana*. Mexico City: Instituto Nacional Indígenista.

DIGEPO (Dirección General de Población de Oaxaca). 2000. *Marginación municipal Oaxaca*. Oaxaca: DIGEPO y Instituto Nacional Indigenista.

Durkheim, Emile. 1971 [1915]. *The Elementary Forms of Religious Life*. London: Allen and Unwin.

Earle, Duncan. 1990. "Appropriating the Enemy: Highland Maya Religious Organization and Community Survival." In *Class, Politics, and Popular Religion in Mexico and Central America*, edited by Lynn Stephen and James Dow, 115–139. Washington, D.C.: American Anthropological Association.

Eber, Christine. 1995. *Women and Alcohol in a Highland Maya Town*. Austin: University of Texas Press.

El Guindi, Fadwa. 1977. "Lore and Structure: Todos Santos in the Zapotec System." *Journal of Latin American Lore* 3:3–18.

———. 1986. *The Myth of Ritual: A Native's Ethnography of Zapotec Life-Crisis Rituals*. Tucson: University of Arizona Press.

El Guindi, Fadwa, and Henry A. Selby. 1976. "Dialectics in Zapotec Thinking." In *Meaning in Anthropology*, edited by Keith Basso and Henry A. Selby, 181–196. Albuquerque: University of New Mexico Press.

Fabian, Johannes. 1974. "How Others Die: Reflections on the Anthropology of Death." In *Death in American Experience*, edited by Arien Mack, 177–201. New York: Schocken Books.

Farriss, Nancy. 1984. *Maya Society Under Colonial Rule*. Princeton, N.J.: Princeton University Press.

Fernández Kelly, Patricia. 1975. "Death in Mexican Folk Culture." In *Death in America*, edited by David E. Stannard, 92–111. Philadelphia: University of Pennsylvania Press.

Finkler, Kaja. 1994. *Women in Pain: Gender and Morbidity in Mexico*. Philadelphia: University of Pennsylvania Press.

Foster, Donald W. 1971. "*Tequio* in Urban Mexico: A Case from Oaxaca City." *Journal of the Steward Anthropological Society* 2:148–179.

Foster, George M. 1948. *Empire's Children: The People of Tzintzuntzan*. Mexico City: Smithsonian Institution, Institute of Social Anthropology.

———. 1960. *Culture and Conquest: America's Spanish Heritage*. New York: Cooper Square.

Franco, Jean. 1999. "What's in a Name? Popular Culture Theories and Their Limitations." In *Critical Passions: Selected Essays*, 169–180. Durham, N.C.: Duke University Press.

Friedlander, Judith. 1975. *Being Indian in Hueyapan: A Study of Forced Identity in Contemporary Mexico*. New York: St Martin's Press.

Fuentes, Carlos. 1964. *The Death of Artemio Cruz*. New York: Farrar, Straus and Giroux.

Gallinier, Jacques. 1989. "Conceptions of Death in Mesoamerica: An Ethnographic Outline." Manuscript, Department of Social Anthropology, Cambridge University.

García Canclini, Néstor. 1993. *Transforming Modernity*. Austin: University of Texas Press.

———. 1995. *Hybrid Cultures: Strategies for Entering and Leaving Modernity*. Minneapolis: University of Minnesota Press.

Garcíagodoy, Juanita. 1998. *Digging the Days of the Dead*. Boulder: University Press of Colorado.

Gijsbers, Wim. 1996. *Usos y costumbres, caciquismo e intolerancia religiosa*. Oaxaca: Centro de Apoyo al Movimiento Popular Oaxaqueño AC.

Gillow, D. Eulagio. 1978 [1880]. *El Diocesis de Oaxaca: Apuntos históricos sobre la introducción del cristianismo en la Diocesis de Oaxaca*. Mexico City: Ediciones Toledo.

González Crussi, Frank. 1993. *The Day of the Dead and Other Mortal Reflections*. New York: Harcourt Brace.

González Esperón, Luz María. 1997. *La celebración de muertos en Oaxaca*. Oaxaca: Instituto Oaxaqueño de las Culturas, Fondo Estatal para la Cultura y las Artes.

González Medina, Rogelio. 1993. "El Panteón Municipal de San Miguel de la ciudad de Oaxaca." *Alcaraván* 4:38–40.

Goody, Jack. 1975. "Death and the Interpretation of Culture: A Bibliographic Overview." In *Death in America*, edited by David E. Stannard, 1–8. Philadelphia: University of Pennsylvania Press.

Gramsci, Antonio. 1971. *Selections from the Prison Notebooks*. Translated by Quentin Hoare. New York: International.

Greenberg, James. 1981. *Santiago's Sword: Chatino Peasant Religion and Economics*. Berkeley: University of California Press.

_____. 1989. *Blood Ties*. Tucson: University of Arizona Press.

Gross, Toomas. 2003. "Protestantism and Modernity: The Implications of Religious Change in Contemporary Rural Oaxaca." *Sociology of Religion* 64:479–498.

Gruzinski, Serge. 1993. *The Conquest of Mexico*. Cambridge: Polity.

Hall, Stuart. 1981. "Notes on Deconstructing 'the Popular.'" In *People's History and Socialist Theory*, edited by Raphael Samuel, 227–240. London: Routledge and Kegan Paul.

Hamnett, Brian R. 1986. "La iglesia en las primeras décadas del siglo XIX." In *Lecturas históricas del estado de Oaxaca*, edited by María de los Angeles Romero Frizzi, 3:71–82. Mexico City: Instituto Nacional de Antropología e Historia y Gobierno del Estado de Oaxaca.

Handler, Richard. 1988. *Nationalism and the Politics of Culture in Quebec*. Madison: University of Wisconsin Press.

Harris, Olivia. 1982. "The Death and the Devils Among the Bolivian Laymi." In *Death and the Regeneration of Life*, edited by Maurice Bloch and Jonathan Parry, 45–73. Cambridge: Cambridge University Press.

Harvey, H. R., and Isabel Kelly. 1969. "The Totonac." In *Handbook of Middle American Indians*, edited by Evon Z. Vogt, 8:638–681. Austin: University of Texas Press.

Herrasti, Lourdes, and Alberto Aguirre. 1985. "El mexicano y la muerte: Consequencia de una especulación: Entrevista a Arturo Warman." *México indígena* 7:18–21

Hertz, Robert. 1960 [1907]. *Death and the Right Hand*. Aberdeen: Cohen and West.

Higgins, Michael J. 1974. *Somos gente humilde: Etnografía de una colonia urbana pobre de Oaxaca*. Mexico City: Instituto Nacional Indígenista.

_____. 1979. "Social Relations Among the Urban Poor of Oaxaca." In *Social, Political and Economic Life in Contemporary Oaxaca*, edited by Aubrey Williams, 103–142. Nashville, Tenn.: Vanderbilt University Press.

_____. 1983. *Somos Tocayos: Anthropology of Urbanism and Poverty*. New York: University of America Press, 1983.

_____. 1990. "Martyrs and Virgins: Popular Religion in Mexico and Nicaragua." In *Class, Politics and Popular Religion*, edited by Lynn Stephen and James Dow, 187–204. Washington, D.C.: American Anthropological Association.

Higgins, Michael J., and Tanya L. Coen. 2000. *Streets, Bedrooms, and Patios: The Ordinariness of Diversity in Urban Oaxaca*. Austin: University of Texas Press.

Howell, Jane. 1997. "Turning Out Good Ethnography, or Talking Out of Turn? Gender, Violence, and Confidentiality in Southeastern Mexico." *Journal of Contemporary Ethnography* 33:323–352.

Humphreys, S. C., and Helen King, eds. 1981. *Mortality and Immortality: The Anthropology and Archaeology of Death*. London: Academic Press.

Hunt, Linda Lee Mergentime. 1992. "Living with Cancer in Oaxaca, Mexico: Patient and Physician Perspectives in Cultural Context." Ph.D. diss., Harvard University.

Huntington, Richard, and Peter Metcalf. 1979. *Celebrations of Death: An Anthropology of Mortuary Ritual*. Cambridge: Cambridge University Press.

INEGI (Instituto Nacional de Estadística Geografía e Informática). 1991. *XI Censo de población y vivienda, 1990: Oaxaca: Perfil sociodemográfico*. Aquascalientes: INEGI.

_____. 1997. *Oaxaca: Resultados definitivos: Conteo de población y vivienda, 1990–1995*. Mexico City: INEGI

_____. 1999. *Anuario estadístico del estado de Oaxaca*. 2 vols. Oaxaca: INEGI.

_____. 2000. *XII censo general de población y vivienda, 2000: Resumen general*. Mexico City: INEGI.

_____, ed. 1998. *Oaxaco hoy*. Oaxaca: INEGI.

Ingham, John M. 1970. "The Asymmetrical Implications of Godparenthood in Tlayacapan, Morelos." *Man* 5:281–289.

_____. 1996. *Mary, Michael, and Lucifer: Folk Catholicism in Central Mexico*. Austin: University of Texas Press.

Joseph, Gilbert, and Daniel Nugent. 1994. *Everyday Forms of State Resistance*. Durham, N.C.: Duke University Press.

Kahn, Peter. 2003. *All Religions Are Good in Tzintzuntzan: Evangelicals in Catholic Mexico*. Austin: University of Texas Press.

Katz, Friedrich. 1988. "Rural Uprisings in Preconquest and Colonial Mexico." In *Riot, Rebellion and Revolution: Rural Conflict in Mexico*, edited by Friedrich Katz, 65–94. Princeton, N.J.: Princeton University Press.

Kearney, Michael. 1972. *The Winds of Ixtepeji: World View and Society in a Zapotec Town*. New York: Holt, Rinehart and Winston.

_____. 1986. "From the Invisible Hand to Visible Feet: Anthropological Studies of Migration and Development." *Annual Review of Anthropology* 15:331–361.

Kearney, Michael, and Carol Nagengast. 1989. *Anthropological Perspectives on Transnational Communities in Rural California*. Davis, Calif.: Institute of Rural Studies.

Kemper, Robert V. 1977. *Migration and Adaptation: Tzintzuntzan Peasants in Mexico City*. London: Sage.

_____. 1981. "Obstacles and Opportunities: Household Economics of Tzintzuntzan Migrants in Mexico City." *Urban Anthropology* 10:212–229.

Kligman, Gail. 1988. *The Wedding of the Dead: Ritual, Poetics, and Popular Culture in Transylvania*. Berkeley: University of California Press.

Knight, Alan. 1990. "Racism, Revolution, and *Indigenismo*: Mexico 1910–1940." In *The Idea of Race in Latin America, 1870–1940*, edited by Richard Graham, 71–114. Austin: University of Texas Press.

Lafaye, Jacques. 1974. *Quetzacoatl and Guadalupe: The Formation of Mexican National Consciousness, 1531–1813*. Chicago: University of Chicago Press.

Lancaster, Roger. 1988. *Thanks to God and the Revolution*. New York: Columbia University Press.

Leach, Edmund. 1976. *Culture and Communication*. Cambridge: Cambridge University Press.

Leslie, Charles. 1960. *Now We Are Civilized: A Study of the World View of the Zapotec Indians of Mitla, Oaxaca*. Detroit: Wayne State University Press.

Levine, Daniel. 1980. *Churches and Politics in Latin America*. Beverley Hills, Calif.: Sage.

Lewis, Oscar. 1951. *Life in a Mexican Village: Tepoztlan Restudied*. Urbana: University of Illinois Press.

——. 1959. *Five Families*. New York: Basic Books.

——. 1961. *The Children of Sánchez*. New York: Random House.

——. 1965. "Urbanization Without Breakdown: A Case Study." In *Contemporary Cultures and Societies of Latin America*, edited by Dwight B. Heath and Richard N. Adams, 424–437. New York: Random House.

——. 1966. *La Vida*. New York: Random House.

——. 1968. "The Culture of Poverty." In *Man in Adaptation: The Cultural Present*, edited by Yehudi Cohen, 406–414. Chicago: Aldine.

——. 1969. *A Death in the Sánchez Family*. New York: Random House.

Limón, José. 1994. *Dancing with the Devil*. Madison: University of Wisconsin Press.

Lipp, Walter J. 1991. *The Mixe of Oaxaca: Religion, Ritual, and Healing*. Austin: University of Texas Press.

Lizama Quijano, Jesús J. 2002. "La máxima fiesta de los oaxaqueños: Algunos comentarios sobre la Guelaguetza de los Lunes del Cerro." *Cuadernos del sur* 7:7–18.

Logan, Kathleen. 1984. *Haciendo Pueblo: The Development of a Guadalajaran Suburb*. Tuscaloosa: University of Alabama Press.

Lomnitz, Larissa. 1977. *Networks and Marginality*. New York: Academic Press.

Lomnitz-Adler, Claudio. 1991. "Concepts for the Study of Regional Culture." *American Ethnologist* 18:195–214.

——. 1992. *Exits from the Labyrinth: Culture and Ideology in the Mexican National Space*. Berkeley: University of California Press.

Lutz, Catherine. 1982. "The Domain of Emotion Words on Ifaluk." *American Ethnologist* 9:113–128.

Lutz, Catherine, and Lila Abu-Lughod, eds. 1990. *Language and the Politics of Emotion*. Cambridge: Cambridge University Press.

MacNabb, Valerie, and Martha Rees. 1993. "Liberation or Theology? Ecclesiastic Base Communities in Oaxaca, Mexico." *Journal of Church and State* 35:723–749.

Madsen, William. "Syncretism." 1957. In *Handbook of Middle American Indians*, edited by Manning Nash, 6:369–391. Austin: University of Texas Press.

Mahar, Cheleen. 1992. "An Exercise in Practice: Studying Migrants to Latin American Squatter Settlements." *Urban Anthropology* 21:275–309.

Mahar Higgins, Cheleen. 1974. "Integrative Aspects of Folk and Western Medicine Among the Urban Poor of Oaxaca." *Anthropological Quarterly* 48:31–37.

Malinowski, Bronislaw. 1948. *Magic, Science, and Religion*. London: Faber and West.

Mallon, Florencia E. 1995. *Peasant and Nation: The Making of Post-Colonial Mexico and Peru*. Berkeley: University of California Press.

Mangin, William. 1967. "Latin American Squatter Settlements: A Problem and a Solution." *Latin American Research Review* 2:65–98.

Mannheim, Bruce. 1991. *The Language of the Inka Since the European Invasion*. Austin: University of Texas Press.

Margolies, Barbara Luise. 1975. *Princes of the Earth: Subcultural Diversity in a Mexican Municipality*. Washington, D.C.: American Anthropological Association.

Marroquín, Enrique. 1989a. *La cruz mesiánica*. Oaxaca: Universidad Autónoma de Benito Juárez, Palabras Ediciones.

———. 1989b. "Iglesias, religión popular y relaciones de poder en Oaxaca." Manuscript, Instituto de Investigaciones Sociológicas de la Universidad Autónoma Benito Juárez de Oaxaca.

———. 1992. *El botín sagrado: La dinámica religiosa en Oaxaca*. Oaxaca: Instituto de Investigaciones Sociológicas de la Universidad Autónoma Benito Juarez de Oaxaca y Comunicación Social del Gobierno del Estado de Oaxaca.

Martin, Joann. 1990 "Motherhood and Power: The Production of a Women's Culture of Politics in a Mexican Community." *American Ethnologist* 17:470–489.

Martínez Vásquez, Victor Raúl. 1990. *Movimiento popular y política en Oaxaca: 1968–1986*. Mexico City: Consejo Nacional para la Cultura y las Artes.

Merrill, William. 1988. *Rarámuri Souls*. Washington, D.C.: Smithsonian Institution Press.

Mitchell, Timothy. 1988. *Colonizing Egypt*. Berkeley: University of California Press.

Monaghan, John. 1987. "We Are People Who Eat Tortillas: Household and Community in the Mixteca." Ph.D. diss., University of Pennsylvania.

———. 1994. *The Covenants with Earth and Rain: Exchange, Sacrifice, and Revelation in Mixtec Sociality*. Norman: University of Oklahoma Press.

Montes García, Olga. 1997. "Movimientos religiosos en Oaxaca: Sus características." *Religiones y sociedad* 1:43–88.

Morris, Earl W. 1991. "Household, Kin, and Nonkin Sources of Assistance in Home Building: The Case of the City of Oaxaca." *Urban Anthropology* [special issue] 20:49–65.

Mullen, Robert J. 1975. *Dominican Architecture in Sixteenth-Century Oaxaca*. Phoenix: Center for Latin American Studies, Arizona State University.

Murphy, Arthur. 1991. "Introduction and Overview." *Urban Anthropology* [special issue] 20:1–13.

Murphy, Arthur, and Martha A. Rees, eds. 1991. "City in Crisis: The Case of Oaxaca, Mexico." *Urban Anthropology* [special issue] 20.

Murphy, Arthur, and Alex Stepick. 1989. "Adaptation and Inequality in Oaxaca." Manuscript, Instituto Welte de Estudios Oaxaqueños.

———. 1991. *Social Inequality in Oaxaca: A History of Resistance and Change*. Philadelphia: Temple University Press.

Nagengast, Carol, and Michael Kearney. 1990. "Mixtec Ethnicity." *Latin American Research Review* 25:61–93.

Napolitano, Valentina. 1995. "Self and Identity in a 'Colonia Popular' in Guadalajara, Mexico." Ph.D. diss., University of London.

———. 1997. "Becoming a *Mujercita*: Rituals, Festivals, and Religious Discourses." *Journal of the Royal Anthropological Institute* 3:279–296.

———. 1998. "Between 'Traditional' and 'New' Catholic Church Religious Discourses in Urban, Western Mexico." *Bulletin of Latin American Research* 17:323–339.

———. 2002. *Mujercitas, Migration, and Medicine Men*. Los Angeles: University of California Press.

Navarro, Marysa. 2002. "Against *Marianismo*." In *Gender's Place: Feminist Anthropologies of Latin America*, edited by Rosario Montoya, Lessie Jo Frazier, and Janise Hurtig, 257–272. New York: Palgrave Macmillan.

Nebel, Richard. 1995. *Sta. María Tonantzín/Virgen de Guadalupe: Contuidad y transformación religiosa en México*. Mexico City: Fondo de Cultura Económica.

Norget, Kristin. 1991. "*La Mujer Abnegada*: Notes on Women's Role and Status in Oaxaca, Mexico." *Cambridge Anthropology* 1:1–24.

———. 1997a. "The Politics of 'Liberation': The Popular Church, Indigenous Theology, and Grassroots Mobilization in Oaxaca, Mexico." *Latin American Perspectives* 24:96–127.

———. 1997b. "Progressive Theology and Popular Religiosity in Oaxaca, Mexico." *Ethnology* 36:67–83.

———. 2004. "'Knowing Where We Enter': Indigenous Theology and the Popular Church in Oaxaca, Mexico." In *Resurgent Voices in Latin America: Indigenous Peoples, Political Mobilization, and Religious Change*, edited by Edward L. Cleary and Timothy J. Steigenga, 154–186. New Brunswick, N.J.: Rutgers University Press.

Nutini, Hugo. 1976. "Syncretism and Acculturation: The Historical Development of the Cult of the Patron Saint in Tlaxcala, Mexico (1519–1670)." *Ethnology* 15:301–321.

———. 1988. *Todos Santos in Rural Tlaxcala*. Princeton N.J.: Princeton University Press.

Nutini, Hugo, and Betty Bell. 1980. *Ritual Kinship: The Structure and Historical Development of the Compadrazgo System in Rural Tlaxcala*. Princeton, N.J.: Princeton University Press.

Obeyesekere, Gananath. 1968. "Theodicy, Sin, and Salvation in a Sociology of Buddhism." In *Dialectic in Practical Religion*, edited by Edmund Leach, 7–40. Cambridge: Cambridge University Press.

Ochoa Zazueta, Jesús A. 1974. *La muerte y los muertos: Culto, servicio, ofrenda y humor de una comunidad*. Mexico City: Secretária de Educación Pública.

O'Gorman, Edmundo. 1986. *Destierro de sombras: Luz en el origen de la imagen y culto de Nuestra Señora de Guadelupe del Tepeyac*. Mexico City: Universidad Nacional Autónoma de México..

Ortiz, Andrés. 1985. "Santos, calaveras y muertos: La búsqueda de una raíz: Entrevista a Carlos Navarrete." *México indígena* 7:4–12.

Otero, Gerardo. 1996. *Neoliberalism Revisited: Economic Restructuring and Mexico's Political Future*. Boulder, Colo.: Westview Press.

Pacheco Vásquez, Pedro D., Earl W. Morris, Mary Winter, and Arthur D. Murphy. 1991. "Neighborhood Type, Housing, and Housing Characteristics in Oaxaca, Mexico." *Urban Anthropology* [special issue] 20:31–47.

Parsons, Elsie Clews. 1936. *Mitla: Town of the Souls*. Chicago: University of Chicago Press.

Pastrana, Daniela. 2001. "Religión y pueblos indios: De la intolerancia a la convivencia." *La Jornada*, April 8.

Paz, Octavio. 1961. *The Labyrinth of Solitude*. Harmondsworth: Penguin.

Pérez, Ramona. 2000. "Fiesta as Tradition, Fiesta as Change: Ritual, Alcohol and Violence in a Mexican Community." *Addiction* 95:365–373.

Portillo, Andrés. 1910. *Oaxaca en el centenario en la independencia nacional*. Oaxaca: Ayuntamiento de la Ciudad.

Prince, Zachary, and Arthur Murphy. 1988. "Haciendo Colonia: The Making of a Community Near Oaxaca, Mexico." Manuscript, Instituto Welte de Estudios Oaxaqueños.

Radcliffe-Brown, Alfred R. 1964 [1922]. *The Andaman Islanders*. New York: Free Press.

Redfield, Robert. 1930. *Tepoztlan, a Mexican Village: A Study of Folk Life*. Chicago: University of Chicago Press.

Redfield, Robert, and Alfonso Villa Rojas. 1990 [1934]. *Chan Kom: A Maya Village*. Prospect Heights, Ill.: Waveland Press.

Ricard, Robert. 1966 *The Spiritual Conquest of Mexico*. Berkeley: University of California Press.

Romero Frizzi, María de los Angeles. 1973. "Los Días de Muertos en San Juan Atepec, Ixtlan, Oaxaca." *INAH Boletín*, 2nd ser., 73:37–40.

———. 1996. *El sol y la cruz: Los pueblos indios de Oaxaca colonial*. Mexico City: Centro de Investigaciones y Estudios Superiores en Antropología Social–Instituto Nacional Indigenista.

Romney, Kimball, and Romaine Romney. 1966. *The Mixtecans of Juxtlahuaca, Mexico*. New York: Wiley.

Rosaldo, Renato. 1984 "Grief and a Headhunter's Rage: On the Cultural Force of Emotions." In *Text, Play, and Story: The Construction and Reconstruction of Self and Society*, edited by Edward M. Bruner, 178–195. Washington, D.C.: American Ethnological Society.

———. 1989. *Culture and Truth*. Boston: Beacon Press.

Rowe, William, and Vivian Schelling. 1991. *Memory and Modernity: Popular Culture in Latin America*. London: Verso.

Rubel, Arthur, C. W. O'Neill, and R. Collado-Ardon. 1984. *Susto: A Folk Illness*. Berkeley: University of California Press.

Rulfo, Juan. 1959. *Pedro Páramo*. Translated by Lysander Kemp. New York: Grove Press.

Sault, Nicole L. 1985. "Zapotec Godmothers: The Centrality of Women for *Compadrazgo* Groups in a Village of Oaxaca, Mexico." Ph.D. diss., University of California–Los Angeles.

Scheper-Hughes, Nancy. 1992. *Death Without Weeping*. Berkeley: University of California Press.

Schirmer, Jennifer. 1994. "The Claiming of Space and the Body Politic Within National Security States: The Plaza de Mayo Madres and the Greenham Common Women."

In *Remapping Memory: The Politics of Time/Space*, edited by Jonathan Boyarin, 185–220. Minneapolis: University of Minnesota Press.

Selby, Henry A., Arthur D. Murphy, and Stephen A. Lorenzen. 1990. *The Mexican Urban Household: Organizing for Self-Defense*. Austin: University of Texas Press.

Sepúlveda, María Teresa. 1973. "Día de Muertos en Iguala, Guerrero." *INAH Boletín*, 2nd ser., 73:3–12.

Seremetakis, C. Nadia. 1991. *The Last Word*. Chicago: University of Chicago Press.

Stephen, Lynn. 1991. *Zapotec Women*. Austin: University of Texas Press.

Stephen, Lynn, and James Dow, eds. 1990. *Class, Politics, and Popular Religion in Mexico and Central America*. Washington, D.C.: American Anthropological Association.

Stoll, David. 1990. *Is Latin America Turning Protestant?* Berkeley: University of California Press.

Strathern, Marilyn. 1992. "Parts and Wholes: Refiguring Relationships in a Post-Plural World." In *Conceptualizing Society*, edited by Adam Kuper, 75–104. London: Routledge.

Székely, Miguel. 2000. *The Economics of Poverty, Inequality, and Wealth Accumulation in Mexico*. New York: Macmillan.

Taylor, William B. 1972. *Landlord and Peasant in Colonial Oaxaca*. Stanford, Calif.: Stanford University Press.

———. 1979. *Drinking, Homicide, and Rebellion in Colonial Mexican Villages*. Stanford, Calif.: Stanford University Press.

———. 1985. "Between Global Process and Local Knowledge." In *Reliving the Past: The Worlds of Social History*, edited by Olivier Zunz, 115–190. Chapel Hill: University of North Carolina Press.

———. 1987. "The Virgin of Guadelupe in New Spain: An Inquiry into the Social History of Marian Devotion." *American Ethnologist* 14:9–33.

———. 1996. *Magistrates of the Sacred: Priests and Parishioners in Eighteenth-Century Mexico*. Stanford, Calif.: Stanford University Press.

Thomas, Louis-Vincent. 1975. *Antropología de la muerte*. Mexico City: Fondo de Cultura Económica.

Todorov, Tzvetan. 1997. *The Conquest of America*. New York: HarperCollins.

Turner, Victor, and Edith Turner. 1978. *Image and Pilgrimage in Christian Culture*. Oxford: Blackwell.

Uzzell, Douglas. 1974. "*Susto* Revisited: Illness as a Strategic Role." *American Ethnologist* 1:369–378.

Van Gennep, Arnold. 1960 [1909]. *The Rites of Passage*. London: Routledge and Kegan Paul.

Vásquez, Miguel Angel. 1999. "Voz de la comunidad: Panteón San Miguel, la enseñanza de Juárez." *Noticias*, October 16.

Velasco, Perez. 1989. "El costo de morirse y la defensa del ingreso." *La muerte en México* [special issue of *Jueves*, a supplement of the Mexico City daily *Excelsior*], November 2.

Vélez-Ibáñez, Carlos G. 1983. *Rituals of Marginality: Politics, Process, and Culture Change in Central Urban Mexico, 1969–1974*. Berkeley: University of California Press.

Villaurutia, Xavier. 1966. *Obras*. Mexico City: Fondo de Cultura Económica.

Voekel, Pamela. 2000. "Piety and Public Space: The Cemetery Campaign in Veracruz, 1789–1810." In *Latin American Popular Culture*, edited by William Beezley and Linda A. Curcio-Nagy, 1–25. Wilmington, Del.: Scholarly Resources.

———. 2002. *Alone Before God: The Religious Origins of Modernity in Mexico*. Durham, N.C.: Duke University Press.

Wade, Peter. 2000. *Music, Race, and Nation: Música Tropical in Colombia*. Chicago: University of Chicago Press.

Wagner, Roy. 1975. *The Invention of Culture*. Englewood Cliffs, N.J.: Prentice Hall.

Warner, Marina. 1976. *Alone of All Her Sex: The Myth and Cult of the Virgin*. London: Pan.

Warner, W. Lloyd. 1959. *The Living and the Dead*. New Haven, Conn.: Yale University Press.

Westheim, Paul. 1953. *La calavera*. Mexico City: Antigua Librería Robredo.

Whitecotton, Joseph. 1977. *The Zapotecs: Princes, Priests, and Peasants*. Norman: University of Oklahoma Press.

Williams, Aubrey. 1979. "Cohesive Features of *Guelaguetza* System in Mitla." In *Social, Political, and Economic Life in Contemporary Oaxaca*, edited by Aubrey Williams, 91–141. Nashville, Tenn.: Vanderbilt University Press.

Williams, Raymond. 1976. *Keywords: A Vocabulary of Culture and Society*. New York: Oxford University Press.

Wolf, Eric. 1979. "The Virgin of Guadalupe: A Mexican National Symbol." In *Reader in Comparative Religion*, edited by W. A. Lessa and Evon Z. Vogt, 149–153. New York: Harper & Row.

INDEX

Numbers in italics refer to pages on which figures appear.

263–264; government organization of, 194; graves during, *210–211*; in Janitzio, 240; local complaints about, 259–261; local writings about, 237–238; meaning of, 213–217; moral principles of, 229; moral stories about, 187–192; as national holiday, 235–236; origins of, 12, 192–194, 237, 239; other celebrations of, 286nn.4, 5; past celebrations of, 259; past recognition of, 253–254; public lectures for, 237; as ritual reversal, 226; sacred versus public celebrations of, 259; schedules of events for, 242–248, *243, 244–247*; tradition of, decline in, 227–228

Day of the Dead and Other Mortal Reflections, The (González Crussi), 9–10

"Day of the Dead in Oaxaca, Mexico, The" (Web site), 249–250

Day of the Holy Cross, festival food for, 218

Day of the Little Angels (Día de los Angelitos), 196, 212

de la Madrid, Miguel, 227

de la Serna, Jacinto, 279n.39

dead, 282n.8; adults, as sinners (*difuntos*), 117–118, 120, 122, 124, 164, 189, 282n.12; body disintegration of, 141–142; children, as little angels (*angelitos*), 80, 118–120, 196, 212, 282nn.11, 12; as community members, 135; Day of the Dead meaning for, 183, 213–217; faithful, 193; indulgences for, 126; as intermediaries, 178; and living, 115–116, 119, 164, 177; prayers for, 117; procession of, 188; socialization of, 183; trouble with, 86

death, 281nn.2, 3; anniversary (*cabo de año*) of, 4, 150; anthropomorphization of, 10; "bad," 163–164, 169; fear of, 215; "good," 114, 117, 154, 158, 161, 170, 177; of infants, 3; in marginal communities, 266; Mexican meaning of, 6–8, 12, 244, 266–267; in Oaxaca, 266–267; personal experience of, 3–4, 266; "popular" claims of, 215; preparing for, 214–216; relationships reaffirmed by, 265–266, 269; as revitalizing for community, 114; as social disruption, 113–114; social life contributions by, 182; as social relation, 116; spaces of, 118–119; timing of,

161–162; women's organization tasks of, 143

death, rituals of, 1–2, 4–6, 30, 93, 100, 109, 113–114, 116–118, 216–217, 269–270; body and soul placement in, 122; Christian influences on, 114; community revitalization by, 18, 114; consumerism leveled by, 18; as ideal social interaction, 154–159; independent of church, 182; interpretation of, 13–14; maintenance practices of, 149–150; as obligation of living, 163–164; patterns and contradictions in, 5; remembrance of, 269; "right" practice of, 150; rural–urban ties strengthened by, 182–183; for soul's rest, 116; toward continuous community, 16–17; values invoked by, 165–166; women's leadership in, 123–124, 147

Death of Artemio Cruz, The (Fuentes), 6, 11

Death Without Weeping (Scheper-Hughes), 3

democracy, 52, 55

D.E.P. *See* Rest in Peace

Department of Education, Culture, and Social Welfare (Dirección de Educación, Cultura y Bienestar Social), 242

Department of Public Education, 242

Día de los Muertos. *See* Day of the Dead

Díaz, Porfirio, 36

DIF. *See* Integral Family Development Program

dioceses: of Mexico, 98; of Oaxaca, 98, 100, 101, 192–193; of Puebla, 98; of Vallodolid, 98

"Dios nunca muere" (God Never Dies [funeral march]), 125

documentation, 44–45

domestic church (*la iglesia doméstica*), 71, 72

domination/subservience, 46–47

Dominicans, 32

Don Juan Tenorio (Zorrilla y Moral), 237, 288n.14

Durán, Diego, 279n.39

Durkheim, Emile, 170

"Dust of the Seven He-men," 84

Earle, Duncan, 96

Easter, 222–223

eat dirt (*comer tierra*), 10